O N

DIARMAID FERRITER is one of Ireland's best-known historians. He is Professor of Modern Irish History at University College Dublin and a columnist for *Irish Times*. He is a regular broadcaster on television and radio. His previous books include, *The Transformation of Ireland* (2004), *Occasions of Sin* (2009), *Ambiguous Republic* (2012), *A Nation and Not a Rabble* (2015) and *The Border* (2019).

DIARMAID FERRITER

ON THE EDGE

IRELAND'S
OFFSHORE ISLANDS:
A MODERN HISTORY

P

PROFILE BOOKS

This paperback edition published in 2020

First published in Great Britain in 2018 by
Profile Books Ltd
29 Cloth Fair
London EC1A 7JQ
www.profilebooks.com

1 3 5 7 9 10 8 6 4 2

Typeset in Garamond by MacGuru Ltd
Printed and bound in Great Britain by
CPI Group (UK) Ltd, Croydon CR0 4YY

A CIP catalogue record for this book is available from the British Library.

ISBN 978 1 78125 644 2
eISBN 978 1 78283 252 2

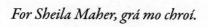

For Sheila Maher, grá mo chroí.

CONTENTS

ACKNOWLEDGEMENTS

Material relating to the history of the Irish offshore islands is located in a variety of institutions and archives and I am very grateful to those who facilitated access to that material and provided help in locating various sources, including Brian Kirby of the Capuchin Archives, Crístoír Mac Cárthaigh of the National Folklore Collection, Fr Kieran Waldron of the Tuam Diocesan Archives, Moira Hughes of the Raphoe Diocesan Archives, Eamon Lankford of the Cape Clear Archives, Kieran Hoare of the James Hardiman Library, NUI Galway, Kate Manning and Orna Somerville in the UCD archives and the brilliant staffs of the National Archives of Ireland, National Library of Ireland, Irish Military Archives, Public Record Office of Northern Ireland, Manuscripts and Research Library TCD and the James Joyce and Richview libraries in UCD.

I am also grateful to Catríona Crowe, to my colleagues in the School of History, UCD, for their support and collegiality, to Andrew Franklin and Penny Daniel in Profile Books for their positivity, patience and professionalism and to Trevor Horwood for his dexterous copy-editing. I extend deepest gratitude for their love and support to the Ferriter and Maher families and to my close and valued friends for their solidarity over many years. My deepest debts are to my marvellous, captivating and cherished daughters, Enya, Ríona and Saorla, for their patience in the face of my impatience, and to the sublime, perceptive and provocative Sheila Maher, to whom this book is dedicated.

INTRODUCTION

'a restless anxiety'

When doing research in the National Archives of Ireland in relation to the founding of the Irish Free State in 1922, I came across a very bleak account of life on Tory Island, nine miles off the coast of Donegal. Informed by the views of Fr Carr, the Catholic priest then administering to the islanders, it included the following assertions:

> The rock formation is granite, the soil is poor and shallow, therefore the people are dependent on kelp [seaweed] burning and fishing for a livelihood. Last year there was no market for kelp and the principal buyer of fish went smash, owing money to everyone. There is a population of 350, of whom two thirds are said to be destitute. A school roll of 45 of whom 30 attend regularly. Father Carr says he has not the heart to force the balance to school, knowing that they would have to go there hungry, at the same time some of the 30 go hungry to school. The islanders are native speakers, politics have penetrated there, the majority are free staters but there is a minority adherence of a lost cause ... The deputation ask for help for the 30 families until the herring fishing season begins which will be about the middle of May. The Rural District Council of the mainland, under whose sway they are supposed to be, will do nothing for them as they pay no taxes – in which they

are no doubt right as they never got any benefits such as police, JPs, poorhouse officials, contracts etc.[1]

The letter made reference to a number of themes that were central to life on the islands dotted around Ireland's 7,800-kilometre coastline: poverty, relations with the mainland, the role of the clergy in highlighting island conditions, the islands as repositories of Irish language and culture and the difficulties their residents faced in being heard. The files in the National Archives relating to island life are mostly about crises; poverty, bad weather and desperation combined to produce begging letters, telegrams or deputations. Over the course of the twentieth century some islands remained populated; more were abandoned. That bald fact represented in one sense a great failure on the part of the revolutionary generation that established the Free State in 1922; a number of them had spent time on the western islands in pursuit of cultural and linguistic purity, and extolled them as containing the essence of an ancient, distinctive Irish civilisation worth nurturing and championing. Matching the rhetoric with practical help was to prove tortuous and frustrating, but was it true that islanders were 'treated with suspicion, prejudice and hostility by those who could have helped them'?[2] There is no doubt that they were sometimes so treated, but this is by no means the full story.

What hope was there that newly independent southern Ireland would see the islands as representing an opportunity regarding regional planning? In 1936 Dr Lester Klimm, a professor of Economic Geography at the University of Pennsylvania who had spent time on Donegal's most populated offshore island, Arranmore, two miles west of Burtonport on the mainland, in the summer of 1934 doing fieldwork, noted that 'there is no one in the country doing work on economic geography'. He referred to the 'great problems' of the western islands, including inadequate or absent harbours and lack of pasture and fuel. He suggested the solution to the problems would lie not in agriculture but in identifying a general island problem and responding through regional planning. He ended his advice to the Irish government on a positive note:

'Ireland is a new, young and vigorous nation. It has problems, serious ones, but also the advantage of a "youthful" outlook. It is my belief that the principles of regional planning may contribute to a solution of some of these problems.'[3]

At the heart of this book is an exploration of why that was not the case. There were a number of state and local initiatives undertaken to assist some islands, but in relation to their overall population it is a story of a long decline. In 1841 there were 34,219 people living on 211 offshore islands; in 1911, 24,700 living on 124 islands; in 1961, 14,473 living on 92 islands, and by 1991, just 9,569 living on 66 islands. By 2002 there were only 58 populated islands, as recorded by the Central Statistics Office. Furthermore, 'between the censuses of 1986 and 1991 ten islands lost their population. These included some which had once supported extensive communities such as Rutland Island (Co. Donegal) which had a population of 125 in 1841.'[4] Although there was a very slight increase from 2002 to 2006, 'it may be too soon to claim this as an established trend', while Gola Island in Donegal regained a presence in the census for the first time since 1966, this was as a result of holiday makers'.[5] There was no uniform increase in the early twenty-first century; County Cork's Sherkin Island, for example, experienced a 16 per cent increase in population between 1996 and 2011, while in the same period, County Mayo's Inishturk Island saw its population drop by 36 per cent.[6]

By 2016 the census revealed that the number living on the inhabited offshore islands was 8,756, down from 9,029 in 2011, suggesting a degree of stabilisation.[7] Overall, however, the majority of island populations have dropped by 90 per cent in the last 170 years, and the theme of island evacuation is an emotive, haunting one that produced powerful images and words as the population decline continued. There is only one populated offshore island in Northern Ireland, Rathlin, off the coast of Antrim, and as a percentage of the overall population of the island of Ireland, the offshore islands population in 2016 is tiny at 0.13 per cent. The Scottish census of 2011, in contrast, listed ninety-three inhabited islands (including those joined by road to the mainland) with a total population of 103,700, which was then 2 per cent of the population of Scotland.[8]

In relation to the wider European context of islands, when, in 1988, the European Communities Economic and Social Committee compiled a report on disadvantaged island regions it identified a population of

European island regions of over 7 million people ('this alone justifies concern over their future'). Denmark headed the list of the ten EEC states, with 60 per cent of its total population being island dwellers; the next highest was Italy (16.6 per cent), followed by Greece (14.7 per cent), Spain (5.5 per cent), Portugal (5.2 per cent), France (0.5 per cent), UK (0.4 per cent) and Ireland (0.3 per cent). Netherlands and West Germany were joint lowest on 0.1 per cent. At that stage the overall island population in the EEC was 4.4 per cent of the population.[9] Whether the Irish islands, however, were seen as part of Europe at all is another question; renowned Irish poet Seamus Heaney described the Aran Islands, Inishmore, Inishmaan and Inisheer, eight miles off the coast of Galway, as 'three stepping stones out of Europe', while Cole Moreton described the Blasket Islands, off Slea Head in County Kerry, as 'the end of the world'.[10]

It was observed in 1996 that a proactive policy to keep the Irish islanders on islands was of 'fairly recent date', though what constituted a 'proactive policy' was contested, with talk of the denial of 'fundamental rights' (medical, educational, economic and social services) and lack of consistency in state policy. Greater access to the islands was also, for some, a double-edged sword. Reg Hindley, who had a particular interest in the fate of the Irish language and travelled the Gaeltacht (Irish-speaking) areas and Cape Clear, a Cork Gaeltacht island in 1957, observed in 1990 that 'the cultural costs and benefits of greatly improved accessibility are always greatly debatable'.[11] What constitutes an island is also debatable, depending on tide and connection to the mainland. Achill, for example, has not strictly been an island since it was linked to the mainland by a bridge, opened in 1887, but it has been maintained that Achill remained in essence an island and it is included in this book: 'It held all the islander's susceptibilities to the outside world although only a few hundred yards separated [it] from the mainland' according to artist Paul Henry, who found it the ideal haven for his art ('Achill spoke to me, it called to me as no other place had ever done').[12]

The appeal of the Irish islands is partly because if, in the words of Tim Robinson, the cartographer and historian of the Aran Islands, Ireland was intriguing as an island off the west coast of Europe, then its offshore islands were even more intriguing as 'Ireland raised to the power of two'; simple, bare places and yet making one aware 'of the overwhelming richness of even the tiniest fragment of reality'.[13] Rich in antiquity, unspoilt heritage and archaeological remains, 'Islands, by their very definition, beg the question of beginnings'.[14]

There is a long tradition of seeing islands as 'distinct and special places',[15] but for the social historian they also magnify fundamental themes relevant to the wider Irish historical experience: the fate of cultural and linguistic identity, the experiences of communities on the margins, the gulf between rhetoric and reality in state building, the construction of the myths of independence and the relationship between the centre and the periphery. Irish historiography in recent years has benefited much from an approach that seeks to look at 'history from below'[16] (with a particular focus on marginality and resistance); island narratives and experiences have the added attraction of also providing history from the edge.

Islands are intriguing for multiple other reasons, including their historic vulnerability, and 'no other type of territory has been so affected by the colonial endeavour as [the] island'.[17] They were prime targets for some of the earliest invaders of Ireland and were some of the first territories to be snatched in the European Age of Discovery. They attracted pirates and became sites of defensive warfare while also proving fruitful for numerous religious congregations. For cultural nationalists they were both haven and symbol of Irish independence. Associated with all these endeavours was control, and it was to prove a contentious issue.

The islands of Ireland have generated a rich and distinct literature from both natives and visitors, a body of work that provides much illumination of the themes mentioned above, often with great vividness, and an antidote to a perception of the islands as being either isolated and insular or fulfilling a Utopian ideal of escape from oppressive urbanisation.[18]

A central preoccupation of this book is to investigate what island life meant to the native islanders and whether their experiences equated with the characterisations of them by outsiders: variously resilient, hardy, God-fearing and industrious, on the one hand, or unruly, lazy, ungrateful and anarchic, on the other. The islands have provided a canvas onto which various idealisations and resentments have been painted. Most often, however, the islanders were characterised as representing a national ideal, and in the words of the Catholic Bishop of Cork, Cornelius Lucey, when writing to Taoiseach (prime minister) Eamon de Valera in 1957: 'they deserve to be saved for the nation'.[19]

In truth, however, by the mid twentieth century, the words celebrating them also became their elegies, and even as their renown grew, their populations shrank until in some cases they were evacuated; the future, simply and cruelly 'slipped out of their hands'.[20] What needs to be explored is whether this was because, although independence was a product of a culture that was dynamic and invigorated, in the early years of self-rule the 'sense of Irish possibility froze'.[21] The fate of the islands also developed a cynicism about 'the romantic and sentimental lovers' of the remote districts who had, according to an activist in the Irish Countrywoman's Association, 'one thing positively in common. Few of them derive their income from the land. Even fewer of them live on it.'[22] As a chronicler of Inishmurray Island, off the coast of Sligo, wrote in 1955, after it had been abandoned, 'today, the only life apparently is rabbit life ... there is no real living for a community of people on these few acres. There is a paradise for the archaeologist and the historian and there is an exciting new experience for the tourist.'[23]

Many islands possess a physical beauty and dramatic setting that seems tailor made for memorable images; as veteran photographer Eric Luke noted in relation to Tory Island, which he had been visiting for forty years, 'it cannot fail but to provide a perfect photo opportunity'.[24] But beauty and ugly reality could sadly collide. In his 2014 novel, *Beatlebone*, Irish novelist Kevin Barry dwelt on the story of the most famous seeker of an Irish island idyll, John Lennon of the Beatles. Lennon bought the island of Dorinish in Mayo in 1967 ('nineteen acres of rocks and bloody rabbit holes'; he needed to go there 'and scream and let nobody find him'). Barry imagined it was not long 'before the idyll of a new west was smeared by the great dreariness that Ireland attempts to stay quiet about. Imagine the near perpetual assault of rain.' Lennon only very briefly visited it twice and passed it on to hippies, some of whom lasted nearly eighteen months there; the longest resident, Sid Rawle, would later maintain 'Dorinish was heaven and it was hell.'[25]

Harshness and softness often co-existed in descriptions of both the islands' environments and their people. J. M. Synge, who first visited the Aran Islands in 1898 and generated a literary bounty from his visits, was more lyrical than most in explaining the attraction of the islands to loners and artists: 'the continual passing in this island between the misery of last night and the splendour of today seems to create an affinity between the moods of these people and the moods of varying rapture and dismay that are frequent in artists and in certain forms of alienation'.[26] The poet W. B. Yeats was later to suggest that Synge on Aran had made it clear he loved 'all that had edge, all that is salt in the mouth, all that is rough to the hand, all that heightens the emotions by contest, all that stings into life the sense of tragedy'.[27]

Over a century later, when novelist Colm Tóibín wrote of his trip to Inishmaan, the middle Aran island, in 2007, he noted that 'I was moving into a world of nature governed by wind and weather, sharp and soft lines of horizon, disappearing perspectives, high skies and great banks of cloud and a world of people governed by careful politeness, watchful slow glances and deliberate understatement'.[28] *Peig* (1936), the autobiography of Peig Sayers, who lived on the Blaskets and became its most famous resident, depicts existence on the island as vibrant but also occasionally harrowing, when it became 'this dreadful rock ... remember, you who read this, I was in a predicament if ever a poor woman was. I had to wash and clean my fine young boy and lay him out in death.'[29]

Sayers was one island author who achieved renown and as a result of this kind of literature there was a new dimension to the depiction of the islands and their inhabitants as something special, a process that began with the publication of *An tOileánach* (*The Islandman*) by Tomás Ó Crohan in 1929, a unique account of Blasket island life chronicling the battle against nature and the sea but also a story weaved around humour, irony and philosophy. In 2016 this book found its way into a list of *Modern Ireland in 100 Artworks*, where it was suggested it was 'far more complex and ambiguous than any simple ideological reading might imply' and its sparse style was 'a conscious aesthetic effort much admired by later writers including John McGahern'.[30]

But Ó Crohan's book was also relentlessly parodied by one of

Ireland's great satirical writers, Brian O'Nolan (Flann O'Brien) in *An Béal Bocht* (*The Poor Mouth*), published in 1942 and featuring the degenerate, ignorant and immoral character Bónapárt Ó Cúnasa and 'the reality of the state's failure to sustain viable Gaeltacht communities pokes through O'Nolan's savagely brilliant satire'.[31] It included such section headings as 'Hardship', 'the bad life', 'Black sadness', 'death and ill fortune' and 'hunger and ill fortune'. The character Sitric Ó Sánasa is praised to the skies for his poverty by Dubliners who attest that they have never seen anyone so poor and so truly Irish; the same enthusiasts mistake the grunting of a pig for beautiful melodious Irish because they cannot understand it.[32]

For all the lauding of the islands' purity, therefore, a cynicism coexisted about their exploitation and those who supposedly embodied the traits of the 'ideal national type' made precious little profit from it. An exchange between a Blasket Islander and inquiring visitor is instructive: Tomás Ó Crohan's son Seán remembered 'I let fly at them ... that the high up learned professors and people with a sound knowledge of Irish were well paid to tease out the knotty problems for them.'[33] Breandán Ó hEithir, a brilliant journalist and broadcaster and native of the Aran Islands, was also wary of the idea that the islanders were a people apart and 'loved the fact that the islander's blood group pattern turned out to be similar to that of Northern England'.[34]

Some outsiders became integrated and intrinsic to island life, including a number of island priests who emerge as a remarkable group. Some of them were minded to encourage acceptance of drudgery on the grounds that the islanders would be rewarded in the next life. One such priest, Revd J. T. Greally, writing in the *Catholic Bulletin* in 1925 about the islanders of Inishbofin and Inishark in Galway, referred to 'their fortitude amidst their sufferings, their generous instincts, their high ideals of Christian virtues and above all, their devoted and happy attachment to their Catholic faith'.[35]

But others were much more trenchant and demanding. Fr Murtagh Farragher, parish priest of the Aran Islands from 1897, was one of the most vocal champions of the islands in the twentieth century, but was also a tyrant and bully. In a 1913 letter to the Congested Districts Board (established by the British government in 1891 to assist the more impoverished districts of the west of Ireland) he insisted 'my' islanders were 'not lacking in either brains or muscle and only await the opportunity of exercising both'.[36] From 1980, Fr Diarmuid Ó Péicín, a Jesuit priest, became a voluble and relentless champion of the Tory islanders, carrying on the long tradition of the troublesome island priest, and he took his complaints about their treatment all the way to the European Parliament. On his death in 2008 he was characterised as the 'turbulent priest who saved Tory Island'; he did it partly with 'the venom of his tongue' and was forced to leave the island in 1984 by the Bishop of Raphoe, in whose diocese the island lay.[37]

But it was that same marginalisation and estrangement that enabled islanders to cultivate their own culture, way of life and manner of expression with aplomb. English classical scholar George Thomson, one of the many academic visitors to the Blasket Islands, cogently summed up the attraction of the community and its language: 'The conversation of these ragged peasants, as soon as I had learned to follow it, electrified me. It was as though Homer had come alive. Its vitality was inexhaustible.'[38]

This is a reminder of another central theme: the impression of visitors to the islands; not just those of a literary bent but also painters, students of the Irish language and filmmakers, most famously Robert Flaherty, whose *Man of Aran*, filmed on Inishmore, won Best Film at the Venice Film Festival in 1935. Flaherty was an artist who 'deliberately never made any clear distinction between reality and reconstruction' and did not feel any compunction about depicting reality as it was then. As with some of his other work, he 'went to great lengths to keep the modern world ... literally out of the picture', most memorably with the staging of a dramatic shark hunt, a pursuit long abandoned by the Aran islanders. Yet, 'given that some definitions of myth suggest that part of their purpose is to convey an essential truth, Flaherty may have gotten some things right along the way'.[39] He did, but he also contributed to the broader cultivation of Gaelic myth; as Cork writer Seán O'Faoláin was to comment acidly in 1944: 'To the historian few spectacles are so fascinating as mass-delusions.'[40]

Liam O'Flaherty's work provided a powerful antidote to the cult of the Gael. Born on the Aran Islands in 1896, one of his best novels,

Skerrett, published in 1932, powerfully depicts a real-life feud on the island between two remarkable characters, a priest and a teacher, a reminder that island life featured many disputes and territorial rows and that, for all the sense of community, there were ruptures that went deep.

O'Flaherty was also well placed to describe both the pain and fleeting joys of island life, a place where

> the struggle of life was terribly intense. There, not only extreme poverty, but the very position of the island, foster in the human mind those devils of suspicion and resentment, which make ingratitude seem man's strongest vice. The surrounding sea, constantly stirred into fury by storms that cut off communication with the mainland, always maintains in the minds of the inhabitants a restless anxiety, which has a strong bearing on character ... a good catch of fish can send a whole village into a frenzy of excitement, while an outbreak of swine fever may cause a panic comparable to that of an earthquake among people differently placed on the earth's crust. This instability, in the same manner, turns friends into foes and foes into friends with startling suddenness. It corrupts the dictionary of human qualities, making the stolid neurotic in their spleen and showing by fits a ghoulish barbarism in natures ordinarily of sweet temper.[41]

But the notion of the island as a sanctuary, far removed from the divisive politics or violence of the present persisted. Another writer of O'Flaherty's era was Michael McLaverty, whose first novel, *Call my Brother Back* (1939), came to him on a visit to Rathlin Island, where he had spent a short period as a child, because it 'reilluminated for him the tranquillity of the island life compared with the pitiable waste of blood that was spilt in the poorer quarters of Belfast'.[42] This idea of escapism was also apparent much later in relation to the Troubles in Northern Ireland. In the mid 1980s Irish singer Paul Brady's 'The Island' contrasted the 'women and children dying in the streets' of his native Northern Ireland and those 'still trying to carve tomorrow on a tombstone', with a desire

to take you to the island
and trace your footprints in the sand
and in the evening when the sun goes down
We'll make love to the sound of the ocean.

Brady's 'endemic getaway' could not be more removed from the harshness of the other images in the song, 'leaving the listener all the more haunted by the disparity between what is and what could be'.[43] The song was played in February 2017 when retired stunt man Pascal Whelan, the last permanent resident of Omey Island, a tidal island near Claddaghduff in Connemara, was laid to rest. A native of the island, he had left it aged six but retired to Omey in the 1980s; in more ways than one he 'lived life on the edge'.[44]

The islands continue to be presented as sites of innovation and tradition; landscapes of worry but also creativity and the ultimate getaway but practically, often struggling to survive. This is true, not just of the Irish islands, but of many island communities internationally. The Scottish islands, for example, suffered many similar problems and, as with the Irish islands, their fate generated heat, light and insight from many observers over centuries. It is still fascinating to read the account by Samuel Johnson, one of the greatest literary figures of the eighteenth century, of his sojourn to the Scottish islands, including Skye, Mull, Raasay, Col and Iona from August to November 1773, published in 1775 as *Journey to the Western Islands*. It was a period described by his trusted companion Boswell, who accompanied him, as 'never passed by any man in a more vigorous exertion'.[45]

Johnson was then aged sixty-four and 'had not otherwise been out of England, had always spoken as if he scorned the Scots and had certainly shown no love of wild nature'.[46] He was fascinated by the islanders' strange culinary habits ('they do what I found not very easy to endure. They pollute the tea table by plates piled with large slices of Cheshire cheese.') He witnessed an 'antiquated' life and 'a people of peculiar appearance', but also 'hospitality and elegance' and the impact of emigration: 'an island, once depopulated, will remain a desert as long as the present facility for travel gives everyone, who is discontented and unsettled, the choice of his abode'.[47]

Approaching Iona, there was 'no convenience for landing', but he was so conscious of the antiquity of the island and its religious past that it 'advances us in the dignity of thinking beings'. There was archaeology on a ground 'which has been dignified by wisdom, bravery or virtue', but also inhabitants that are 'remarkably neglected. I know not if they are visited by any minister. The island, which was once the metropolis of learning and piety has now no school for education nor temple for worship, only two inhabitants that can speak English and not one that can read or write ... perhaps in the revolutions of the world, Iona may be sometime again the instructress of the western regions.'[48] It is remarkable how so many of these observations of nearly 250 years ago resonate in modern accounts of island life, in Ireland and elsewhere, along with the sense of the city inhabitant moved by experiencing something so at odds with their usual experiences.

Rather than documenting the minutiae of all the individual islands, this book is thematic in approach, examining the emergence of greater awareness about some of the main and minor islands and their pasts from the nineteenth century, how Irish island issues were handled by both British and Irish governments, the impact made and impressions generated by island visitors, and life on the islands for the natives and their pastors. In taking this approach – by no means exhaustive – the book explores how the islands of western Ireland in particular were used, observed, celebrated and neglected, the cultural impact they had, the interest they generated in archaeologists and antiquarians, their survival and adaptation or abandonment and where they stand now in relation to Irish identity and modernity.

The archival material relating to the islands is as scattered as the islands themselves. State files, local authority records, private collections, diocesan archives, newspaper reports, folklore collections, archaeological surveys and the collections preserved on individual islands combine to allow a comprehensive and textured overview of the islands; their heritage, plight, depiction and fate. Many of the archival documents are published here for the first time. The book also draws on the work of local historians who have filled many pages of local history journals with accounts of the archaeological, ecological, social and maritime history of islands off the shores of their respective counties.

When an interdepartmental government review of Rathlin Island was conducted in 1975 it suggested succinctly, in a description applicable to all the islands, 'Rathlin has enjoyed and suffered a long and chequered history'.[49] This book seeks to explore social, political, cultural and literary aspects of those histories in order to document life on the edge of Ireland and, therefore, on the edge of Europe.

ONE

THE ISLAND QUESTION IN THE NINETEENTH AND EARLY TWENTIETH CENTURIES

'as to rent, I might as well look for diamonds in the ocean'

From the middle of the eighteenth century, the population of Ireland expanded at an unprecedented rate and by 1821 had reached almost 7 million, representing a growth of well over 4 million in the previous 200 years. At its apex, before the Great Famine of 1845–9, it reached 8.5 million. With such expansion came demand for more places of settlement and the attraction of some of the offshore islands increased as a result. The 1841 census indicated there were 211 inhabited islands with a population of 34,219.[1] Although various islands are likely to have been inhabited for centuries, details of individual islands before the nineteenth century and the first state census in 1821 are sketchy – in Kevin Whelan's description 'only stray references that flash occasional light on a murky landscape' – though the post-famine sources are more detailed.

What is clear, however, is that on certain islands, including Clare Island in Mayo, 'a fully mature settlement system was well in place by the end of the eighteenth century'.[2] Abundant natural resources including seaweed, fish and grass were a considerable attraction. The population of Clare Island in 1835 was roughly 1,600. Rents also rose as the west of Ireland economy expanded and the fishing industry developed in tandem with the cultivation of land. The system of dividing land into ever smaller parcels and excessive reliance on potatoes created demand for land 'in the most isolated places', including the Blasket Islands in west

Kerry, where turf, fertile soil, rabbits, drinking water and fish facilitated population expansion. In the mid eighteenth century there had been five or six households on the island comprising approximately forty people; by 1841 there were twenty-eight houses and 153 people.[3] The combined population of Inishbofin and Inishark, off the coast of Connemara, was 1,612 in 1841, with the islanders, like others, leasing their holdings from an English landlord, and in the early part of the century Inishbofin experienced its first era of thriving herring fishing.[4]

Further south, Cape Clear Island, off the coast of Cork and Ireland's southernmost inhabited Irish-speaking island, had in the region of 400 households in the mid eighteenth century with an estimated population of 1,600, but this had dropped to 1,057 in 1831, a reminder that local factors were also relevant to island demographics, including isolation, economic fluctuations, disease and, in the case of Cape Clear, the closure of the coastguard station in the mid 1830s.[5]

Economic and population expansion created both opportunities and problems for the island communities, which, combined with their location and the economic and military importance of maritime affairs, meant they were increasingly likely to come under the scrutiny of central government. There were many examples in the nineteenth century of enduring island themes: periodic vulnerability due to food shortages, the importance of champions of the island harrying those in authority, reliance on private charity, the potential of the fishing industry, the issues of accessibility and distance from the mainland, and doubts about the character of the islanders, their trustworthiness and their penchant for illicit distillation.

As with the rest of Ireland, the islands were also affected by the crucial issue of land ownership and the attitude of landlords. From the seventeenth century, the establishment of English and Scottish plantations, supposedly to reform and civilise the Irish or to reward Crown loyalists, meant the demise of many Gaelic landlords and new, often absentee owners who, by leasing their acquisitions, imposed new landlords on the native populations. In Cork, for example, Cape Clear had been ruled by the dominant O'Driscoll clan but by 1641 the island was the property of Sir Algernon May and subsequently Sir William Wrixon Beecher. In the early nineteenth century the bailiffs Wades and Tobins from Waterford dispersed native islanders 'in their greed for themselves and their families'.[6] The Earl of Cork became the landlord of the Blasket Islands, where the islanders 'never had any wish to pay the heavy rent demanded of them'. The 'middlemen' sent to collect rent could be severe and there were raids to enforce payment, although Lord Cork was also open to occasional reductions in rent at the request of clergy.[7]

Clare Island in the nineteenth century was owned by Sir Samuel O'Malley, who mortgaged it to a London Insurance Company, after which it was leased to a land agent; this island also witnessed confrontation over non-payment of rent. The Aran Islands had been acquired in the seventeenth century by Richard Butler, the Earl of Arran, and from the mid eighteenth century belonged to the Digby family of Kildare; at time of the famine in the 1840s the owner, Elizabeth Digby, was criticised for sending only two tons of meal as relief to her hungry tenants; as was the case with other islands, 'its owners knew little of such a remote source of a tiny fraction of their rents' and the island was administered by agents 'who themselves visited only periodically'. There was also resentment at the landlord's agent, who wanted to 'persuade the lower orders of the sinfulness of papistry'.[8]

In contrast the Gage family, who purchased a long lease of Rathlin Island from its owners the McDonnells in the eighteenth century, had much more of a presence, farmed land on the island and were seen as enlightened landlords.[9] By the early nineteenth century 'it is possible to detect two contrasting styles of administration on the islands', one guided by the philosophy of 'estate improvement', the other a 'distrustful and dismissive' approach by absentee landlords. While the Gages took a 'personal and direct' interest in the welfare and economy of Rathlin Island, Marquis Conyngham was the opposite in how he treated the Donegal islands, including Tory, that were part of his estate. Conyngham lived in England and ran his estate through a London agent and subagents in Donegal; 'pleas for help with rents, or for maintenance of the estate were met with refusal, passed on to agents for decisions, or ignored'.[10]

In the early nineteenth century, the registered papers for the Chief Secretary's Office in Dublin – one of the principal offices of state in

Ireland – revealed that correspondence about the offshore islands was dominated by concerns about lighthouses, smuggling and distress arising from poverty. In June 1822 there was much urgency about the need for a grant for fever relief in Galway and an inquiry into the 'state of health' on the Aran Islands. These were the three islands (Inishmore, Inishmaan and Inisheer) that dominated the sea lanes of Galway Bay, which, given their antiquity and strategic importance, and association with the Irish Christian and monastic tradition, had long been important and fought-over territory and were attracting ever greater interest. Like the rest of Ireland, Aran's population was at its peak before the famine, with 3,521 on the three islands: 'the fragmentation of the terrain into tiny fields expresses the desperation of those nineteenth-century generations, hoarding every tuft of grass for their cattle'.[11]

In 1822 Galway doctor Thomas Whistler was requested to report on conditions on these islands whose inhabitants were said to be 'in very great distress, from the want of food and the extensive spread of contagious fever'.[12] Two days later, civil engineer Alexander Nimmo wrote to the undersecretary William H. Gregory from Clifden about poverty and proposals for relief works and referred to distress on Gorumna Island, also in Galway and with a population in the region of 1,900, which 'far exceeds anything I have yet witnessed'. A further letter to Gregory from Arthur French, Anglo-Irish peer, MP and landlord in Oranmore, referred to the lack of means of the 'lower orders' and the distressed state of Gorumna: 'as to rent, I might as well look for diamonds in the Ocean'.[13] The following month, additional relief funds were also sought for a public work scheme on Achill Island in Mayo, the largest of the Irish islands, which covered an area of about sixty square miles, and recorded a population of 4,901 in 1841.

A few months later Richard Thorpe, local inspector of fisheries in Skibbereen in west Cork, wrote to the Lord Lieutenant (the chief governor of Ireland) Richard Wellesley seeking £100 to aid the fishermen of Inishturk and Cape Clear.[14] This followed on from Cork MP William Beecher's demand for public works on Cape Clear and Sherkin islands, part of his estate: 'they have not a single road in either of them'. He offered to contribute personally an equal amount towards the work.[15]

There were also many requests for the building of lighthouses on islands, for reasons of both safety and trade.[16] In some cases, private enterprise provided the precedent; the Clare Island lighthouse was built by the Marquis of Sligo in 1806 before being taken over the by Dublin Ballast Board. When they were built with state funds – and the nineteenth century can be seen as Ireland's 'golden age of lighthouse development'[17] – there were also numerous requests for appointment as lighthouse keeper. Denis Burke from Skibbereen sought this job on Cape Clear and he cited his service in the Royal Navy, during which he had endured shipwreck and imprisonment in France in 1812: 'from his knowledge and experience of the sea faring line he would be adequate to the duty'.[18] Requests such as this, including applications as tide surveyors and tide waiters, went to the Ballast office in Dublin.

George Halpin, the Inspector of Irish lighthouses in 1820, highlighted the need to erect two lighthouses on Skellig Michael Island in Kerry. According to Halpin, there was a general need for sea-warning structures to be 'a faithful leading light for vessels bound north and south and keep them clear of all danger'.[19] The Skelligs (consisting of Michael and a smaller one) were uninhabited at that stage and were famed in folklore as the place from where St Brendan, the sixth-century navigator, sailed before discovering America and also because at the summit of the rock were the ruins of a monastery, a popular place of pilgrimage requiring 'iron nerve to make the ascent' and also where eligible, unmarried young men and women went if they failed to secure a love match, 'to find consolation'.[20]

Halpin had become Inspector of Lighthouses in 1810 following an act that vested all Irish marine lights and beacons in the Ballast Board and the achievement of the Board in that area 'contrasted with the dismal state of marine safety outside Dublin. He reported immediately on the condition and requirements of coastal lights (then numbering fourteen), which he subsequently revolutionised by designing and constructing dozens of new or improved lighthouses around the coast with staff accommodation.'[21] Halpin's achievements were remarkable; new lighthouses were built almost every year during his inspectorate, with 'many famous examples as far apart as Inishtrahull [over six miles east of Malin Head and one of the most northerly of the Irish islands] and Tory Island,

Co. Donegal (1813, 1832), Skellig Michael, Co. Kerry (1826), and possibly the most dramatically situated of all Irish lighthouses at Fastnet Rock, four miles south-west of Cape Clear Island, Co. Cork (1854)'. Crucially, he 'established a tradition of world-renowned Irish lighthouse pioneers of the nineteenth century, including John Tyndall and John Wigham', and was ably assisted by his son, George Jr, who succeeded him.[22]

The lighthouses were certainly badly needed. Samuel Lewis, whose topographical dictionary of Ireland was the first detailed study of its kind in Ireland, noted in 1837 that prior to the Skellig Michael lighthouse in 1826 'scarcely a winter previously elapsed without frequent and fatal ship wrecks'.[23] Two lighthouses were necessary on Skellig 'because of the peculiar layout of the island', while on Inishmore the lighthouse in operation in the early 1850s was 'ineffective in cloudy or misty weather' and a new one was built with the local 'very hard crystalline limestone'.[24] This burst of lighthouse building may also have generated some social tensions on the islands given that, for example, on Tory Island, where the lighthouse had been requested by the Harbour Commissioners and merchants of Sligo in 1828 and was established in 1832, 'the contrast between the affluent lighthouse staff at the station and that of the islanders was very obvious'. Lighthouse keepers' children posing for photographs decades later were noticeably well dressed and the quality of offshore accommodation for those involved in the service 'give[s] some indication of lightkeeper's rank and status in Irish society'.[25]

Tory was particularly interesting because of numerous ships wrecked in its treacherous vicinity; it was one of the most remote islands but had been inhabited for over 4,000 years and may have had a population of up to 600 in the early nineteenth century. Only 250 of its 785 acres consisted of arable land and its peat was overused for burning kelp, an essential nineteenth-century island industry.[26] Brown or red seaweed was harvested for both food and fertilising purposes and seaweed was burned for its ash as a source of soda and later iodine for such industries as glass making and linen bleaching. The income it generated was essential for rent payment, especially in the north-west; on Tory Island in 1853 it was described as a 'most profitable business' and it survived on the islands longer than elsewhere.[27]

Island lighthouse keepers also made daring rescues; in March 1821 Mary Walsh, wife of the lighthouse keeper on Mutton Island, petitioned the Lord Lieutenant the Earl of Talbot for remuneration for her husband 'following his rescue of four individuals from a boat which was about to capsize'.[28] Mutton was the largest island off Clare's western coast and fourteen miles south of the Aran Islands. The presence of a lighthouse on Rathlin Island from 1856 – necessitated because Rathlin was located in a busy seaway between Scotland and Ireland – also meant the east of the island 'was a lively place', with six keeper's houses.[29] The first mention of coastguards on Rathlin Island, seven miles off the coast of Antrim, relates to 1823 and they appeared to have had 'little to do with lifesaving, but had a great deal to do with catching smugglers'.[30] Rathlin was likely to have been populated for 5,000 years, with an extraordinarily rich and varied history marked by invasion and refuge; its population stood at 1,150 in 1810 before emigration to Scotland and America reduced it to 1,010 by 1841. Kelp burning on the island generated £20 per ton in 1812 and it exported barley to Scotland for whisky distilling, but the fishing industry was underdeveloped because of the lack of a safe harbour.[31]

Tobacco smuggling was another concern that brought attention to the islands; one of the principal smugglers in the early 1820s was John McColgan; a file of reports from Major Samson Carter, the chief police magistrate for County Donegal, related to efforts to prevent tobacco smuggling and illicit distillation in the vicinity of the Donegal coast and the particular need to patrol Rathlin Island. In parallel, George War-burton wrote to Charles Grant, the chief secretary, about the expected arrival of a ship loaded with tobacco at Mutton Island 'and of bodies of armed men on land, ready to protect the cargo from the police'; the caves on Mutton Island were frequently used by smugglers and a cave on its north side was called Poul Tabach (tobacco hole).[32]

On Inishmurray, six miles out in Sligo Bay – another island with a significant monastic settlement and with a population of roughly 100 in the 1880s and land mostly of shallow peat – during the winter months islanders were employed in distilling poitín (often referred to as poteen), a traditional, potent drink distilled from grain supplied by farmers on the mainland. The island became 'notorious' for poitín in the nineteenth century, which necessitated great vigilance on the part of the Royal Irish Constabulary (RIC, created in 1836).[33] John Wynne, who held the lease for Inishmurray Island, maintained in 1846 that 'their great evil is their habit of illicit distillation which they carry on now for the purpose of providing their cattle with food in winter ... but the practice is very demoralising'.[34]

Samuel Waters, who was stationed at Grange on the mainland, across from Inishmurray, in the late 1860s as an RIC officer, soon learned that during the winter months the islanders, numbering about ninety-five, were 'mainly employed in distilling poitín' and that he and his fellow officers 'invariably made considerable seizure', but he also turned a blind eye. One island woman had been so civil to him 'I left her quietly most of the illicit material which we had seized'. She was so grateful that she asked him to taste a drop of the special brew of poteen, which she reserved for herself and her family. She gave it to him in an eggshell as during a raucous Christmas party the drunkards 'had a free fight and smashed every article of glass or crockery in the place'.[35] The RIC barracks was evacuated in 1893, meaning there was new scope for the enterprising distillers, but they did not have it all their own way and it was reported in 1897 that the RIC had discovered and destroyed 195 gallons of wash on Inishmurray.[36]

Whatever about potential riches from smuggling, shipwrecks or illicit pot stills, islands in the nineteenth century were more likely to come to the attention of the authorities because of neglect and impoverishment, in tandem with the wider west of Ireland. There was no system of poor relief in Ireland before 1838 and in the early nineteenth century the government encouraged local relief efforts, adding one third to private relief efforts or importing food to be sold at subsidised prices.[37] A serious famine in 1822 represented a new challenge and local and government relief had to be organised; on the islands both government and private relief were used but the operations 'did not run at all smoothly'. On the Aran Islands the landlord was the absentee Revd J. W. Digby of County Kildare, 'who never visits these islands nor gives any encouragement whatsoever'; famine relief was administered by members of the islands' 'very small' middle class.[38] There were disputes about transporting aid and 'little gratitude' on the part of some islanders, but 'perhaps it was felt they did not have much for which to be grateful'. In relation to public works, there were also problems with monitoring the system of payments through food. The Church of Ireland Archbishop of Tuam, Power Le Poer Trench, also personally raised considerable relief for the islanders, though given his evangelical leanings this was hardly a completely selfless act. The relief resulted in the construction of a pier at Killeaney on Inishmore.[39]

Advantage was also taken of the distressed state of some islands to encourage conversion from Catholicism to Protestantism during an era when the Protestant ascendancy had been placed under increasing pressure following Catholic emancipation in 1829 and a more organised, assertive and confident Catholic Church attending to the religious and educational needs of the majority. Achillbeg, just south of Achill Island, with 326 acres, had a population before the famine era of 200; in the sixty years after 1841 its population declined from 178 to 104 (it was evacuated in 1965). In 1854 the islanders' landlord, William Pike, wrote to the residents warning them he would have them evicted if they were guilty of 'persecuting or annoying' people who had converted to the Protestant faith on account of the influence of Edward Walter Nangle, the Protestant evangelical.[40]

Nangle in the early 1830s had observed the destitution of the Achill islanders and decided to live among them as a missionary; he was so struck 'by the desolate beauty of the island and by the primitive but noble "savagery" of the people' he decided to establish a Protestant colony 'with the aim of bringing Christ and the Bible to this forgotten part of Ireland'.[41] Achill's main landlord, Sir Richard O'Donnell, duly granted Nangle some land at a nominal rent, and enlisted the aid of Robert Daly, the future bishop of Cashel, who encouraged other evangelicals to oversee the foundation of the new mission which began in August 1834. The mission eventually purchased much of the island from the O'Donnell estate and it included an impressive infrastructure of schools, a church, hotel and printing press and the missionaries used the Irish language of the islanders. There was determined opposition from the Catholic Church, especially from the Archbishop of Tuam, John MacHale, who characterised the proselytisers as 'these venomous fanatics' and 'who sent a succession of hostile parish priests to counter Nangle's initiatives'.[42]

Seen by many Catholics as nothing less than aggressive and exploit-ative proselytism, converts could face ostracism; allegations at the time and since that 'the Achill mission was the apotheosis of "souperism" largely arose from what happened in the famine years, when meals were provided for the children in the schools and conversions increased'.[43] By 1847 Nangle was giving employment to over 2,000 labourers and feed-ing 600 children in the schools; in the region of seventy per cent of the island's population at one stage were in receipt of relief from the mission, though the backlash from the Catholic Church was ultimately effective in lessening its reach and effectiveness.[44]

But the islands had markedly different fortunes during the Great Famine of 1845–9. It was noted by the Famine Relief Commission in 1849 that 'the poverty of Cape Clear with a population of about 1,300 is likely to be particularly great'.[45] Clare Island was devastated, a reminder of the robust level of its population with all the attendant pressures on land and crops, and it was unusually fertile for an island. In 1846 its par-ish priest, Fr Peter Ward, appealed desperately for relief works and aid, estimating in July 1846 that 200 would starve as a result of the potato blight; he believed the island's landlords were 'disposed to let the people die without the least desire to subscribe one farthing'. Relief works com-menced but from a pre-famine high of 1,600 the population dropped to just 545 by 1851.[46] The Blasket Islands had a population of 153 in 1841 and as a result of the famine its population 'fell noticeably but not drasti-cally'; by 1851 there were ninety-seven residents but they did not depend on the potato to the same extent and, crucially, the island was not over-populated. Whether or not blight reached the island is contested, as is the assertion there were no famine deaths, but it is likely the island had 'partial immunity'.[47]

In the early nineteenth century Rathlin Island had a population of 1,150. There was a Rathlin Island Relief committee during the famine but it did not last 'owing to the government's refusal to alter the rules to suit the peculiar circumstances of Rathlin as an island', although grain and rice were purchased, with landlord Robert Gage subscribing £40. Nonetheless, the island's depopulation was stark, down to 753 by 1851. Some islanders went to the Belfast or Scottish shipyards, while Gage negotiated with a shipping line in Derry for the transport of more than eighty people to America; in the spring of 1847 alone, 107 people left the island.[48]

On Valentia Island, which had a population of just over 3,000 in 1845, the numbers had fallen to 2,500 by 1851; other parts of Kerry suffered steeper falls and renowned naturalist and chronicler of the island, Frank Mitchell, wondered what the 'cushioning effect' was on Valentia and suggested the waters around it were not yet overfished and still offered 'plentiful harvests'.[49] The population of Inishmore continued to rise beyond the Great Famine; the potato blight did not reach the Aran Islands and in 1853 it was proudly claimed that 'the islanders have had the singular good fortune never to have been visited by the potato blight; never to have had a death from destitution, and never to have sent a pauper to the poor house', but pressure was also relieved by migration.[50] Clearly the Aran Islands fared better than most during the famine, a catastrophe described by one of the members of the Royal Commission on Congestion in 1908 (see below) as a consequence of over-reliance on the potato: 'nature's remorseless punishment of disregard for her laws, a warning for all time'.[51]

In the second half of the nineteenth century there were intermittent crises for various islands. In May 1861 reports of distress on Cape Clear included the observation that the population was 'bordering on starvation'. At a House of Commons sitting the following year, it was noted that a government officer had been dispatched to investigate the locality; his finding that 'there was much distress there but it was not more than prevailed in ordinary seasons' was disputed.[52] It was private charity rather than state intervention on which islanders had to rely most; at the end of the following decade it was reported that a religious order, the Sisters of Mercy, were visiting the island 'accompanied by some of the female inmates of the workhouse' in Skibbereen to attend the sick: 'One man has lost five children. A young girl who visited the mainland where measles was present first introduced the contagion. She, on her return home, was attacked.'[53] Of forty cases, sixteen proved fatal; one of the reasons it spread was because 'the abodes of the poor people are low, dark and ill ventilated cabins, the whole family in some instances occupying one small sleeping apartment affording less cubic feet than would suffice for one person'.[54] There was also a measles epidemic on Cape Clear in December 1887 which caused fatalities.[55]

The population of Inishbofin, off the coast of Galway, was 1,612 with 285 houses in 1841; an inspector of fisheries in 1873 referred to 'distress amounting almost to destitution' on the island where sheep had died of starvation and there was no fishing gear. An indication of the mindset at that stage with regard to assistance was that he surmised: 'as the system of giving money gratuitously is not considered a good mode of affording relief, it is proposed to raise a fund by private subscription to enable loans to be made to the fishermen on their own security to surmount their present great difficulties'.[56] Inishbofin was considered one of the best areas for basking sharks that provided valuable oil but in 1891 the population of the island had fallen to 985 and there was an illiteracy rate of 46.4 per cent.[57]

Agricultural depression and the land war era of the late 1870s and early 1880s, as the Land League sought to transform tenant demands for rent abatement into a wider battle to end landlordism, also posed serious dilemmas. In response, one relief organisation suggested the islands could be characterised as 'desolate prisons amidst the Atlantic ... if ever there was poverty genuine, poignant, terrific and unmerited, it was theirs'.[58] It estimated the western islands 'number about thirty in all and contain 22,510 souls'.

The islands were not immune from the land war evictions and clearances; such uprooting on Castle Island in south-west Cork, at the behest of landlord Thomas Henry Marmion in 1890, caused quite a political storm and absorbed, among others, William O'Brien, the agrarian campaigner and MP who was imprisoned at various stages for his land agitation. Castle Island was described in 1837 as 'tolerably fertile, it produces no plant higher than the creeping furze. It is about a mile and a quarter distant from the mainland, between Long island and Horse island, and contains only fifteen small cabins indifferently built' with an estimated eighty-nine inhabitants. At the time of the Castle Island evictions O'Brien had timber houses built on the mainland for the victims opposite their former island homes, while another sympathiser marooned the men sent to the island to stop the islanders returning by cutting their boats adrift. One of the islanders wrote that 'the rents were 50 per cent over and above what any human being could knock out of the land'. Eventually about six families returned.[59] In contrast, the Heir Island landlords, the Beechers, 'did not evict any tenants'.[60]

Outside of temporary if devastating crises there was also much to be positive about. The experiences of Valentia, for example, are a reminder of the need to avoid generalising about the islands. Daphne Mould, who chronicled Valentia's history in the 1970s, insisted it did not fall 'into any of the normal island categories'. It was not as remote and inaccessible as many others and alongside its antiquity and culture it was also associated with 'another world entirely of technology and high living standards – the world of the transatlantic cable, the Met and radio stations', as well as subtropical gardens created by the Knight of Kerry. In the 1850s and 1860s Valentia was the location of the European end of attempts to lay the first transatlantic telegraph cable; success came in 1866 and contemporary newspapers marvelled at this 'triumph of mind over matter'. It also had an important weather station because of its location, and weather reports began to be made from the island with an observatory established in 1867 (moved to the mainland in 1892). It was also subsequently used as a base to provide radio services to shipping.[61] While the island had been relatively prosperous, its slate quarry closed in 1880 causing considerable unemployment. A number of island families were involved in an assisted emigration scheme in 1883; the condition was that the whole family must go together and the school roll dropped dramatically from 220 to 56.[62]

North and South Inishkea, off the Mayo coast, with sixty whitewashed cabins and some 300 people, had a healthy cash economy and had also been relatively unaffected by famine, and 'piracy and poitín brought resident coastguards and three RIC constables' (the islanders displayed an 'adaptable morality towards their piracy and plunder'). Schools were built on both islands in 1886 and 1894 (a state-funded national education system had been introduced in 1831), with the children taught both English and Irish. The island also had to endure a typhus epidemic in 1897.[63] In 1876 Fr John Healy, the curate of Grange and a future Archbishop of Tuam, visited Sligo's Inishmurray and observed that in the national school most of the children could now read and write but it was a school 'where the poorly clad children put in a shivering and reluctant attendance in winter. The annual visit to the school for the results examination is a source of terror to most of the Board's inspectors.'[64] Healy, a 'literary pilgrim to the shrines of Ireland's vanished past', had a passion for antiquarian sites and was greatly interested in the monastic schools of old: 'he liked to end his essays by speculating that the ancient monasteries might one day be revived and the islands of the west once more attract hermits'.[65]

In 1862 a British newspaper sent a correspondent, Henry Coulter, a native of County Down who had worked with Irish newspaper the *Freeman's Journal* (established in 1763) to investigate conditions in the west of Ireland. His travel accounts were first published as a series of letters 'in relation to the condition and prospects of the people, consequent upon the partial failure of agricultural produce, caused by unfavourable harvests during the last two years'. While he found dwellings that were 'degraded and wretched' he also identified some prosperity, the product of a society in transition.[66] In its annual review of 1871, the *Freeman's Journal* highlighted 'abundant and substantial evidence of prosperity ... marks of contentment and comfort abound' in rural as well as urban areas.[67] Many islanders, including those from Heir Island, south-west of Cork, which had a population of 358 in 1841 and still 294 in 1911, joined the British merchant navy, as did natives of Cape Clear.[68] Bere Island, in Bantry Bay, Cork, suffered a drop in population from 1,152 to 876 between 1861 and 1911, but in the decade 1891 to 1901 there was a 9 per cent increase in population as outsiders were brought in to work on batteries and the building of military houses. It had a tradition of fortified army bases stretching back to the late eighteenth century and included five Martello towers dating from the Napoleonic wars; the island was used as both training ground and anchorage for the British navy, and such presence made a significant contribution to the economic life of the island.[69]

The health of the fishing industry was, of course, paramount for the welfare and prosperity of the islands and their experiences differed. A Fisheries Act of 1819 had established a Fisheries Board but a parliamentary inquiry in 1836 suggested an industry in sharp decline and poorly equipped; though the east coast was faring better, there was little domestic demand for fish. Internationally, the mid nineteenth century witnessed great change due to improvements in fishing methods, travel and refrigeration, but progress in Ireland was uneven. The numbers at work in fishing are estimated to have declined from almost 65,000 in 1829 to roughly 39,000 by 1865.[70] There were up to 500 sailboats and rowboats fishing from Valentia in 1825 with 400 people working in its onshore fishery the following decade and a curing station was based there from the 1840s.[71] Sherkin Island, with a long tradition of seafaring, was home in the nineteenth century to island families who 'owned and skippered their own coastal trading vessels, many built on the island'; on the north shore, a horseshoe-shaped cove served as the 'dock' for the island shipbuilding industry. Sherkin had a population of 1,126 in 1841 but by 1851 it had fallen to 896; the *Margaret Hughes*, a Sherkin-built schooner launched in 1842, took emigrants to America at the time of the famine.[72]

Breandán Ó hEithir, a well-known journalist and Aran Island native born in 1930, sought to chronicle the rise and fall of the fishing industry on the islands and noted in 1978 that, despite escaping the worst horrors of the famine, it did not escape the agricultural and economic crisis of 1879–80 and things got sufficiently bad for the islands' new Catholic parish priest to send a starkly worded telegram to the chief secretary in Dublin: 'Send us boats or send us coffins'.[73] It was one of the great island telegrams (see chapter 4) and there were to be many more. It was also seemingly effective, with a grant of £20,000 made available under poor relief to improve harbour facilities and over the next decade a fishing industry was created in Inishmore: 'the industry reached a peak twice and twice almost vanished into the folk memory'. By 1900 there were sixty-three boats and 350 men fishing out of Kilronan on Inishmore.

When the new Free State government established a Commission on the Gaeltacht, its report in 1925 noted that on islands, including Cape Clear and Aran 'a considerable number of the younger men between 1895 and 1920 became whole-time professional fishermen', but that 'a collapse of the markets in the latter year followed by the scarcity of fish, bad weather and political disturbances in the three years following brought about a serious setback in this development'. Some full-time fishermen had adopted power vessels in 1912, the year 'in which steam and motor power were for the first time applied to the fishing industry in Ireland' with loans made by the Congested Districts Board.

There were 150 such vessels up to 1920, following the herring fishing around the coast; 'these loans were advanced on the security of the vessels, combined with the character of the fishermen'. With the outbreak of the First World War, herring curing almost ceased as the chief markets for herrings were Germany and Russia, but the withdrawal of Scotch and English steam trawlers for naval duty enabled Irish fishermen to secure a market for their fresh mackerel and herring in England and prices soared. Many invested in motor boats at high prices, but with the post-war return of the British vessels there was a great decline in the value of the fish: 'added to the misfortune of collapsed markets was the most unusual failure of the mackerel and herring shoals to make their seasonal visits to our coast in 1921 and 1922'.[74] One veteran of the fishing boom years on the Aran Islands told Ó hEithir 'there was as much money made as could cover the islands in one pound notes' but 'by 1928 fishing on a large scale in Aran was dead and those who hadn't emigrated were full of suspicion and cynicism. Nobody wanted to hear about trawlers or co-operatives.'[75]

In 1887 the parish priest of Rath and the islands in Cork, Fr Charles Davis, reportedly brought a delegation of islanders from Cape Clear to meet Queen Victoria, who arranged for Davis to meet Baroness Burdett Coutts, philanthropist and one of the wealthiest women in England, who became involved in the promotion of the fishing industry in Ireland by helping to start fishing schools and provide boats. She had also advanced substantial funds in 1880 for supplying seed potatoes to the impoverished tenants. When Fr Davis drew up a report on the island it led to the setting up of an interest-free purchase loan fund, towards which Coutts contributed £10,000, and within a year fifteen Cape Clear boats were bought under the scheme.[76] Six years later, Fr Davis organised and led a deputation to meet the chief secretary for Ireland and got the idea of a fishery school for Baltimore, on the mainland in west Cork, adopted, the first of its kind. Davis later became a very active member of the Congested Districts Board and there were piers built at both Sherkin and Cape Clear islands as well as a lighthouse at Sherkin. As Fr Davis saw it, fundraising for island ventures was particularly problematic as 'few were found to trust the distant islanders'.[77]

Part of the reason for such distrust was because collecting rent and taxes from islands was problematic and fraught. In June 1844 a letter of appointment for the bailiff 'and caretaker' of the three Aran Islands, Martin Herman of Kilmurvey, on Inishmore, was issued by landlord John William Digby. The position carried a salary of ten guineas per annum, 'which shall be increased to twelve guineas if I shall think he deserves it from his increased attention to his duties – he is to be sober, vigilant and attentive to directions and to keep peace and good order amongst the tenants as far as he can do so – he is to go through the three islands at the least once a month to see that all goes on right – he is not to permit any new cottages or houses to be built on any pretence whatever'. His main mission had to be 'Mr Digby's advantage in the islands at all times'.[78]

The most dramatic manifestation of disputes over the islanders and their dues occurred in September 1884 when a British gunboat, HMS *Wasp*, was wrecked off Tory Island in Donegal. It had made a journey from Westport in Mayo to (depending on which account is read) collect overdue taxes or perform evictions, or both, when disaster struck; fifty-two soldiers and sailors were drowned with just five survivors; eight bodies were recovered and buried on the island.[79] Contemporary reportage was suitably exclamatory, with news arriving in Dublin by telegraph from London of 'terrible calamity off the Irish coast ... The wreck of the WASP will be a date by which the people of this wild and rugged coast will regulate the chronology of a generation, for it is the saddest tale of the sea ever yet borne to their homes by the tempestuous winds of that northern ocean.'[80]

It must have sunk quickly, it was surmised, because it was 'well supplied with boats and lifebuoys'. The focus of the mission was not, apparently, Tory, but the island of Inishtrahull, five miles north of Malin Head: 'A telegram from London this evening states that the gunboat Wasp was coming round to Moville for the purpose of taking the sheriff and an evicting party to the islet of Inishtrahull ... where a number of persons were today to have been removed from their dwellings. It is believed that the Wasp struck a rock on this wild coast and foundered directly afterwards.' Ironically, the Tory islanders were deemed to be 'gallant rescuers' who used their fishing boats to reach survivors and took them to the island lighthouse, 'where they were most kindly treated'. But there was comment also that in transporting the team of evictors to Inishtrahull, the boat was on a voyage to 'a most wretched place. The whole rent recoverable is only a few pounds.'[81]

The men saved 'refused to leave Tory island until officially ordered'. One of the survivors was a cook who was subsequently interviewed and was 'especially eloquent in his praise of the kindness with which he had been treated whilst on the island'.[82] The cause of the sinking was later deemed to be careless navigation; the commander of the rescue ship, *Valiant*, Captain Marrack, also 'spoke in the highest terms of the manner in which the islanders had treated the men and desired it to be stated, remarking that the inhabitants of the islands along the coast had been too frequently spoken of with harshness'.[83] Inishtrahull experienced a large population increase in the 1880s and had a community of thirteen families up until 1928, when it was evacuated; a tragedy, when a mailboat from Malin was swamped and an islander drowned, hastened its demise. It was eventually made into a bird sanctuary in the 1970s.[84]

The Blasket islanders also dined on tales of their resistance to those seeking rates and rents in the nineteenth century: 'Any boat that dared to approach the island to collect rent or to take the cows in lieu of rent was met with a shower of stones from the overhanging cliffs, some of them big enough not alone to injure the attackers but to hole the boats.'[85] In his memoirs, Henry Robinson, on the staff of the Local Government Board for Ireland established in the early 1870s, and who frequently prefaced the words 'island distress' with 'alleged', noted that the admiralty lent the Local Government Board HMS *Albacore* to get medicines and provisions to the Inishkeas during an outbreak of typhus:

> The multifarious functions of the gunboats on the West were very puzzling to the islanders. The same vessels that came with food supplies for the people and departed with bonfires blazing on the beach in their honour would return in a few days with bailiffs, process servers and police to sweep the island bare for rents or

rates. Then, after a pitched battle, away would go the bailiffs with their seizures and back again would come the gun boats after a few weeks interval with tons of meal to help the people to tide over the further distress caused by its previous visit.[86]

As with most of Robinson's memories there was something far too neat and exaggerated about this. It also seems far fetched that during the Irish crisis of 1879–80, as recorded by the Dublin Mansion House Relief Committee (see below), there was 'a misery so abject that when a gunboat was despatched a short time before to one of the Blasket Islands to enforce payment of county cess the crew of the gunboat no sooner saw the unhappy creatures they had come to overawe than they clubbed together and paid the amount of the demand out of their own wages'.[87]

But the raids and resistance were real and continued, including that by HMS *Britomart* in July 1890, targeting the Blaskets at the behest of its landlord Lord Cork, which generated much media and even parliamentary attention, a reminder that such raids could be completely counterproductive. There may have been a hundred policemen on board the gunboat, which, considering the island had a population of 130, underlines the heavy-handedness; there was little for them to take in lieu of rent, so they took the currachs (rowing boats used by the islanders) to Dingle town, over twelve miles away, which the islanders had to pay to retrieve. The unwelcome visitors were also accused of leaving typhoid in their wake; some reports suggested up to seven years' rent was due.[88] The local *Kerry Sentinel* was scathingly sarcastic in response: 'a victory that sheds additional lustre on the name of England! ... the tact and courage displayed by the members of our great Irish force in this daring enterprise ...' It was also raised in Parliament by Kerry MP Edward Harrington, who wondered 'is it the intention of the Admiralty to continue this practice of lending Her Majesty's ships of war?' MPs speaking in favour of the islanders secured a commitment that 'Her Majesty's ships' would no longer be used to confiscate goods in lieu of unpaid rent.[89]

Despite their distance from the mainland, islanders were not necessarily oblivious of politics and the state. Eoin MacNeill, a clerk in Dublin's Four Courts and Irish language enthusiast, was staying on the middle of the three Aran Islands, Inishmaan, in the summer of 1891 when Ireland was engulfed in the tragic drama of the downfall of the iconic Irish nationalist leader Charles Stewart Parnell. His personal life had resulted in the split of the nationalist party he had led and the previous month he had married his lover, Katherine O'Shea. MacNeill wrote to his brother: 'I find that the people are not so ignorant of the details of politics ... I haven't spoken to anybody here would touch Parnell now with a ten-foot pole or be seen with him in a forty-acre field ... I came across one man here who professed himself a good nationalist but said he didn't know what material good home rule was going to do.' MacNeill told the man, however, there were about twenty men on relief work on Inishmaan at a rate of one shilling a day, road making, which amounted to £1 a day, but that the cost of overseeing it with a policeman, a steamship subsidy and an engineering subsidy meant it costs ten times as much as was paid in relief to oversee it; it would be a lot more cost efficient, MacNeill concluded 'under an economic and careful government, not centralised'.[90]

In 1889 the curate on Tory Island, Fr D. E. Coyle, wrote to Bishop Patrick O'Donnell thanking him for a cheque for £3 he had sent and noted that a 'few strangers' had recently visited the island, including an MP, who had asked 'what would they do in case they were evicted'. In response, 'one of the islanders answered "We couldn't be sent to a worse place"'.[91] Fever had emerged on the island for 'want of fuel'; the previous month O'Donnell had written to another local priest, Fr James McFadden: 'the news you gave me of Tory Island is very sad. As the people have no hospital it might be well to call the attention of the sanitary officers to the state of things.'[92]

In the 1890s there were also seizures for rent and seed rate due on Achill, which was often distressed, so much so that the founder of the Land League, Michael Davitt, wrote in 1886 that its residents were 'compelled to eat what an ordinary pig would turn aside with an indignant snout'. Bart Molloy, the largest provisions dealer in Achill, was said to be owed £600 by the 'poor creatures'.[93] Significantly, the following year a bridge connecting Achill to the mainland was opened and named after Davitt, the fishing industry was extended and it was made accessible by railway in 1892, meaning the concerns raised by the travel writer Harriet Martineau in *Letter from Ireland* (1852) – 'the traveller is annoyed at the loss of time and the fatigue incurred by the great circuits that have to be made to get from place to place' – were addressed.[94]

The winter of 1880 was particularly notable for evidence of distress in the west. The voluntary Mansion House Relief Committee was set up in Dublin in January 1880 and identified Donegal and Mayo as the most afflicted counties. The Relief Committee was established under the auspices of the Lord Mayor of Dublin, Edward Dwyer Gray, and funds were raised in Europe, America and even Australia and India; the money was distributed to local committees, with the proviso that it be spent on Indian meal. A special subcommittee was established to 'relieve the western isles' and four gunboats were placed at its disposal by the government: 'When they reached the islands they found the people surviving on turnips, coarse dried fish and boiled seaweed.'[95] The Relief Committee, which oversaw the distribution of £130,000 to some 800 religiously mixed local committees, certainly made a significant impact and succeeded in communicating Irish distress to a wide international audience.

Commissions were established the following year, when the harvest improved, including the Bessborough, chaired by the sixth Earl of Bessborough, F. G. Ponsonby, a substantial landlord in Kilkenny, who looked at the workings of land legislation. His report influenced Prime Minister Gladstone's 1881 Land Bill, which was transformative and far reaching in establishing the principle of dual ownership between landlord and tenant and resulted in the establishment of the Land Commission, empowered to fix rents and purchase estates with a view to transfer to tenants. These initiatives, subsequently built on, were to be instrumental in enabling tenant ownership of land, including on the islands. It was from this type of reforming mindset that the words 'congestion' and 'congested districts' began to find their way into popular usage and also brought the Quaker and philanthropist James Hack Tuke to prominence with his publication *Distress in Ireland* (1880). There were also parallels with Scotland in relation to land war, the Crofter's Act and a Scottish Congested Districts Board.[96]

Achill came under the sharp gaze of Tuke, who in many ways was the father of the Congested Districts Board (CDB) for Ireland. He was deeply affected by visits to Ireland during the Great Famine and then the 1880 severe food shortages in western Ireland ('turf dwellings near the road which my friends, who were not acquainted with the West could not believe was a human habitation') and was a vocal exponent of economic reforms for the congested districts, including land reform, local industries, railways and fishing. Because of the failure of government to embrace the idea of assisted emigration he took it on himself and 'by 1884 had assisted some 9,500 emigrants to travel to America and Canada. Tuke, who personally selected many of the emigrants, also used his contacts in America to secure aid and employment for the Irish on their arrival overseas.'[97] During another food crisis of 1885–6 he was called on by the government to assist once again and raised substantial funds. It was recorded in 1892 that the Tuke Fund had enabled a 'considerable number' of families to emigrate from Achill in 1883–4: 'most of these families resided in the north-eastern corner of the island and an improvement in the general circumstances of the people in this part of Achill is plainly to be seen'.[98]

Tuke's endeavours and the establishment of the Irish CDB in August 1891 are a reminder that one of the striking themes of the late nineteenth century is the number of private philanthropists and public servants who were engaged with the travails of the west and the islands, including Henry Robinson, who was frequently dispatched on Local Government Board missions to the West of Ireland. The following decade in relation to distress on the Aran Islands in 1894, Robinson suggested 'the decisive test for the Board was how it would match long-term objectives with short-term need'.[99] James Arthur Balfour was the chief secretary for Ireland who established the CDB, and, though dismissive of Irish nationalism, was anxious for a 'constructive' unionist policy for Ireland. He regarded the Irish land system as 'essentially and radically rotten', and made funds available for tenants to purchase their own land and facilitated railway construction. In truth, he believed the solution to the rural crisis was mass emigration from poorer districts but realised how unpalatable that would be to nationalists; at the end of 1890 he visited distressed parts of Mayo, Connemara and Donegal and met with those suffering.

The CDB proved to be a successful government initiative in Ireland, and its work drew praise from many quarters. It was invested with wide-reaching powers to encourage agriculture and industry, initially along the west coast (where 20 per cent of residents lived in congested electoral districts) but subsequently extended inwards, covering eighty-four districts and a population of over 500,000. It drew together representatives from state, churches, landlords, business, the professions and the local community and employed agricultural instructors, promoted improved methods of land cultivation, cottage industries, fisheries, road, pier and bridge building and also purchased land for resale to tenants. Although there were numerous criticisms of its financial management, Balfour was certainly proud of the Board's achievements, claiming that it had done more good for Ireland than a hundred domestic parliaments would ever do. Although nationalist MPs mocked his policy of 'light railways and heavy punishments', many of their constituents 'were grateful for his ameliorative measures'.[100] By 1909, the CDB had an annual sum of £250,000 at its disposal and it has been described by its historian, Ciara Breathnach, as a 'radical new departure' because of the way it pinpointed areas of distress, was an advance on previous 'quick fix' solutions based on outdoor relief overseen by the Board of Works under the Poor Law, and was not put under the control of a political assembly.[101]

It was especially relevant to the islands, as overall, between 1891 and 1923 it erected or substantially improved over 9,000 rural dwellings, reduced the number of traditional byre dwellings and 'almost completely' replaced the housing stock on the offshore islands as part of this overall process.[102] Decades later a priest on the island of Arranmore in Donegal observed that 'the CDB got the people to build better homes. Since then the health bill of the island has been good.'[103]

Crucially, it also bought off landlords. In the 1890s the CDB bought out the Aran Islands from their owners, supplied a pier and a fishery store and stone-built, slate-roofed houses, though that did not necessarily prevent depopulation.[104] The transformation of Clare Island as a result of the CDB was remarkable; in effect the CDB 'entirely remodelled its landscape'. It purchased the island in 1895 and resold it to the tenants five years later; the fertility of the land meant that its nineteenth-century expansion had witnessed great pressure on limited space, and the fragmentation of farms by the 1890s was such that 'consolidation through enclosure of land was not possible without the intervention of an outside agency'.[105]

The complicated pattern of land division inherited from the rundale system (common in pre-famine Ireland, but lasting well after it in some poorer districts, where the land was leased to one or two tenants who then divided it amongst numerous others for crops and grazing, based on land quality) was reflected in the fact that in two small fields shared by three tenants, one tenant had twenty-two separate plots, another sixteen and the third fourteen, many of the plots no bigger than a single tillage ridge. By the time the CDB intervened three years' rent was owed by the Clare islanders (some £1,800) and twenty of ninety-eight tenants had been evicted. It was purchased by the CDB after the intervention of a local priest and guarantees given by the Archbishop of Tuam Dr MacHale and William O'Brien MP. The CDB consolidated farms and resold to seventy-eight tenants; the scale of the works was 'immense' from 1895 to 1901, completed almost exclusively by the islanders including the building of a seven-mile-long commonage wall along with roads and drainage; the CDB spent £13,600 on the project.[106]

The chairman of the CDB, William Lawson Micks, was later to observe of the CDB that its land purchase function 'greatly eclipsed all its other proceedings and activities',[107] a development of great significance to islanders. During its lifetime (1891–1923) it purchased 951 estates for over £9 million and £2.25 million was spent improving these estates for in the region of 60,000 tenants, including those on Clare Island, the Blasket Islands, the Aran Islands and the Inishkea Islands, whose residents were 'troublesome folk to get money out of', according to a Land Commission official.[108]

Detailed insight was provided on the state of the islands by the CDB's local (baseline) reports of the 1890s compiled by various CDB inspectors; the reports highlighted the main island industries, mainly fishing, poultry and kelp manufacture. Knitting, weaving and spinning were in decline due to mass machine-spun textiles and for some islands, there was a heavy reliance on seasonal migration. Fish, tea, stirabout and potatoes were the staples of diet and sales of eggs and butter were vital. Barter – eggs and fish exchanged for tea, sugar and tobacco, for example – was also common.

The assessments of the CDB inspectors were frank and sometimes cutting. F. G. Townshend Gahan surveyed some of the Donegal islands in 1896 and on the largest, Arranmore, with a population of 1,103, noted several families were 'living on the holdings of their parents', cattle of 'a very inferior type', with land cultivated 'entirely by spade labour' and men and girls away at harvest and potato digging. The CDB had sent superior bulls to the island, which 'people seem to appreciate very much'; there was, however, only a single pig.[109]

He pointed out that the islanders paid £150 yearly in county cess 'and deserve better treatment at the hands of the grand jury' (later that decade the 1898 Local Government (Ireland) Act replaced a number of household taxes including the county cess payable to the grand juries and the poor law rates payable to the boards of guardians with a single charge payable to the new county and borough councils). Roads were poor, there was no telegraphic communication or adequate pier and 'about 60 per cent of the men and the same proportion of the able-bodied girls migrate each year to Scotland', where wages ranged from ten to twenty-five shillings a week. There was practically no weaving or spinning left in the district, but the kelp industry was significant and the most important after fishing, with about 200–250 tons of kelp made annually, while there were about sixty boats engaged in herring fishing and there were four curing stations in the district of Arranmore, on the mainland: 'each man earned at least £15 this season and in many cases much more'; one boat's crew fished salmon last season 'and had a nice profit for themselves'.

But they needed a curing station on the island to save them from going to Burtonport and back, and 'from a moral point of view it would be a great advantage as the amount spent on drink at Burtonport during the fishing is enormous'. The island also had a good supply of turf (though 'about ⅔ of the mountain belongs to the landlord'). Tea and sugar were largely paid for in eggs and butter and there was a six-month credit system for purchasing meal and flour but that was problematic: 'The great drawback of the credit system on which the people work is that being as a rule illiterate, they have absolutely no check on the dealer – anything he chooses to put down they must accept.' The average family spent about £43 per year on clothing, fishing gear and food with some money made from sale of eggs, butter and kelp, and there was a large dependence on Scottish earnings; expenditure on whiskey was estimated at an annual average of £1.10s: 'about 30 per cent are teetotallers, 40 per cent moderate, the remainder drink a good deal'.[110]

What was also clear from these reports was that there was no single island experience. The way Townshend Gahan summed up life on Arranmore was hardly positive: 'Their home life is simple and monotonous, their only diversions being weddings and wakes. The herring fishing too lends at that particular time an element of excitement to their lives. They have no peculiar local customs, so far as I could find out. In the winter months they practically do nothing.'

But compare that to his assessment of the island of Inishkeeragh, where industriousness was absent and the islanders were

> apathetic and hopeless ... live very wretchedly and if not removed will in the course of a few years be driven from the island ... there are in all eleven families living on the island and to me they seemed the most wretched, without exception, in the district. There is a national school on the island – a room, about ten feet square, if so large and hardly fit to be a byre. They have no well water but get it from the furrows between the ridges and the ditches.[111]

Inishkeeragh still had a population of 117 in 1911 and in 1955 it was stated in the Dáil (Irish Parliament) that there were still twelve families in a 'helpless situation' and 'sad plight' who would no longer be able to habitate it.[112]

But Townshend Gahan also made the observation that, Inishkeeragh aside,

> the general condition of this district is more prosperous than

many of those on the mainland. The people have more energy and although the great profits they reap from the herring fishing has a rather deadening effect on them, from an industrial point of view, still, on the whole, they seemed to me more industrious than the people of other districts on the mainland.[113]

Tory Island was the subject of Townshend Gahan's inspection in February 1897 at a time when its population was 320. During a period of distress in 1890–91, 'every family on the island except two were on the relief works', while there were no green or root crops, though the methods of cultivation 'are in some respects more advanced than those on the mainland'. There was little or no migratory labour and the turf supply was 'practically exhausted'. But fishing was in a good state with a curing station on the island opened three years previously. The CDB had erected a substantial pier but industry was needed. They were a 'shrewd, healthy race, such a thing as an imbecile or person of weak intellect is practically unknown'. In the previous six years no county cess had been paid; they complained that they did not get services and the rents were historically excessive. Townshend Gahan was crystal clear in his recommendation that 'the Board should purchase the island ... should the Board become owners of the island many things would be possible which are now unattainable'.[114] This happened in 1903, when it was purchased form the Joule family who had owned it since the 1860s. This proved to be a serious modernising influence and the islanders were given grants to replace thatched cottages with two-storey stone-built houses.

Clare and Inishturk were visited by Robert Ruttledge-Fair of the CDB in May 1892: on Clare 'the people, some of them from pure laziness, will not climb the mountain where the turf of good quality can be obtained but cut scraws, half peat and half clay in the vicinity of their houses'.[115] Residents of both islands were generally 'well-clad' with 'fairly good houses' but they had lost 'almost all habits of industry and self-reliance ... they live very extravagantly and in good years make no effort to lay by anything to meet adverse circumstances'. One of his key recommendations was 'the most important of all: discouraging gratuitous relief being given under any circumstances, except that administered under the poor law'.[116]

He also visited Inishbofin in August 1892 and noted a curing station had been recently established there: 'the Inishbofin and Inishark islanders are the best and most practical fishermen on the west coast'.[117] Improvements to piers had already been made by the Fishery, Piers and Harbour Commissioners, but again there was a sting in relation to the islanders' relationship with officialdom: 'Unfortunately, they have learned to look to government for assistance in the smallest enterprise and they never seem to think that a little energy on their part would tide them over many difficulties'.[118] Redmond Roche visited Cape Clear in January 1893 and noted that, while a boat slip had been built on Heir Island, 'more accommodation in the way of slips and shelter is needed in various places'.[119]

The Aran Islands were inspected by Robert Ruttledge-Fair in the spring of 1893 at a time when the population was 2,907, comprising 562 families, sixty of whom were deemed to be living in 'very poor circumstances' but with good breeds of both cattle and sheep (Aran cattle always got high prices at fairs). A telegraph office had also recently opened up at Kilronan but there was scarcely any employment for labourers outside of spring and summer.[120] Islanders did little lobster fishing; better boats were needed and 'much time is lost in enforced idleness' due to poor weather. There were 116 currachs, twelve small sailing boats ('third class') and four large trading boats: 'the pier at Kilronan is the most availed of but it was wrongly placed and at low water is inaccessible even for small hookers'. Houses were fairly well furnished: 'in every respect, particularly as regards cleanliness, they are far superior to the houses occupied by the Connemara peasantry', another reminder that the assessments of the islands could include assertions of superiority over the mainland.

The Aran people were also deemed to be 'fairly industrious and hard working and may, I think, be depended upon to take advantage of any opportunity that may be afforded to improve their circumstances. Like most of the islanders of the west coast they are very suspicious ... I am not aware of any organisational effort having been made to develop the resources or improve the conditions of the people of this district ... the islanders hitherto could not be considered fishermen', but efforts made recently by the Board were bearing fruit, especially in relation to the transit of fish.[121]

Robert Ruttledge-Fair visited Achill in April 1892 and noted that five different landlords owned different tracts of the island. While postal arrangements were good and a telegraph office had opened the previous year, there was no kelp industry or lobster fishing, no facilities for the sale of fresh fish and no knowledge of fish curing. Most houses were stone, though a few were still 'sod huts'. He suggested there was no reason cottage industries could not thrive on the island, but for fishing to be developed places of refuge and shelter for the boats were needed.[122]

Achill was greatly dependent on seasonal migration and the island suffered unbearable tragedy in June 1894 when 400 gathered to board currachs to take them to hookers, which were then travelling on to Westport and then by steamer to Glasgow or Liverpool for seasonal work. That same year, the Westport correspondent of the *Irish Daily Independent* had described the islanders as 'people living in the most miserable hovels that ever sheltered man or woman'. Four years previously Arthur James Balfour, the chief secretary, had visited the island to witness the poverty; £4,000 worth of seed had been made available but islanders were pursued for payment after the crop failed.[123]

There were 126 passengers on board the *Victory* hooker and when it foundered, overladen, thirty-two died: 'fond relatives were recognised, the wailing rent the air and the scene was heartrending'. The victims included Mary Patten, aged eighteen, 'who was going to Scotland to provide for her mother and five other children', and it was observed by a contemporary newspaper that 'what is even more appalling than the tale of death is the revelation of life on Achill Island which the evidence [of the inquest] discloses'. They went to Scotland to earn the landlord's rent and the seed rate while a 'benevolent liberal' chief secretary imposes 'this white slavery'.[124]

But on the positive side, on foot of the detailed reports of the CDB inspectors the role of the CDB in the development of the islands became vital. It bought the Blasket Islands from the Earl of Cork in 1907 and spent ten years reorganising the land and building roads and houses.[125]

The Board also invested heavily in developing a fishing industry for Tory, with a curing station, eight boats, a pier and a slipway. On Arranmore it oversaw house building and fish curing and reorganised the division of land; significantly, the island prospered from 1891 to 1920; its population was 1,163 in 1894, which had increased to 1,650 in 1911. It also had a nurse and domestic training classes; the improvements from 1980 to 1920 were considered 'real and long-lasting'.[126] In its twenty-seventh annual report in 1920, the CDB reported average expenditure per household in the south Connemara islands was just over £63, up from just under £18 in 1891; there was significant increase in expenditure on oil lamps and clothes, both of which were considered luxury items.[127]

Aran became such an important centre for mackerel fishing that it was necessary to employ an agent to market the Aran produce in London. Aran fishermen seemed to be happy with the Board's operations, though there were criticisms in 1898 that it was charging too much for freight. But historian Ciara Breathnach emphasises that the Board engaged with the fishermen, encouraged price scaling and intervened when there was a glut in the market; as mackerel had left American coastal waters, the cured mackerel trade flourished until 1900. From 1912 fish were shipped from the islands to Galway city on the steamboat *Dún Aengus*; at a cost of £7,500 it represented 'the largest single investment in a vessel by the CDB', which was also spending over £25,000 annually on fisheries and harbours after 1910. Quite simply, the CDB 'transformed sea-fishing in West Galway, and this was especially true of the Aran Islands'.[128] Nonetheless, the hoped for local voluntary co-operatives did not emerge on the scale the Board had hoped; Aran islanders did establish a fishing co-op but it did not thrive and did not cover fishing equipment; it was also difficult to persuade people to engage in fisheries full-time.[129]

The CDB could certainty be credited with aiding commercial fisheries and speeding up the delivery process, given the steamer service between Aran and the mainland, yet it was maintained that Connemara men 'had no regard' for the tuition provided by the Board, 'possibly because it was free ... and they did not seem to care for investment in the future'.[130] It was also significant that the marine engineer advising the

Board insisted all marine works in congested counties be made of concrete for durability.

There was always going to be inconsistency in fishing owing to the 'notoriously unpredictable herring', but the CDB's curing stations were regarded as a great stride forward. They were set up 'under the direction of skilled immigrant instructors from the Shetland Islands'. At Gola Island in Donegal (which had 169 residents in 1911) the CDB provided a stone pier, boats and fishing gear; in the 1960s the pier on Gola still had 'excellent' anchorage unaffected by the tide.[131] On Inishmurray, off the Sligo Coast, where kelp was an important enterprise, the CDB assisted when 1,000 tons of kelp was shipped out of the island in 1895 alone. The same year the CDB proposal for a curing station on the island did not progress, but the Board 'did send John Duthie of Oban, Scotland, to teach the best methods of fishing' and he stayed for a year.[132]

Efforts to develop the island resources also raised tensions in relation to how the authorities would work with islanders and their representatives and relations between the CDB and the Department of Agriculture and Technical Instruction (DATI), established in 1899, were also often fraught. John McCuaig, the only shopkeeper on Rathlin and a spokesperson for the island fishermen, wrote to the DATI in October 1900 complaining bitterly about 'the deplorable state of the fishing ports of the island owing to the gales of late years ... with the result that many of us holding small patches of farms were served with ejectments'. At that stage there were 365 people living on Rathlin and depending largely on fishing, and if the ports were not improved they might be compelled to 'emigrate to some more favourable place'.[133]

The DATI observed in response that 'none of them, however, follows fishing exclusively'. A DATI inspector's report in February 1902 noted the islanders were represented on the local district council by two members 'who, however, live on the mainland and cannot be expected to take the interest in the wants of Rathlin as if they lived on the island'. The inspector told McCuaig that Antrim was a rich county and, 'as according to his statement the islanders paid their rates', they should get the county council to do the work.[134]

Things continued to deteriorate. In 1906 Fr Joseph McGlave, a priest on the island, informed the DATI that the only deep-water harbour was 'completely closed'. He noted that the island forefathers

> went far out to sea and fished the rich banks that are off our shores but which cannot be reached on the small boats which now alone we can use. Our population then was more than treble what it is now and they were more comfortable and better-off than we are. Now agriculture is the industry – and a very poor one – and fishing the recreation.

There was also damage done by potato blight: 'we are sorry to admit potatoes are our staple food'.[135] While the DATI was 'somewhat doubtful whether the possibilities of fishing are so good as has been represented', it was acknowledged that an improved harbour was needed, but also noted that a bull provided by the department was 'neglected and was not properly fed' and when returned to DATI at the end of the season 'was in a starved condition, although the person in whose charge the bull was placed was paid for his keep'.[136] Bureaucratic wrangling was apparent in relation to the development of the harbour; the piers and harbours committee was due to travel to the site in June 1907 but there were disputes over who should fund it as 'the work cannot be said to be for the benefit of the fishing industry'. It was later deemed to be 'a matter of transit of produce' and the CDB was asked to contribute £600.[137]

Fr Murtagh Farragher served as curate on the Aran Islands from 1887–91 and then returned as parish priest in 1897. There were to be many extraordinary island priests (see chapter 4) and Farragher, more than any other, exemplified their best and worst traits and crossed swords with the authorities at various stages. An energetic, egotistical bully, he sent a memorandum in colourful and exaggerated language, full of bathos, self-promotion and self-regard, to the CDB in November 1910 and referred to the 'complete transformation' of the islands in the previous fourteen years. He had been curate before the CDB when, 'with pain and sorrow, I saw the poor people starving', but then with the operation of the CDB he witnessed the 'cloud lifting' and elaborated on his 'gratification to see the beaming countenances of those whom I had known before and known to have never even a smile'.[138]

He noted that he was 'called upon to play a rather prominent part' as a 'people's advocate ... because I am so passionate in intervening for them' but not all hopes had been realised. He simultaneously and erroneously referred to himself as the islanders' 'humble pastor', which could not have been further from the truth. Arrears had built up regarding loans for boats and fishing gear; there were those who spent unwisely to 'have a whack out of it' while funding lasted, but there was now a depreciation in the value of mackerel and a need for cod nets and more marketing of the fish. A better service by the Galway steam boat was also demanded but crucially, 'It may be gratifying to know that there has been no appeal for charitable purposes since the advent of the Board'.[139]

Farragher's relationship with the CDB worsened. He claimed in 1913 that its property had been 'misused and misapplied' and that the Board's local representative, Coleman Costello, 'has been allowed to use his position more in the object of discrediting his parish priest and endeavouring to lower him in the estimation of his flock than seeing that the operations of the Board are directed with the interests of the fishing and the fishermen'. He wanted Coleman to 'mend his manners'.[140] In reacting to the CDB's annual report for 1913 he thundered that 'my islanders are not lacking in either brains or muscle and only await the opportunities of exercising both', but insisted the CDB was not doing its job properly and that he was no 'carping critic'.[141]

This was an indication of how Farragher defined the islanders according to what he was looking for. Three years earlier he had referred to them as 'poor unsophisticated people whose lives have been spent cut away from every civilising influence'.[142]

Two years later, he insisted that the days of sailing boats were numbered; that motor boats were required along with a new system of loans. Fishermen were getting fleeced, and the CDB was not performing well as it was 'choked by red tape' and smothered by 'officialdom'.[143]

The complaints continued in subsequent years. By 1919 he was insisting that the 'good intentions of the Board are grossly miscarried'; he had also complained about storage facilities at the docks in Galway and the branding of mackerel barrels but also, in 1916, about the 'unscrupulous action of the fish buyers ... even the friendly intervention of the Board fell on the deaf ears of those parasites'. This necessitated the formation of a co-operative, but it did not do well and needed the assistance of the CDB.[144] In turn, the CDB insisted it needed clearer accounts from the co-op and clarity about 'financial results'. Farragher accused it of being jealous of the success of the co-op; the CDB insisted all it was concerned with was making the best of fisheries.[145] Farragher was also at the centre of a number of notorious boycotts (see chapter 4); one of them was the subject of questions in the House of Commons in November 1911. It was alleged that Colman McDonagh 'has been boycotted, with his aged mother and a young family of children ... McDonagh, having been employed in 1909 and 1910 by the Congested Districts Board in charge of an ice hulk in Aran was this year refused employment and the secretary of the branch of the United Irish League [UIL, founded in 1898 to agitate for redistribution of land to small farmers in the west] appointed in his stead'. Farragher was the president of the UIL branch in question. McDonagh attended a UIL meeting to plead for the boycott to be removed and was 'turned out' by Farragher; McDonagh subsequently attempted suicide and ended up in an asylum.[146]

Further attention was devoted to distressed parts of Ireland with the Royal Commission on Congestion, which first met in London in 1906 and reported in 1908. One of its members was Sir A. P. Mac Donnell, a senior civil servant and native of Mayo, regarded as a 'liberal imperialist', who had overseen famine relief efforts in India in the 1870s. He doubted the Irish fitness for home rule (though he eventually came round to the idea), was recruited as undersecretary for Ireland in 1902 and helped to pass the Wyndham Land Act of 1903, which laid down the parameters for agreements between landlords and tenants to be automatically approved by the Land Commission. He referred to the relief of congestion as

the most difficult administrative problem of the time in Ireland. A permanent and radical solution to that problem is only to be found in a policy of state-aided emigration to the colonies, or in a policy of migration which means removing people from congested

districts to new holdings carved out of untenanted land bought
for the purpose ... the first alternative is a counsel of despair.[147]

The Report noted that the districts scheduled under the Congested
Districts Act of 1891 consisted of 3,626,381 acres, more than one-sixth of
the total area of Ireland with a population in 1901 of 505,723, more than
one-ninth of the total population of Ireland.[148] Eighty thousand families
were living in congested districts and seven of every eight holdings in
those districts were under £10 valuation. Of particular relevance to the
islands was the finding that the average earnings Irish migratory labourers brought home after five or six months' seasonal work varied from £12
to £15, but that in bad years the failure of the crop 'results in a condition
of semi-starvation'. Beer, whiskey and tobacco consumption was 'excessive ... stimulants for a badly fed population rather than as ordinary luxuries ... nevertheless the death rate is low, a testament to the virility of the
race'.[149]

This was a significant point as the death rate in these districts was
14.6 per 1,000 compared to 19.4 for the rest of the country. One contributor also noted that 'acute intelligence and quickness of perception are
striking characteristics of the people to be dealt with'.[150] The report also
gave insight into how the process of the CDB buying islands worked and
how, in practice the CDB could bring considerable improvement to the
islands. It noted that the Board spent more on improvements on Clare
Island than they had paid for the island, but as they resold it for £10,000,
'they recovered a large part of their expenditure from the tenants in the
shape of the enhanced price and lost on the whole transaction only a
comparatively trifling amount'.[151]

Despite such improvements, or because of the increased expectations,
persuading islanders to pay rates remained a tall order. In 1908 Michael
Doogan, a rate collector in Donegal, wrote to Patrick O'Donnell, the
Catholic Bishop of Raphoe. O'Donnell was an administratively gifted
cleric who served with the CDB from its creation until its dissolution in
1923 and was a firm supporter of the co-operative movement. Doogan
outlined 'a matter of grievance' as 'the unfortunate collector of Donegal
rates'. He had taken up the collection of rates fourteen years previously

and had made some efforts, 'without success to get a landing on the islands and the question fell through'. More recently, island communities, including Gola, refused to pay 'although I made all possible efforts but lately no boat would go there with me and I am now held accountable for the amount ... I have a large family to support.' He also insisted that councillor Patrick Gallagher was 'working heart and soul against me'.[152]

Gallagher was a native of the Rosses district of Donegal and a renowned co-op organiser who two years previously had established the Templecrone co-op society and was trying to defeat the financial stranglehold exercised by local gombeen men, the wheeler-dealer money lenders and exploiters, who, after he had visited Gallagher's co-op store, writer George Russell insisted were worse than greedy landlords: 'the landlord owned the land. The gombeen men owned the people and the profits the gombeen men got out of the men was greater by far than the profit the landowner got out of his for the holding'.[153] Gallagher also insisted that the gombeen man, who 'can ruin any man who crosses him for he is all powerful in his own district', was more harmful than any bad landlord.[154] But a rate collector was unlikely to get much sympathy from Bishop O'Donnell; indeed, James Ward, a trader on Tory, wrote to O'Donnell five years later noting 'we escape rents, rates and taxes thanks largely to your Lordship and Tory, though remote and insignificant always, has moved a bit away from its perennial destitution'; so much so that he was able to enclose 'a wee cheque'.[155]

But the non-payment of rates created other problems. In December 1914, Fr John Boyle, the parish priest on Tory, wrote to O'Donnell noting that the Dunfanaghy guardians, who had been contributing £30 annually for a nurse on the island, '[have] ceased to contribute towards the maintenance of a nurse on Tory. They took this course because of the non-payment of rates by the islanders ... anyone can see what a blessing such as a nurse was to a people who are, for months at a time, beyond the reach of medical aid'. He also noted that William Lawson Micks, chairman of the CDB 'seems to think the question of dealing with defaulting islands must some day be settled', concluding there was a necessity to 'submit a reasonable scheme' to the islanders.[156]

In 1909 there was much dispute about the supply of water to the

Aran Islands, which was out of order; at a monthly meeting of the Galway Rural District Council a letter from Fr Farragher to the Local Government Board was read concerning this issue, pointing out the inhabitants of Inishmaan and Inisheer had experienced 'frightful privations for want of water ... yet it is asked that these people should pay rates. This they refuse to do, on my advice'. Farragher insisted he would do everything 'in my power' to prevent them paying rates 'until there is some attempt made to treat them as ordinary human beings'. One member of the council advised Farragher to first get the islanders to pay their rates as they had refused for the past six or seven years.[157]

Islanders were also, like their mainland counterparts, to benefit from some of the measures associated with the evolution of the welfare state. Augustine Birrell, the chief secretary for Ireland, visited the Aran Islands in June 1911 accompanied by a party including Henry Robinson, by then vice president of the Local Government Board. Although Birrell travelled by the CDB steamer, 'the visit was of a private character'. He was welcomed on behalf of the islanders by Fr Farragher, who specifically referred to the Liberal government's introduction of the University Act, the Congested Districts Act, the Old Age Pensions Act and 'other beneficial acts and pledges'. Birrell replied 'in a forcible speech' and said he hoped the CDB would continue to improve the welfare of the islanders 'until the advent of home rule when he hoped the people would attain a high level of prosperity and comfort'. The visitors were 'enthusiastically cheered', especially by the old-age pensioners.[158]

Island visits could also be used to make other, contrary political points for nationalists or to hone their burgeoning linguistic and nationalist commitments, as in the case of Roger Casement, who wrote in the summer of 1912, 'I am now on the wing for Ireland – to Rathlin Island.'[159] Casement from 1913–14 also spearheaded a humanitarian relief campaign for Connemara islanders, depicting them as 'an Irish Putumayo' (as a member of the British consular service Casement investigated reports of atrocities in the region of the Putumayo, a remote tributary of the Amazon where the Peruvian Amazon Company was collecting rubber; his report revealed the horrific treatment and enslavement of the indigenous population of the Putumayo including flogging, rape,

starvation, mutilation and murder). In May 1913 there was a typhus outbreak in Connemara, which promoted the evocation of the ghosts of the
Great Famine. Casement, with the zeal of the convert to Irish nationalism, generated controversy with his insistence on the need to 'remove the
stain of this enduring Putumayo from our native land' and was accused
of 'inexcusable exaggeration'.[160] He knew well this was precisely what he
was doing, but as he saw it, the publicity generated justified the distor-
tion. It was a time when, given the collapse in kelp prices (the £6 once
commanded for a ton of kelp had dropped to £2 10s) there were suggestions that some of the island communities needed to be relocated inland,
but the parish priest at Carraroe in Galway complained of 'disfiguration
of facts'. Casement sought to cash in on the publicity by writing public
letters about a Connacht 'on the verge of chronic famine' in a 'dispos-
sessed Ireland', the victims being the 'white Indians of Ireland'. The CDB
took exception to these assertions. Casement, with others, including the
historian Alice Stopford Green, had a wider agenda, which was to attract
sympathy to the cause of Irish independence.[161]

A report on the Connemara region that included some of the western islands, sent to the CDB in 1914, was published in the *Irish Review*,
a major publication of the Irish literary revival filled with contributions
from many of the major figures of the political and cultural revival including Douglas Hyde, the founder of the Gaelic League in 1893, and Roger
Casement, whose suggestion led to the 1914 report which was signed by
Alice Stopford Green in London, as well as promoters of agricultural
improvement. The authors complained that 'no notice' had been taken
by the CDB of the report.[162] Its authors had paid a 'series of visits' to the
islands and noticed that the price of kelp had dropped from £9 a ton to
between £2 and £3; 'it no longer pays to burn it'. They wondered would
scientific methods be used to establish the industry on new lines. They
also highlighted the importance of remittances from America and the
poor quality of the land, on which 'as a German visitor put it, a central
European goat would die of hunger'.[163]

Then there were the wretched dwellings: 'House 12 ft by 12 ft. Floor,
living rock, natural drainage hole in the middle. One door, pig in the
room. Bed fills up one end of room. A half starved pet kitten. Man has

a quarter share of a boat's work. The boat can work only six months. No fence round house. Bedding consists of sacks filled with straw.'

They also insisted reform needed to be achieved through the Irish language and argued that dependence on relief generated the threat of the disadvantaged western people being turned into a 'mere horde of ingenious beggars'. There was also an unapologetic idealisation of these people as 'a remarkably handsome race ... beautiful and courtly manners. For sheer good looks, both among men and women, they are not to be surpassed in the world ... far superior in qualities of mind and body to the slum dwellers of our great cities'.[164]

During the subsequent revolutionary period from 1913–21, islands featured as places of internment or useful hiding or resting spots for those on the run or those seeking to hide seditious materials. Island-ers had mixed feelings about the revolution. The islands contained no shortage of committed nationalists, and when in 1914 the *Asgard* landed arms at Howth for the Irish Volunteers, later used in the 1916 Rising, two members of the crew, Patrick McGinley and Charles Duggan, were from Gola Island in Donegal, a reminder not just of their politics but also their seafaring prowess.[165] In Richard Power's novel *The Land of Youth* (1964), for some islanders the revolution 'seemed a smugly academic interest' but islander Seán, on the run as a republican, found himself 'tormented by rumours from the mainland of ambushes, derailments and burnings. Seán felt frustrated for want of a purpose.'[166]

Fr Patrick Doyle, the former rector of Knockbeg College in Carlow, which had been used as a refuge by some nationalists, hired a returned 1916 Rising internee Gearóid O'Sullivan as a teacher. O'Sullivan was active in a training camp for Irish Volunteers (which evolved into the IRA) in west Cork and

> one day Gearóid arranged for me to go to Baltimore for a boat trip to the islands of the harbour and out to Cape Clear. The local captain of the Volunteers provided a motorboat for the trip. I visited several of the islands where we deposited strange longitudi-nal parcels. The wily volunteer had taken advantage of the innocent priest's trip to distribute rifles to the Volunteers on the islands.[167]

Cork IRA officer Liam Deasy also recalled looking at the possibility of landing arms on small west Cork islands, including Rabbit Island 'then inhabited by one family named O'Driscoll and friendly to the national cause'.[168] (There were, according to the 1911 census, two families comprising seventeen people on the island at that time.[169])

Laurence Ginnell, director of the underground republican Sinn Féin government's department of publicity, having been imprisoned for four months, went to the Aran Islands in September 1919, according to his wife 'for health reasons, as a restful place and remote from roar'. He stayed for over five months.[170] Islands even featured in the republican dispensing of justice after Sinn Féin had established tribunals and republican courts in its attempt to supplant the British administration of justice. In Clare, in the summer of 1920, before the formal courts system was inaugurated, two men who disobeyed an order from a Sinn Féin tribunal to rebuild a wall they had demolished 'were left on an island off the Clare coast for three weeks. A party of the RIC who arrived by boat to rescue them were pelted with stones and abused. The castaways proudly declared that they were citizens of the Irish republic and the police had no right to interfere.'[171]

Spike Island in Cork, at the entrance to the harbour – which from the 1840s to the 1880s had been used as a prison for convicts bound for the penal colonies in Australia and beyond; over 1,000 convicts died on the island during that period – still had a population of roughly 600 in 1911 and held internees and men convicted by courts martial under the Restoration of Order in Ireland Act and by military courts in the martial law area during the War of Independence. The first batch of internees arrived in February 1921 and the following month Bere Island in Bantry Bay, another strategically positioned island at the mouth of one of Europe's deepest harbours, whose population dropped from 1,152 to 876 between 1861 and 1911 and with a tradition of fortified army bases stretching back to the 1790s, opened for prisoner business. By the end of June there were 381 internees on Spike and 106 on Bere.[172]

Before that, the officer commanding of the Bere Island IRA, attached to the Castletownbere battalion, was James Sullivan; a volunteer unit had been formed on the island in 1917 and he estimated its strength at 'about forty'. What was most interesting was that 'training was carried out under our own officers, who acquired their knowledge of military training from British military training manuals obtained from members of the British garrison on Bere Island'. In June 1918 members of the Bere Island Company, in co-operation with men from Adrigole, 'seized a large quantity of gun cotton primers and detonators from the military stores on the island'; over fifty boxes were carried to a boat on the pier then rowed across the harbour and hidden in the Adrigole area.[173]

On Spike Island, prisoners complained that they were charged with making habitable buildings that had historically housed a hospital for treatment of soldiers suffering from VD. In November 1921, seven escaped from Spike at nightfall and 'there were at least four successful escape attempts from Bere Island involving as many as eighteen internees'.[174] Patrick Burke, a Waterford IRA volunteer, was moved from Spike to Bere and 'helped in various attempts to construct tunnels, to enable prisoners to escape. Our contact with friends on the mainland was made through the boy who accompanied the priest saying mass in the internment camp.'[175]

Michael Burke, an IRA captain in the Cobh company, was involved in the planning of rescue of prisoners, including Seán Mac Swiney, the brother of Terence, former Lord Mayor of Cork, who had died on hunger strike in Brixton prison in 1920, from Spike Island in April 1921. His instructions 'were simple ... to be at the back of Spike Island with a boat at 11 a.m. ... the boat to fly the Union Jack'. The prisoners managed to escape 'but then our engine started to give trouble' as 'weeds had got into the water pump' but they managed to get ashore by paddling and wading.[176] Richard O'Connell, a Limerick IRA commandant, also gave details of an escape from the Bere Island internment camp. He had been in various prisons and told a priest, 'I am getting out, even if it is in a box.' Seven of them escaped to a small boat, having cut fences with pliers given to them by an ex-RIC man living on the island, and 'our lads would row like the divil'.[177]

Denis Collins, a Cork IRA lieutenant, was with about 150 prisoners on Bere Island at the time of the truce between British Crown forces and the IRA in July 1921: 'nothing eventful happened ... for some months', but they had a 'very big compound with plenty of room for exercise' and 'our intelligence in the internment camp was in communication with the volunteers on the mainland'. They continued their work digging a tunnel for escape 'until some days before we were released and then we were still twenty yards from the finish'. They were permitted to go down to the sea-shore under armed escort to bathe and in October, 'by agreement with the people outside, five selected men succeeded in escaping while going down to bathe. They slipped away through the open door of a stable as the party passed through a farmyard being shielded by tall men in front and rear. They got to a dugout prepared for them and after dark got away to the mainland by boat.'[178]

Tensions abounded; by the summer of 1921 there were 473 internees on Spike, most threatening hunger strike over the legal status of their detention, but the strike was not approved by the IRA's GHQ and was called off. On Spike Island prisoners, as distinct from internees, who were in separate camps, were poorly fed and not permitted to smoke and as Seán Moylan, commander of Cork's IRA No. 2 Brigade and a future cabinet minister, who had been sentenced to fifteen years in prison, recalled, 'the hunger for tobacco seemed to overshadow every other concern'. But it was not uncommon on the islands for the prisoners to get friendly with some of the guards and in return for butter and cake cigarettes were given:

> The dark cloud that floated over Spike Island that afternoon was not caused by any weather conditions but by the smoke arising from the cigarettes in the mouths of 300 prisoners. Everybody smoked. Some, like myself, for the first time. From that [day] forward the internees supplied us from their own store and after constant raids and punishment the rule against smoking went into abeyance.[179]

It was frustrating for the marooned republicans to hear rumours of negotiations between Sinn Féin and the British government. Prisoner P. J. O'Neill thundered that 'nobody outside seems to care a damn what becomes of us ... we are not stones but men'. By October the situation

on Spike got violent and ugly and almost half the convicts were transferred to Cork prison. Likewise, as noted by historian William Murphy,
tensions boiled over on Bere Island at the time of the truce, when most
internees were sharing a hut with about twenty fellow prisoners, and the
leader of the prisoners there wrote to the *Irish Independent* to complain:
'the only effect of the Truce has been a serious aggravation of our treatment'. He wondered if the camp was 'debarred from all mitigations and
concessions consequent of the Truce'. The island camp emptied speedily
in December 1921, the month the Anglo-Irish Treaty was signed, creating a new Irish Free State for the twenty-six counties of southern Ireland,
a dominion rather than the republic the IRA aspired to. Overall it has
been maintained that the relationships between island prisoners and successive British officers commanding were more good than bad.[180]

For those seeking to recover from the excesses of the conflict, islands
were deemed to be suitable boltholes: Thomas Flynn, a captain in the
Belfast IRA, was ordered after the truce to 'go to Rathlin Island for a
rest'. He travelled with his wife and three other volunteers, but rest had
to wait; instead, they decided to try to capture explosives on the salvage
vessel *The Bouncer* that was salvaging HMS *Drake*, which had sunk there
years previously:

> We organised a social evening on the island and invited the captain
> and his whole crew ... when we got the crew of the Bouncer
> properly enjoying themselves and getting under the influence of
> drink we took their small boat, went out in it and raided the ship
> and removed all the explosives which we disappeared early the
> next morning in a boat to Belfast ... we were never suspected.[181]

During a debate on the peace negotiations that would ultimately
lead to the signing of the Anglo-Irish Treaty, Sinn Féin TD for Sligo-
Mayo East, Alexander MacCabe, expressed the view that 'they could
never bring N.E. Ulster into an Irish Republic whilst the British Empire
was what it was and his attitude was that at all costs they should dig
themselves in somewhere in Ireland, even in the islands of Aran, as an
Irish Republic'.[182] This was specifically remembered by Una Stack, the

widow of Austin Stack, a Sinn Féin minister who opposed the treaty and died in 1929.[183] But MacCabe had tempered his bluster by the time the treaty was debated in January 1922, suggesting 'opponents of this Treaty should remember that there are other principles and ideals involved in the issue besides Republicanism. There is, for instance, the ideal of a peaceful and happy Ireland ... the abyss into which a blind and reckless pursuit of one principle leads and the danger to any nation of having people of such mentality in charge of its destinies.'[184]

For the time being the Aran Islands would have to take their compromised place in the new Free State and hope for a proactive state approach; after all, Frank Fahy, as a member of the first Dáil, had toured the Aran Islands 'on behalf of a committee examining options for revitalisation of the Irish fishing industry, a prominent feature of Sinn Féin's economic programme.'[185] Piaras Béaslaí, a TD for Kerry East who took the pro-treaty side, also invoked the Aran Islands to underline the possibilities of a new dawn, an indication that evoking the name and image of the islanders was a useful political and cultural shorthand:

> Some of those who oppose the Treaty have claimed to be idealists and take a superior pose against those who speak of plain realities. I say it is those who vote for the Treaty that are the true idealists. They have the vision and the imagination to sense the nation that is trying to be born – the poor, crushed, struggling people who never got a fair chance, the men and women of all Ireland, the Orangemen of Portadown, the fishermen of Aran, the worker of the slum and the labourer in the fields, that nation whose fate lies in your hands and whom you are dooming to another and, I fear, a final disappointment if you reject the Treaty. Save that poor nation, give it a chance to be born, have the courage to throw away the formulas which you call principles. Seize this chance to realise the visions of Thomas Davis, of Rooney and Pearse, of a free, happy and glorious Gaelic state. Do not have it said of your work what was said of the doctors who performed an operation – 'The operation was a complete success, but the patient died.'[186]

TWO

THE ISLANDS AND THE
IRISH STATE, 1922-53

'Except for an odd trifle, the policy seems to be speak Irish and starve'

From the foundation of the Irish Free State in 1922, there was no shortage of reminders of the precariousness of offshore island existence, and admonitions that served to illustrate the difficulties of delivering on the rhetoric of Irish nationalists born during the era of the cultural revival. Neither side of the civil war divide had a monopoly on lyrical depictions of supposedly blessed rural existence, despite a tendency to credit Eamon de Valera, a dominant force in Irish politics for fifty years, with especially idealised notions. After Michael Collins, a leading politician and soldier who had contributed greatly to the war of independence, was killed during the civil war in 1922 a posthumous collection of his speeches, *The Path to Freedom*, was published. Slight and folksy, it was filled with clichéd meanderings about the restoring of what he characterised as an ancient, glorious and democratic Gaelic civilisation. This was the kind of indulgence in myth beloved of many of that era. The idea was that the male patriots would restore what Collins referred to as an epoch when

> the people of the whole nation were united, not by material forces but by spiritual ones ... the Irish social and economic system was democratic. It was simple and harmonious. The people had security in their rights and just law ... their men of high learning

ranked with the kings and sat beside them in equality at the high table.

How was Collins going to reinstate this blissful civilisation for the new Free State? By looking to the 'remote corners' of the south, west and north-west of the country, and especially to the authentic Irish women of Achill Island in Mayo, the inheritors and keepers of the flame of Gaelic civilisation:

> Today, it is only in those places that any native beauty and grace in Irish life survive. And these are the poorest parts of our country! In the island of Achill, impoverished as the people are, hard as their lives are, difficult as the struggle for existence is, the outward aspect is a pageant. One may see processions of young women riding down on the island ponies to collect sand from the seashore, or gathering in the turf, dressed in their shawls and in their brilliantly coloured skirts made of material spun, woven and dyed by themselves, as it has been spun, woven and dyed for over a thousand years. Their cottages are also little changed. They remain simple and picturesque. It is only in such places that one gets a glimpse of what Ireland may become again.[1]

There is no evidence that Collins actually visited Achill, but that was hardly required in order to wax lyrical about the islands in such superficial terms. Collins had indulged in what Paddy Hogan, a Labour Party TD from Clare, was later to refer to as 'sentimental slop'.[2]

As it transpired, however, the relationship between the islands and the state was a reminder of how limited 'freedom' would be. In 1925 Seán MacGrath, an official in the Land Commission, responded to reports of distress on Achill by mentioning the work of the CDB and the Land Commission:

> As much has been done in that way to better Achill for the islanders as can be done. The appeals of the islanders and of those acting for them have, perhaps, been too generously met in the past and I

am keenly alive to the spirit of depravity that exists among them and as a result of which they look outside the resources of the island for the wherewithal to live on.

He acknowledged the need for government to remove the necessity for emigration and accepted that 'the existence of a native government alters the whole outlook', but

on the other hand it should be the aim of a native government to even up conditions all over the area of its jurisdiction and to put an end to any drain on the Exchequer that promises to be continuous and unproductive of permanent results. It is plain that the island and the surrounding district is an undue drain on the resources of Co Mayo and of the Saorstát [Free State].[3]

This private bemoaning of benevolent pre-independence British governments for supposedly eroding the independence of islanders existed in parallel with an official narrative that was particularly evident in the report of the Commission on the Gaeltacht (Irish-speaking areas) in 1925 which looked at the challenges facing the areas where Irish was spoken. There were approximately 544,000 Irish speakers and almost 2.5 million non-Irish speakers at that time in the Free State and a number of islands, including the three Aran Islands, Arranmore, Cape Clear and Tory, were Gaeltacht. In relation to the residents of the Irish-speaking districts, the official narrative from the Commission (the commissioners visited some of the western islands) was that 'the neglect and contempt, the ignominy and the abuses to which it has been subjected are a part of our tragic history'.[4]

In tandem, the images of the west generally and the islands specifically continued to serve useful rhetorical and propagandist purposes, and when the *Irish Free State Official Handbook* was published in 1932 it relied heavily for its illustration on the work of Paul Henry and his paintings of Achill and depictions of Aran by Maurice Mac Gonigal, the landscape and figurative painter, who had visited the Aran Islands in 1924, the start of a life-long fascination with the western isles. This book cited the findings of the Royal Commission on Congestion in Ireland, published in 1908, which suggested the inhabitants of the congested districts in the west of Ireland were 'to a large extent the wrecks of past racial, religious, agrarian and social storms in Ireland and of famine catastrophes ... yet, if men be the test of the wealth of a nation, they are a most valuable potential asset'. A. O'Brolcháin, secretary of the Department of Land and Fisheries, asserted: 'these words were still applicable when Saorstát Éireann assumed control. The problem is now being tackled in a comprehensive manner', though details were scant.[5]

More detail, however, was provided on the archaeological wonder that was the stone fort on Inishmore, Dún Aonghusa, 'standing as it does on the very edge of the precipice with the swell of the Atlantic thundering against the towering cliff'. It was impossible to forget 'the overwhelming grandeur of this view'.[6] Stephen Gwynn, former MP, soldier and cultural nationalist and author of numerous guidebooks, developed this theme, suggesting in relation to the western islands 'the Atlantic swell comes in, its thunder can be heard and there is always exhilaration, even when there is softness'. He encouraged the visitor to get a steamer to the Aran Islands to see the fortifications of the Stone Age and the tiny churches 'when Ireland was beginning to be a potent centre of Christianity in a Europe trampled over by pagan hosts'.[7]

This focus on the distant past facilitated a glossing over of a crucial point in relation to the administration of affairs relevant to the islands: the winding up of CDB in 1923, after which there was 'no longer a body which had a definite policy for island issues'.[8] This was to remain a complicating factor for decades. The bald reality, and deep irony, was that more was done for the islands under British rule than was done in the early decades of native rule. The historian of the CDB, Ciara Breathnach, has convincingly argued that, because it identified areas of acute economic difficulties and then implemented measures that improved standards of living, the CDB 'excelled in its performance', especially when compared with the 'inaction' of the Irish Free State.[9] This was of particular relevance to the islands, which had been specifically targeted by the CDB. A commission on agriculture in 1922 did not make provision to deal with congestion, and the pleas of members of the CDB as it was being wound up that the new state's department of agriculture, into which the CDB was to be absorbed, needed to pursue separate policies for the west were not given the attention and action they needed.[10]

Instead, successive governments reacted to island crises in an ad hoc manner, convening intermittent interdepartmental inquiries in light of specific transport problems, drowning tragedies, food shortages or demands for evacuation. There were six such inquiries from the 1930s to the early 1960s before the central development committee of the Department of Finance was given responsibility for co-ordinating the work of different departments in relation to the islands. While the inquiries resulted in some improvements in communications and government intervention to ease some island burdens or to facilitate certain island evacuations, there was a determined refusal to set up a separate island authority on the grounds that island affairs were already the responsibility of a number of government departments.

As early as May 1922, in relation to the grant of relief for distress, which had an estimate for £100,000, the minister for local government and soon to be head of the executive council of the Free State (prime minister) William T. Cosgrave acknowledged that 'the situation in certain counties is little short of economic distress of the most pronounced order. It is approaching famine in some areas.' But there was also a barb thrown in the direction of Tory islanders, for whom relief of £308 was earmarked: 'It seems from information received from our inspector that they do not pay rates in Tory Island and an inspector remarked that they were good judges. They had advantages of government without payment of rates.'[11]

In 1922, Thomas O'Connell, Labour Party TD for Galway and future party leader, asked in the Dáil about relief of distress on Aran – 'the first season within living memory in which no kelp has been sold in the Aran Islands' – and the minister for local government, Ernest Blythe, was steely in his reply:

A sum of £1,000 was allocated from the Distress Fund to the Aran Islands. The Galway Rural District Council would have arranged the scheme for the expenditure of this money in the ordinary course but owing to the persistent refusal of the Islanders to pay their rates the Council have declined to accept any responsibility regarding them. An inspector has been sent to Aran to consult with the local Clergy as to the further steps to be taken in the matter. No allocation from the Unemployment Grant was made to the Aran Islands.[12]

In January 1924 the minister for local government, Séamas Bourke, was informed of distress on Heir Island in Cork, 'bordering on starvation, due to the failure of the fishing industry and other causes'. Bourke's reply was, 'In this case it does not appear that the Skibbereen Guardians have invoked the special powers of the county council concerning exceptional distress contained in Section 13 of the Local Government (Ireland) Act, 1898.'[13] The question of the division of responsibility between central and local government was to persist and the issue of the payment of rates remained contentious.

The plight of the islands in the early and mid 1920s was part of a wider, dire need in congested areas. By October 1924 people in Connemara were reported to be surviving on seaweed and shellfish; the ghost of the 1847 famine was evoked and the *Freeman's Journal* reported that '75 per cent of the people now have no potatoes, their chief diet of the last two months, and the harvest prospects were never worse in living memory. There is no employment.'[14] In February 1925 the *Manchester Guardian* reported on 'The famine in Ireland', though the government preferred the more euphemistic description 'acute distress', and included a photograph of the interior of a cabin in Gorumna Island, County Galway. In early 1925 references were made to parallels with the distress of the 1890s and allusions to famine raised the hackles of government ministers, who saw a need to counteract this 'famine propaganda', though the government did establish a 'distress in the west' cabinet committee.

Nonetheless, the *Connacht Tribune* was adamant in its reporting of 'deaths of starvation in Connemara' and the 'plight of people on [the] mainland and the islands'. It also reported that on New Year's Eve 1924, a doctor was called to the home of Michael Kane on Omey, a tidal island on the western edge of Connemara, but he was 'starving and too far gone to benefit from medical attention ... lying on the stone floor near a small turf fire'.[15]

While the government vacillated and private relief funds struggled to cope, the *Connacht Tribune* reported that 'the poor people conceal their poverty sometimes even from one another. They reveal a strange mixture of pride and fatalism.'[16] So, too did some politicians and those charged with framing solutions for the west of Ireland. This was apparent in the evidence that was given to the government's Commission on the Gaeltacht, which highlighted the yawning gap between the rhetoric and the reality when it came to the islands. Not for the first or last time it was island priests who dispelled the myths with a frankness that was at times caustic (see also chapter 4).

In his letter to the Commission members at the outset of their delib-erations, William T. Cosgrave referred bitingly to the fate of the Irish language: 'our language has been waylaid, beaten and robbed and left for dead by the wayside'.[17] The report was to highlight the extent to which convenience and material realities trumped language revival: 'it is the fact and not the sentiment which impresses the Irish speaking population'.[18] That was abundantly clear in the evidence given to the Commission by those residing on the islands. Fr Duggan, the curate on Arranmore Island in Donegal, referred in his evidence in August 1925 to the extent to which the fishing industry had failed in recent years, while none of the islanders had succeeded in becoming teachers and only one had got into the public service, and he had been educated to secondary level on the mainland. For parents, 'they would like their children to be taught English at school because there is no prospect before them but emigration to America or Scotland'. Regarding their rights as Irish speakers, 'they have never given it a thought one way or the other'.[19] When asked by the chairman if the islanders thought 'Scotland and America are better to them than Ireland' he responded, 'That, I would be inclined to say is their attitude.'

Revealingly, state officials who came to the island to deal with issues such as agriculture, welfare, policing and fisheries spoke English and 'gen-erally require the services of an interpreter'; it looked rather strange that in relation to the census there were Gardaí (Police) 'not knowing Irish going into the island to find out who did'.[20] Another telling exchange witnessed the chairman asking, 'Do they realise they have got something which the rest of the country has not got?' The response was 'No'.

Fr Duggan also reckoned that the people seemed 'to have lost hope in Dublin' in the last few years: 'they don't find the government authorities as friendly to them as they might be'. Duggan was told by another questioner that the island inhabitants, by speaking Irish, 'are certainly a great asset to the nation if they keep the island in that way with that spirit alive among them', but Duggan's main concern was that there was a need for compulsory attendance at school up to age fourteen: 'there is no useful purpose served by sending children to Scotland under 14'.[21] (Compulsory attendance was required under legislation the following year; previously, children could be exempt from compulsory attendance when they reached the age of eleven.) Overall, Duggan insisted the island was 'in an impossible position economically. Something must be done. Things cannot go on indefinitely as they are,' and capital was needed for deep-sea fishing.

Also giving evidence that month, Fr S. J. Walsh, the parish priest of the Aran Islands, communicated similar sentiments but in more robust language; emigration was encouraging an embrace of the English language and the focus now was on America, England or Scotland.[22] Those at home were depending 'largely on the American cheques'. He saw few grounds for hope:

> I regret to say that after consultation with a good number of people, I cannot suggest a remedy unless perhaps supplying the islanders with boats for deep sea fishing, which would entail a very considerable expenditure and must fall in with the universal feeling which find[s] expression here, that if the fishing, the natural industry of these islands goes down, then the people go down with it and the land would not be able to support the existing numbers.[23]

Fr Walsh's main message to the Commission was not about the survival of the language but the survival of the people and his message was firmly directed at the state: 'It is absolutely essential for the people of Aran to get government assistance to enable them to pursue the fishing industry. There seems to be an objection on the part of the government to the giving of assistance' as some fishermen still owed money on previous boat loans, but if government did not assist 'it is practically signing the death warrant of the fishing industry'.[24]

Two years later in the Dáil, in a debate on the Department of Fisheries (which, in effect was a junior ministry) came the most stern admonishment about the fate of the islands in light of the transfer from British to Irish rule: 'Mr Duffy said the islands of the west coast had been greatly encouraged by the CDB but were now abandoned, neglected and at a stage of destitution.'[25] The CDB spent an annual average of £26,008 on fisheries and harbours from 1911 to 1923, the year of its disbandment. But there were new complications. While the cured mackerel trade with the US had thrived until about 1900, by now the mackerel had returned to US waters and it led to a drop in price from $14 to $9 a barrel. After the war the British deep-sea fleet was also recommissioned 'and the British market for Irish-landed fish disappeared'.[26]

Western fishing was also hampered by loans arrears that had amassed as a result of a generous CDB approach, and it had continued to loan even when prospects were gloomy; the loan scheme was stopped by the Free State government in 1923, but without a replacement scheme; instead an 'Eat more Fish' campaign was adopted aimed at fostering domestic markets for fish.[27] It became increasingly difficult to get people to engage in fishing whole time; while, in 1923, successful commercial fisheries with full-time workers were operating from Donegal and the Aran Islands there were less than 1,000 full-time fishermen in Ireland by the mid 1920s.[28] The main economic focus at that stage was on agriculture and this had adverse consequences for the sea fishery sector, which could not capture markets lost during the First World War and the disruption caused by the war of independence and civil war periods alongside increased competition from foreign trawlers were further complications. Leading nationalists had insisted marine resources had great potential but fisheries minister Fionán Lynch struggled to persuade the government to invest in sea, inshore and river fisheries. In 1924 the total estimate for the Department of Fisheries was just £25,318, which Lynch admitted was 'parsimonious'.[29] As Lynch put it in 1927:

I have to state that the deep sea fishing industry of the Saorstát is still a long way behind as compared with other countries ... there are difficulties operating which render our rate of progress very slow. These difficulties are due to international as well as domestic causes. We do not eat much fish ourselves – about 14 lbs. per head per year. We export the bulk of our catch, either fresh or cured, to other countries. We eat all the fish other than herrings and mackerel that we catch, and we import a considerable quantity of fresh and canned fish besides. We export the bulk of the salmon, herrings and mackerel that we catch. The markets for cured herrings and mackerel continue to be depressed, and the low prices realised are reflected in the earnings of our fishermen. This inevitably reacts upon the activities of the men, who are without capital and, therefore, find it most difficult to carry on. The unusually stormy weather and the scarcity of fish during the past few years have contributed, with low prices, to keep the working fishermen practically on the margin of existence.[30]

Where the balance should lie between self and state help remained a vexed issue. Also in 1927, a memorandum on state financial loans for fisheries, which outlined schemes of state financial loans in Norway and Denmark where joint community guarantee operated as opposed to independent security, included the assertion by Fionán Lynch that these schemes were highly commendable but that the government would still want to retain a degree of control over operations. Lynch insisted 'the need to infuse a higher spirit of self-reliance and independence among them [the western people] is one of the first things to be attended to'.[31] But the previous year, Richard Mulcahy, former IRA leader and minister for defence, who had served as chairman of the Gaeltacht Commission, was told by a correspondent from Mayo: 'The Western peasantry are crushed down by poverty, even hope is dead or dormant. They have not the heart or the courage necessary to organise. Who, in place or power is big enough to devise a scheme?'[32]

By 1928, fisheries was no longer assigned its own government department; instead it came into the Department of Lands, and by that year ten motorboats and four sailboats had been repossessed by the state in lieu of unpaid debts, though the state continued to subsidise the loss-making steamboat service to the Aran Islands. By 1929 CDB loans arrears stood at £128,500; eventually, a Fisheries (Revision of Loans) Act in 1931 was passed, a Sea Fisheries Association was formed whose members could avail of loans from a modest fund, and many debts were cancelled. The Cleggan tragedy in 1927, sometimes referred to as the west coast disaster (see below) prompted greater urgency about fishing policy; the amount available for loans had been a mere £7,000 that year, compared to £30,000 in Denmark.[33]

State building and straitened finances in the 1920s raised the questions of whether there was an exaggerated belief in the ability of governments to bring about social, cultural and economic change in rural areas, whether proposals for change being advanced were deep enough and also the attitude of the rural people themselves and the role emigration would continue to play. But there was also the key theme – so relevant to islands and their autonomy – of state centralisation (a key legacy of the civil war but also a part of the state's inherited political culture) and in particular the marked centralisation of executive bodies that administered rural affairs.

But those engaged in the social problems of rural Ireland also pondered other questions, including the degree to which an anti-urban philosophy crafted by Irish nationalists was not matched by a strong alternative philosophy, or the extent to which the partial resolution of the land war that resulted in most tenants owning their own land had deprived the rural population of the 'slight social coherence that they formally possessed as tenants of the same landlord'.[34] All these issues were magnified for the islanders given their distance, psychological and physical, from the mainland, and created tensions that dominated state/island relations in subsequent decades.

The writer Peadar O'Donnell captured some of these themes in his novel *Islanders*, published in 1927, his narrative based on an island in Donegal and focused on the heroics of Mary Doogan and her son Charlie. There were 'three beds in which ten children were packed away at night'. There was nothing to eat but potatoes and 'we have the roof nearly ate from over our heads as it is'. Mary laments the 'scatterin of my childer ... It's away to the Lagan with the childer to earn a few shillins, then away to Scotland, an it ends up with America'.[35] Ultimately it was 'starvation that was crushing his mother'. Agents of the state were distrusted, including the chief of the local coastguards, who was 'unpopular ... for he had secured a conviction against Jack Doney for failing to report a cask of petrol that had been washed ashore' ('bad scrant to him!'). Charlie was told that he would make a fine policeman but he insists 'they'd put me in a sack and drown me if they heard on the island that I was joinin the police ... I'll stick to the sea.'[36]

Sticking to the sea, however, was a high-risk endeavour. The same year O'Donnell's book was published, a devastating tragedy hit the islands in the form of the Cleggan disaster. On 28 October 1927, forty-four fishermen lost their lives, leaving behind 174 dependants; the victims included nine fishermen from Lacken Island, ten from the Inishkeas, nine from Inishbofin and two from Aran. The Cleggan disaster came about due to a violent storm without warning; one survivor, Pat Reilly, when interviewed as a very old man in 1990 said pithily 'there was no heed of nothing ... one puff came and hit us and threw us up straight on the land'.[37]

Reaction to this tragedy followed what was to become a pattern; a fundraising appeal was issued by government with a national committee established headed by Cosgrave and the Catholic Archbishop of Tuam, Dr Thomas Gilmartin. Newspapers also issued appeals with the money incorporated into a national fund. From all sources, almost £37,000 was raised (equivalent to over €1.5 million today) and it was noteworthy that this 'remarkable figure included subscriptions from almost every part of the world as well as from every town and village in Ireland' (schoolboys on the Isle of Wight were 'among the earliest to respond'[38]) with local committees headed by parish priests.

It was a horrific reminder of the islanders' vulnerability, but there was controversy over how the funds should be distributed, criticism over the inadequacy of weather warnings and much media comment on the preponderance of flimsy fishing boats. The *Irish Times* in October 1927 reported that the view from Galway and Mayo indicated that 'if there had been some system of supplying the fisher folk with daily weather reports there might have been no loss of life' and that one clergyman had a private wireless set and heard that a gale was forecast 'but when he tried to warn the departing fleet he was too late ... now that weather forecasts are prepared with a considerable degree of accuracy there ought to be little difficulty in supplying at least daily reports to every fishing village in Ireland.'[39]

A few days later it was reported that two Irish army aeroplanes were searching for bodies and that 'survivors had remarkable escapes in some cases, riding the gale for seven hours before being dashed ashore'.[40] What was significant also was a sense of the need to investigate a wider context; the *Irish Times* referred to the 'pitiful hovels' the islanders were living in and their 'starvation diet'. Cosgrave characterised the islanders as a 'God-fearing, thrifty, hardworking race' and, significantly, he asserted 'they were content with their lot and sought to bring their children up to face the dangers of the deep and the hardships of the daily round with the courage they inherited from generations of sea folk like themselves'. The job of government was 'to bring succour to those whom the hand of the Lord hath touched'.[41] Dr Michael Lavelle from Letterfrack gave medical evidence at the inquest and was given permission to make a statement extraneous to the medical evidence: 'In the absence of a jury he said that he wished to convey to the proper authorities the criminal folly of people being compelled to go out to sea in crafts that would not be used as pleasure crafts even in good weather'.[42] This was a reference to the 'nobby' boats that had been introduced by the CDB to the area in 1909, chosen because they provided a fully decked craft and could travel further afield than the traditional and basic currach, but they were still relatively fragile.

Within a few months a second disaster occurred in the vicinity of the Aran Islands, leaving thirteen dependants to whom the benefit of the Cleggan fund was extended. They were supplied with fifteen boats with full equipment by the Department of Fisheries while a sum of £100 was allocated to each family to pay debts and stock their holdings, which was reported to have 'freed these people from their pressing pecuniary embarrassments'.[43] A deed of trust was then established for the relief of distress amongst 'the fisherfolk of the western coast or islands which may arise by reasons of storm, flood, famine disease or other misfortune of a public nature'.[44] It was decided larger, motorised boats were not the answer as they were not viable economically or practically, though the disaster committee did approve a grant of £500 for a motorboat service between Cleggan and the islands of Inishbofin and Inishark. But even the relief committee, in the words of its honorary secretary, was unable, owing to weather conditions, 'to cross over to the island'. It was also stern in the assertion that 'no extravagance in the allowances should be permitted'.[45] There was serious dissatisfaction with the distribution of relief. Inishbofin islanders in 1930 insisted 'we have not been allocated sufficient money', to which a local priest responded that they were exaggerating; another issue was 'the size of the [relief] committee along with the lack of representation from among the fishing communities themselves'.[46]

While much money was raised after the Cleggan disaster, including £150 from the British royal family, historian Jude McCarthy points out that 'the state made no direct contribution to the fund' and that a local Galway priest, Fr O'Malley, was 'not behind the door in his criticism of the authorities'. He maintained, 'it is sadder still to think that it needs a tragedy to arise in the minds of the authorities a consciousness of the terrible realities for the poor man's struggle for existence'.[47]

Some left the Inishkea islands soon after; the loss of eleven breadwinners too much to bear, with a Land Commission inspector lamenting that 'it is absolutely impossible to put the people back on their feet again'. The first stage of the migrations did not take place, however, until 1931/2. By 1934 the evacuation was compete and they moved to Land Commission houses on the mainland in an operation that cost £13,000. McCarthy points out that, significantly, hereafter the Land Commission denied islands were its responsibility; in any case the islanders were not given enough land to make a living and still depended on the island to graze cattle and sheep: 'the islanders were left, literally, neither here nor there'.[48]

Tragedy also rocked Donegal in 1935 on Arranmore, the Donegal island with a population of 1,500. Such was its impact that the Irish Folklore Commission's school project, just two years later, received a submission from Ballintra, County Donegal, that included a poem about it:

There's a broken hearted mother
On the Isle of Arranmore
Her eyes are dim from weeping
And her heart is laden sore
She gazes on the raging tide
That mourns around her door
And she prays to God to comfort her
On the Isle of Arranmore.[49]

A yawl had left Burtonport harbour for Arranmore in November 1935; on board were fifteen islanders returning from harvesting in Scotland along with five others; it ran upon a rock, throwing the passengers to the sea. The *Irish Times* described it succinctly as 'One frightful calamity', with nineteen dead and only one survivor, Patrick Gallagher, aged twenty-six: 'their boat met the fate that hangs always over islanders who make their living upon the sea'. The *Irish Press* referred to the nineteen victims who 'struggled in the water and disappeared one by one in the darkness'.[50] The *Irish Times* made a heartfelt appeal for subscriptions to a relief fund:

> If some disaster were to kill 8,000 citizens of Dublin in a night the loss would be no greater to her than the death of nineteen men and women to the tiny community of Arranmore. Indeed, the blow might be less severe, for everybody on one of these small islands is linked with everybody else by the tie of blood, of marriage, or of intimate acquaintance.[51]

Particularly tragic and gripping was the experience of the sole survivor, who

> held on to the keel of the upturned boat while he tried to keep hold of his father and brother, but the father was carried from his grasp after an agonising struggle for life of about two hours and sank immediately, being, by this time, it is believed, dead. Gallagher still retained a grasp of his brother and remained clutching

the boat until the awful tragedy was discovered at 9 o'clock yesterday morning. His brother was then dead.

As he clung to the boat, he watched the cottage lamps on the island extinguished 'one by one ... I almost gave up hope.'[52]

Much was made about the idea of Arranmore as one of 'the few surviving outposts of Gaelic civilisation' but with sons and daughters who were sent as 'harvesters to the lowlands of Scotland', while once again 'and this time without warning, the sea has gathered in its pitiless harvest'.[53] Mrs Edward Gallagher was 'the most tragic figure' having lost her husband, four sons and two daughters, 'but is still under the impression that she lost her husband and one son only. She believes that the other children are still in Scotland at the harvesting.'[54]

Peadar O'Donnell wrote excoriatingly in the aftermath of this tragedy and he was better placed than most to write about the islanders. His first teaching post was on Inishfree, a mile out to sea from his Donegal home, and he began to write on Arranmore when he took over as headmaster of a national school there in July 1916. It was an island where 300 families supported two schools and nine teachers. O'Donnell wrote about their humanity but also with a searing realism about their poverty and was not going to indulge in resigned acceptance of the power of nature and physical environment. His first and only play, *Wrack*, about poor island fisherfolk, had been written, he told his publishers 'in a rage' (and was staged at the Abbey Theatre in Dublin in 1932).

In relation to the Arranmore tragedy, he wrote:

> The world says it was a rock ... and the world says it was a fog. But it was not a rock. It was society. The world has spelled out one of its crimes in corpses ... but if the agony of that moment of breathed prayer that comes as close to us as our own breathing does not flash into a decision to end the impounding of the Gael and the trek to the Scottish tattie field then the suggested beacons around Arranmore are not a remedy for a wrong but a hush hush to easy settled consciences.[55]

Much that he wrote was also a rallying cry for the rural poor, whom he believed needed to be 'startled into a sense of their own stature'. The following year Sheila Kennedy, a lecturer in history at University College Galway, wrote more generally about the western seaboard, which was suffering from the centralisation of power and the endurance of abstraction: 'romantic portrayals of western scenery and western peasant life are blinding the Irish people to the ugly truth that Connemara is a festering sore on our body politic'. The government, she insisted, needed to undertake a serious migration scheme.[56]

In the aftermath of the Arranmore drownings the recently appointed *Irish Times* editor, Robert Smyllie, was anxious to have a central committee to administer funds, and a week after the tragedy he was in a position to forward a cheque for £3,000. The local priest, Fr MacAteer, suggested that any national committee should have a few local representatives, but 'necessarily few' as it would be 'a most delicate affair on account of local cross-currents' (there could hardly have been a more inappropriate and insensitive choice of words) and might involve him in difficulties.[57] At the request of both Smyllie and the editor of the *Irish Press*, John O'Sullivan, head of government Eamon de Valera, who had taken over from Cosgrave after Fianna Fáil's electoral victory in 1932, had invited people to act on a general committee to administer the funds. The amount involved was £3,500 from the small-circulation *Irish Times* (reflecting its wealthier reading base), £1,802 from the *Irish Press* and £4,426 from the *Irish Independent*, the two largest dailies.[58]

By December 1938 the Bishop of Raphoe, William MacNeely, noted that, despite notice of closing of appeals, money was still coming in 'pretty freely' and the fund eventually reached £17,316.[59] But that created its own difficulties. A scheme was approved in July 1937 stipulating that £1,000 would be allocated to Patrick Gallagher, £2,450 to Mrs Annie O'Gallagher and family and £1,350 to Michael and Nellie Gallagher and family with a portion to be paid up front and the balance invested in trustee securities with a monthly income paid. The Attorney General was a guardian of the charities and the scheme was approved before Justice George Gavan Duffy of the High Court; he paid tribute to Francis Gallagher, a solicitor and secretary of the trust fund who was said to be familiar with the 'islanders' conditions'. Duffy hoped Gallagher would act as 'guide, philosopher and friend to the dependants'.[60]

A week before that scheme was approved, Patrick Gallagher, the only survivor, wrote to de Valera (the letter was written in an impeccable hand by the secretary of the local Fianna Fáil cumann, Hugh O'Donnell) 'as the only survivor. Please note my grievance.' His father, four brothers and two sisters had drowned and he had

> spent sixteen hours on the keel of the ill-fated boat caressing my brother whom I managed to drag from the water ... I lost complete memory after being taken off the keel. As a result of the exposure and shock and sorrow I am nervous, in poor health and unable to do even light work. I shall never be able to provide for myself and I have no one to maintain me, I being left with my mother and two brothers (schoolchildren). My grievance is and I earnestly request your Excellency to rectify same is that I was asked to sign for 15s per week as allowance out of the fund. I refused on the grounds that this is inadequate for my support.

He needed, he insisted, £6 a week and 'I beg also on behalf of my mother who is now completely adrift'. He maintained that 'the party who lost only one member of their family are receiving an allowance twice as much as my mother ... this is surely unfair and inhuman'.[61]

Gallagher received a curt response on behalf of de Valera, devoid of even an expression of sympathy for his gargantuan losses, the reply maintaining that de Valera could not take any action, as there was a central committee to administer the funds.[62] The following week another letter, also written by Hugh O'Donnell, was sent on behalf of Nellie Gallagher; she had lost her parents in the tragedy and was left to look after her blind sister. She had been asked to sign for £40 a year but maintained that the other rates were £65 for the mother or father of a victim and insisted 'we are victimised ... a family who lost only one member may receive more than our family who lost two'. Nellie received the same reply as Patrick Gallagher.[63] Yet another islander, John Ward, whose son, the family breadwinner, had also drowned maintained he was getting nothing and 'must suffer through lack of nourishment'.[64] That was another letter written in vain, even though in December 1936, the *Irish Independent* reported that the disaster fund now stood at £18,450 supposedly for the welfare of the nine families and thirty-two dependants.[65] Fifty years after the tragedy Patrick Gallagher, then aged seventy-seven, was still living in a small cottage on the island and was 'crustily adamant in his refusal to open the floodgates of the memory of that fateful day'.[66]

The Arranmore tragedy shook the government, not just because of its scale but because it brought unwelcome attention on the reason why so many islanders were travelling to Scotland for work. In its wake, the executive council (cabinet) of the Fianna Fáil government asked the minister for lands, Joseph Connolly to obtain a report on the question of providing a state-aided transport service between the mainland and the principal islands off the west and south-west coast. Connolly, however, did something more personal and immediate. In a strictly confidential report he wrote of his day on the island for the funerals of nine of the victims: 'as I was only on the island for the day of the funeral it was not easy to make particular or detailed investigation'. He noted that the Office of Public Works (OPW) had started work, prior to the tragedy, on erecting beacons 'but that disagreement arose amongst the islanders themselves as to the proper location of these beacons and that accordingly, operations were suspended'. Some who thought poor weather had been the reason for the suspension of works did not accept such an explanation.

Curiously, Connolly noted that 'nothing in the nature of complaints was made to me either by the people of the island or the people of the mainland' (presumably, the day of the funerals and the level of grief would not have been conducive to such conversations), but two islanders did maintain that if beacons had been in place 'the accident would not have happened'. Among the questions he wanted raised were what, if any, representations had been made regarding transport to and from the mainland ('during, say, the last thirteen years') and he wondered would it be advisable 'to have a full report or survey on the transport arrangements that exist, the markings of courses etc. to ensure that all possible precautions can be taken by the state without delay'. A communication cable that used to exist was 'broken or destroyed during the Trouble' (a reference to the war of independence or civil war period). He made 'discreet but close inquiries' as to whether some of those on board had been drunk, celebrating their homecoming and was told, 'All, without exception, were sober ... at Burtonport the only drinks consumed were two small whiskies and one bottle of stout by three of the men' and those travelling were 'amongst the very best types of families on the island'.[67]

It was interesting that it was the minister for lands who had compiled this report and attended the funerals, given that it was the minister for industry and commerce who was responsible for sea transport, but other departments were also relevant including Local Government, Fisheries, Posts and Telegraphs and, outside of that, the OPW. This was a reminder of the degree to which responsibility for the islands was spread so thinly with the result that, in reality, no government department was really responsible, but what was also clear, from this and other episodes, was the degree to which it was the Department of Finance that held most sway when it came to the islands, for the very obvious reason of expenditure.

One result of the Arranmore tragedy was that it was decided in November to set up an interdepartmental committee on transport to the islands with representatives of the above departments and the Department of Justice. At the end of November, a memorandum from the Department of Finance regarding the disaster noted that the information on record in the department was 'incomplete and scrappy'; that in 1925 the Department of Finance had twice refused to authorise wireless telephonic communication from a neighbouring post office but had then approved it at a cost of £14, 'mainly on humanitarian grounds', because 'on the basis of the volume of postal traffic it was admitted that there was no case for its establishment'.

But there was a graver point to be made about sea travel: no matter what arrangements were made regarding transport to the islands or marked channels of safety,

> familiarity always tends to breed contempt for the daily dangers inherent in such island life. The islanders will always go their own way in their own boats and could not be compelled to travel by a

public service which would be available only at a particular time and only a particular route. It would be well to bear this in mind in considering any suggestions for the establishment of 'safe and regular' services which can carry no guarantee of preventing a recurrence of disaster.[68]

That was perfectly true, but it was also a conclusion suited to a Department of Finance and was also about the department pre-empting the findings of the interdepartmental committee. It reported in February 1936 and concluded 'the stretches of water between the mainland were in themselves mediums of transport no less than roads'.[69] That suggested both local and central responsibilities and that legislation was needed to institute, regulate and control the sea traffic and therein lay problems. The real reason the beacons project for Arranmore had not been completed was 'differences of opinion with the county council as to the precise type of Beacon for the maintenance of which the council would be liable'. The committee suggested responsibility for legislation should lie with the Department of Local Government and Public Health (DLG).

The Department of Industry and Commerce maintained that the Galway–Aran steamer was justified but DLG did not think it feasible to impose on local authorities the licensing of sea-going ferries. In April 1936, however, the Department of Finance insisted that 'no case has been made in the report for the provision of state-aided transport services in communication with the islands'.[70] Finance believed these issues were for local government and industry and commerce. These questions of responsibility were to endure; the following year, for example, the Archbishop of Tuam, Dr Thomas Gilmartin, made representations to de Valera on the subject of the provision of piers and beacons for the Aran Islands and a note from DLG highlighted the farce that 'local authorities do not appear to have any statutory authority to undertake such works' (this is precisely the kind of work that the CDB had been actively engaged in on the islands).[71] Gilmartin had also forwarded a letter he had received from the parish priest on the Aran Islands, Fr Killeen, who was, like some of his predecessors, trenchant:

As regards the fishing, there is a feeling of despair everywhere in the islands. The unwillingness of the government to help is very discouraging. In Inishmaan and elsewhere the poor people are helpless. All they have is the frail currach – currachs can't reach the steamer and school children lose the free meal ... for several the school meal was actually the first meal of the day. Except for an odd trifle, the policy seems to be speak Irish and starve. Piers and boats are an absolute necessity for both Inishmaan and Inisheer.[72]

De Valera was concerned about this; after more departmental wrangling about who was responsible he got annoyed and insisted 'the question at issue be pursued to a definite conclusion'.[73] The reason why the Aran Islands got a state-subsidised steamer service under 1936 legislation was because the Department of Industry and Commerce felt the size of the islands' population justified it; DLG had insisted it was not feasible to impose on local authorities the licensing of sea-going ferries because technical expertise and centralisation were necessary.[74]

Even with that centralisation, there was still the issue of responsibility for communications with the islands. Eight islands were listed as having telephonic or telegraphic communication with the mainland (Tory, Arranmore, Clare, the three Aran Islands, Inishbofin and Bere Island). In February 1938, 'considerable difficulty was experienced in determining precisely the nature and extent of the functions' appropriate to Industry and Commerce and DLG regarding wireless, in regard to which thirteen islands, each with a population of over a hundred 'remain to be dealt with', though agreement was subsequently reached.[75]

The year 1937 also witnessed tragedy for some Irish islanders in Scotland and this brought the issue of migratory labour once again to the fore. Ten young migrant workers from Achill, who were working on the potato harvest in Scotland, died in their accommodation in the town of Kirkintilloch just outside Glasgow. They were staying on land owned by Glasgow potato merchants. Their accommodation consisted of a simple shed (or a bothy, as they were known), with a sliding door fastened by a simple slip-bolt. Bedding was inverted potato boxes covered with straw and old blankets. Probably due to an overheated stove, the bothy was ablaze at one o'clock in the morning, but the workers were trapped; the door could not be opened, and remained closed until one of the potato merchants arrived. It was then that the scale of the tragedy became apparent. The fire claimed the lives of ten boys and men between the ages of thirteen and twenty-three. Their bodies were found huddled together beside a wall opposite the door. The distress in the village of Achill Sound when news reached there was overwhelming.

Such migratory work had long been a reality for the Achill islanders and many others in the west, and they counted for little. As historian Barry Sheppard has noted, 'Irish migrants to Scotland have been described as the "Cinderellas" of the Irish diaspora, occupying the bottom of the league ... they had even less rights than the Scottish workers who occupied the bottom rungs of the workforce.'[76]

Only one of the coffins bearing the remains to a Catholic church in Kirkintilloch had a name on it, as the rest of the bodies could not be recognised. When the bodies were returned for funerals in Achill there was widespread national mourning, and the newspapers launched appeals to raise funds for the victims' families. Those who reflected on the cause of the fire were quick to point to the dire state of the accommodation as the major factor, and the responsibilities of those who could and should have done something about it. In the aftermath, rules were issued to Scottish local authorities to improve the accommodation of migratory workers, but whether they were enforced depended on the whim of the local authorities.[77]

The Kirkintilloch fire also prompted an Irish government report on seasonal migration, which arrogantly maintained there was 'so much information in government departments that the examination of local individuals or bodies and evidence was not necessary'. It concluded, 'The improvement of the conditions under which migratory workers are employed lies entirely in the hands of the workers themselves.'[78] Peadar O'Donnell contributed an article on the Kirkintilloch tragedy to *Ireland Today*, suggesting it was 'unthinkable that all this will not bring forth a real effort to better the conditions'. But cynicism that anything would change was reflected in his prediction that 'Once the ballyhoo dies down ... the affair is about closed.' Those with power, he insisted, 'will never wreck the social set to which they surrender themselves so charmingly just to break through to the lives of the poor'. What was needed was 'to make them listen while they get told that their little social flutterings are tiresome'.[79]

O'Donnell also published a pamphlet, *The Bothy Fire and All That*, which castigated the Irish government for failing to deliver on its promises and called for aggressive state intervention to address rural poverty and provide land for those that required it, which would involve challenging the 'thickening of the defences of capitalism'. The following year the first delegate conference of Irish migratory workers was held at Achill and appealed to the government to provide free travel to Scotland for the working season, as travellers had to borrow to travel, money that was then deducted from wages, necessitating a longer stay. The delegates reminded the government 'we go to Scotland each year to work for the Scotch "tatie" merchants because otherwise it would be impossible for us to keep our homes together'. They also demanded that the provisions of the dole 'be extended to women on the same terms as men'.[80]

There was an extraordinary compartmentalisation going on at government level about the islands in the sense that, coterminous with these harsh, material and desperate realities, there was a parallel effort, through the Irish Folklore Commission (IFC) established in 1935, to preserve for the future the stories of rural Ireland, which included the folklore of the islands. Until 1970 the IFC, 'under funded and at great personal cost to its staff', assembled one of the world's largest folklore collections and maintained contact with scholars on five continents; what it amounted to was 'a great salvage operation'.[81] But ensuring its survival was a constant battle. It had a close association with the rural population – closer than 'any other cultural institute' – but was starved of adequate funding.

The contention of its director, Séamus Ó Duilearga, as expressed in a letter to de Valera in 1947 was that 'it has become clear that, given facilities and power we can make Ireland the centre of West European scholarship in the field of oral tradition and European ethnology', but this was not fully realised. Full-time collectors were poorly paid (£300 a year) and the work of transcription was arduous; on some occasions they even had to 'share a bed with an informant'.[82] But much island history and lore was preserved, even while the travails of the islanders were bringing evacuation into focus. Brian McLoughlin worked as a full-time collector with the Commission in County Galway and on some of the coastal islands from 1936 to 1939 and recorded in extensive detail the lives, customs and folklore of the islanders; he made an enormous contribution to capturing their contemporary and historic essences.

The plight of island communities was also relevant to the government of Northern Ireland because Rathlin Island off the coast of Antrim came under its jurisdiction. At the end of 1926, Northern Ireland's minister for commerce, Milne Barbour, reflecting on the need for the pier at Rathlin to be repaired (it had been built between 1912 and 1915 and its construction had been 'faulty') and a new one to be built at Ballycastle, the nearest mainland town to the island, because of the difficulty of landing fish ('this occupation has largely been abandoned'), noted he had 'considered depopulating the island and transferring them to the mainland', but 'the people themselves would absolutely refuse to leave the island'. He suggested half of the cost could be borne by the state, and half by Antrim County Council.[83]

The non-payment of rates by islanders was also an issue in Northern Ireland. In 1932 the prime minister, James Craig, wrote to Charles Blackmore, the secretary of the Northern Irish cabinet, in relation to representations that had been made to Lord FitzAlan, the last Lord Lieutenant in Ireland and a leading Catholic layman with a strong interest in social issues, about 'the grave conditions attached to Rathlin ... I observe by this morning's *Newsletter* that they have refused to pay their rates'. Fitz-Alan suggested what was required was an 'apparently small amount of government help'.[84] Craig responded that he was not aware of any 'outstanding difficulties'; he had paid the islanders a visit in October 1932 and had been assured by a resident priest that all was well. There was also the building of a new quay at Ballycastle to facilitate crossing and shelter. Craig's impression of the inhabitants was that 'they were, comparatively speaking, well off owing to the derating of their agricultural holdings and the fact that under the land acts they were subject to a minimum payment of annuities'.[85] The same day Harold Barbour, a well-known promoter of agricultural improvement, chairman of Antrim County Council, senator and younger brother of the minister for commerce, sent an extraordinary letter to Craig in relation to Rathlin and the rates. He noted that the county council had 'appealed to their sense of honour' and had written off in the region of £1,500 of irrecoverable rates 'on them agreeing to be decent in the future ... all in vain'. He claimed that a rate collector had sought to travel to the island to attempt seizures but 'not a boatman from Larne or Portrush would lend his boat as they claim – possibly with some justification – that if their boat went to Rathlin for this purpose it would not leave the island intact'.

What made the letter even more interesting, however, was Barbour's drastic suggestion as to how to up the ante in the rates war:

> It has been brought to my notice that HMS *Hood* [the iconic battle cruiser for the Royal Navy, launched in 1918, with a crew of almost 1,500 and weighing 44,600 tons] is in the vicinity at the moment. This, I understand, is the largest battleship in the British navy and seeing that it is so convenient it might be a favourable opportunity to send it to Rathlin to collect these rates. I really believe this measure would be effective ... I do not believe the visit of HMS *Hood* would be accompanied with any casualties even if a few cattle were seized on the island and deported.

Hardly surprisingly, Craig's response was a curt 'out of the question'.[86] Barbour's wife, Anna, subsequently wrote to Craig's private secretary to insist that the suggestion he had made was 'a joke' and he was perturbed that Craig took it seriously.[87]

But it was also noted that Antrim County Council had refused to spend any money on roads on the island 'in view of the fact that the islanders refused to pay rates and have paid no rates for many years ... various attempts have been made by the county council to collect but owing to the difficulty of having execution [sic] these efforts have always been abortive'.[88] Craig remained of the view that 'on the whole I do not think the islanders have much to complain about'.[89]

It was also made clear the following year that the government could not afford to fund a proposal made by Norah Gage (the Gage family had taken possession of the island in 1746 when it was purchased by Revd John Gage; the Manor House on the island was home to the family for over 200 years; see chapter 1) to repair the old mill so that the islanders would not have to take all their grain to Ballycastle to be ground. Gage however, continued to press Craig for help, noting in September 1933 that 'the kelp is not selling well, which is the only industry', pointing out that the tenants had now bought out their farms, making the Northern government landlord. She was also careful to express gratitude for Craig's 'kindly interest in Rathlin island'.[90]

Blackmore joked with a Home Affairs civil servant that, given all the representations being made on behalf of Rathlin, especially in relation to a revitalised mill, 'it looks as if you will have all the residents in Rathlin Island up at parliament buildings before you finish'. He saw it as his mission 'to prevent whole hordes of them clattering up to Stormont to plead their case. They are very keen to do this.'[91]

The islanders were advised to approach the Carnegie Trust (established by Scottish-American industrialist Andrew Carnegie in 1913 to improve the well-being of the people of the UK and Ireland) for funding, which was refused. Home Affairs saw this as a great pity, given that 'old Carnegie's money would be far better spent in assisting these unfortunate islanders to deal with their crops than in teaching farmers' wives how to execute fancy patch work quilts and folk dances.'[92]

Norah Gage proved to be a remarkably persistent lobbyist for the cause of Rathlin, even seeking the help of the British royal family, writing to Prince Henry, son of the king, and the Duke of Gloucester (who also had the title Earl of Ulster) in 1937 seeking £250 to restore the mill: 'the people are a loyal set of farmers and fishermen and the severity of the storms lately have isolated them completely'. She referred to them as '360 people half-way between Ireland and Scotland'. Basil Brooke, the minister for agriculture, had proposed a loan 'which I could not accept for the people as they could not pay it back'.[93] The plea was in vain as 'their majesties are unable to give a donation'.[94]

Rathlin islanders faced many of the same problems as their southern island counterparts, including impediments to a successful fishing industry. The Ulster Sea and Coastal Fisheries Association wrote to Craig in 1937 about the absence of marketing, and the need for a better loan scheme ('as at present in force in the Irish Free State') to obtain suitable boats and fishing gear: 'the fishermen of Rathlin island have ceased to fish beyond their personal needs owing to the absence of marketing facilities'. It requested the minister of commerce, Milne Barbour 'to consider the establishment of a suitable curing station on the island'.[95] But there was scepticism about that proposal as the islanders only fished 'the rough class of fish' ('black pollack' or 'half-grown saithe') and it was believed that curing 'belongs to another age'.[96] Storms, however, were timeless, and one that hit hard in January 1938 resulted in a telegram to Craig: 'Rathlin Island storm bound for three weeks. Islanders without food or firing'. Eventually, the RAF was able to make a landing and the government committed itself to continuing to 'ease the lot of the hardy farming and sea-faring stock of the island'.[97]

How to deal with storm-bound islands was a persistent challenge for the southern Irish state also, but there was suspicion during the 1930s that Tory islanders had a tendency to exaggerate their plight. It was reported in January 1938 that it was five weeks since the mail boat had been able to travel to Tory and the islanders sent a telegram to de Valera on 10 February: 'Island in deplorable plight for want of foodstuffs for several days owing to storm'. Inquiries in the Department of Justice revealed conflicting reports from the mainland Gardaí about the extent of the privation.[98] There was an interesting twist to these Tory tales of woe, as one of the islanders was suspected of being behind the telegram, a 'fake', according to one local TD, Cormac Breslin, 'with a view to obtaining notoriety and cheap food'. But de Valera insisted if things were truly bad the option of sending military planes to the island 'must be considered without delay'.[99]

Another source of information – further evidence of the sprawling nature of island responsibility – was the Inspector of Services with Posts and Telegraphs, who assured the government that the islanders normally kept six to eight weeks' supply of foodstuffs in expectation of emergency, but that 'there was only one man in Tory whose word he would rely on in the matter, Fr McFadden'.[100] It was telling that such distrust existed, but in this case, the suspicions were justified, as the following week it was confirmed that the telegram had been sent by one of the islanders, William Rogers (sometimes he signed himself Paddy Rogers or Pádraig Óg or James; even more confusingly, he had a cousin on the island who was also named William Rogers), who was fraudster and a rogue, or in the more formal language of the civil service 'has an unsavoury reputation'. He had managed, for example, to obtain money from the Southern Loyalists Association on the plea that 'the islanders were Loyalists' (supporters of union with Britain) which they were emphatically not.[101]

These various spotlights on Tory did prompt a memorandum on the island from a DLG inspector who noted in September 1938 that the position of the island was 'satisfactory'; there was 'quite a fair amount of money' in circulation because of unemployment assistance; nor did it use its full free school meal allowance.[102] But he noted that the islanders were 'too lazy' to avail themselves of the plentiful turf available close to Magheroarty Pier, the mainland point closest to the island:

> In other islands the inhabitants appear to be more industrious and are therefore more comfortable. Not so with the Tory islanders where the young men appear to hang idly around. To emphasise this I have been informed that two of the islanders recently joined the Garda Síochána but resigned and returned home after a short period of service. They are regarded as bad fishermen with bad boats and bad gear. They pay no rates.[103]

The government was no doubt embarrassed by a report in the *Daily Express* in February 1939 that a 'famine SOS' had been radioed from Tory to the mainland. The newspaper reported that 280 residents 'have been fighting famine for five weeks'. The *Daily Express* in Belfast chartered a plane from the Northern Ireland Aero Club but it could not land and instead made an airdrop of 'bread, tinned milk, tobacco, cigarettes'. The next day the newspaper reported that the island was fighting 'Flu as well as famine' on what it called 'Famine Isle'. According to Fr McFadden they were living on poor-quality potatoes 'and periwinkles'.[104] In the midst of all this a memorandum from the Department of the Taoiseach observed of DLG, Defence, Agriculture and Lands, that 'none of these departments ... appeared to be in a position to suggest any way of having relief brought to the Tory islanders'.[105]

A further memorandum on Tory Island from a civil servant early that summer after he had visited on 19 May observed the cows 'might be described as the usual island type – poor and hungry looking', but with regard to fuel, 'the persons willing to cut, save and transport it are discouraged by the existence of less industrious persons who would steal it'. He noted that 'the islanders are well housed, more so than most other islanders ... no rent, rates or taxes are paid. The people are very peaceful, dancing being their only amusement.' Regarding the recent storms 'with a less hardy race the result might have been serious' but there had been no deaths among the 280-strong population. De Valera took a specific interest in this and asked a number of questions.[106]

These memoranda were notable for a pattern; a response to a short-term, adverse event and then an assessment that was often contradictory by declaring islanders to be both hardy and lazy, resourceful and slothful. During these years, in his capacity as private secretary to the minister for local government, writer Brian O'Nolan was dealing with some of the correspondence arising out of the plight of islands, which may well have whetted his satirical appetite to be later manifest in his book *An Béal Bocht* (*The Poor Mouth* – see Introduction and chapter 7).

One thing the focus on Tory did generate was an interdepartmental conference on food shortages on islands during storms, with information gathered on sixty-eight islands, it being observed that communications had been interrupted in the case of fourteen. But there was also an insistence that reports of distress on Tory had been exaggerated and that 'the residents of Tory had the reputation of not being very strict in the matter of discharging debts; they were unlike other islanders in this respect'.[107] Seán Ó Moráin, director of Gaeltacht Services in the Department of Lands, noted that he had undertaken the responsibility of sending food stuffs to Tory by the SS *Muirchú*, a ship in the service of the state's Coastal and Marine Service, but 'in reality, he did not believe that he had any responsibility in the matter'. He was glad to report that most of the money owed for the food had been repaid; the difficulty, however, was that 'no government department admitted liability for dealing with a situation such as that which arose at Tory' and the government needed to nominate one department of state for that purpose.[108]

References were also made to the 'peculiar' circumstances of Inishmurray Island in Sligo, which had no shop or church, but just a school, 'little tillage ... and only one cow'. Two months later no department had taken responsibility for submitting recommendations to government. The following month DLG insisted food supply for the islands was not its responsibility, though in February 1940 it undertook to see to the duty of 'studying conditions etc.'.[109] In January 1944 William Rogers sent another SOS telegram from Tory that was regarded as unduly alarmist when there was 'no need for alarm'.[110]

But in May of that year, the Department of the Taoiseach was still looking for a response from DLG, especially after the Archbishop of Tuam, Joseph Walsh, had sent a memorandum to the Taoiseach regarding conditions on Clare and Inishturk islands in which it was insisted 'the principal difficulty in regard to these islands is one of isolation and not of poverty ... the islanders generally appear to be able to make a living with the aid of pensions, money from abroad etc.'. It was suggested that what was needed for those islands was what was provided to Aran in the Aran Islands Transport Act of 1936 – the payment of an annual subsidy for the operation of the steamer service (limited to £300 and guaranteed until only 1945) and occasional subsidies to meet the cost of overhauls of the *Dún Aengus* vessel used in the service; it had originally been purchased with a loan from the CDB in 1912.

In accordance with the provisions of that Act, an agreement was made with the Galway Bay Steamboat Company (established in 1872) for the operation of a regular service. It was also noted that a medical officer could not be found for Clare and Inishturk and that 'evacuation should only be adopted as a final resort'.[111]

Archbishop Walsh's eight-page report in April 1944 was frank and unsentimental about life on Clare and Inishturk, and also direct in calling the state to account. A few years earlier, Fr J. Cannery, chairman of the Clare Island parish council, insisted the islanders should only be paying half rates as the historical valuation of Clare Island was 'totally out of

proportion' to its productive value and the cost of living for the islanders was high owing to distance from the mainland and 'advantage taken
by buyers of islanders at fairs owing to difficulty in taking stock home
again'.[112] As far as Walsh was concerned 'they can hardly be classed as
fisherfolk any more than they can be classed as farmers' and there was
a notable reliance on 'American and now English cheques'. It was frustrating that summer visitors could get the impression the islanders were
'comfortable and carefree'.

Inishturk had a population of 125 that was dependent on the resident
doctor on Inishbofin: 'within the last 2½ years although a number of children were born I am not aware that he was ever present'. Walsh had visited
the islanders on New Year's Eve to give Mass after an arduous journey 'of
about five hours'. Many of the islanders were suffering from influenza and
were cut off from post; a few weeks earlier three of the islanders arrived at
the presbytery 'asking me to be ready in the morning to go with them as
the mother of one of them was dying'. After a lengthy voyage to the island
he ended up having to stay until the weather turned. The previous year
the Inishturk islanders 'all signified their willingness to leave the island'.

Walsh was also concerned that island intermarriage, 'which must
have gone on for generations, has left its mark in a number of ways. There
are albinos and squints and a dullness of intellect very noticeable in the
school'. In relation to Clare Island, he pointed out that in 1938, a mother
of ten children had died in childbirth after attempts to get assistance had
been foiled by adverse weather: 'one would expect that such a tragedy
would awaken public consciousness on the needs of a small community'.
He was also pointed in his reference to the issue of non payment of rates:
'Are we coming at last to the underlying reason for this reluctance on the
part of local authorities to consider the needs of Clare Island?'[113]

There were two issues relevant here; the overvaluation of the holdings and the lack of services provided. Five months later, the main concern of DLG, however, once again, was to disclaim responsibility for
'the islands generally'. There was an acute sense of defeatism, denial and
prejudice about the islanders who were, it seems, to be left to their own
devices, both because the 'nature of the problems permit of no fixed or
final solution' that came within DLG's brief, and because the minister

can accept no absolute responsibility in contingencies against which it would be impossible to provide ... there is practically no staff of state or local officers on any of these islands and any arrangements which may be made must be left to the operation of the people themselves. In these circumstances the minister could take no responsibility for any lack of honesty or discipline on the part of the islanders which might defeat the plans for financing a food shortage scheme or lead to the consumption of such stores in advance of an emergency.[114]

In relation to Tory, the Donegal county manager, S. D. MacLoughlin, noted in 1944 that there was only one house on the island 'which is not receiving assistance from public funds of one kind or another'. When the island had been storm bound the previous winter 'the priest, the teacher and the nurse ... were absent on the mainland' and during the storm there were adequate supplies of oatmeal: 'were it not for the local agitation organised by the notorious Paddy Rogers, very little complaint would have been heard'.[115] So who was this notorious Rogers? Some insight was provided in a confidential report on supplies for Tory Island by two inspectors from the Department of Supplies. There were sixty-four inhabited houses and a population of 262; six islanders were working in Scotland 'and about eight girls from the island working in service on the mainland' along with thirty-four OAPs and seven widows. The islanders 'appear to be a quiet, easy-going type of people. From all accounts they cannot be prevailed upon to go to the mainland to work, even for attractive wages, being apparently satisfied to struggle along on the island. They live for the most part in conditions of extreme poverty. Their attitude appears to be extremely insular'. There were three shops on the island and the inhabitants displayed much animosity towards non-native Andrew Shields ('a widely travelled energetic man ... they regard as an intruder from the mainland') who ran one of the shops on the island and was its only fish buyer, while they tolerated William Rogers, also a trader but a native, 'although both these traders are overcharging at the same rate'.[116]

Total income to the islanders from fishing was about £400 a year, with £60 from wool (75 per cent of householders had a cow and 90 per cent a few sheep and there were five horses). Pádraig Óg Rodgers (who, as seen earlier used different names at various stages) was an islander who had fallen out with many and was 'notorious for his penchant for writing letters of complaint or appeal to all and sundry' and liked to present himself as the island's representative. He had served a year in Mountjoy Prison in Dublin for forgery of a cheque: 'some of the residents have great admiration for Padraig Óg while others dislike him intensely for drawing notoriety on the island'. Another trader, Eamonn Duggan, had a small business selling flour: 'he is illiterate and appears to be a guileless type of man'.[117]

Considerable effort was expended to get to the bottom of Rogers's mischief. W. Leen from the Chief Superintendent's Office in Letterkenny in Donegal, suggested he was 'very clever' and 'occupies his time by inventing schemes whereby he can defraud some individual, society or company ... there never is, however, or never was any real shortage of provisions on the island. When the island is cut off for even a few days there is press publicity, the information published being invariably untrue'. This was the fault of Rogers; with any kind of a storm he 'sees an opportunity to attract attention to Tory'. During the winter of 1943 he had sent numerous letters and 'received in reply many subscriptions of amounts varying from 2/- to 10/- ... these come mostly from PPs, Bishops etc in the south of Ireland'.[118] Rogers 'usually describes himself as holding some office indicating a position of prominence on the island. A favourite description of himself is the District Representative, Western Area, 66 Morsherer Buildings, Tory Island. This looks more like a Manhattan address than a Tory Island one. There is, of course, no such building on Tory.' What it all amounted to was that for years, Rogers had been running a 'Tory Island racket ... we also suspect that this man is fraudulently obtaining dole in respect of a wife and child absent in Belfast'.[119] Another scam of Rogers, this time using the name James P. Rodgers, was revealed in a letter of 5 February 1944, wherein he suggested 'the inhabitants of Tory Island would be grateful if a licence be granted the island for selling spirits as medicine to the poor sick people of the island'.[120]

Further illumination of the life and times of Rogers and indications that he was not as clever as he thought was provided in a press report from 1949, when, aged forty-five, he was sentenced in the Dublin Circuit Criminal Court to three years' penal servitude after pleading guilty to charges of fraud. It was stated that he had received orders from Scotland and England as a result of advertisements in a Scottish periodical soliciting orders for fishing nets. He was in receipt of the large sum of £534 by false pretences and also admitted attempting to obtain £218 by fraud; the investigating Guard 'said that because of his knowledge of English, Rogers was regarded by Tory islanders as a sort of solicitor-cum-scribe'. He told Justice Shannon that he had left Tory 'because his wife, a Belfast girl, could not get used to the ways of the people there'.[121]

In relation to the ongoing question of island communications, transport and the interdepartmental committee set up in November 1944, there was much foot-dragging; the Department of the Taoiseach was still asking for the report in May 1946. It was submitted that July, recommending that the Gaeltacht services division of the Department of Lands 'should be charged with the administration of any legislation which may be contemplated'. The minister for lands was opposed to this: 'he considers there is no connection between Gaeltacht services and Ferry services ... a specialised task for which it has not the necessary experience'. But Industry and Commerce insisted it was relevant to it, the Office of Public Works and DLG, as the provision of ferry services 'does not fall within the statutory functions of any one minister'.[122] There was no Department of Transport (and Power) until 1959.

The same year it was reported that the inhabitants of Inishmurray were anxious to evacuate and had approached the Land Commission; the Commission's officials in Sligo were reported to have visited the island 'and carried out an exhaustive inspection' (the island had about twenty-five acres of arable land).[123] Those islanders had also been caught between different stools of officialdom at various stages. In March 1939 it was reported that 'protracted negotiations regarding responsibility for expenses' had prevented the departure of the Sligo Harbour Commissioner's vessel *Tartar* to relieve the islanders. DLG had insisted it was a matter for the Gardaí, while Sligo Gardaí insisted it should be dealt with by the Board of Health. *Tartar* eventually reached the island two days later through a sea 'lashed to fury by a gale which reached a velocity of fifty miles an hour'. Islanders had resorted to lighting distress fires; twelve islanders had attempted to get to the mainland: 'among them went a woman – fearless Mrs Mary Herity'.[124]

It was no wonder the islanders felt they had endured enough by the 1940s given this level of exhausting ordeal, and the island was evacuated by the end of 1948. The exodus happened relatively quickly as Sligo County Council had agreed to provide cottages on the mainland and the parish priest of Grange on the mainland aided the islanders in their lobbying of government. But there was also a particular issue for these islanders that contributed to their decline in fortune – the problems that had arisen in poitín making, it being so difficult to secure raw materials during the war.[125] Michael Waters, the island 'king', blamed skewed government priorities: 'it cost £10,000 to put up these cottages. For less than that we could have built a harbour on the island, which we have pleaded for sixty years. The lack of a harbour drove us to the mainland.'[126] There was delusion in that assertion also; a harbour alone could not have alleviated the other problems, including thirst for migration and lack of marriage opportunities, not to mention storms. In any case, a defiant verse generated by the islanders now seemed sadly hollow:

We have kept our own distillery, no taxes do we pay
May the Lord protect my island home that lies in Sligo Bay.[127]

As head of government, Eamon de Valera maintained his interest in the islands in different ways and was particularly interested in the Gaeltacht islands' contribution to the survival of the Irish language. In power since 1932, a key part of de Valera's state- and identity-building agendas was to stress the distinctiveness and positives of Irish rural identity in contrast to that of industrial Britain. His approach had a 'firm basis' in nineteenth-century nationalist philosophy, and he continually pointed to the ancient pedigree of Ireland and its religious and civilising influence as well as the need for it to maintain its attachment to language as a bulwark against cultural absorption. One of his most famous assertions, from 1933, was that

The Irish genius has always stressed spiritual and intellectual rather than material values. That is the characteristic that fits the Irish people in a special manner for the task, now a vital one, of helping to save western civilisation. The great material progress of recent time, coming in a world where false philosophies already reigned, has distorted men's sense of proportion, the material has usurped the sovereignty that is the right of the spiritual.[128]

The difficulties being experienced by some of the islands made such assertions hollow and de Valera was sensitive about that. Given his rhetoric and the islands' associations with antiquity and cultural and linguistic purity, their plight represented both a personal and a political challenge for him. In response, he embarked on an ambitious tour of the western islands in 1947 on board a corvette of the Irish navy. Some of the political charges made against de Valera about this trip were wide of the mark, given his genuine interest in the islands and given there were few votes to be garnered on them, but he did leave himself open to the accusation that he was being somewhat self-indulgent and nostalgic and establishing direct contact with the island communities at far too late a stage.

Notes about the itinerary for the trip in de Valera's papers reveal the tightness of the schedule and the reasons why critics saw the voyage as being as much about photo opportunities as anything else: 'Inis Mór, 3 p.m.–7 p.m. ... Inish Bó Finne [Inishbofin] 5.45–6.45 p.m.'[129] The voyage generated plenty of newspaper coverage, but only minor improvements in the lot of some of the islanders. On the Blasket Islands, the oldest inhabitant, Seán Ó Catháin said 'he had welcomed him once before, as de Valera reminded him, when he had come after the civil war on the Tír Mhór (mainland) with an Dochtúr Padhraig de Brún and stayed on Blasket for a rest', where it was maintained that 'soldiers from Valentia had come looking for him' (an incident not recorded by his biographers and one that was more likely folklore).

De Valera was told of the islanders' wants, including nets and flour, and told them 'the islanders could show many wealthier people on the Tír Mhór how to deal with waste ground'. He promised to lighten their hardships before travelling to Cape Clear, where he urged the children to help in the restoration of the Irish language. When he got to the Aran Islands 'dressed in the simple garb of the local fishermen ... [he] made a striking but homely figure in contrast with the brass and braid of the military and naval uniforms of his escort'.[130] Matt Mullen addressed him on behalf of the islanders and maintained they 'were well aware that were it not for what Mr de Valera had done for the country there would not be many left on the island to welcome him that day'.[131]

A few days into his trip he was described as 'bronzed and sunburned'. He was a picture of relaxed good health during his sojourn, helped by his doctor, who had given him tablets to prevent sea sickness with a stern instruction: 'Do not take them more often than at six hourly intervals. Crippen used this drug to poison his wife.'[132] This was a reference to Hawley Crippen, one of the most notorious killers in British history, a homeopath based in London who had been hanged in 1910 for poisoning his actress wife Cora. But others were more interested in concrete diffi-culties and the government had, in correspondence, been made aware of them. In June, Patrick Gibbons of Mayo County Council had written to the county manager in Castlebar outlining the 'three most outstanding needs of the people of Clare Island', which were the services of a doc-tor (lives had 'already' been lost due to the difficulty of the dispensary doctor in Louisburgh reaching the island), harbour facilities and 'lack of flour', while potatoes in '75 per cent of the homes' were used up.[133] De Valera received a handwritten welcome in Irish from the islanders on Clare; one of those in the welcome party was John O'Malley 'who wore a [war of independence] service medal'; he said 'they were glad to see the chief of the Irish people coming to the island on an Irish ship. He said it was a great advance on the time when a British gunboat came to collect rents in Clare Island and the police were driven away with stones by the people.'[134]

These visits were undoubtedly gratifying, if not momentous occa-sions for the islanders and some of them tickled de Valera's belly. On Tory, an address was read in Irish by the teacher John Gallagher, who said 'that since Colmcille came to Tory [Colum Cille, founder in the sixth century of the monastery of Iona off the west coast of Scotland] ... no one was more genuinely welcome than the Taoiseach, whose care and concern for the welfare of the people, especially in the Gaeltacht was much appreciated'. The pressing material needs, however, were not alluded to, including over-dependence on fishing and a shortage of boats and inadequacy of port facilities, de Valera merely promising 'he would give consideration to any schemes submitted to help the lot of the people'.[135]

Fine Gael's Thomas F. O'Higgins denounced the 'mad scheme of extravagance' with the assistance of the navy 'in order that Mr De Valera could carry out a pre-election tour of the coast and islands' (a general election was held seven months later with Fianna Fáil losing power after sixteen years in office). Fine Gael's Liam Cosgrave described it as a 'joy ride' demonstrating the government's 'loss of sense of reality' and 'an effort to emulate the British royal tour in South Africa'.[136]

There was some follow-up. A month after the trip, the Department of Finance received representations from the Office of the Taoiseach regarding the widening and deepening of the landing place at Tory Island and it was pointed out that in 1941 the government had offered Donegal County Council a 75 per cent grant to do this if the council contributed the balance, but it would not as the islanders did not pay rates, 'and since then the case has remained in abeyance'. It was now believed a full grant should be given as Tory 'is one of the strongholds of the Irish language and of Gaelic culture and tradition' so young people needed to be kept on the island.[137] This obviously had de Valera's imprimatur as he had stated at the outset of his islands tour that 'if there is one thing I would ask the Irish people to do today it would be to restore the language'.[138]

There was also follow-up from the Department of Health in looking at medical services on Clare (the minister for health 'will not raise any objection to the appointment of a residential medical officer on the island') and an exploration of minor employment schemes in knitting and weaving on Tory.[139] Perhaps more substantially, and an indication that he was more than posturing, was that de Valera interviewed the chairman of the Electricity Supply Board (ESB) regarding an electricity supply to the Blasket Islands but was told that the distance between the Blaskets and the mainland (6 km) 'precludes the consideration of supply of electricity to the islands from the Board's network'; what were needed were oil-driven generators for each cluster of houses at a cost of £12,800.[140]

These scraps of improvement or potential improvement hardly amounted to enough. At the time of de Valera's visits *The Kerryman* newspaper published a thunderous editorial, a reminder that newspapers, both national and provincial, were frequently robust in addressing the plight of islanders: 'The island's disease is purely economic. Independence has not improved the lot of the islanders. Rather the reverse because the functions of the old CDB have not been since efficiently discharged along our coastal hinterland. These islands should be rent and rates free ... too long they have been left alone, crying in the wildernesses'. In Sligo there was satire about de Valera on the national corvette: 'is he not, notionally, the boy who stood on the burning deck when all but he had fled?' The Tory islanders, it noted, 'told him that he was dearer to them than anything except nets which, they keened, are twice the price here that they are in Scotland'.[141]

De Valera had declared during his trip 'Now I have seen and they will know that the government will not neglect them.'[142] But some islanders felt the hollowness of that assertion was exposed in subsequent years. In November 1948 a Radio Éireann programme, *Letters from Listeners*, broadcast a scathing complaint from an Aran islander, Mrs M. Gavin, so splenetic that it was deemed worthy by one minister of being raised at cabinet level, though it was ultimately withdrawn from the agenda. The text of Gavin's letter witnessed her

> in a furious rage, furious with our government. Where are the members of it? Asleep? Why oh why did they not go to the aid of the Aran islanders, or were the people there not 'big fry' enough to be taken notice of? No, they could die of hunger for all our so-called government care. Surely it is a national scandal that three weeks have elapsed before anyone came to the rescue of the people of Aran. Babies could die for want of food, but no one cared ... they are the nicest people in Eire – or are they in it? For all any of our ministers cared, they might have been in Jamaica.[143]

The headline-grabbing island event of that era, however, was the evacuation of Great Blasket Island in 1953. Its end as a populated island was powerfully depicted in 2000 by Cole Moreton, an English author, in his book *Hungry for Home*, and he pointed a finger squarely at de Valera for his failure to do more. Moreton also documented the exodus, both to the mainland and to Springfield, Massachusetts, where there were more descendants of the islanders than on the island itself; one drove a car with the registration BLASKT. Morton recreated the visit of de Valera to the island in 1947 in order to reiterate the assertion of George Thomson, the English classical scholar and Marxist who had visited the islands, had a brilliant command of their language and had encouraged the islanders to write: 'A social system which could let such a culture die must be rotten in some way.'[144]

What sent the Blaskets hurtling towards evacuation was the death of islander Seán Carney from meningitis in 1947. The telephone on the island was not working and bad weather meant Seán's dead body lay for three days on his father's bed. When his corpse eventually reached the mainland his cause of death had yet to be officially determined and Seán's brother Mike recorded 'my father told them to write down that the government killed him'.[145] Such anger and grief was hardly surprising; the tragedy for the Carneys was part of a much wider plight for those living on the various inhabited islands. For their way of life to be sustained they needed investment, proactive governments and a matching of the rhetoric that eulogised them as the inheritors and protectors of an ancient and valued culture, with resources to withstand the challenge of what *The Kerryman* newspaper in 1953 referred to as 'the supremacy of the Atlantic, which dominates the lives of the Blasket Island people'.[146]

Mike Carney wrote to de Valera after his brother's death, wondering why, if his government placed such a premium on the survival of the Irish language, it failed to support the way of life of those who preserved it.[147] After the death of Seán, Fine Gael leader Richard Mulcahy asked for a tribunal of inquiry into the circumstances of his death, to which the minister for industry and commerce, Seán Lemass, replied tersely that the radio telephone was out of service: 'I do not see what purpose a tribunal could serve.' Mulcahy's outrage was 'for some of the remnants of the Irish speaking population on our islands to die in such circumstances', a telling description.[148] Communication with the island had been 'wholly interrupted' for twenty-eight days in January 1947; in April that year, the government received a telegram from the Blaskets: 'Stormbound, distress. Send food. Nothing to eat. Blaskets.'[149]

On 6 August 1947 a Department of the Taoiseach memo on conditions on the Blaskets included a powerfully bleak opening paragraph:

> The Blasket islanders are mostly housed in hovels as bad as anything in Gardiner Street or Gloucester Street [in inner city Dublin, location of many tenements] in their worst days. They have no church, no priest, no doctor. There is not a single tree on the island and probably not more than half a dozen bushes. They have not a public house, a cinema or a dance hall in which to find distraction from their woes. Their land is untillable. They have no cows that I saw and apart from the doles, their only means of livelihood are the grazing of mountain sheep and lobster fishing. They are dying out and perhaps it is better for them so. I fear it is too late but I believe they could have been saved at relatively a very small cost.

They were described as 'the ageing and despairing people of the Blaskets'.[150] It could only conclude 'the Blaskets would be a good place for a holiday for anyone who is satisfied with simple pleasures'.

In tandem, de Valera presided over a conference in his room in Leinster House to discuss the Blaskets, an indication of a very personal concern. He said his visit had brought home to him the deterioration in conditions and while civil servants told him evacuation was inevitable and he accepted such a course might eventually be 'unavoidable', an 'exhaustive effort' was needed to prevent it. At that meeting it was agreed that two civil servants from the Gaeltacht Services and the Department of Education would spend a few days on the Blaskets and 'not announce themselves as being government officials but would spend some time on the island as ordinary visitors' to prepare a report.[151] In October 1947, the islanders wrote directly to de Valera: 'Dear leader. We want you to let us know what you are going to do for us. Please let us know immediately for winter is coming. If you can't help us we will have to go across the Atlantic to seek our fortune.'[152]

P. O'Cochláin of the Department of Education's technical instruction branch wrote one report on the Blaskets. By 1947 there were 600 sheep ('they thrive on the island') and fifteen donkeys but just fifty-one residents, nine of them over the age of seventy and eleven aged between sixty and seventy. What was most obvious was the abandonment of the island by young people, 'particularly by the girls'.[153] The islanders were reported to be 'indifferent to improving their holdings. They have no desire to avail of any assistance obtainable under the improvement schemes of the Department of Agriculture'. The Gaeltacht Services division had made an attempt to improve transport in 1929 with an engine boat by way of a £400 grant but it was dropped owing to insufficient demand. This issue was revisited in 1937 'subsequent to the publication of a good number of letters in the newspapers' but terms could not be agreed with local fishermen regarding the operation of the service, a reminder that the story of the Blaskets and indeed the islands generally was not solely one of state neglect.

A sock-knitting enterprise had failed, the radio telephone service installed in June 1941 was often out of order and the national school had closed that year. But the islanders were not, comparatively speaking, especially poor. Through payment of £292 in old-age pensions and £210 in unemployment benefit assistance along with money generated from the sheep and fishing they were 'reasonably well off … in comparison with people in other districts in the west of Ireland … they do not and never have paid rates or annuities'.[154] The islanders had made it clear they wanted to be treated on the same terms as the islanders of Inishkea, with Land Commission houses on the mainland, near the island and retention of land on the island for sheep grazing.

A. Ó Gallchobhair, who had visited the island in August 1947, also submitted a report, remarkable for its vividness and candour, in which he observed that the islanders 'were expecting some result from the Taoiseach's visit', but the reality was that 'they were not prepared to remain there any longer'.[155] The women also 'mentioned the everlasting terror they experienced while the men are at sea in stormy weather' (a fisherman the previous decade had described the currach as an 'odd shaped coffin'[156]). He was 'unable to obtain any favourable account' of the life of the people 'because of their burning desire to leave ... it is said that women are not at present prepared to marry on the island'. He observed that 'there is no wireless on the island, but from the point of view of Irish, perhaps this is just as well.' There was no safe place for boats to land, though Currachs were 'wonderful little boats and the cleverness and bravery of the men who handle them is still more wonderful'. His account also contained indirect but cutting indictments of government failures:

> When one thinks of the coastguards that used to be stationed about the coast of Ireland under the British regime and the splendid housing accommodation they had for themselves and their boats and the fine slips that were built for them although rarely used more than perhaps a few times each year, it seems extraordinary that the CDB or some other government department did not provide facilities of that type for the people of the Blasket seeing that they would be of great assistance to them.[157]

He feared

> it is now too late to attempt to keep the people on the island ... I must say that the island reminded me of one of the internment camps that used exist in the Troubled times, the difference being that the internees were in no way troubled about food supplies and other requirements and had the hope of freedom sooner or later ... it is the desire of the Taoiseach, however, to keep the people on the island if possible.

It was revealing that a report like this could conclude that the island internees of the war of independence fared better than the inhabitants of the much-vaunted and eulogised islands under native rule.

The total estimated cost of resettlement was about £12,000. The foot-dragging was to continue; reports were still being compiled in subsequent years, including by J. F. Glynn, a civil servant who visited in 1950 on behalf of the Land Commission, and who recalled in August 1952 that he still retained 'a vivid picture of the hopeless condition of the residents' and that, if settled in Dunquin on the mainland, overlooking the island, there could be a 'swift assimilation' that would 'strengthen the native language'.[158] By November 1952, a memo from the Department of Education estimated a migration scheme would cost £23,000 but was worried about a chain effect with other islanders demanding the same, and it 'might set in train a continuous and expanding outlay ultimately amounting to a £¼ million or more'.

The minister for finance, Seán MacEntee, was opposed to the migration of the Blasket islanders because 'economic or other conditions may change to the benefit of the islanders'. How he could conclude this was astonishing; what he was really hoping was that 'the natural drift to the mainland should be allowed to continue' even though such a migration would 'destroy the distinctive Blasket tradition'. By March 1950 there were only thirty people left on the island and just a single child. Much was made of four-year-old Gearóid Ó Catháin's status and he achieved national and international fame as the last child of the island and a child with no school to go to. The *Irish Press* reported in August 1951 that he was 'the last child on the Great Blasket, a dying island that is the last outpost of the Celtic Empire'.[159]

Significantly, the minister for education, Seán Moylan, was 'of opinion that the problem is a national and humanitarian one'.[160] On 8 November 1952 the government decided that the minister for lands should arrange for the islanders to be migrated to Dunquin. That decision came two months after four of the islanders, out of a population that was now just twenty-eight (and only two cows) asked in a petition to be 'released from our island fortress ... if people at this stage of civilisation and standard of living only realised what hardships of mind and body we endure, we are sure that they would raise their voices and rally to our cause'.[161] But on 9 November 1953 it was reported that six residents were to remain on the 'deserted' island; postman John Kearney and his mother and four elderly bachelors who insisted they were not being provided with suitable accommodation on the mainland. A clue as to their consternation was contained in a Department of Lands memorandum four months earlier: 'the intention is to install four elderly unmarried men in one house'.[162] But they, too, departed. Jude McCarthy has argued that 'the overall impression is that no department wanted, or had, any responsibility for the migration of the community, nor, indeed, did anyone appear interested in any policy initiative'.[163] For those reasons, but also others that were arguably beyond state control, the demise of the Blaskets was only one of a number of dispiriting island narratives during that era.

THREE

THE STATE AND THE
ISLANDS, 1953–2016

'public men who pay lip service to the last outposts of the Gael'

The evacuation of the Blaskets was only one island tale of woe (though not necessarily for the evacuees) in the 1950s. In 1951 three families were migrated from Dursey Island off the Beara peninsula in west Cork to the mainland. Dursey was bare, treeless and exposed, with a population of just ninety-five (a cable car from the mainland was opened in 1969, making it unique among Irish islands), but it was maintained in the Dáil in June 1953 that conditions on the islands off the west Cork coast were 'much better than on most of the islands off the west coast'.[1] While it was reported that year that twelve of the larger islands off the south, west and north-west coasts were to be linked with the mainland by public telephone, starting with Inishmaan and Inisheer, two years later the minister for posts and telegraphs, Michael Keyes, told the parish priest of the Aran Islands, Fr Tom Varley, that the state could not increase the frequency of postal deliveries to Aran owing to the prohibitive cost. CIE, the state-owned transport company, was already losing heavily on each trip, with a state subsidy making up the loss. The annual cost of this service to the department was £843 and revenue was just £586; Varley was requesting a daily service but was told 'the department's information is that the islanders are not dissatisfied with the existing service'.[2]

Varley, however, was loath to accept that and wrote to the Taoiseach, Fine Gael's John A. Costello, who had replaced de Valera in 1948: 'It is the only parish in Ireland that is treated in this deplorable way ... it is quite obvious that an attitude of "couldn't care less" prevails in the dept of P+T in regard to Aran.' He also maintained, signalling new priorities, that it was damaging to tourism: 'Scores of people were left behind on the pier in Galway at all the mid summer sailings.' Costello assured him of the government's commitment to the Gaeltacht areas ('the very special concern of the government') but regretted that his request could not be granted.[3] There was more positive correspondence, however, in October 1956, from Revd John Walsh on Cape Clear, who thanked Costello for authorising the building of a new mail boat so that the islanders did not have to endure 'such dangerous and outdated transport facilities'.[4]

While the Fine Gael-led coalition governments from 1948–51 and again from 1954–7 were able to oversee some minor improvements arising out of de Valera's island visits in 1947 and their own initiatives, the crucial, consistent problem in relation to the government and islands remained that of departmental responsibility and it was not solved. What was clear towards the end of that decade was that civil servants were likely to be more vocal and pointed about this. Unfortunately, it was too often distressed isolation and tragedy that generated the frankness. In February 1957, the *Sunday Press* reported

> Last weekend, a 58-year-old farmer, Anthony Cloonan, of Inishark, married with two children became gravely ill. In a frantic effort to obtain help, neighbours lit huge fires and sent up flares to attract attention from the nearby island of Inishbofin where the doctor and priest reside. The flares were seen and a currach set out from Bofin into a full scale gale to find out what was wrong. The currach succeeded in crossing the three miles separating the two islands but when they reached Inishark a landing was out of the question because of the huge seas. During the next twenty-four hours the currach made several attempts to land but in the end was forced to turn back and Mr Cloonan died without medical aid.[5]

John Garvin, secretary of DLG, pointed out that island welfare was no longer the responsibility of that department, but of the Department of Social Welfare, established in 1946. Yet Garvin noted that the DSW 'disclaim responsibility for action ... it is, however, unsatisfactory that no department should be prepared to accept responsibility in such circumstances. Our experience is that we are often asked to intervene at short notice when the emergencies occur.'[6] Similar noises emanated from the Department of Justice; a memorandum from its secretary, Tommy Coyne, insisted one department had to have responsibility for the islands, pointing out that in relation to distress on Inishark, 'each department disclaimed responsibility for taking the initiative in getting relief to the islanders'.[7]

In June of that year, at a time when the population of Inishark was just thirty-three (there were 281 people living on nearby Inishbofin), Fr Charles O'Malley from Inishbofin wrote to Galway West Fianna Fáil TD Gerald Bartley regarding Inishark (whose residents had petitioned the government in 1952[8]) suggesting he had not done enough 'beyond mentioning the matter once in the Dáil'. The priest did not want to make a statement to the press as

> that would injure your high standing ... but can you blame me if I am beginning to feel a little disappointed in your efforts for us ... they are not asking for charity. All they want is a chance to earn their living and rear their families where the danger of death and starvation is not always hanging over them. Living conditions in Inishark in the winter are sub-human.[9]

Bartley was annoyed and told him he had made representations to the Land Commission: 'I have in fact accumulated quite a considerable file of papers in relation to the matter', and asked him not to single out FF to be charged with neglect. The Department of the Gaeltacht, established the previous year, had no intention of getting involved, as the island was not in a Gaeltacht area (see below).[10]

The minister for lands, Erskine Childers, in response to a letter from the Archbishop of Tuam, who had visited and been 'appalled' by conditions on Inishark, insisted it was not an issue for the Land Commission. This was an interesting assertion; it is true the Commission's job was to relieve congestion, not the opposite, but it had provided land holdings for migration from Inishkea in 1931 and the Blaskets in 1953.[11] It was noted that any transfer of Inishark residents to neighbouring Inishbofin was 'likely to be strongly resisted' by Inishbofin, and that moving them to the mainland 'might lead to a similar request from the inhabitants of Inishbofin'.[12] A note from the Special Employment Schemes Office observed in relation to Inishark that there was only one smallholder 'considered suitable for a farm and since the Land Commission could make no use of his present holding he was really a landless man from the Land Commission point of view; he had nothing useful to offer'.[13] The minister for local government, Paddy Smith, insisted that rehousing them was not an issue for the local authority as its function was to rehouse those in unfit accommodation, but the islanders 'occupy good slated houses'.[14]

It was agreed to set up an interdepartmental committee and its report in 1958 noted that the population of fifty on Inishark in 1951 was reduced to just thirty-three by 1957. There was neither priest nor doctor on the island, no post office and no telephone link, and the school had been closed in December 1957. Social welfare assistance to the islanders amounted to £872 annually and there was an annual income from fishing of about £450. No rates were paid; there was a single horse, ninety-six sheep, a hundred poultry, 'no pigs' and 'Irish is no longer the language of the island', though it was widely spoken 'up to around 1930'.[15] Most importantly, the islanders were anxious to leave and 'they must experience a strong feeling of impending extinction' with only two single women and ten single men in the 19–40 age bracket: 'It is a well known fact that women are most reluctant nowadays to marry and settle down in island homes.' There was a good case for migration 'if only on humanitarian grounds ... there is also the consideration that should there be further intermarriage on the island it might have undesirable consequences due to the close relationship already existing between the eight families already there.'[16] Spending the estimated £19,000 needed to build a new pier would be money 'largely wasted'; it would be cheaper to migrate them, but settling them on the mainland would mean a 'violent change' in their way of life, an interesting choice of words.

But as usual, there was disagreement as to under whose auspices evacuations should proceed ('this is not in the scope of normal land settlement work') and who should pay. The Land Commission noted that Finance and itself were in dispute over the allocation of exceptional funds for this and since 1953 applications for migration and resettlement had also come from Dursey (population of 95, down from 210 in 1911) and Heir islands, (population of 116, down from 294 in 1911): 'some migrations from these islands were effected on an individual basis but it was decided to take no action on the question of general resettlement'. The fear was that, after Inishark, more requests would follow. A fund of £14,000 was needed for the Inishark migration; this expenditure was agreed by cabinet in June 1958.[17] Even after that, as highlighted by Jude McCarthy, some islanders complained about the poor quality of the land they were migrated to: 'we got nothing but rocks'.[18]

There was also controversy in October 1957 when four men and a woman 'who put out in a motor-powered currach from Clare Island for the Mayo coast as dusk was falling' disappeared. Civilian volunteers searched the coastline from Louisburgh to Achill, but such was the extent of the islands in Clew Bay that the Irish air corps was asked to send aircraft to search the area: 'the Department of Defence said however, that the request had come too late', which generated an outcry.[19] Those in the currach were two Board of Works colleagues who had been on the island to carry out a survey, two fishermen who had agreed to transport them (one was a father whose youngest child had been born a few days earlier) and Bríd O'Toole, aged twenty-five, a native of Inishturk 'who was going to England to seek work' and had essentially hitched a lift on the boat. The army plane was involved in the search the day after in poor visibility, and the tragedy led to demands for a lifeboat or helicopter stationed in Clew Bay; critics of the delays in the search referred to a 'callous and indifferent approach' to air-sea rescue.[20]

A resolution from Galway County Council in May 1957 demanded a helicopter to be stationed in Galway to convey patients from the islands to the mainland, but it was decided by the Department of Industry and Commerce that weather conditions could also make a helicopter unsafe and that the commercial operation of helicopters was not viable due to lack of demand.[21] The following winter Mayo County Council called on the government to alleviate the plight of Clare and Inishturk and provide an air-sea rescue service. Fr Gleeson on Clare called for 'proper harbours' and Dr O'Toole, the district's medical officer, maintained 'as far as medical and spiritual aid was concerned, at most times during the winter a priest or doctor might as well be in the centre of Europe because they were absolutely powerless to get to the island'.[22] The following month during the Christmas holiday there were reports of 'storm-lashed' marooned islanders on Clare, where there were 450 people: 'beer runs out, flour goes short and sixty-two young Irish folk are cut off from their jobs in England. They sent telegrams to their bosses yesterday explaining the hold up.'[23]

Disputes also raged on about the Aran Islands steamer service, rows which by now had reached major saga status. In the early 1940s, twice-weekly sailings had been reduced to one owing to the worsening financial position of the Galway Bay Steamboat Company running the 120ft vessel *Dún Aengus*, meaning those wishing to transact business on the mainland 'have to stay a week. Many are compelled to dispose of their livestock and other produce to middle-men who may exploit their position.'[24] There was intense lobbying – from the Archbishop of Tuam, clergy, the Galway county manager and Galway Chamber of Commerce – for the restoration of a second weekly sailing, as 'many islanders normally have no opportunity for replying to correspondence for a week'. But it was noted at government level that 'the financial position of the company is desperate'.

Unusually for a government department, Industry and Commerce insisted 'a twice weekly service is essential to the well-being of the islanders and the additional cost should be borne by the Exchequer'. The Department of Finance, however, was having none of it; it could not see the justification for increasing the subsidy and in revealing language insisted 'the disabilities of the islanders have not become any more acute' and that owing to improvement in social services, tourism and livestock prices their financial position had improved with 'an apparently substantial traffic in small boats to and from the islands'. The claim that islanders were delayed in Galway 'seems to be exaggerated'. The government, however, agreed to look at the possibility of CIE taking over the steamer service from the Galway Bay Steamboat Company, which was agreed in August 1951.[25]

Pressure on the government over this and other island issues frequently came from the opposition in the Dáil in the form of emotive, accusatory questions laced with dramatic language. John (Jack) McQuillan, for example, a politician who came to prominence on the back of a stellar Gaelic football career with Roscommon and was elected in 1948 after campaigning with the new Clann na Poblachta political party on a radical land and agricultural platform (and also 'tapping a streak of small-farmer radicalism'), asked in November 1950 'if this house looks on the people of the Aran Islands as inhabitants of Devil's Island or of a leper's colony. For a long time past these people have been cut off from the mainland except for a once a week service.'[26]

There was further disquiet in March 1953 when CIE was planning to withdraw the *Dún Aengus* for an 'annual survey' for an indefinite period. According to the *Sunday Independent*, such cavalier treatment, with no substitute to be put in place, could be 'regarded as an indication of how official circles really regard this last great outpost of the Gaelic nation'. It was parish priest Fr Tom Varley who had asked the newspaper to intervene on the grounds that 'a native government should not allow them to be treated as outcasts'.[27] A week later the same newspaper published an editorial under the title 'The Western Outcasts':

> The Aran folk are a sturdy and stoical breed. They are indeed well used to being ignored and treated as if they were of no account. But when they are victims of treatment like this, is it any wonder they become cynical when they read of public men who pay lip service to the last outposts of the Gael and the bastions of Gaelic civilisation and the treasure house of our ancient culture and all the rest of the phrases so often mouthed in the Dáil and on platforms. Can they be blamed if they wonder is this their reward for their loyalty to Irish traditions or if they question the sincerity of all the high-flowing platitudes about the need for preserving the Gaeltacht? ... it should not be left to any newspaper to have to stir the conscience of those who guide the destinies of the country. It has been said

over and over again that the remnants of the western Gaels are a sacred trust to the nation. There is precious little evidence that the trustees appreciate their duties and responsibilities.[28]

A substitute for the steamer, a small fishing boat provided by CIE, could not travel the following month owing to bad weather. Fr Moran, the curate on Inisheer, suggested 'in a few days our diet will consist of potatoes and salt ... paraffin oil supplies were exhausted a week ago', while Fr Varley criticised the 'veil of silence'. Relief arrived the following day.[29] De Valera, Taoiseach again from 1951–4, was prompted to intervene and the chairman of CIE told him he would tell his board of de Valera's wish that a proper substitute be provided when the *Dún Aengus* was withdrawn from service.[30] By the end of 1954, when John A. Costello was back leading a coalition government, Fr Varley was once again calling for a daily service to the islands; islanders were 'often on board ship for as long as six or seven hours even when they are going to or coming from hospital' and he demanded 'just rights' for the Gaeltacht.[31]

Industry and Commerce suggested that if the boat was to travel from Rossaveal, twenty-three miles from Galway city, as was demanded by some who felt it was a better option than the city itself, then £60,000 would be needed for navigational facilities and improvement work and another £100,000 for the construction of a proper harbour. When Costello sent this information to Fr Varley he dismissed it out of hand, but Costello, tiring of the remonstrations, insisted, 'I am in the hands of the ministerial advisers whose advice I forwarded to you.'[32] Varley's reply was that those ministers 'are guided by officials who just look out over Galway Bay and take the safest line and the line of least resistance, viz., to advise to leave things as they are. They have a feeling that people who have put up with it for so long will stand it for ever.'[33] Later that year, Varley pointed out that the island of Inishbofin, with a population of 300, 'all English speaking', situated eight miles from the nearest mainland harbour, 'has a postal service four times a week'. The Aran Islands, with a population of 2,000 'all Gaelic speaking' and nine miles from the nearest mainland harbour, 'have a postal service twice a week ... can you reconcile these facts with the sentiments for the Gaeltacht?'[34]

Early the following year the Aran islanders formed a protest committee about the lack of service from the *Dún Aengus* from February to April, the period during which the bulk of the Aran livestock was due to be shipped to Galway (about 300 cattle and 1,200 sheep were shipped from the islands each season). Varley could only resort to threatening media attention: 'the position is so serious that it is bound to bring about an outcry in the public press'.[35]

The constant emphasis placed by Varley on the Gaeltacht status of the Aran Islands was a reminder of so many historic aspirations that had been dashed. From the 1920s state policy for the Gaeltacht had essentially taken on the character of a regional development programme, but policies such as grants and loans for housing, land reclamation and kelp production and free school meals did not stabilise the west, which was ravaged by emigration in the 1950s, a decade when half a million left Ireland. By 1956, when, remarkably, the official Gaeltacht was defined for the first time, having been assigned its own government department (like the islands 'the problems of administering the Gaeltacht were passed from one ministry to another'[36]), it contained only 85,700 people out of a total population of just under 2.9 million. As officially defined, there were Gaeltacht areas in seven of the state's twenty-six counties – Donegal, Mayo, Galway, Kerry, Cork, Meath and Waterford – and it omitted areas that had experienced a decline in Irish language use. By 1961 the number of Irish speakers in the state had fallen to 78,524 and ten years later to just 70,568.

While the focus had traditionally been on agriculture and the education system, the emergence of Gaeltarra Éireann in 1958, a state board to administer and promote rural industries, indicated a new emphasis; it had 700 employees by the 1960s, and while state resources were sometimes put to good use, the approach was too patchy. There simply had not been, in Gearóid Ó Tuathaigh's description, a 'coherent plan of language-sensitive socio-economic regeneration for the Gaeltacht'.[37]

Another man very familiar with island issues and, like Fr Varley, adept at generating press headlines, was the Catholic Bishop of Cork and Ross, Cornelius Lucey, who frequently sermonised on all and sundry. He had little time for those who believed an independent state could afford to bask in the glory of its fight for freedom, and many of his beliefs could be summed up in his statement that 'it was a misguided idealism to be prepared to die for one's country, but not to live for it, or to work for it, or to make it a better place for more to settle down in'.[38] This explained why he spoke out so strongly against emigration and the plight of the islands. In November 1957 he wrote to de Valera about the islands attached to his Cork diocese, suggesting it was a 'thousand pities' that their populations were falling as 'they are a sturdy people, a great stock, and, at least in the Cape [Cape Clear Island], still half Irish-speaking. They deserve to be saved for the nation ... I feel so much for the islanders and their passing.'[39]

Lucey demanded the de-rating of occupied houses and holdings. A court case the previous year against rated owners on Whiddy (there were seventeen farms on the island with a population of eighty) for the withholding of rates had ended in defeat for the islanders. De Valera, who served his last term as Taoiseach from 1957–9, brought up Lucey's concerns at a government meeting and a memorandum was prepared by the Department of Local Government insisting the law should not be changed regarding rates: 'it would be difficult and invidious to sponsor legislation for relief in these special cases without encountering numerous demands for similar concessions'.[40] There was also the question of the writing off by local authorities of rates deemed to be irrecoverable and in the 1920s and 1930s numerous complaints had been made to the department about the failure of islands in Mayo and Galway to pay rates: 'even when decrees were obtained against defaulters the local authorities found it impossible to have them executed due to their inability to effect seizures of either stock or goods on the islands'.

In Galway, rates were paid in full on Inishmore but not on the two other Aran Islands; on Clare only three individuals paid rates; the curate, the rate collector and the (local authority) assistance officer: 'the remaining occupiers have refused to pay rates for many years. These rates are written off as irrecoverable each year.' In Donegal, Arranmore islanders paid rates, but those in Gola, Tory and Inishbofin did not. The memorandum insisted 'it cannot be taken for granted that islanders are in poorer circumstances than the residents on the adjoining mainland', but it was true that valuations of island holdings could be excessive as they were fixed when the fishing industry was thriving 'and when seaweed was much more valuable than it is now'.[41] But it was pointed out that they got the maximum allowance of rates remission (three-fifths of remission for agricultural land) and deductions were made for inaccessibility: 'rates cannot be regarded merely as a payment for services rendered ... also there is not necessarily any connections between the amount a local authority spends in a particular area and the amount received in rates'.[42]

Armed with such information, a civil servant drafted a letter of response to Lucey, referring to the 'insuperable practical difficulties'. It was best to leave it as it was, especially when some local authorities were, in any case, deciding they were irrecoverable. But de Valera insisted on a much more comprehensive response to the bishop and expressed the wish to devise 'some helpful scheme', while being mindful of 'financial considerations'.[43] De Valera took a hands-on interest in this; as he was going to be in Cork a few days later he offered to call on the bishop, which he did, after which 'the bishop understood the position'. He may well have, but that did not stop him stirring it up, as usual, a few months later, at a confirmation service in Kilcoe, Cork, where he was reported as saying 'Islanders on Cork's west coast should not be asked to pay the same rates as mainlanders.'[44]

A month later, the refusal of Whiddy islanders to pay rates was again in the news. A planned visit in May by the county sheriff, Edward Healy, intended as a 'final warning', had to be abandoned owing to bad weather, but that was not the end of the issue. In June 1958 Sheriff Healy arrived in Bantry with Gardaí and court officers to enforce the order; £800 arrears were owed by thirty-eight island defaulters who claimed they did not get the services those on the mainland got. What was described as the latest 'invasion', when three Gardaí went over first, was a surprise. The officials followed and entered into negotiations with the islanders with proposals to be referred to the minister.[45]

The following year, the issue was raised in the Dáil by Labour Party TD for Cork West, Michael Pat Murphy, who moved a motion in November 1959 to revise the valuations of all island holdings 'in view of the grave lack of amenities on islands around the coast'. There was, he suggested, 'a moral duty' on the government to give some grant-in-aid, which he suggested should be 50–60 per cent rates relief.[46] In light of this, the Department of Finance pointed out there 'were some sixty islands around the coast' and asked various departments for information. The collective replies suggested 'no department has in mind the sponsoring of any special concessions to islanders and the department of the Gaeltacht did not accept that any committee might fall within its province' as only twelve of the islands were in the Gaeltacht.

This exercise led to a general overview of what individual government departments were doing for the islands. Committees had been set up to look at transport (1944) the situation on the Blaskets (1947) and Inishark (1957), and now consideration was being given to forming a committee to investigate the question of resettlement of the Inishturk population.[47] Where pupil numbers were too low to warrant local education, subsidies for transport or boarding out would be provided so that they could be schooled on the mainland. Other assistance highlighted included the grant towards the cost of bottled-gas installations for those living on Gaeltacht islands and a new boat operating between Cape Clear and the mainland. The Department of Health insisted, 'apart from transport difficulties due to inclement weather [quite an understatement] island inhabitants are in many cases as convenient to district hospitals as inhabitants of remoter districts on the mainland'. There were resident dispensary doctors on Valentia, Inishmore, Clare, Arranmore and Inishbofin, while the Land Commission pointed out curtly that 'islanders are persistent defaulters in the payment of land annuities [payments owed on money borrowed by tenants to become landowners] and the arrears to date are £18,000'.

The Department of Land and Fisheries referred to its credit scheme for the supply of boats. Other developments mentioned included piped water in Kilronan on Inishmore and Valentia, causeways and bridges provided to connect the Galway islands of Lettermore and Gorumna with the mainland, and the fact that the twenty-one largest of the islands, those with a population of a hundred upwards, had a local post office, while the steamer service to Aran was operating at a loss to the state. Rural electrification, which had began in earnest in 1946, had been extended to Arranmore, Achill, Valentia, Bere, Spike and Little Island off Dunmore in County Waterford.

These lists suggested the accusations that the state did nothing for the islands were inaccurate, but as was often the case with the compilation of government memoranda on the islands, there was also the casting of aspersions on islanders' characters:

> Islanders get the full social welfare benefits – old age pensions, widows and orphans pensions, public assistance, blind pensions etc. – in fact, they are believed to do better than persons living on the mainland since the department have not got so good an opportunity for detecting fraudulent claims from islanders. It is understood that a recent survey of Tory Island showed that every family there save one was in receipt of some form of social welfare benefit.[48]

In September 1960 the cabinet decided an interdepartmental committee would examine the general condition of the islands and report within two months.[49] The committee's report was ready in June 1961 when a significant decision was made, given the decades of responsibility being disclaimed by various departments: 'the primary responsibility for island matters should not be assigned to any department', but that a permanent interdepartmental committee with representatives from Finance, Local Government, Lands and the Gaeltacht would be established to co-ordinate and 'act as a clearing mechanism'. It was recommended that the minister for education should prepare a scheme for the award of limited state scholarships to island children; there would also be an extra £5,000 grant to improve roads on the islands along with a telephone service for four different islands as yet unconnected, as well as bottled gas schemes and improved landing facilities.[50]

Whether these gestures were too little and too late remained to be seen; what was apparent at this stage, however, was the considerable tourist potential of the islands.

The 1960s often witnessed islands being heralded as providing a sanctuary from stressful commercialism, essential oases or stopping off points for the discerning archaeologist or language scholar or families in need of nature. This marketing of the islands was particularly pronounced in *Ireland of the Welcomes*, the official publication of the National Tourist Publicity Organisation for Ireland, and published every two months from 1952 (Bord Fáilte Éireann, the Irish Tourist Board, was established in 1955). It was noted in 1962, for example, that 'as with all retreats, Achill is being discovered'. The challenge was to present the islands as both archaic and adaptive: 'The primitive, poetic and paradoxical are all part of Achill ... gone are the days of oil lamps and primitive facilities. Ireland's vast rural electrification scheme has reached Achill and may upset many a girl's matrimonial schemes' as bachelors now had electric plugs that 'can't talk back'.[51]

Likewise, in relation to the Aran Islands, 'the simplicity of life ... has a strong appeal for people of more progressive, but perhaps less happy communities', but one older islander did fear 'that the islands were in danger of becoming a show piece'.[52] It was reported in 1962 that the first 'CIE Educational tour' to the Aran Islands was imminent.[53] This did nothing to dilute the purple prose of the tourist generators, however; in the summer of 1964, the 'sturdy and colourful' fishermen of Aran were deemed to represent 'something of the artistic beauty of medieval life'.[54] The following year, an article on Inishark referred to the evacuation of four years previously, when the 'last seven of the eighteen families were rehabilitated [an intriguing but presumably mistaken choice of word] on the mainland and they are almost a legend', forced off Inishark 'by the sea and the weather'.[55]

Newspapers, however, focused on more prosaic realities in relation to government policy and the islands. It was reported at the end of 1963 that Rutland Island off the coast of Donegal 'has become deserted'. Sixty-three-year-old Hugh McCole and his sister 'were taken off the island where they had been marooned with little food and without fire for several days'. At one stage there were twenty-four families living on the island and it had a post office and pub but 'now it will be given over entirely to cattle from the mainland'. McCole had initially refused to leave but 'now he realises that Rutland is dead'.[56] The same fate awaited Gola; the last residents left in November 1969 and one of them, Fergal McGee, was photographed with his two suitcases as it became 'deserted'.[57]

In the *Irish Times* in May 1968, journalist Denis Coughlan wrote of

Cape Clear; while it 'rises majestically from the sea ... the land is sick; sick with the cancer of indifference and lack of capital'. He noted that recently the Fianna Fáil Taoiseach Jack Lynch had visited the island to present them with a prize for their efforts in promoting the Irish language but it still had no electricity: 'It is especially galling when the islanders can look across to their sister island Sherkin and see the lights shining mockingly across the narrow stretch of sea which separates them ... all water on the island must be drawn by hand ... the tourist potential of the island has, as yet, not even been scratched on the surface.'[58] While the number of schoolchildren on the island had increased since 1946, 'some families have been almost wiped out by emigration and one native remarked with pride that he had forty-two first cousins in the US'. But Coughlan could finish on what, for so many observers and visitors was a positive note: the island was 'by passed by most of what is bad in our present-day civilisation'.[59]

A few years previously, Córas Tráchtála, the Irish trade board formed in 1959 to market Irish goods abroad, shipped an authentic twenty-four-foot currach from the Aran Islands to Montreal for display at an Irish trade promotion drive.[60] But Aran was frequently in the news in the 1960s for other reasons, including the difficulty of getting a doctor to serve the islands. When Dr Alan Delaney arrived to take the post in April 1967 'at the inflated salary for the position of £2,000 a year', it was front-page news for the *Irish Independent*, which had noted that before his arrival there were '1500 without a doctor on Aran Islands'. Both of his predecessors 'resigned after six months duty' and islanders were still waiting 'for the promised cottage hospital'. A spokesman for Inishmaan insisted the situation on the island 'merits immediate top level investigation' because of winter isolation and insufficient educational and religious facilities: 'the complete absence of modern facilities is a disgrace. Those in authority seemed to satisfy their conscience by simply doling out a few extra shillings to the islanders. Their attitude seemed to be "How can we keep them quiet"? rather than "How can we improve their standard of living with human dignity?".'[61] The following year, however, it was announced that government approval had been given for a two-bed cottage hospital and nurse's quarters on Aran, and a medical officer's residence, involving expenditure of almost £10,000.[62]

Even better news for the Aran Islands came with the dawn of a new decade and a new air service; the air strip was opened in August 1970 on Inishmore at a cost of £20,000, with the ten-seater plane averaging three flights a day. The main focus now was on how it would increase tourism. Initially, it was the possibility of the withdrawal of the tourist ferry, *The Galway Bay* from the island that initiated the air link project.[63] The air service transformed the lives of the communities there: 'Electricity, post-primary education and industry all came to the islands as a result of the flights, along with hundreds of thousands of tourists. One hundred in 1969 became 14,000 in 1976.' Before such flights, the residents of these islands faced a thirty-mile journey to the hospital in Galway in lifeboats 'through crashing black waves and wailing winds' and it could take three hours to reach the island by ferry.[64]

Tourism was also very much in the frame in relation to a bridge to Valentia Island in Kerry. The 1,300-foot span, which cost £500,000 and took two and a half years to construct was opened 'by the man who made a by-election promise that it would be built', Neil Blaney (who had been minister for agriculture on the eve of a south Kerry by election in 1966), meeting a twenty-year demand (see also chapter 4).[65] Its opening prompted an assertion by the county manager, Séamus Keating, that, with it, 'the people of Valentia had gained more than they had lost'.[66]

But the wider plight of islands continued to generate considerable emotion, with pleas to devise special policies to assist them, including cost-of-living subsidies and telecommunications, while others sought assistance to enable island residents who so desired to transfer to the mainland. In 1971 there were eighty inhabited islands off the coast, with a population of 11,737, which dropped to 10,866 in 1979.[67] Gaeltacht status came to the fore in relation to island controversies. In November 1971 junior Gaeltacht minister Michael Kitt was on Cape Clear for the launch of the island's new electricity scheme and was reported as saying that the islanders, 'unless it is clear they are adhering to the Irish language ... should not expect assistance' from his department, suggesting the status of the island as a Gaeltacht was being queried. There was also the contention that the islanders had wanted an island child to switch on the light 'as a symbol of the future of the youth of Cape Clear ... the implication was that the department had insisted that Mr Kitt should throw the switch.[68]

In 1973 Liam O'Rocháin, one of those involved in the Cape Clear co-operative established in 1969 to administer electricity on the island, authored a 'Manifesto for the Islands' suggesting the incoming Fine Gael–Labour coalition government 'should devise a special policy for the islands' including the abolition of income tax for islanders in employment 'because of the inequities between island and mainland living costs' and cost-of-living and building subsidies, maintaining that a house that would cost £6,000 to build on the mainland would cost more than £8,000 to build on an island.[69] His suggestions gathered dust, but versions of them were to re-emerge at various stages.

Despite modernisation and improved access and communications, evacuation was still a recurring theme. Six of the seven families on Inishturk (with a population of eighty-three in 1971) off the coast of Mayo, for example, wanted to move to the mainland, as did twelve of the sixteen families on Galway's Inishturbot (with a population of sixty-five).[70] The combined cost to the Land Commission of their resettlement was estimated at £80,000 (the Department of Finance, unusually, was supportive). The islands were 'small, low-lying, bleak' and the residents were living in primitive conditions:

> There is no priest, doctor or nurse on the islands and mass is said on each island only on one Sunday per month. There is no electricity; some islanders use bottled gas for lighting and cooking. Contact with the mainland is by radiotelephone. All the men on both islands over eighteen and under pension age are reported to be getting social welfare assistance. These are not Irish speaking communities. The islanders, who own lands ranging from three acres to eighteen acres plus a share of commonage, cannot be described as farmers in the true sense. The Turk islanders are in the main fishermen.

It was reported that those who wished to stay on Inishturbot 'comprise three elderly bachelors and an elderly couple whose family have emigrated.[71]

In 1974 Fr Pádraig Staunton, based on Inisheer, lamented the decay of that island but realised the limitations of island living were becoming hazardous: 'There was a time when the last thing I would do would be advise someone to leave the islands. I'm not so sure now.' There were twenty-seven unmarried men and two women between the ages of fourteen and thirty, dependent on unemployment assistance. While he wondered why there was not more effective co-ordination of the efforts of various government departments, he did not see it as just an issue of government neglect: 'what are the churches or the clergy doing? Are they too comfortable to care? Are they waiting to muzzle anything in a dog collar that pisses on the sacred cows of church or state?'[72]

The secretary of the Department of the Gaeltacht in 1975, Liam Tobin, thought it was 'wrong to have wholesale evacuation of islands': he did not want to see any part of the national territory becoming 'a deserted black spot'.[73] Minister for transport and power, Fine Gael's Peter Barry, informed Taoiseach Liam Cosgrave in May 1975 that it would be too expensive and simply not feasible to provide electricity on Clare and Inishturk, and Inishturbot residents were reported to want to move to the mainland at Clifden in Galway 'before next winter'. Barry also insisted in communication with Cosgrave in July 1975 that 'the Gaeltacht islands ... have benefited because of the existence of a department with the particular duty of promoting the general well-being of Gaeltacht area'.[74]

Despite the existence of this department, however, confusion about just who was responsible for island life and communities continued. The islanders' welfare still essentially fell between the stools of different government departments. There was also an enduring tendency to depict them as almost alien and deliberately lazy. A memorandum regarding the evacuation of seven families from Inishturbot in 1975 recorded:

> the people are poor and uneducated, without resources and completely lacking in initiative; their income is derived from fishing on a very small scale, social welfare payments and – in some cases – contributions from the St Vincent de Paul Society [a Catholic Church charity] ... morale on the island is reported to be very low as a result of the drowning of three islanders while returning

from the mainland last September [they had been socialising and watching the all-Ireland hurling final on the mainland].

The cost of the resettlement was estimated at £250,000 over three years. Minister for finance Richie Ryan was opposed to central government financing this, insisting it was a housing issue for the local authority. The minister for lands insisted his department had no funds available and the minister for local government 'strongly disagrees with the suggestion that the islanders should be forced by government policy to leave their island homes for the wholly unsuitable environment of a semi-urban housing scheme'. It was ultimately decided that it should be the responsibility of the Land Commission.[75]

Marie Mannion, Inishturbot's teacher, said that because they were not told about their options 'there wasn't one person on the island who realised that it was possible for them to live in their homes with the same facilities as on the mainland'. Journalist Brian Wilson concluded that 'islands and islanders seem to be regarded as irritants rather than assets in present-day Ireland'. Eighty-four-year-old islander Michael Ward described the move as going 'from heaven to hell', but another life-long resident thought that, due to the 'living conditions and associated hardships, women and children deserve the chance of something better'.[76]

As to complaints that the non-Gaeltacht islands were being discriminated against, Fianna Fáil's Bobby Molloy, representing the constituency of Galway West, wrote to Cosgrave in 1975: 'your recent voyage around our coast must have sharply demonstrated that the hardship of island life is not determined by the language spoken, but bears heavily on all'.[77] In 1977 the government announced a £750,000 grant for the Gaeltacht islands; residents of English-speaking Clare had complained of discrimination against the non-Gaeltacht islands, which as well as Clare (population 150), included Inishbofin (population 250) and Inishturk (population 67), all three maintaining that all requests for assistance had been refused.

In September 1977 the minister for the Gaeltacht, Tom O'Donnell, promised them equal status with the Gaeltacht islands.[78] There were disagreements as to whether the islanders' problems were social or financial;

minister for finance George Colley did not accept 'without qualification that the same services as on the mainland must be available to islanders'. There were reports of 'intentions to desert Tory island' and the vacation of Inishturbot. It was felt in the Department of the Taoiseach that 'in view of the trend for the populations of islands to fall and eventually disappear ... the question of capital investment should be approached with great caution'. There were only thirty-one residents on Long Island off west Cork: 'it is proposed to canvass the population to ascertain if they want electricity'.[79]

Rescuers were not contacted in time to save the lives or recover four of the six bodies lost on the *Evelyn Marie* trawler off the coast of Donegal in January 1975. The family of one of the victims, Hughie Gallagher, living on Arranmore Island in Donegal, picked up news of the disaster on CB radios, after the trawler struck rocks off Rathlin O'Birne Island and 'vanished without trace'. This family, and others, spent years unsuccessfully searching for answers about the inadequacies of the response to the tragedy, the failure to send a helicopter to attempt a rescue and the lack of transparency around the official government inquiry into the event. Almost two years later, in November 1976, the *Carraig Una* trawler went down at the same spot with the loss of five lives.[80]

Another island, Whiddy in Bantry Bay, Cork, achieved prominence because of its oil refinery. In January 1979 disaster struck when an explosion occurred while a French tanker was unloading its cargo; all forty-three crew members were killed as well as seven workers on the Gulf Oil terminal. A subsequent inquiry held two transnational oil companies, Gulf and Total, responsible for the disaster. Total, owners of the tanker, had not kept the vessel properly maintained while knowing it was in poor condition, while Gulf Oil was criticised for not taking adequate measures to ensure the safety of the men on Whiddy. It has also been suggested that the Whiddy disaster 'may have played its part in reducing the government's enthusiasm for building a nuclear power station. Only twenty-seven of the fifty bodies were recovered; the *Irish Independent* headline referred to it as a 'Holocaust'. Whiddy's inhabitants, numbering just fifty-seven, 'fled in a flotilla of small boats', while those who fought the flames were commended for their bravery. Survivors accused the Gulf

Company, which paid $120 million in compensation for the clean-up operation, of 'closing ranks when investigations began'. The terminal was never fully repaired.[81]

In 1975 the Taoiseach Liam Cosgrave was asked by Fianna Fáil TD for Mayo West, Denis Gallagher, if he would consider the establishment of an 'island authority', but the Department of Lands pointed out that primary responsibility for Gaeltacht islands rested with the Department of the Gaeltacht and that the Central Development Committee (CDC) of the Department of Finance had been given responsibility for co-ordinating the work of departments in relation to the islands.[82] The CDC completed a report in 1976, under the auspices of the Department of Economic Planning and Development, covering many facets of island life in order to 'avoid dealing with island problems in an ad hoc way'. It suggested that if problems were rectified 'a reasonable population structure could be maintained on a number of islands' and listed non-Gaeltacht islands with their populations in 1975: Clare (150), Turk (67), Bofin (250), Bear (274), Dursey (35), Heir (52), Long (31), Sherkin (88) and Whiddy (60) making for a total overall population of 1,007.[83] They needed ferries, telephones, electricity, piped water, landing places, housing, tourism and 'female employing projects' for women of 'marriageable age' and to 'motivate islanders towards self-help and improvement', grants for community premises at 75 per cent of costs and a permanent subcommittee of the CDC for island development. Overall, capital of £707,500 was needed, but in the view of one civil servant, 'it would be unwise ... to make substantial investments on islands where the populations are going to migrate to the mainland in any event.'[84]

In general there was a 'gross imbalance' between the numbers of marriageable males and females on the islands and none of the islands in the survey had a resident doctor. But most islanders were willing to stay, 'given certain improvements, mainly in communications ... or perhaps resigned to stay given the lack of suitable alternative holdings and housing on the mainland'. The following year the minister for industry and commerce, Des O'Malley, was 'strongly opposed' to a subsidised electricity supply for the non-Gaeltacht islands because the ESB was obliged to operate on a commercial basis and there was concern that isolated communities on the mainland would agitate for the same.[85] The minister for agriculture, Jim Gibbons, also thought these draft proposals for the islands were 'too committal'.[86]

There was also political focus on Rathlin Island in the 1970s, including an interdepartmental review of the island following a visit in June 1975 by John Concannon, who was parliamentary undersecretary of state at the Department of Housing, Local Government and Town Planning in Northern Ireland. Another official in the department noted of this review, 'we do not want this exercise to become public since this carries the risk of raising local expectations too high'.[87] Findings included a primary school with a classroom 'built between 1850 and 1899', 'no playground' and an island population of 103, representing a 58 per cent decrease since 1937, when the population had been 245. Educationally, the islanders were 'relatively well provided for' but electricity and water were problematic (they were still dependent on 'small lakes, springs and wells sunk') and there were too many constraints on tourist development, which had to be balanced with the need 'to avoid destroying the island's own character'. Ideas about potential cottage industries had been mooted at various stages, given the high level of unemployment, but these were 'often based more on misplaced optimism than on economic reality'.[88] The most pressing worry, however, was lack of electricity, an issue not solved until the 1990s.

Newspapers covered many other aspects of the state's fractious relationship with the islands during the 1970s, including calls for increased protection for island antiquities. In 1975, members of the National Monuments Advisory Committee appealed to Sligo County Council regarding Inishmurray, which had been evacuated in 1948. The island contained unique remains of Irish Christian settlement ('one of the most complete and exciting in Europe', which included an eighth-century grave slab – see chapter 5). The best of the carved stones had to be removed to the National Museum and there had been a decade-long effort to persuade the OPW to purchase the island from its owners, the former residents.[89]

There was no Irish equivalent of the Highland and Islands Board in Scotland, which had been established in 1965 to enable those communities 'to play a more effective part in the economic and social development of the nation'; by the early 1980s it had an annual budget of £28 million and staff of 262. The population of the Highlands and Islands was 353,000 at that time.[90] Nonetheless, there were numerous Irish state bodies that had an association with the development of island enterprises and economies. In 1974, twenty-seven-year-old Tarlach de Blacam, a Dublin native living on Inishmaan ('does not physically look like most island men. Not bulky, hardship-honed and bronzed. He looks, in truth, rather pale') was Islands Development Officer for Gaeltarra Éireann, having been initially drawn to the Gaeltacht Civil Rights movement by writer Máirtín Ó Cadhain. He was charged with the task of promoting small industries based on local raw materials and crafts, fishing and tourism. He called for a co-operative spirit that could be formalised into pressure groups to 'exercise the maximum force in all directions' for the benefit of the islands.

De Blacam also noted that those state agencies whose work involved the islands included county councils, county development teams, regional development groups, the Board of Works, CIE and Bord Iascaigh Mhara (the Irish state agency responsible for developing the seafood industry): 'the list is seemingly endless'. He suggested 'much has been done to educate the mainland about the special needs of island communities', but much remained to be done and he insisted islanders also needed to be taught how to develop their own community, while the mainland needed to be educated 'out of the old banishment syndrome'.[91] De Blacam went on to establish the highly successful Inis Meáin knitwear company (see Postscript); other industries and enterprises were supported by Údarás na Gaeltachta, established in 1980 to promote the economic, social and cultural development of the Gaeltacht.

In 1974 De Blacam had suggested there was a good case for creating an association of islands, but this was not to happen for almost twenty years. The islands federation was inaugurated on Cape Clear Island in September 1984, initially founded by representatives of sixteen islands but which grew to a membership of thirty-three islands, partly because, unlike in Britain, Irish islands were all offshore parts of mainland administrative areas. The press release for the federation (Comhdháil nOileáin) suggested that, with its creation, 'no populated off shore island however small, remote or disadvantaged, need be alone in the struggle for survival'. One of its chief demands was that the government should set up a separate authority responsible for the islands and it sought to exert pressure regarding schools, water schemes and electricity. Significantly, Rathlin was included in its membership, though the islanders were said to be in dispute about this as Rathlin was part of Northern Ireland rather than the Republic.[92] Did the new federation live up to its press-release promise? Coverage of island issues in the 1980s would suggest not, at least in the short term, and due to funding shortages it temporarily ceased functioning.

Even at the end of the 1980s, Dáil debates about transport to the Aran Islands featured and there was criticism of the expense of the air fare (£30) and the dilapidated condition of the state-funded boat, the *Naomh Éanna*. Michael D. Higgins, Labour Party TD for Galway West, pointed out that the people of Aran were still not linked to television and 'deprived of connection to the mainland'. Ministers still liked to get personal about the islands, with the minister for tourism and transport, Séamus Brennan, assuring Higgins, 'I spent many of my younger days on the *Naomh Éanna*. I know the islands well, so there is no lack of goodwill on my part.'[93]

But what did goodwill mean in practice? Islanders frequently were reliant on their own initiative or support from the EEC, which the Republic had joined in 1973, along with the UK, through its structural funds and other 'regional development instruments' in the alienating language of Brussels bureaucracy. From the earliest stages of membership, the development of the EEC's regional policy was a major focus of Irish efforts, with considerable success, but there was ambiguity attached to the description 'region'. For certain purposes, the entire country was termed a region up to 1999, which attracted criticism as a paradox of EEC regional policy as it lessened the pressure to formulate a balanced development of all regions in the country. A report from the EEC's Economic and Social Committee in 1988 referred to the 'precarious situation of most island regions' with a combined population of almost 10 million 'of whom a large proportion are disadvantaged or poor' with the issues of inaccessibility, transport infrastructure, water and energy supplies and housing and social facilities most problematic. It also pointedly referred to the failure of member states to give due attention to these matters, which was 'due less to lack of resources than to the fact that these island populations are not large enough or sufficiently organised to exercise any significant electoral pressure'. The danger of their neglect was that they could become 'desert islands providing a haven for a few social "drop outs" or international tourist colonies'. One of the great dangers was that fishing was being 'spurned' by a younger generation.[94] But, as shall be seen, the EEC's own subsequent policies on fishing also played their destructive role.

In Ireland, accusations of a hierarchy of priority for islands persisted. In 1982 stormbound inhabitants on Inis Bó Finne off the Donegal coast (often also cited as Inishbofin, the same name as the island off Galway) were isolated over Christmas by raging storms. A local councillor complained that the islanders were always overlooked when it came to 'mercy missions' and wanted to know why 'army helicopters were used to fly across Inishbofin to bring supplies to Tory Island'.[95] Local Fine Gael TD Dinny McGinley waded in earlier that summer by describing the living conditions on Inis Bó Finne as 'more reminiscent of the Third World than an inhabited Irish island' and he insisted it needed a rescue package to prevent its abandonment: 'it has been by passed entirely by the twentieth century'. Its seventy residents had no electric light, proper landing place for boats, shop or school, with 'goat tracks' instead of proper roads.[96] In January 1983 there was further controversy about whether this island needed the air corps to deliver supplies, McGinley thundering that when snow fell heavily the previous year 'the Air Corps were able to send helicopters to Wicklow to feed animals'.[97]

In 1982 the MEP and leader of Northern Ireland's SDLP, John Hume, made an impassioned intervention on behalf of the Rathlin islanders when writing to the minister for the environment at Stormont in Belfast. He was particularly interested in comparing their experiences with that of other island communities and wanted the minister to meet a delegation from Rathlin. At that stage the island had a population of 114:

In every civilised society island communities like Rathlin are recognised as unique phenomena and every effort is made to help them survive and to preserve their individual way of life. Prodigious efforts have been made these last twenty years to reverse the decline of the western isles of Scotland. Even a small and relatively poor country like the Republic of Ireland has made enormous efforts to assist its island populations. In Sweden, the inhabited offshore islands are pampered by the central government with every conceivable service and subsidy. By comparison, Rathlin has been grossly neglected.[98]

He pointed out that the island had first got a radio telephone link only seven years previously, that it had no service from Northern Ireland Electricity, no proper cargo boats, no mains water supply or public sewer, no public authority houses since the 1920s, no tourist amenities, doctor or decent harbour. If improvements could not be made 'it will be a sad reflection on our society', he concluded.[99]

Hume had certainly laid bare a litany of privation, but whether island communities in the Republic would have agreed with his assertion that 'enormous efforts' had been made to assist them is doubtful. There were interesting reactions to Hume's intervention within the civil service in Northern Ireland. It was acknowledged that children often remained on Rathlin as 'over age pupils in the primary school'. When the minister for the environment met with Hume and the Rathlin Island Community Association, Hume referred in particular to the assistance given to the Scottish islands by the Highland and Islands Board, and insisted that an overall development plan for the island was necessary, but 'the minister pointed out that the present ad hoc way of dealing with Rathlin's problems had resulted over the past few years in some significant improvements involving substantial government funding'.[100] It seemed extraordinary that it would be deemed better not to have an overall plan for the island but to deal with issues on an ad hoc basis, but in truth, that had been the approach to dealing with the island communities, north and south, historically, periodically allowing governments to compile lists of intermittent infrastructural improvements or small-scale initiatives for the islands.

Voices demanding something more substantial, however, were getting louder. The previous year, 1981, the parish priest of Tory Island, the redoubtable Fr Diarmuid Ó Péicín, accused Donegal County Council of 'genocide' on the occasion of a visit by the minister for the Gaeltacht, Paddy O'Toole, to Dungloe. Ó Péicín was adamant in maintaining the council had drawn up a plan for the 'speedy elimination of Tory', including the cutting off of essential supplies, refusing to develop the island and coaxing people into new houses on the mainland. There was a determination, he insisted, to 'destroy one of the most independent-minded living Gaeltachts in the country' and the county council had 'forgotten the primacy of the spirit ... man can survive even in extreme circumstances'.[101] (See also chapter 4.)

Significantly, Ó Péicín blamed both state and church as he described conditions on Tory as 'worse than he had experienced in the worst slums of Africa', where he had been a missionary.[102] Ó Péicín was especially adept at generating publicity for Tory's plight ('using the media was something that I knew would work'), and in his memoirs castigated 'officials back on the mainland, hiding behind their impenetrable bureaucratic smokescreen', but he also 'suffered as much from Church bureaucracy as I did from the lay or governmental kind'.[103] He also had stand up rows with officials from the Department of the Gaeltacht, who 'immediately criticised the quality and paucity of my Irish'.[104]

He ended up working closely with Winifred Ewing, an MEP and vigorous campaigner on behalf of the Scottish islands, who encouraged him to 'hit Strasbourg'. Ewing did not believe Irish MEPs were doing enough for the islands, and, as Ó Péicín saw it, 'the efforts and encouragement which should have been coming from one of the 15 Irish MEPs were instead coming from a Scottish MEP'. Ó Péicín also made his way to the US and met with Speaker of the House of Representatives, Tip O'Neill.[105]

In November 1990, at the outset of voting in the Irish Republic's presidential election, during which the winning candidate, Mary Robinson, had made much of appealing to marginalised communities, an air corps helicopter arrived with ballot papers and polling staff on Inis Bó Finne in Donegal to discover that the islands thirty voters had abandoned the island for their winter homes on the mainland. The polling station remained open for four hours, but, not surprisingly, nobody turned up. On Inishfree, three miles out from Burtonport, the ballot box and a single ballot paper arrived by boat, but officials discovered that the island's only registered voter had emigrated to Peru eighteen months ago.[106]

Nonetheless, the 1990s was notable for more focused debate on the islands from politicians and the creation of a government department that included islands in its title as well as the attempt to latch the islands on to a contemporary political narrative that sought to bring hitherto excluded communities into the political frame. The Islands Federation was re-established as the Irish Islands Federation (Comhdháil nOileáin na hÉireann) in 1993; it became a co-operative and succeeded in getting recognition as a rural economic development company and was granted £1.3 million, enabling it to open an office on the Aran Islands. While it was robustly asserted that islanders were denied many fundamental rights in relation to regular economic, medical, educational and social services, it was also pointed out that islanders needed a 'realistic, prioritised list of planning objectives'.[107]

A Dáil debate in March 1996 highlighted the consistency of themes relating to the islands over seven decades; it came on the back of a report on island development by an interdepartmental committee that had sat for three years. Its mission statement was 'to support island communities in their economic, social and cultural development, to preserve and enhance their unique cultural and linguistic heritage and to enable islanders to secure access to adequate levels of public services so as to facilitate full and active participation in the overall economic and social life of the nation.'[108] The report emphasised the islands' unique cultural contribution and maintained that economic criteria alone should not dictate a strategy for their development. The report's main recommendations included an initial £1 million outlay on island access services as well as the establishment of a 'minimum standard' for such services, the investment of £4.6 million for harbour development on Tory Island, a 'financial envelope' into which all current government spending on access to the islands could be placed, and more financial assistance to facilitate island children going to secondary school.

The proposed strategy was slated by some opposition TDs as containing meaningless general statements and the absence of commitment to air services and tax concessions for islanders. At that stage Fine Gael minister of state (junior minister) Donal Carey, a member of the Fine Gael-led coalition government, had responsibility for 'western development and rural renewal ... with special responsibilities for the islands'. Cork Fine Gael TD P. J. Sheehan congratulated Carey

> on the manner in which he has tackled the neglect of island communities off our coastline to whom mere lip service has been paid since the foundation of the State. The rigours of living on an island are not understood by many people. I come from a constituency that has seven of the islands and I know only too well that those island people have suffered. I have seen a strong virile population on those islands thirty or forty years ago dwindle to a very small group. The islands are part and parcel of our culture and history, so much so that a former Taoiseach saw fit to buy an island off the Kerry coast. That island is not mentioned in the report. Perhaps he restored that island to its former glory and it does not need any State assistance.[109]

This was a reference to controversial politician and Taoiseach Charles Haughey, who in 1974, for £25,000, had bought the island of Inishvickillane, one of the six that comprise the Blasket archipelago and only intermittently inhabited by very small numbers until the early twentieth century. From the 1960s, as owner of racehorses, a stud and a Georgian mansion, Haughey sought to combine aristocratic trappings 'with an image as a modern and glamorised reincarnation of Gaelic chieftainry'.[110] Long rumoured, it was firmly established by a tribunal report decades later that his 'wealth' was built on payments from some of the country's richest men, 'sometimes disguised as political donations'. He also had large debts written off by banks as much smaller debtors were pursued and had acquired luxuries while imploring the Irish public to tighten their belts. Haughey's purchase and development of Inishvick-illane was a manifestation of his 'fiefdom' approach; material to build the new island house had to be transported by helicopter; a wind-powered electricity generator was also installed on it at the state's expense 'for experimental purposes'.[111] Ever crass and messianic, he even had a rep-lica of an Ogham [an ancient alphabet] stone from the island made and transported to his retreat, also at taxpayer's expense. [112]

The island acquisition also allowed him to internalise 'the mystique of the Great Blasket Islands, in the process challenging the assumption that he was an effete dilettante'. He presented a television programme, *Charles Haughey's Island*, in January 1988 and waxed lyrical about learn-ing from the O'Donnelly brothers, who had sold the island to him: 'they taught us about island life. How to judge the weather, to understand the moods of the sea and tides and currents. About the puffins, the storm petrels, the black headed seagulls, the seals, where to put down our lob-ster posts and where to catch a fine big mackerel.'[113]

While Haughey enjoyed the splendid isolation of his ill-gotten gains, Donal Carey allocated the £1 million promised in 1996 to facili-tate greater access to the islands on the grounds that 'each island should be entitled to a socially desirable minimum standard of access service'. In relation to the 1996 report, Carey made the interesting observation that 'it was our intention initially to include in the report a photograph of the last people to leave the Blasket Islands, taken in the late 1940s or early 1950s which is on display in Dunquin. Because it was felt it would send the wrong message it was omitted.'[114] He also suggested desertion of more islands would 'represent a major tragedy for the entire people of Ireland' and suggested a positive way forward by pointing to local authority island committees in Cork, Mayo, Galway and Donegal, which comprised local authority members and islanders.

Carey also identified a question that, again, had been raised for decades: just who was responsible for islands? He said the 'biggest single difficulty' facing islands was 'the barrier encountered by small, isolated communities in accessing and co-ordinating the many diverse agencies and departments concerned with their development', bringing to mind the observation of islanders in 1931, quoted by Jude McCarthy. When seeking assistance they said they were 'referred from Herod to Pilate until we didn't know where to go'.[115]

Fianna Fáil's Éamon Ó Cuív, a TD for Galway West, was adamant that what was needed was a Department of the Gaeltacht and the Islands; islanders needed a government department that was a 'one stop shop' so that their needs would be put ahead of 'departmental empire building'. What was also demanded for them was a clear 'charter of rights'.[116] The following year, after Fianna Fáil returned to government, Ó Cuív was appointed as minister of state at the Department of Arts, Heritage, Gaeltacht and Islands. This was hardly a 'one stop shop', but given the extent of the wrangling over decades about who had responsibility for the islands this was significant: in the words of Jude McCarthy, 'after sixty-six years the ideological jump was made, the islands were considered a peculiar problem and they were assigned to a specific department'.[117]

In another reminder of historic concerns, Ó Cuív insisted 'Islanders do not want to become guinea pigs, they do not want to become a protected species; they do not want tourists to be sent out to look at them as if they were some type of strange people. They are ordinary Irish citizens'. He did not like what he termed 'the reservation mentality that some people adopt towards people living in rural areas'.[118] This was redolent of an insistence that had been made by Ernest Blythe, Cumann na nGaedheal's minister for finance in the 1920s and a minister with an exceptional commitment to the promotion of the Irish language. When reacting to various proposals from colleagues and the civil service in 1931 about how to promote the welfare of the inhabitants of rural Ireland and, in the words of a memorandum from the Department of Education, the need 'to provide a centre for the struggling western villages, now that the crossroads are frowned upon', Blythe seemed irritated that the rural populace was being officially assessed as a class apart, insisting that they 'will not consent to be made a sort of "peculiar people" in their own land'.[119]

Another illustration of the endurance of this theme was the assertion in 1996 that Dubliners had a tendency to romanticise island life, which is 'all very well when one is sitting back watching island life on TV'.[120] Fine Gael's Ted Nealon was undoubtedly correct in asserting 'all of us have a certain romantic attachment to the islands'. During the debate on the islands report in 1996, some politicians could not help themselves, indulging in emotive, semantic excesses. Fine Gael's Dinny McGinley, referred, for example, to the 97 per cent decline of the population of Donegal's Inis Bó Finne from 1961 to 1991 and the 35 per cent overall decline in the island population from 1961 to 1991: 'During the famine one million people died while another one million people emigrated. The depopulation of the islands is on a par with that catastrophe.'

Others preferred to concentrate on the contemporary cost of living, pointing out that a 1994 survey showed that a basket of twenty-three common food items cost 16.6 per cent more on the islands than on the mainland.[121] A 1993 survey of the cost of living on Cape Clear had found likewise.[122] While people on that island 'in general appear to be quite comfortable financially', there were tensions about the operation of the co-op, grants and enterprise.[123] Cork County Council also conducted a west Cork island study in 1994, concluding the west Cork islands were 'sensitive and complex' and 'include some islands in danger of complete depopulation' with the main challenge being to achieve 'an adequate pool of young people from which new island families can be formed'.[124]

A year previously it was noted that there were seven inhabited offshore islands in west Cork; the three largest were Bere (population 240), Cape Clear (140) and Whiddy (90); the smaller ones had populations of fewer than thirty permanent islanders. A combined delegation of these islanders attended a meeting of the western committee of Cork County Council, 'where they insisted that it was time that the Cork islands take their rightful place in the administration of the county'.[125]

Cape Clear's co-op, formed in 1969, was described in 1990 as operating 'almost like a government in miniature', reflecting an island that abounded 'with endeavour and pride'. A wind-energy project – two windmills on the island were producing over 60 per cent of its required electricity – was also an indication of that dynamism. It was described in 1992 as 'the country's only private working wind energy project', but its future had been 'tangled up in political and bureaucratic wrangling'. It was 50 per cent funded by a German company but there were, allegedly, difficulties in getting the ESB to co-operate.[126]

The issue of electricity was also central to the welfare and modernisation of Rathlin and its population of 107 (including five lighthouse keepers), and this became controversial in Northern Ireland in the 1990s in relation to the feasibility of a mains supply and who would pay for it. In November 1990 Jim Anderson of NI's Department of Economic Planning pointed out that NI Electricity (NIE) had made a profit of £80 million that year and there was an onus on it to supply rural areas, but the board of NIE concluded that supplying Rathlin was 'inherently uneconomic'.[127] Its chairman remained 'firmly opposed'. However, Richard Needham, NI's economy minister, had promised the islanders a mains supply when he had visited the previous summer. He had been advised 'not to give any undertakings to the islanders but he chose to go his own way'.[128] Needham had told NIE he took 'a close personal interest' in this and referred to the 'strong moral obligation' on NIE, given that other islands around the British Isles had mains electricity (the North of Scotland Hydro-Electric Board had a statutory commitment to connect remote areas and had been doing that since 1947). It was estimated it would create a deficit of only £25,000 per year: 'frankly, I consider this to be a very small sum'.[129] It was clear, he maintained, that the islanders deserved the basic services the mainlanders took for granted.[130]

The islanders still had their political champions, not just John Hume, but also MEP Ian Paisley, leader of the Democratic Unionist Party, who visited the island to express support and suggested a European grant would be available: 'there is no reason to let Rathlin go into the twenty-first century in the dark'. Paisley had for many years pursued the claims of the islanders (a reminder that he was not sectarian in his approach to his constituents, given the religious composition of the island, which was majority Catholic).[131] The islanders were reported to be looking for an underwater electric cable at an estimated cost of £1.77 million; the NI Housing Executive was supportive. NIE met with Paisley and the islanders and said it would look at EEC funding options, but it 'dodged the question' of its own contribution, instead focusing on what the state contribution would be.[132] Further explorations of what would be involved suggested a cost of £911,000, with the EEC providing 55 per cent of the cost and NIE 40 per cent for 'the only community in Northern Ireland

without access to the NIE grid', but it was pointed out that the islanders could not afford to pay the balance, which would amount to £3,200
each. In the event they had to pay about £1,080 per property.[133] It was
also apparent in private correspondence that the islanders were not
committed to running a co-operative for this purpose, or as the Rathlin
Development and Community Association spokesperson put it, 'I don't
think attitudes on the island are ready for this change ... we cannot force
a co-op on people.'[134]

The 1990s and beyond witnessed substantial investment of state
and European structural and development funds in the islands and their
infrastructure. Because of their 'peripheral location and island status',
official government policy was to support the islands' economic and
social development 'in an effort to overcome any disadvantages they
face as island communities'. Funding for capital improvement projects
on the islands was available under various schemes; in 1997 £1.75 million
was available from the Department of the Taoiseach for capital projects on the islands while £1.3 million was allocated for marine works on
Tory Island funded from the Department of Arts, Heritage, Gaeltacht
and Islands, though it was noted in the Dáil in 1997 that '82 per cent of
the allocation to the islands for 1996 was not spent'.[135] Investment was
available under European programmes and the National Rural Development Programme with an allocation of €1.845 million under that programme for the period 2002–6. Access, tourism and renewable energy
were major priorities and there were many improvements in these areas.
The Irish Islands Federation in turn became a new company (Comhar
na nOileán Teoranta) to take over responsibility for LEADER (Liaison
entre actions de développement de l'économie rurale, roughly translated
as 'Liaison among actors in rural economic development'), RSS (rural
social schemes) and other programmes for the islands; under the Rural
Development Programme for 2007–13, €4.6 million was approved for
the islands.[136]

Roads, harbours and airstrips were provided for some islands, while
the 2007–13 National Development Plan announced '€126 million will
be invested in our offshore island communities to facilitate programmes
of pier construction (including major improvements to the piers and

harbours of the three Aran Islands), tourism facilities, ferry and air services and the promotion of small enterprises, renewable energy and social, health and educational facilities on the islands'. A new €14 million harbour for Inishmaan was opened in 2008 by Eamon Ó Cuív; he was 'regarded as a hero on many islands for his efforts to improve transport services and infrastructure' during his time as Fianna Fáil minister with responsibility for rural, Gaeltacht and island affairs from 2002 to 2010.[137] Ó Cuív also sanctioned a €2 million airstrip for Inishbofin in 2003 but it did not come into use. In 2004 he noted that his department had spent more than €1.35 million to improve access to and improved infrastructure on the Mayo island of Inishbiggle with a population of forty.[138]

Journalist Kevin Myers, however, decried what he regarded as such lavish expenditure on sparsely populated small islands (on Inishbiggle, 'Creating slipways, a helipad and new roads – nearly £34,000 per resident') satirising the government department with responsibility for islands as 'the department of superior Irishness'. The term 'island-proofed' also began to be employed in relation to national plans and development strategies.[139] The budget for expenditure on the islands was €6.543 million in 2014 with annual subsidies of nearly €1.7 million provided for passenger and cargo services to offshore islands.[140] In 2016 a budget allocation of €9.275 million was announced to assist island communities, consisting of €6.631 million current expenditure and €2.644 million capital expenditure.[141]

But there remained reasons to doubt the level of commitment to sustaining island populations in the early years of the twenty-first century. Some of those reasons were highlighted by French filmmaker Loïc Jourdain in his documentary *In Éadan an Taoide* (Against the Tide), which charted the efforts of fisherman John O'Brien of Inis Bó Finne to regain the right to fish, on a small scale, like his father and uncles before him, for wild Atlantic salmon. When the Irish government in 2007 insisted on pushing through an EU ban on drift-netting for salmon, O'Brien, along with a small group, including fishermen from neighbouring Arranmore, refused to accept the €18,900 (before tax) offer of compensation, as 'I didn't want to sell out my children's rights'.[142] For all the preoccupation of the EU with endangered species, and for all O'Brien was reading 'about

EU measures to create sanctuaries for fragile species, there was no word about humans'.[143]

O'Brien found himself in 2006 as one of roughly 1,500 commercial licence holders 'pitted against some 30,000 anglers and as one of 10 per cent of bona fide commercial salmon netsmen who do not want to quit their activity for any compensation'. The licence to drift net for wild salmon during two months of the summer 'has been a vital piece in the economic jigsaw that sustains his small community in [Inis Bó Finne] and on the neighbouring island of Arranmore'. Private fishery owners and angling organisations insisted salmon needed to be restored to rivers and supported the drift-net ban. O'Brien viewed the issue as a class, not conservation, war: 'the loss of a public right among coastal communities to private fishery owners who will charge for access'.[144]

Ironically, because of the loss of the salmon option, the O'Brien family had to turn to lobster and crab fishing, which put too much pressure on lobster stocks, while further EU restrictions on whitefish landings meant live bait for crab was unavailable. He took the issue to the European Parliament, where, eventually, he and a small band of committed supporters working the corridors of EU power, managed to secure a clause in a new common fisheries policy permitting member states to protect their island communities. O'Brien also pushed the issue in parliament, with the Oireachtas Joint Sub Committee on Fisheries, which in January 2014 published its *Report on Promoting Sustainable Rural Coastal and Island Communities* and suggested the government examine 'the feasibility of heritage licences to be issued ... for rural coastal and island communities. Such licences would optimally facilitate traditional fishing practices'. O'Brien was still waiting in 2016; as far as he was concerned this was also about 'the right of island communities to survive'.[145]

Aspects of O'Brien's battle revealed much about heritage, islands and the EU – and, indeed, the Irish government's deference to the EU, as it chose to interpret fisheries policy in too extreme a way in its desire to be seen as a 'good' EU member. Quite legitimately, O'Brien also highlighted the contradictions of governments that proclaimed their commitment to the viability of Gaeltacht communities while metaphorically throwing the likes of O'Brien overboard, even though he represented the very

essence of the Gaeltacht and island communities that had been rhetorically championed since the foundation of the state. While the population of inhabited Irish islands decreased by 35 per cent between the 1960s
and the 1990s; Inis BÓ Finne's declined by over 95 per cent.[146]

As O'Brien rightly pointed out, this was also about heritage and the
Gaeltacht being sacrificed on the altar of privatisation: 'a transfer of the
resource, the loss of a public right among coastal communities to private
fishery owners'. A pertinent observation was also made by Loïc Jourdain,
who was 'struck by the fact that other EU member states have pushed for
heritage status for their islands'.[147] As for O'Brien, 'if he was an Iberian
lynx, a Spanish imperial eagle or a brown bear living in Greece [all desig-
nated threatened species worth of EU protection], he reckons he would
have more of a chance'.[148]

Rows also continued into the twenty-first century about transport
to the Aran Islands; air travel to the islands from 1970 had transformed
the lives of the communities there, but in 2015 islanders once again
found themselves up in arms about a refusal to listen to them after it was
revealed by the minister for the Gaeltacht Joe McHugh that Executive
Helicopters was the 'preferred tenderer' for the state's public service obligation to provide flights for Aran. If confirmed, this would mean, instead
of the existing Aer Arann service, a helicopter service would operate out
of Galway airport on the other side of the county, fifty-two kilometres
away from the airport used by Aer Arran.[149]

These developments came at the end of a summer that witnessed
another protest; this one over the sole primary school on Inishmaan,
which lost its second teacher in 2012 as the number of pupils fell below
Department of Education regulatory levels. There were nine pupils
enrolled, with children in every class from infants to sixth class. The pro-
testors' spokesperson insisted, 'Unless we take the necessary steps now to
protect Inishmaan's future, its people, its heritage, its language, island life
will disappear as completely as it did on the Blasket Islands.' A temporary
solution was achieved with Zurich Insurance agreeing to fund a second
teacher, but only for a two-year period.

The same year, on a visit to Cape Clear, the president of Ireland,
Michael D. Higgins, stressed the need for the state to protect and sustain

the life and culture of Irish islands at a time when the Irish islands federation was thirty-one years old and represented 2,900 people; Higgins
insisted the islands were 'this living part of our heritage'.[150] Meanwhile,
Údarás na Gaeltachta submitted a doomed plan to the Commission on
Taxation aimed at injecting life to the islands that would allow individual
residents 'to earn up to €100,000 before paying tax' and capital allowances to be written off.[151]

A report on the west Cork islands in 2014 warned that the year-
round habitation of some of those islands was 'clearly at threat' and recommended integrated development strategies and community council
structures representing all the islands in the area. There were ongoing
complaints that many national policies were not 'island-proofed' and that
most of the island communities worked 'independent of each other'.[152]
The following year, the report of the parliamentary subcommittee on
fisheries, which had made twenty-nine recommendations regarding
aquaculture, fishing tourism and heritage licences to support traditional
fishing practices was described as 'gathering dust'.[153] A year later, when
Noel Harrington, a Fine Gael TD for Cork South West lost his seat in
the general election, it was observed that his work interest was the 'niche'
area of the fishing and seafaring community of this large constituency,
but he lamented that the media was focused elsewhere: 'Nobody else
gives a damn about the islands.'[154]

FOUR

THE ISLAND PRIEST

'more than the spiritual head of the island communities'

In 1920 the *Irish Ecclesiastical Record*, a monthly Catholic journal that began publication in 1864, published an article on the history of the islands of Inishbofin and Inishark by Revd John Neary. Replete with superlatives about the sea ('mountainous ... tumultuous swell ... desolate ... storm swept ... wild weltering chaos of the open ocean'), the author also had much to record about the islanders and island life: 'Inured to hardship, they lead a dangerous existence and win a precarious subsistence from the deep ... quick witted, shrewd, nimble, wiry, energetic, their lives are lives of endeavour and endurance, of grit and audacity.' Because necessity was such a 'hard taskmaster', many islanders 'lie beneath the waves submerged'.[1]

The combined population of these two islands had been 1,500 at the beginning of the nineteenth century but in 1911 stood at just 801; the main occupation for the men was fishing ('no more daring or intrepid seamen exist') while the women spun and knitted with home-grown wool. They were also house proud, with 'a deep-seated and abiding love for their sea-compassed homes', and in their nature, were not just shrewd but also

> guileless, friendly unsuspecting ... sometimes overly so, for there
> have not been wanting occasions, which they justly resent, when

cynical and high-sniffing pundits have been received by the
islanders with open-hearted, cordial kindness and welcome and
afterwards they were rewarded by publications which girded and
poked fun at their religious observances, traditions, customs and
beliefs. It is an ungrateful, unrefined quack and ill-conditioned
person who, under the guise of science, repays homely, courteous,
unpurchased friendship and wounds sensitive feelings by covert
sneer or open contempt, mockery or derision.[2]

Understandably, Neary had a particular focus on religion on the
islands and its long, troubled but defiant history. He referred to Fr Red-
mund Martin Fadden, who in 1834, during a cholera outbreak, had reputedly buried the Inishark dead with his own hands before succumbing
himself, but Souperism – the attempt to convert Catholics to Protestantism through the inducement of food – had 'looked in vain at the island'.
In 1860 Henry William Wilberforce had bought the islands for £11,000
from the Sligos before Cyril Allies obtained them in 1876. By about 1910,
negotiations were well advanced for the purchase of the Allies estate by
the Congested Districts Board, but Neary suggested the CDB that succeeded Allies (this 'ideal, sympathetic landlord') 'cannot boast overmuch
of its deeds of high achievement since its acquisition of the islands'. Neary
was not necessarily accurate in these criticisms; in 1892 a curing station
had been built at Inishbotin pier under the auspices of the CDB and the
CDB acknowledged that the fishermen of this island and Inishark were
'the best and most practical on the west coast', while another pier was
built on the east end. The CDB had also set about providing bigger boats
for the fishermen by making loans available while instruction was given
in drift-net fishing.[3] But the overriding point Neary wanted to make was
that the islanders were now as 'firm in the faith as their own stout mountains, and strong as the sea that lashes their shores'.[4]

Neary was no detached champion of the islands; a native of Bally-
haunis, Mayo, and educated at Tuam and Maynooth, where he had been
ordained in 1900, he had ministered as a curate in Inishbofin and was an
accomplished historian and archaeologist who focused on the past of the
parishes he administered in.[5] His defensiveness about how the islanders

were characterised by outsiders may have been prompted by a number of factors, including tourism and the growing interest of ethnographers and anthropologists in island communities (see chapter 5). Neary was one of numerous island priests in the nineteenth and twentieth centuries who became robust defenders of their parishioners and their faith, were sensitive to outside criticism about them, and harried others with power, money or influence to do more to ensure the islands remained populated.

The CDB recognised that some island priests had made great efforts to improve island welfare and prospects, amongst them Revd Charles Davis, the parish priest in the Cork district of Baltimore, which included Cape Clear Island. His contribution to the development of the fishing industry was singled out by the CDB as 'a remarkable and conspicuously successful effort'.[6] Davis looms large in the history and archive of Cape Clear, and, as noted previously, in the 1880s he had even led delegations of islanders to Queen Victoria and the chief secretary for Ireland and got the idea of a fishery school for Baltimore adopted. Davis died in 1892 and poetic tributes were paid to him to underline his impact on the island and coastal communities:

> The tears of woe, that spring we know
> From feelings the heart cannot speak.[7]

He was particularly remembered for the 'munificent gift' of over £2,000 from philanthropist Baroness Burdett Coutts which had happened 'at the instance' of Davis to assist the Cape Clear islanders in their fishing.[8]

Later that decade, Fr Michael O'Donoghue on the Aran Islands performed a similar function when he reputedly sent a starkly worded telegram to the chief secretary in Dublin: 'Send us boats or send us coffins'. As Breandán Ó hEithir noted, 'the authorities responded with unusual speed and an immediate grant of £20,000 was made under the Poor Relief (Ireland) Act to improve harbours on the three islands'. This was critical, as over the following decade a fishing industry was created on Inishmore; islanders subsequently got Dublin sculptor James Pearse, whose son Patrick went on to lead the 1916 Rising, to carve a Celtic cross in honour of O'Donoghue.[9] O'Donoghue was eulogised in the international weekly Catholic journal *The Tablet* as a priest 'who worked wonders for the islanders when they were in dire distress'.[10]

But what impact had his correspondence created at the time? It was common subsequently for exaggerated claims to be made about his impact, including the assertion that his 'ultimatum' to the government 'made world headlines' in 1886 (it was not even reported in the *Irish Times*, established in 1859 and conservative and unionist). Yet, in March 1886, the strongly nationalist *Freeman's Journal* reported from its 'special commissioner' that there was 'appalling distress among the inhabitants'. Speaking to the journalist, Fr O'Donoghue noted that the islanders were 'dependent for their very existence on the alms of private benevolence' and that 'judging from the communications received by Fr Donohoe [sic] from both the chief secretary and the under-secretary the government intend to leave to the charitably disposed the work of saving its subjects from hunger and death'.

Four years later the *Irish Times* gave much prominence to the views of Revd John Verschoyle, the imperialist journalist and deputy editor of the *Fortnightly Review*, about the impact of the CDB, suggesting the Aran Islands were 'not by any means the dismal and desolate place of untravelled imagination. The lot of the islanders is not so miserable as is supposed' and the crop for that year was looking positive.[11] Perhaps Tim Robinson, the great chronicler of the Aran Islands a century later, struck the correct balance, suggesting that O'Donoghue's 1886 telegram was 'an act which, if not so miraculously or electrically causative of the Congested Districts Board intervention as oral history would have it, is the perfect emblem of his dedicated representation of his flock in the face of governmental delay and the [landlord] agent's rapacity.'[12]

Or is that too generous? If the memories of Henry Robinson of the Local Government Board are to be relied upon (which is doubtful), the episode was not so much a manifestation of starkness but something of a pantomime:

Send relief or coffins was another dramatic effort on the part of a
Galway priest to waken the government to the necessity of relief

works, and the effect of this portentous telegram would not have alarmed the government very much less than it did had they seen the parish priest taking it around the town and showing it with the utmost hilarity to his friends. Among others, he took it to his old friend the late member [MP] for Galway, George Morris, the Vice President of the Local Board. The official utterance of the Vice-President on this occasion was 'Begorra, Father James, you are the boy who knows how to talk to them'. No one really took the telegram seriously except the Irish Office, who were rather upset about it, as although they referred it to the Local Government Board for observations, the Vice-President could not very well explain that he himself on the previous day had highly commended the parish priest for the humour of it.[13]

How reliable is Henry Robinson's account, given that he did not even get the priest's name correct? And would the islanders have gone to the trouble of erecting their cross with the inscription – 'In memory of the Rev Michael O'Donoghue, for eleven years the beloved priest and benefactor of Aran' – if he had been a self-satisfied clown? And yet, Robinson was touching on something he had referred to in his previous memoir; the idea of exaggeration, generating what the *Freeman's Journal* in 1882 defensively referred to as sceptics 'who know or care little about Ireland', assuming accounts of island distress were a kind of 'stock article' or 'the cry of "wolf"'.[14]

As an inspector with the Local Government Board in the 1880s, Robinson was often dispatched on missions to the west of Ireland and recalled in his memoirs how the parish priest of Achill, Fr Healy ('a wild and emotional creature') 'worked up' a 'distress agitation' on the island. He came up to Dublin determined to see the Lord Lieutenant, head of the British administration in Ireland, and on seeing him tearfully begged for the lives of his parishioners to be saved. The Lord Lieutenant said he would send Robinson to the island to assess the situation. The priest then had certain arrangements to make so that 'all the thinnest people in the island should be at Achill Sound in rags and tatters' to meet Robinson: 'the people were all paraded after chapel and the leanest and most sickly selected. They were instructed to be lying about in listless attitudes, leaning up against the walls, too utterly weary even to speak except to whisper to the government official that they were starving.' Robinson, however, was late arriving and by the time he got there 'a furious faction fight' was raging between the Sweeneys and the Lavelles: 'the "starving islanders" fought on like wild cats ... not a word was ever heard again of famine in Achill'.[15]

It was clear that island advocates were also getting used to the novelty of using newspapers to increase the profile of their causes; the issue of publicity was vital in relation to island welfare and priests were centre stage in this process in the late nineteenth century, taking advantage of what was now a proliferation of newspapers. The abolition of taxes on the press after 1855 was crucial for the growth and availability of a cheaper press, which coincided with the evolution of nationalism. Alongside the national titles, 'the size of the feast in terms of material is demonstrated by the sheer bulk of Irish newsprint available between 1850 and 1892 when about 218 provincial papers appear to have been in print'. Illiteracy also continued to fall, from 47 per cent in 1851 to 33 per cent in 1871 to 25 per cent in 1881.[16]

When, in the 1980s, the Jesuit Fr Diarmuid Ó Péicín became a controversial champion of Tory island, he looked back to the example of the island priest, Fr James O'Donnell, who in 1882 sought to communicate the plight of the islanders by getting vital information to newspapers.[17] This was indeed effective; a plethora of reports in October and November 1882 referred to the 'terrible distress threatened in the west ... on Tory Island, nine miles from the nearest land, over three hundred people are without food and the means of getting any'. The islanders and others in the west were 'entering upon a winter of terrible portent ... it is simply a story of impending starvation'.[18] Increased publicity meant questions asked in Parliament and the elucidation of denunciations of government inaction, and as was the case with Tory in 1882, the admiralty placing a gunboat at the service of the government to convey emergency relief. A letter in the *Freeman's Journal* made it clear that the information and the demands were being conveyed by 'the devoted priest of Tory Island', who highlighted that the 'little crop on which they are expected to live' had been 'completely destroyed' by the great gale of September, and that the Board of Works, responsible for public relief work, needed to respond urgently: 'let help be sent immediately to the West and to the poor priest in Tory'. A few weeks later there was much more specific information on what Tory needed: £200 for fishing nets and a harbour, to make them 'independent'.[19]

The Tablet newspaper in the early twentieth century was keen to see if any priestly reality corresponded to their depiction in what was by then the very popular fiction of Canon (Patrick Augustine) Sheehan in books such *My New Curate* (1900). A contributor to the newspaper recalled that he had been invited to accompany a curate, Fr John Flatley, on some of his perilous pastoral visits to the Aran Islands, including to the smallest island, Inisheer, where he arrived 'just in time to anoint the dying person'. The journalist also relayed this tale of then parish priest of the islands Fr Murtagh Farragher, who

> was some years ago a curate on the island and had a terrible experience one Christmas. As he was crossing to Inishmaan it blew a regular hurricane and the currak [currach] was pitched and tossed mercilessly on the waves. The coastguards at Kilronan [on Inishmore] watched through their glasses the fight for life on the rocky coast of Inishmaan and as darkness fell they concluded that the canoe was wrecked. That Christmas and for five days longer Kilronan and all the island of Inishmore bewailed the fate of the young priest they loved. But happily, Fr Farragher, with his crew, as if by a miracle, succeeded in landing and next day had his Christmas dinner, a chief item of which was cured fish, with the islanders. At the end of the five days when the storm abated somewhat, word was sent over to Kilronan that the priest was safe and great were the rejoicings ... rough as it is, the priests use bicycles to facilitate them in the performance of their duties. In Aran, the parish priest is more than the spiritual head of the island communities. Their temporal welfare receives his constant care. In Fr Farragher's cottage many a scheme has been discussed in recent years for the amelioration of the bad lot of the islanders.[20]

Treacherous journeys across sea could also apply to a mainland priest who had a priestless island within his parish. Fr John Healy, a future Archbishop of Tuam, who was a curate in Grange from 1871 to 1878, had been a literary and archaeological pilgrim to Inishmurray, but 'one wild new year's night' was awoken by a sick call by 'four strong men who seemed as if cast up by the sea'. They had travelled the eight miles from Inishmurray; one of them pleaded that his father was dying and 'was sure to go by the next tide' and Healy 'could not resist that appeal'. He made it to the island, but because it was a stormy night, keeping the police at bay on the mainland, 'the natives were busily engaged making poteen'. At dawn, the crew was too drunk to journey; he replaced the fallen crew with women: 'they could handle the oars as well as the men ... they were more afraid of the storm than me' but were moving too much to one side. Healy had a gun with him and told them 'the first woman who leaves her place, I'll shoot her dead. It was one of the most effective speeches I ever made.'[21]

Others were less fortunate, and the death of Revd J. O'Halloran, a curate on Cape Clear in January 1918, cast a pall over the island. He had been travelling to Baltimore and 'met with an accident by which he was thrown out of the boat'. A non-swimmer, he was fished out of the water but contracted pneumonia and died; he was a 'very popular, pious and zealous young clergyman'. As a native of Kilkenny, he 'had come amongst them as a stranger from the diocese of Ossory and had laboured unselfishly for their welfare' and was characterised as a 'splendid specimen of young Irish manhood'.[22]

Times of tragedy were opportunities to stress the importance of the depth of Catholic faith, or, as was suggested by a former curate on one of the Inishkea Islands in 1927 after the Inishkea disaster, it was only amongst the islanders that a priest could 'really feel the warm, sincere welcome for a minister of religion and experience too the soul-longing of a truly religious people'.[23] This was possibly a dubious boast; Brian Dornan, author of a comprehensive history of the same islands, asserted without ambiguity that independence and stubbornness were at the heart of the island people. During an age in which 'the landlord and the priest form the twin foci of the land war and the devotional revolution, Inishkea seems to have held neither in high regard'.[24] That devotional revolution had witnessed the number of priests in Ireland increase from an estimated 2,200 in 1840 to 4,000 by 1911; by that stage Catholic communities comprised 89.6 per cent of the population of southern Ireland.

The boasts of island faith were born of this wider history of Catholicism and also the attempts to convert Catholic natives. Some islands were cauldrons of these battles and the folklore of the islands was suffused with tales of heroic and persecuted priests and friars, stretching back to the 'murder of six friars' at the time of St Colman, who around 667 established a monastery on the island of Inishbofin, up to the period of the penal laws discriminating against Catholics beginning in the seventeenth century when priests could be sailed over under cover of darkness but would be chased by 'sadistic priest hunters', in the description of an elderly informant on Clare Island in 1942. Bible readers appeared soon after the famine on Clare to set up a school and a boiler for porridge and soup: 'but five days marked the duration of the school ... young men smashed everything up including them and their boiler'. The police sent the proselytisers away and they set their sights on other islands.[25]

In the 1980s, Irish novelist and playwright Sebastian Barry became intrigued to discover that his great-grandmother had belonged to a fundamentalist religious congregation on Sherkin Island in the late 1880s and she faced a personal crisis when the prospect of marrying a man in Cork city emerged. It provided the inspiration for Barry's powerful play *Prayers of Sherkin* (1990). While based on emotion rather than empirical research (Barry had never been to Sherkin), the power of this drama lies in the poeticism of the language used to describe island life and seafaring; the play itself had stemmed from a poem.[26] But the religious theme is also central: Fanny Hawke's departure from the island from a failed community of millenarians to marry a Catholic was illustrative of the wider religious tensions and struggles of that era, more effective for being dramatised on an island.[27]

There was a specific Island and Coast Society mission for the proselytisers ('for the education of children and promotion of scriptural truth in remote parts of the coast and adjacent islands'), which reported in 1847 that 'of Cape Clear and Sherkin, the most affecting details have reached the secretary' but that 'essential relief has been afforded' and that 'these islands were among the first to receive boilers'.[28] A small Protestant church was built on the island in 1849 by means of subscription collected by Revd Edward Spring of the Protestant Cape Clear Mission, amounting to £500: 'the little flock for whom it has been provided have, from their means, also subscribed liberally' while those who could not afford to give money were 'contributing in work'.[29] But things did not progress steadily; in March 1851, Spring reported 'few accessions' since his previous report but also 'few relapses', although even 'this much good has been all in opposition to the constant public denunciations and private example of an unscrupulous and violent priest'.[30] This may have been a reference to Fr Henry Leader, a priest of the Cork parish Rath and the Islands.

Something akin to religious warfare was also apparent in Achill in the 1850s as a result of the mission of Edward Nangle (see chapter 1). The conflict was recounted by Harriet Martineau in her *Letters from Ireland* (1852). Because of the Nangle mission, and 'now that Dr MacHale's [the Catholic Archbishop of Tuam] attention is riveted upon Achill ... scalding seems to be a favourite idea with the priests ... "May the Almighty scald your soul when you come to die" is one of their imprecations, in one case used by a bishop to a convert'.[31] MacHale had appointed Fr John Dwyer as parish priest on Achill to counteract the Protestant encroachment and the priest was told to tell his parishioners to 'have nothing to do with these heretics – curse them, hoot at them, spit in their faces'.[32]

It was common in subsequent years for the missionaries to write of island schools that were in a 'most creditable state' but encountering difficulties with 'the Romish priest ... withdrawing several of the older children from the school'.[33] The Catholic Church was robust enough on Cape Clear in 1860 for seventy-two children to be confirmed, and in May 1868 the Bishop of Ross, Michael O'Hea, visited the island for the purpose of Benediction 'to a large congregation and he states that he found everything in order'.[34]

The Island and Coast Society produced annual reports of its missionary work, which it also trumpeted as a 'record of the dying faith', or, more crudely, the combating of 'heathen darkness and ignorance', and recounted with pleasure in 1865 the story of one unnamed western island:

'the priest disowns the island; he has not had three marriages from it for the last six years'.[35] In 1878, gifts from English 'kind friends' of the Society included 'six blankets for the people in Aran Island' but it also recorded on another unnamed island, violent coastal storms and drowning tragedies and it ensured a 'sheltering wing thrown over the school and also over the fatherless children'.[36]

By the 1880s some specific locations were named, including the school on Valentia, which had thirty-two children, but the Society was also facing, in the western districts, the consequences of 'Catholic agrarian outrages' and 'tumultuous assemblies' in contrast to the law-abiding and obedient 'Protestant peasantry'.[37] The sixtieth annual report in 1894 'noted with regret' that subscriptions and donations had fallen; at that stage it had only thirty-five schools and 991 pupils. Only one island school was mentioned that 'maintains its efficiency'; the following year Valentia school was regarded as 'well worked' but adversely affected by not only severe weather but the 'removal of two coastguard families from the island'. By the early twentieth century, no island schools were mentioned.[38]

Inishbofin was remembered as a place of both refuge and internment for clergy, Brian McLoughlin of the Irish Folklore Commission (IFC) being told in 1942 that 'at one time there were as many as fifty priests interned here by the governing English authorities' and afterwards sold as slaves in Bermuda.[39] Priests could also fall victim to island feuds, but the perpetrators suffered the consequences according to an informant of Ciarán Bairéad, who collected material for the IFC on the Aran Islands in 1966. He was told by Fr Thomas Killeen, who had served on the island for twelve years, that

> there was a Fr O'Flaherty, parish priest of Aran. He was a native of the island. The Franciscan fathers used to keep a priest there up to that, but the O'Flahertys drove him out when they had a priest of their own. I heard that there were twenty-one of the O'Flahertys who were concerned in driving him out and twenty of them were dead within the year and the other died shortly after.[40]

An island posting for a priest was by no means an ideal one. The correspondence in the 1870s between Fr James McFadden, the parish priest of Gweedore, in whose parish Tory Island lay, and the Catholic Bishop of Raphoe, James MacDevitt, contains thanks for financial contributions, and McFadden's 'extraordinary sacrifices for the spiritual needs of the people of Tory island'. McFadden in October 1875 had recommended a curate should stay on Tory 'for a least a year' and one of a high character, as 'better no priest on Tory than one whose conduct was not exemplary'. He was opposed to the bishop's preferred approach of alternating priests on Tory.[41]

In 1879 McFadden wrote to Bishop Michael Logue, MacDevitt's successor, suggesting that 'to supply the spiritual needs of the island' a [fixed] curate was needed; curates were alternating and receiving a £50 subsidy from the Diocesan society. McFadden noted he had remonstrated with Bishop MacDevitt on this to no avail; he saw it as a 'positive injustice ... and an impossible burden on the curates'.[42] McFadden sided emphatically with the tenants during the land war and was arrested over his activism in 1889 and sentenced to three months' imprisonment for incitement to conspiracy. That same year, the curate on Tory, Fr Coyle, wrote to Bishop of Raphoe, Patrick O'Donnell, Logue's successor, noting that 'a few strangers' had visited the island, including an MP who wondered what the islanders would do if they were evicted, 'whereupon one of the islanders answered "we couldn't be sent to a worse place"'. At the same time, fever was a problem on the island from 'want of fuel'.[43] O'Donnell also wrote to McFadden that year about the news from Tory that he thought 'very sad. As the people have no hospital it might be well to call the attention of the sanitary officers to the state of things.'[44]

Correspondence about Tory in subsequent decades was punctuated with concerns about the prevalence of illness, the necessity of poor relief and want of seed.[45] The issue of aid to send a priest to the island and build a church there remained contentious, McFadden noting in 1901 that there was dispute as to whether the parish priest should support another priest on the island: 'the PP doesn't get a farthing from the island, a position unknown to any other parish priest in Ireland'.[46] Seven years later the parish priest, Fr Cunningham, was quoted in the *Freeman's*

Journal reacting to reports of starvation on the island and the decline of fishing due to the arrival of trawlers. The potato crop did not suffice and 'the people were almost entirely dependent on the sea'; the curing station had closed four years previously.[47] According to one account of life on Cape Clear, the priest could also have a say in what fish was eaten; the two fish that the islanders rarely ate were monkfish and skate/ray: 'It was considered sinful, as we believed them to have aphrodisiac qualities. The priests discouraged eating these fish. They were known as bed fish (*éisc na leapan*).'[48]

In the annals of island priest activists none looms larger than Fr Murtagh Farragher, familiarly known as Fr Murty, who served as a curate on the Aran Islands from 1887 to 1891 and returned as parish priest in 1897. While it was true, as obituaries would later put it in relation to his time on the Aran Islands, that 'he took advantage of every opportunity which presented itself to uplift the condition of his people and he was responsible for great improvements in their lot', and that he was regarded as a 'great man in an age and under conditions that demanded great men,'[49] what was not mentioned was that he was also a violent tyrant. Such were the passions he aroused as parish priest that a disgruntled islander went to the trouble of bombing his island abode. But he was also revered by many of them. Farragher saw himself as an advocate for the social, political, cultural and linguistic rights and merits of the islanders. A Gaelic League activist, he was central to the 'Aran controversy' of 1901–2 (the Gaelic League had established a branch on Aran in 1898), as was his curate, Fr Charles White, who arrived on Aran in 1900. White knew no Irish and preached and administered the sacraments in English. The League's newspaper, *An Claidheamh Soluis* (*The Sword of Light*) cited his case as an instance of how the Catholic religion was used as a 'powerful anglicising agency', earning White the title 'A Trinity College Priest', a reference to the university established by Royal Charter in 1592 and regarded as a bastion of the Protestant Ascendancy.[50]

The controversy generated numerous letters to newspapers. Farragher defended White (and Farragher, in his own words, was 'unaccustomed to being challenged in the affairs of his parish'), which led him into conflict with the Gaelic League. White also insisted he would not be dictated to by the League: 'I am the mediator between them and God' he wrote of his islanders in a letter to *An Claidheamh Soluis*, the islanders being in his view 'an innocent minded peasantry'. One scholar of the Gaelic League, Timothy McMahon, has not unreasonably highlighted that 'the condescension towards his parishioners expressed in White's comment is telling, especially coming from a man unable to converse with many of the adult members of his congregation about even the simplest daily matters.'[51] But White had seemingly learned such a style from his parish priest master; Farragher, as was his wont, sought to maximise confrontation, first withdrawing permission to two Gaelic League visitors to stage an open air concert on the island (which he later denied) and then refusing permission for Fr Michael O'Hickey, Catholic priest and a vice-president of the Gaelic League, to say Mass on the island.

Another priest, Fr Jeremiah O'Donovan, also criticised Farragher; Farragher lashed out in retaliation and the debate lingered on in the newspaper before fizzling out. A letter to Gaelic League stalwart Eoin MacNeill from a fellow senior Gaelic Leaguer gives some indication of how Farragher chose to frame this particular battle: 'there is one point at least which I think should not go unchallenged, namely when he says that our policy would now seem to be to keep those who know only Irish in ignorance of English. However this might agree with the ideas of some, it has never been part of the public policy of the League.'[52] What was interesting about this was the extent to which Farragher was determined that the islanders' wherewithal to deal with commercial and modern realities (especially in relation to their fishing transactions) was not going to be sacrificed on the altar of Irish language revival. Farragher weathered the Gaelic League storms to the extent that he took his language revival commitment to Dublin for a lecture in 1904 and claimed that the islanders had 'the purest – the first shot – of the real, genuine, pure Irish tongue ... they had firmly and most tenaciously clung to the faith.'[53]

His relationship with MacNeill also weathered the storm and MacNeill was later to write warmly of him.[54] They had a long association; when he visited the island in 1892, MacNeill had written to his brother about his hunting exploits and noted that Fr Farragher was an expert shot when it came to rabbits: 'he killed as many as a score in one day.

Consequently the rabbits are both scarce and wary now.'[55] That was just one example of Farragher's dominance and force; there were many others, some of which came to notice during the Aran trial of 1908 at the summer assizes before a judge and six jurors in Galway. This was the result of the 'Aran Island outrage', a reminder not just of island priests but also of the feuds and disputes, power struggles and class hierarchies that were intrinsic to island life.

Islander Roger Dirrane was bailiff to the Digby estate that owned the island. In the division of land, Farragher accused Dirrane of favouring himself and his friends while maintaining as parish priest he wanted the land to go only to 'the poor'. Dirrane had desired possession of Killeney Lodge on the island, of which he was caretaker and where he was staying, and the land around it, which Farragher wanted for the parishioners for a school. In addition, Dirrane 'seems to have had some differences of a religious character with Fr Farragher' (he had not attended Mass for eighteen months). On 1 June, Fr Farragher's sister went to bed at 11 o'clock and after half an hour was awakened by a 'great crash ... she thought the house had been struck by lightning'. She went to the bedroom of the servant, Mary Flaherty, and they went downstairs to discover all the windows had been broken and some of the ceiling had fallen in.

The next day, a broken saucepan and bits of fuse were found at the scene, fragments of Dirrane's home-made bomb, hurled in when Farragher was away from the island. The Archbishop of Tuam, Dr John Healy, gave evidence that Dirrane had called to him regarding the dispute over staying in the Lodge. Dirrane had also written two letters of complaint to Dr Healy. The archbishop also revealed that some islanders had complained to him of Farragher's behaviour; as he put it: 'there were some who signed letters and some anonymous. There were 3 or 4.'[56]

Evidence of the bomb-making materials was found at Dirrane's house.[57] He was convicted and sentenced to three years' imprisonment and his brother-in-law and accomplice Martin Kilmartin ('I was not drinking last week as I was not working and had no money to pay for drink') to six months. Justice Kenny, presiding, 'denounced the outrage and said he would have given Dirrane fourteen years'.[58] Farragher was also quizzed about another island row; this one between himself and Pat

Hernan. He acknowledged he had used violence against him and had partaken in another row with an islander, Mrs Griffin, whom he had lent money to: 'I did strike her with a stick, but I didn't get money out of her', which prompted laughter in the court. Farragher had also been involved in disputes about county rate collections, and also, as was mentioned in the trial, with an island teacher, David O'Callaghan. Farragher was manager of the schools on the island with the exception of the Oatquarter School, where O'Callaghan taught.

The judge's summing up in the Dirrane case was instructive about many things, including the power of the priest, the tolerance of violence and the perception of the islanders by mainlanders. He said,

> the inquiry was unprecedented in his experience. They were inquiring into the circumstances under which the house of a Catholic clergyman in this country, living in the midst of a Catholic population, was attempted to be blown up by some members apparently of his own congregation. In a country like Ireland where the population was mainly Catholic, the person and property of a Catholic priest was sacred and therefore the inquiry was a very serious one ... a more serious investigation for a jury to have to make he could not conceive ... it was sought to be shown that he and some of his parishioners had not been on terms of perfect amity [what marvellous understatement that was] ... the Rev Farragher had admitted that there was friction between him and some of his parishioners. A clergyman who had to live in a rough community like the island of Aran was not to be too hardly judged, if with a view of controlling his parishioners, he did take the law a little into his own hands.[59]

The relatives of Dirrane were boycotted at the behest of Farragher and teacher David O'Callaghan who ignored the boycott, was also ostracised.

The dispute with O'Callaghan, a Gaelic League devotee and Sinn Féin supporter at a time when that infant political party's influence was minimal, was just as vicious and came to prominence through a slander action in which O'Callaghan sued Farragher for damages. O'Callaghan had been teaching at the Oatquarter School since 1885 and, like Farragher, was committed to the idea of improving the lot of the islanders, but also had a devotion to the Irish language. He had repeatedly clashed with Farragher over social and economic issues on the island and Farragher had questioned his morality and lifestyle and commitment to religion, but was undoubtedly most irked by O'Callaghan's independent spirit, lack of deference towards him and his support for Dirrane. In January 1911 Farragher denounced O'Callaghan from the altar and a boycott of his school began (Farragher had said he was 'not telling you not to send them there but if you take my advice you won't'). Counsel for O'Callaghan suggested Farragher 'undoubtedly claimed an absolute right to rule the island. He did not suppose that the Tsar of Russia in his own dominions was more powerful or autocratic a person than Rev Farragher in the island of Aran'. Opposing counsel suggested O'Callaghan was 'so full of law and of his own importance ... there was no greater autocrat than the village schoolmaster'.

The jury found that the words complained of were spoken 'in good faith and without malice' and O'Callaghan lost the case.[60] The recovery of the legal expenses ruined him. The *Freeman's Journal* reported that the result of the case had created 'great satisfaction' on the island, 'which culminated in a wild outburst' on the arrival of the priest back to the island: 'all the houses in Kilronan were illuminated and bonfires blazed ... immense crowds were on the pier with torches and as the boat neared the quay, cheer after cheer rang out'. A pious Farragher thanked his faithful; he had always, he insisted, 'been the poor man's friend'.[61] There was no future for O'Callaghan on the island; he left in 1914 having lost his school, and the divisions caused by this dispute and others went deep. O'Callaghan wrote to the *Galway Express* newspaper, unionist in its politics, pointing out that he had been evicted from his home at the behest of Farragher and his lawsuit. He had been on Aran for nearly thirty years: 'It is rather a novel incident for a priest professing national sentiments to play the role of evictor.'[62]

Liam O'Flaherty, a native of the Aran Islands and one of fourteen children, eleven of whom survived into adulthood ('I was born on a storm-swept rock and hate the soft growth of sun baked lands where there is no frost in men's bones. Swift thought and the flight of ravenous birds and the squeal of hunted animals are to me reality'[63]) dramatised the Farragher/O'Callaghan feud to great effect in his 1932 novel *Skerrett*. Skerrett was the teacher and Fr Moclair took the role of Farragher (he also included fictional characters). In the novel he recounted the battle 'with almost journalistic exactness'.[64] This is no surprise, as O'Flaherty went to great lengths to research it accurately. In September 1931 he wrote to his agent A. D. Peters from the Aran Islands:

> all the material I have dug up here I am incorporating into a novel, which I have already begun, in which the main characters are a schoolmaster and a priest. It's called Skerrett. I am anxious to get away from here to Dublin as soon as possible so as to read up the account of a lawsuit in the National Library files and provincial newspapers.[65]

For O'Flaherty it was also personal as, in relation to the protagonists, 'he was taught by one and served mass for the other'. Regarding the wider island sagas, Roger Dirrane was a cousin of Liam's father and the various disputations honed the writer's anti-clericalism and ensured those sentiments endured. The divisions on the island had been underlined by the existence of a group called Lucht na Tincans – the Tin Can Party – named after the metal drums in which Roger Dirrane had mixed the explosives. O'Flaherty was a Tin Can, 'an attitude which lasted a lifetime'.[66]

In *Skerrett*, the teacher, who has a 'fierce soul', denounces the answering of catechism answers by islanders 'like parrots', and has a 'mystical worship of the earth and the old pagan gods'. He is left bereft of all until he 'stood alone in a tiny cabin on a lonely crag by the end of the sea'. Fr Moclair ends up as 'undisputed ruler of the island', partly because he has insisted that those against him be treated on his command as 'social lepers' and partly because the island natives are 'only too eager to sell any birthright for a mess of pottage, and Father Moclair, the man of progress and materialist had the pottage'. If they did not follow the priest in his battles with officialdom to improve the island, he told them, 'you'll have to go back to your rocks and fishing lines'.[67] In 1941 fellow writer

Seán O'Faoláin penned an appreciation of the turbulence and intensity of O'Flaherty's writing and its epic wildness: 'one feels that O'Flaherty writes in a kind of fury'. But he also focused on 'the magnificence and the courage of unspoiled man and his apparently inevitable defeat' as, in *Skerrett*, he stands up to the gombeens 'with the primitive honesty of his own natural instincts'. In O'Flaherty's words the aspiration of the teacher was to be 'a man who owns no master' but he was 'doomed to destruction'. O'Faoláin also lamented that there was not a wider Irish audience for the work of O'Flaherty: 'but I forget. We are not allowed to read Skerrett in this country. Which is a great pity.'[68] O'Flaherty's novel *The House of Gold* (1929) was the first novel to be banned in the Free State for supposed obscenity. *Skerrett* was published in England and America in 1932 but an Irish edition did not appear until 1977.

O'Flaherty had a tendency towards melodrama, but it was honed from the landscape and lifestyle of his island upbringing and his elemental prose also unpacked the complexities of the human condition. He was also keen to explore the extent to which the price being paid for the modernity championed by Farragher – developing the fishing industry and encouraging other industry and commercialism – was simply too high. Breandán Ó hEithir also suggested the conflict between the two 'had as much to do with personal and intellectual pride and with who was to be top dog in the community as it had with principles and attitudes towards social change'.[69]

But in relation to 'top dog' status, it was clear that Farragher held all the advantages. These were highlighted in yet another court case in 1911 over alleged trespass on the island between two island families. Farragher had written the agreement about land boundaries: the judge heaped praise on him and added that 'Father Farragher must have got some legal training, as the document was an excellent one. He did not like clergy dealing in legal matters but supposed in many cases it was unavoidable'. After hearing details of the case – a returned emigrant from America to the islands who was 'fond of drink', a dispute over the portion of land to be given on marriage and a hatred between father and son – the judge 'jocosely suggested that a local tribunal should be set up at Aran with Fr Farragher as chief justice', which prompted laughter.[70] But the reality was that Farragher was already chief justice and much more. The court case also, however, exposed his limitations; the very fact that it ended in court suggested his writ was not sacrosanct or always obeyed, which was precisely why he so often encouraged boycotting, which was also a feature of this case. One witness maintained that Farragher 'was boycotting him without any reason and telling people not to speak to him', but, as was usual, as far as the judge was concerned, 'the strong point in the plaintiff's favour was the evidence of Fr Farragher', and that was what influenced the judgment.[71]

Farragher was able to enforce his writ on most because he was so effective in getting material results for the islanders, or what he, in his endless self-promotion, referred to as 'the long and hard struggle against extortion'. This was his response to controversy over the islanders' withholding rents and rates on his advice in 1907. He had been accused of 'abuse ... laid on pretty thick' of the rent collectors.[72] In 1913 Galway County Council was forwarded a letter from Farragher regarding the saga of payment of arrears of island rates; the islanders had not paid rates, it had been noted by the Council in 1909, for six or seven years 'apparently on Fr Farragher's advice'.[73]

A proposed settlement involving payment of £100 in full discharge of arrears had been accepted but there were no road works or repairs being carried out. Farragher's response was trenchant:

> I have been accused over and over again of leading the people of these islands to what is styled by some, socialism. Should we now not see who is at fault, or who repudiates his first debts? I have the greatest respect for the Galway County Council and its secretary, but I must confess it is not so great as to induce me to overlook the first rights and lawful claims of my parishioners.[74]

In 1915 he presided at a meeting of the islanders protesting against tolls on local fishermen: 'It was unanimously decided to resist the imposition.'[75] In correspondence with the CDB he was scathing about the unscrupulous actions of fish buyers: 'even the friendly intervention of the Board fell on the deaf ears of these parasites'.[76] In other private correspondence with his archbishop he referred to the local fish buyers as 'shapers and sharks'.[77]

Farragher's stridency, however, also generated tensions within the church as the actions of loud island priests frequently did. In January 1906 the Archbishop of Tuam, Dr Healy, received a letter from a local magistrate named Johnston, who noted that Farragher had made claims from the altar one Sunday during his sermon that the magistrate sitting in petty sessions in Kilronan had expressed an opinion about the extent to which the islanders' moral fibre was being compromised 'from excessive drinking at wakes and funerals and as I am the only local magistrate I beg to inform your grace that there is no truth in this statement'.[78] There was further trouble the following year and Healy's correspondence grew increasingly fractious and impatient about Farragher's constant righteousness, which forced an abject climb-down from Farragher:

> I have not given you the measure of generous and filial obedience your large hearted kindness deserved ... I believe it is my duty to be humble and submissive ... I will offer you the most reparation I am capable of ... I happily withdraw unconditionally anything I have said or done to give you any offence and my humble and sincere apology.[79]

Healy was undoubtedly the only figure Farragher would submit to or offer humility to.

As Farragher saw it in a letter to the CDB, he had been 'called upon to play a rather prominent part as people's advocate.'[80] He saw his mission as a wider one in relation to the welfare of the west; in 1918 he corresponded with the new Archbishop of Tuam, Thomas Gilmartin, suggesting some priests were 'very jealous' on hearing that he and another priest were discussing the need for an action plan to combat the 'chronic misery' of the western seaboard. While there was 'plenty of wealth in the sea to relieve that misery', the problem was how to capture it, the suggestion being made that a commission was necessary.[81] On the very same day as he wrote to Gilmartin about this, he was able to enclose a cheque for over £13, the amount 'of papal collection here', a substantial amount, and that was just from Inishmore. He was also at pains to criticise other priests 'on the seaboard' for their 'apathy' regarding fisheries develop- ment 'and this applies in an especial manner to the energetic parish priest of Clifden ... I mention this for your Grace's enlightenment and do not desire to impugn in the least or interfere with the motives and inaction of my respected neighbours.'[82]

Farragher died in 1928; his final pastorate was in Athenry, Galway, but it was Aran that he was remembered for, and those fashioning his legacy tiptoed around his vituperativeness or excused it as merely the zeal of the enlightened social worker: 'if the tumult of some of the battles in which he was engaged still echoes faintly down time's corridors, it has to be remembered that these battles were fought for the upliftment of his people and that in most cases they were fought by him alone against an evil tradition steeped in landlordism'.[83] Such hagiography justified his tyrannical and bullying sides by hiding them under cover of the wider themes of nineteenth- and early twentieth-century Irish history. An alter- native conclusion about Farragher has also been reached – much justified – that those 'who cannot be bought over, silenced or isolated must be broken'.[84] In that sense Farragher's trajectory and dominance illuminated much wider themes of church dominance in modern Ireland.

Other priests may not have made quite the impact of Farragher but their role in island life, whether as resident priests or on the main- land with responsibility for the islands in their parishes remained para- mount. It was no wonder the strong rural priest also found his way into fiction; as priest and writer Joseph Guinan saw it in 1911, 'the intimate and endearing relations that exist between the priest and his flock in Ire- land constitute a peculiar phase of our national life'. Fiction centred on priests was also about highlighting the clergy's growing profile in poli- tics.[85] Guinan found a best-selling formula in 1905 with *The Soggarth Aroon*, writing about a heroic priest protecting impoverished tenants from the evils of landlordism, the priest, it appeared, being more effec- tive in this job than the Land League.[86] Guinan was hostile to grassroots agrarian organisations, an indication of the struggle that the church had with controlling new populist and democratic movements. He was at times both clear-eyed and sentimental about poverty and included sub-themes of drinking, gambling, unhappy marriages, health and even illegitimacy.[87]

Canon Sheehan, also a hugely successful Catholic priest novelist from this era, wrote of generational tensions and the difficulty of striking a balance between materialism and traditional identity and obedience. The priests' novels highlighted various manifestations of this – the discouraging of drunkenness through temperance missions and marriage; insisting livestock be kept outside of houses and the encouragement of local industry – but Guinan also came from a family of strong farmers and saw them as the natural ruling class.[88] Guinan likened the relationship between priests and people to marriage: 'It is a union of love; it is the marriage of true hearts for better or worse, in joy and sorrow, in glory and shame – a union until death'.[89] The relationship between island priest and natives was certainly akin to a marriage, a particularly intense one, and could generate loathing as well as love.

Priests often found themselves acting as intermediaries for the sale of islands from landlord to natives. A priest in Belmullet in Mayo, for example, was the initial point of contact between the Walsh Estate and an inspection committee of the CDB with an agreement that the Inishkea Islands could be sold for ten years' rental; various negotiations followed in subsequent years before the sale was agreed.[90] In 1907 fifty-four tenants from Rathlin sought to have their rent fixed at a fair level by the Land Court and 'were assisted in this by the island priest Fr E. McGowan' (under the Northern Ireland Land Act of 1925 the land of Rathlin was vested in the Land Commission). Fr McGowan had also been active in the Gaelic revival and wanted Irish taught in the school, which was opposed by the Church of Ireland minister, Revd Kerr, but in 1914 a 'School of Irish' was established on the island; many of the enthusiasts and scholars were Presbyterians.[91] This was also a reminder of the uniqueness of Rathlin in its religious and political mix; in 1906 Ulster nationalist and antiquary Joseph Bigger had been told there were twelve unionist votes and sixty-six nationalist votes on the island.

Island priests did not have everything their own way, however. Islanders could treat priests with both deference and distance depending on the circumstances and the island's traditions of independence.

In Peadar O'Donnell's *Islanders* the presence of the priest to administer to the dying necessitated, even in the midst of great poverty and the
'starvation that was crushing his mother ... a small table with a spotless
cloth and clean white towel'.[92] But islanders also had their own traditions
that could render the priest surplus to requirements; in his *Letters from
the West of Ireland* (1884), Scottish novelist and travel writer Alexander
Innes Shand, an old-school Tory, wrote of the Inishkea Islands:

> where the people form an independent state of their own and must
> be pretty near heathens. They acknowledge no landlord, they pay
> no rates, they elect a monarch of their own and though a priest
> does come at intervals to confess, to marry or to christen them,
> they have an idol they regularly worship and propitiate before
> their boats put out to sea.[93]

Shand was not the only one to give this practice a profile; decades
later Henry Robinson dwelt on the subject in a volume of his memoirs
in an amusing if exaggerated way. Reports of distress on the island in 1881
prompted relief efforts and it was known that the islanders 'carried on
some kind of Fetish worship', consisting of 'a wooden statuary swathed
in a flannel', which was brought out to sea to regulate storms. When this
was reputedly reported by a British journalist, the embarrassed and angry
Archbishop of Tuam was said to have ordered a priest, Fr Henley, to travel
to the island and destroy it 'and bring the people back to Christianity'.
Three islanders rowed him to the island, 'where he held mass and gave the
people the Divil's own teaching', and he told them unless they burned the
object of their true worship 'he would have them all turned into grass-
hoppers within a week'. Their compromise was to bury it in the graveyard;
the priest then left but a storm forced his boat to turn back and the priest
managed to survive. On the island the statue had been disinterred; the
islanders demanded the priest should 'recognise in the Holy idol his sav-
iour from the stormy sea. Fr Henley accepted the inevitable but warned
its existence must never be admitted to mortal man outside the island.'[94]
The priests name, however, does not correspond to any parish records of
the era and Robinson was fond of spinning second-hand yarns.

The 'statue' however, certainly existed, and was known as the *Namhóg* (translated by some as the god stone); it was also said that smugglers who once stole it were tormented by storms and the Revenue until they returned it. It was believed to have been left on the island by a priest and it was recorded by another priest, Fr T. A. Armstrong, in 1846 as being stone 'carefully clothed in flannel, while another observer, Colm Ó Gaora, who visited the island a number of times in the early twentieth century, suggested its existence was actually to facilitate access to a priest. In the early nineteenth century 'when there was no priest nearer than Belmullet, if the islanders were in need of a priest and had difficulty in getting to the mainland, they would bring out the Namhóg and dip it in the sea, and the storm would ease, allowing them to go for the priest'.[95]

In Richard Power's novel *The Land of Youth*, at the core of which is the fictional remote western island Inishkeever (Power spent time living on the Aran Islands) and set in the early twentieth century, the experiences of the protagonists – a young seminarian Pádraig and his love, islander Barbara Nolan, who returns after three years in the US – are 'shaped by the closed society of Inishkeever where the islanders make their own rules and maintain their own moral codes'. The older men are sceptical of the curate, whose sermons could be discounted 'with a comforting communal obduracy ... the men barely presented themselves for his spiritual services ... they thought him harmless, not knowing that he gazed on them more sternly than on his mainland flock. Secretly, he was proud of how difficult they were to handle. "A contrary people" he told his friends from the inland parishes. "I sometimes doubt if their baptisms took at all, God forgive me!"'[96]

The parish priest, based on the mainland, resents his island duties. For the annual stations, Fr Wall 'looked forward to his annual tour of his outlying territory with as little enthusiasm as if it were an expedition by canoe to the headwaters of the Congo'. He had a 'dislike' of the islanders 'as if they were a tribe whose ways he had grown too old to get used to'.[97] He will not baptise an illegitimate island child but believes it is a problem for his curate, not him, to deal with. A new curate preaches vigorously from the pulpit about the need for co-operative endeavour and piped water: 'they listened to all he said with as bad grace as was consistent with reverence and when at last he inveighed against the bachelors who showed no sign of marrying ... they write him off finally as being invincibly ignorant of the facts of life'.[98]

While the priests and their demands in many ways epitomised a modernising project in the late nineteenth and early twentieth centuries it remained to be seen if their crusades would be overtaken by other agencies. Significantly, Farragher in June 1919, when writing to Archbishop Gilmartin in the context of contact with the Irish undersecretary, one of the senior British administrators in Ireland, was 'filled with hope that I am no longer to be left to plough a lonely furrow'.[99] This was a reference to attempts to seek commitments for more sources to develop the potential of the western seaboard.

The problem remained, not the shortage of plans, but the inability or refusal to follow them through. During the war of independence (1919–21), for example, the Dáil appointed a Commission of Inquiry into Resources and Industries to investigate how they could be more fully developed. It suggested a national programme to develop Irish sea fisheries through co-operatives but, as seen earlier, political upheaval and straitened financial times hampered meaningful follow through. In giving evidence before the Gaeltacht Commission in Galway in August 1925, Fr S. J. Walsh, the parish priest on the Aran Islands was urgently adamant: 'many of the older inhabitants will tell you they have never seen worse economic conditions than those prevailing at present. This is entirely due to the continued almost complete failure of the fishing. No other industry can take its place here.' He saw 'little grounds for hope' at a time when the prices being offered were six or seven shillings for 126 mackerel; at one point 'they got £2 per 100'. Boats for deep-sea fishing were needed and he was insistent on the need for state assistance.

In effect he was carrying on the Aran Islands' priestly tradition of stark pleas to central government:

In the place that I happen to represent right in the midst of the Gaeltacht, it is the question for the government to consider whether the preservation of the Gaeltacht is of sufficient importance to the nation to justify them in taking monetary risks that are absolutely essential if the people are to be kept at home. For the last twelve months at least between eighty and a hundred people have left my parish for America.[100]

The previous decade, the parish priest of Achill had written to Archbishop Gilmartin: 'the land such as it is wants to be shaped and reclaimed and drained. The peat industry could be developed. There are acres of excellent turf here', but without adequate support, 'little can be done to turn it into cash'.[101] That was why so many of the islanders continued to have to travel for seasonal work or emigrate, but the main focus during that era seemed to be to ensure that such migration did not undermine their morality. This generated considerable correspondence in the diocese of Tuam in the 1920s arising from an assertion by Anita McMahon in Keel on Achill Island that migration gave rise to 'moral dangers' due to the 'vile language which the children bring back from Scotland'. This was 'sufficient proof of the awful class of people they come in contact with', it being suggested it would be 'much wiser if they concentrated on the question of decent accommodation to start with and not press for too high a wage as well'.[102]

McMahon was a Cork-born journalist who had come to Achill in 1911 to learn Irish at the Scoil Acla Summer School. She was vocal about the poverty of the local people and persuaded the Archbishop of Tuam of the need for the Presentation Nuns to begin missionary work in lower Achill. In 1919 these nuns (the number of nuns had quadrupled in Ireland from 1861 to 1911) came to Keel and they eventually had a convent built there in 1932. Writing from the post office in Keel a few months after McMahon's letter, P. J. Joyce lamented the failure to treat the potato workers 'as human beings' which resulted in their 'degradation ... if your grace, with or without the Crozier issue directions to the Achill people personally ... you will have them with you'.[103]

The curate in Keel, Fr John Keavy, visited the migrants in Scotland and reported on his findings to the archbishop. He found nothing objectionable morally, but suggested the islanders 'don't seem to have a proper realisation of their obligation of attending mass on Sundays'.[104] In another letter he pointed out that most of them were 'badly instructed' in religion, had left school early and had spent three-quarters of their lives in Scotland.[105] He was also concerned with their working conditions and their need to be unionised: the work 'leaves them absolutely at the mercy of the weather and the buyers'.[106] He also wrote to Gilmartin about their religious welfare in 1928: 'one priest sent from Ireland could do nothing for such a scattered crowd'.[107]

Ten years later, this issue was still causing concern; in July 1938, Archbishop Gilmartin was again informed, this time by Archbishop William MacNeely of Raphoe, of a need for a priest 'from this side' to spend the harvest period in contact with the workers, but he was 'not a bit keen on having a press discussion' about this matter. Likewise, Bishop of Galway, Michael Browne 'did not think it a matter suitable for public discussion', a view shared by Archbishop Dignan of Clonfert.[108] The following year, Gilmartin was informed that the Achill islanders in Scotland were 'easily the best Irish in Scotland where faith and morals are concerned'.[109] It was, however, not religion, but housing that turned out to be the most dangerous issue when it came to the welfare of the Achill islanders, given what happened in Kirkintilloch in 1938 (see chapter 2).

As underlined by government files however and seen in chapter 2, island priests also devoted much of their efforts to lobbying various government departments on non-religious matters. In relation to the period after independence in 1922, such files are notable for the number of letters concerning the payment of rates, despair about the decline of the fishing industry and food shortages ('in a few days our diet will consist of potatoes and salt'); dissatisfaction with transport to and from the islands ('as backward as it was half a century ago') and the impact of storm damage ('Immediate assistance required').[110]

In relation to the state's Irish language crusade after independence, Fr Duggan, the curate in Arranmore, was sceptical in 1925 about the degree to which the islanders gave much thought to their rights as Irish speakers, but was 'inclined to say' that their attitude was that 'Scotland and America are better to them than Ireland' and that 'in their letters home they write English'.[111] There was a limit to what even the most energised and committed priest could do in relation to the promotion of Irish, according to Fr Duggan: 'I started a little scheme to try and get them to write Irish by offering to give two prizes of £10 each to the two families which received the greatest number of letters in Irish from their people on Scotland. It was not a success.'[112]

But priests could also facilitate the state's business, north and south. In 1938 Milne Barbour, Northern Ireland's minister for commerce, received a deputation from Rathlin demanding better pier accommodation that was headed by two clergymen. Some progress was made as the *Irish Independent* reported in 1939 that the island's priest and Church of Ireland clergyman had been sanctioned by the Northern Ireland Ministry for Home Affairs as local rate collectors for Antrim County Council, having initially been refused permission.[113] But that was no guarantee of compliance; over twenty years later the *Irish Press* highlighted the 'Rebel ratepayers of Rathlin Island ... many of the 130 inhabitants of Rathlin island do not pay rates and this week a deputation of eighteen county councillors went to the island to seek the reason.' The islanders left them in no doubt: 'if you do some work for us we will pay the rates'; they wanted work done on the roads, harbour and pier.[114]

Island priests were not shy of threatening politicians with embarrassment if they did not respond to requests to assist islanders, then wishing them 'every blessing'. Fr Charles O'Malley on Inishbofin in Galway wrote to a local TD regarding publicity for the desire of the islanders to evacuate. The priest said he did not want to make any statement to the press 'that would injure your high standing ... but can you blame me if I am beginning to feel a little bit disappointed in your efforts for us.'[115] Priests also had an important role to play in communicating with both state and their own church superiors about the yearning of islanders to evacuate and compiled detailed information on individual islanders' circumstances, including on Clare and Inishturk in the 1940s and 1950s: 'last rent paid about 1921 ... if they got a decent holding they would leave in the morning.'[116]

Education was also something the priests expressed trenchant views on. In 1883 Fr William Egan, based in Ballyferriter, was the manager of the Catholic school on the Great Blasket Island and in communications with the Board of Education wrote of the difficulties of getting a teacher:

'of course no trained or classed teacher can be got to virtually transport himself to a miserable school on the Blasket Islands'. The school was frequently closed owing to poor weather and for want of teachers, and priests continually lobbied for a new school well into the twentieth century, Fr Griffin asserting in 1923 'there can be but very few cases of greater need'. Ten years later Fr Browne insisted on the need for two teachers but also wrapped up his demand in the language politics and priorities of the era, playing to the Blaskets' now much-vaunted advantage in this area. This was not just a question of local, island needs:

> I think you will agree that it is of much importance to the nation to maintain the efficiency of this school. There is no need to call attention to the perfection of the Irish spoken on this island. The books already written by the islanders show that they not only have a perfect Irish idiom, but they have much literary ability.

The Department of Education nonetheless refused as there were fewer than thirty pupils attending and by 1940 the question of islanders attending school on the mainland was being discussed. The school closed on the last day of 1940 as 'the number of pupils attending had failed, for two consecutive years, to reach the required figure of 7'.[117]

Just south of Achill, on the island of Achillbeg, which was eventually evacuated in 1965 and which had a bilingual population of about a hundred in 1901, the difficulty of getting teachers was also pronounced. A purpose-built school, opened in 1904, had twenty-seven pupils in 1911 and remained open until the early 1960s. There were also numerous disputes between the parish priest, based in Cloghmore, Achill, and a particular Achillbeg teacher, Francis Hugh Power, who taught at the school between 1913 and 1922. Power was a passionate Irish-language devotee who was perturbed by the prevalence of English on the island but the parish priest displayed a naked hostility to Power's priorities. One of Power's pupils recalled that 'he would not let the parish priest away with anything'. Three teachers were in charge for thirty years; at other times there were unqualified or part-qualified teachers. In 1922, in correspondence with the parish priest, Fr Colleran, the Department of Education insisted that a proposed teacher did not have sufficient fluency in Irish, to which the priest replied it was that teacher or none. In 1960 the island priest sent a telegram to the Department of Education about the urgency of finding a teacher, while in 1962 he wrote, 'no girl would be interested, none offered and I wouldn't ask anyone'.[118]

Thomas Gilmartin, Archbishop of Tuam, also energetically lobbied the Department of Education, for example, in 1935, about the school on Inishark. The issue of island schools was emotive but also riddled with practical difficulties given the complication of educating islanders on the mainland. There was a rule that schools had to close if attendance was below seven 'units' for two consecutive calendar years. Gilmartin was informed that 'average attendance at Inishark Island national school for the calendar year 1934 was only 4.8'. There were only six children on the island of school age and it was contended that they needed to be boarded out.[119] The following year Gilmartin was told that the parents on the island 'have definitely refused to send their children out of the school to be educated' owing to the danger of crossing daily to the mainland, 'to which they must necessarily be exposed' (the island was seven miles from Cleggan), but they could not afford to pay half the salary for an island teacher as proposed by the state. By law children were entitled to free elementary education and the archbishop was urged to make that case, but he also made a moral and social appeal, writing to government in January 1936: 'It will not look well to close a school in such a poor district ... if this occurs it looks as if the children in this remote island will be allowed to grow up in ignorance notwithstanding their legal rights to free education.'[120] Unusually, the department compromised and agreed to pay three-quarters of the teacher's salary: 'this concession is ... very exceptional'.[121] In reality, given the demographics of the island, it was only really a stay of execution.

The combined weight of the priests' and bishops' authority and spiky pens over decades could not trump such demographic reality. But, as revealed in diocesan archives, priests were also apt to be frank with their bishops about the perceived shortcomings of the islanders. In 1942 Fr Canning on Clare apologised to Archbishop Joseph Walsh of Tuam (appointed in 1940 to succeed Thomas Gilmartin and praised by a number of island priests for the interest he took in the islands) about complaints of food shortages on the island, but he believed such scarcity was 'teaching them a lesson because up to the present they could not be got to sow vegetables or even enough of potatoes. Their idea of food was simply bread and tea. For that reason I have told them they are to no small extent to blame themselves.'[122]

A film about life on the Aran Islands that was produced by the Catholic Film Society of London in 1932, *Aran of the Saints*, depicted a community completely dominated by Catholicism, with the islanders seen going to Mass, reciting the Angelus and the Rosary and attending communion services and the funeral of a boy. As with the rest of Catholic Ireland, the island was also in the throes of preparation for the Eucharistic Congress in 1932, an international Catholic gathering that offered the infant southern state an opportunity to highlight its impeccable Catholic credentials and the church a stage to emphasise Irish obedience to the faith. But *Aran of the Saints* gave a lop-sided impression of island religiosity; in truth, there had been no shortage of battles by priests to instil discipline. Fr Martin O'Donnell was a curate on the Aran Islands in the 1930s; Archbishop Gilmartin had asked him whether he was leaving him too long on Aran. O'Donnell's reply was that he would stay 'as long as your Grace pleases, yet I must say that I shall have few regrets, however soon I may leave it'.[123] A year after the film he recounted the details of a recent mission conducted by a Redemptorist who found there were 'ten houses engaged in this accursed poitín traffic. One man gave him to understand that he had only a gallon or two of poitín and spilled it out. I learned afterwards that it was only a portion of sixteen gallons he had.' Two sons of the national teacher had got drunk on poitín and 'the eldest of these is not more than twelve years'.

Significantly, O'Donnell also complained that the parish priest had not visited the island sufficiently often; worse than that, 'there are many things that are too painful for me to put on paper ... should your Grace deem it necessary to change me from Aran I only ask that I may not be next or near a poitín district.'[124] Another Aran priest, Fr Martin Heaney, was remembered by older residents speaking to a collector for the IFC, as also declaring war on poitín: '*Bhí Father Heaney an-mhór I gcoinne an*

Phoitín, Sé chuir deire leis' ('Father Heaney was completely opposed to poteen and put an end to it').[125]

Island communities could also become remarkably attached to their priests, something that sparked an intense rebellion in 1942 on Tory and led the Papal Nuncio in Ireland, Paschal Robinson, to write to the Bishop of Raphoe, William MacNeely, about 'this very difficult and delicate situation'. It all stemmed from the refusal of Fr. B. Duggan 'to cede the parochial house' on Tory after his suspension: 'such conduct on the part of any priest must not only give grave scandal to the devout faithful concerned but must also expose him to the risk of incurring still more grievous consequences. It is also obvious that the attitude of those who support a priest in his disobedience to the ecclesiastical authorities merits the most severe censure.'[126]

Not that the islanders seemed remotely concerned about such censure. The parish priest, Fr J. Cunningham, also wrote to MacNeely to describe his attempt to land on the island in order to make them aware of the Nuncio's displeasure:

> Yesterday I went to Tory with the intention of remaining there for a couple of weeks at least and of endeavouring in that time to win the islands back to their duty by every means in my power and perhaps of influencing Fr Duggan also, but my stay there was short. On landing after very rough passage I was accosted by Fr Duggan and told I was to return to mainland at once by the same boat which brought me to Tory. I got my bags ashore. No one would carry them to my lodgings. Twice I was prevented by physical force from leaving the spot where I stepped ashore. Fr Duggan is master there, the poor islanders are maligned, misled by him and there will be no peace nor grace there while he is allowed to remain on the island ... I told them the object of my mission; they laughed me to scorn; no priest for them but Fr Duggan. With heavy heart I had to return home through a raging sea.[127]

A few years later Fr James McDyer, a native of Donegal who had worked in England for seven years, returned to his native county as curate for Tory Island. His particular preoccupation was the lack of local industry, the development of which he believed could stem emigration. It has been noted that 'he came up against government bureaucracy when he was refused a grant to found a knitting industry'. But funding for Tory was always complicated; during the decade when McDyer toiled there Donegal County Council was offered central state grants to improve facilities (for example to widen and deepen the landing place) if the council would contribute the balance, but the council refused as the islanders did not pay rates. In September 1947 'minor employment schemes' for proposed knitting and weaving industries for Tory were mentioned in the Department of the Taoiseach, but there is no evidence of follow-up. Perhaps government bureaucracy was not always the sole stumbling block; it may have been the case that grants were refused because of an inadequate response to government requests for forms to be filled.[128]

McDyer maintained that prolonged negotiations amounted to nothing 'and I was eventually advised by one department to use my powers of persuasion in having the islanders transferred to homes on the mainland'.[129] McDyer requested to be moved from Tory to return to England but instead was appointed to Glencolumbkille on the mainland in 1951, and he went on to achieve renown as an organiser of industrial and agricultural co-operatives, bringing electricity and tourist initiatives to the area. An appreciation of him after he died gives some indication of how the priestly postings to islands were viewed in the overall scheme of church ministry: 'He had a hard life. His clerical postings were never favoured ones – an urban slum in Britain; the wind-lashed deprivation of Tory Island; the remote district of Glencolumbkille – moving, it seemed, from one situation of human hopelessness to the next. It was in the Glen that his "savage indignation" as he called it, really cut loose.'[130]

One wonders why it did not cut loose on Tory. Granted, he was, during his last few months on the island, referred to by a local newspaper as being 'beloved by the island population', but was he stymied or was the stage too small for him to gain the traction among the islanders that he desired? After all, he was often disillusioned by the failure of smallholders to, in his words 'get off their knees'.[131] McDyer was not a remotely contented island priest and was honest about why in his autobiography: 'on an island I could find very few people who were willing to have a good discussion on international affairs or current events'. The islanders were friendly and 'even too courteous' but he was lonely and went as far as to not only request his bishop for a transfer ('his answer was a blank "no"') but even the Papal Nuncio.[132] McDyer was generous about the islanders' abilities; they had a perception and sharpness above that of mainlanders because of their battles with the sea and arising out of the need and practice of self-sufficiency: 'their minds and their deftness were honed to a remarkable degree'. But he felt the island was a waste of his youth: 'I fretted and felt frustrated that some of the best years of my life were being frittered away when there was so much work to be done elsewhere.' Bored, he even found himself simply sitting on the beach singing to the seals: 'I resolved that whenever my transfer came I would release such a burst of energy that others would be amazed.'[133] In that sense, at least, the island was the making of him.

Another Tory priest was Fr Eoghan Ó Colm, who spent the years 1956–62 on the island and wrote about it in *Toraigh na dTonn* (*Tory of the Waves*) (1971). He was keen to document the island's history and folklore but was also adamant that 'the only way for people to earn the right to speak about Tory is for them to settle in the island for a few years'. He did not romanticise island living and resented that 'hardly a year passes without some enterprising journalist squeezing yet another story out of Tory's isolation and misfortune as viewed from the culture of the mainland … the islands are sick and tried of visitors, pen in hand', generating 'hackneyed headlines'.[134] Ó Colm was also honest about the limitations in the powers of the island priest; while he may have had to adjudicate in land disputes, he had to take island life 'as he found it, seeking to read its secrets and follow its ways as best he could'.[135]

Such testimony was consistent with the observations of the anthropologist Robin Fox. His visits to Tory from 1960 to 1965 coincided with the latter part of Ó Colm's tenure. Fox eventually published his book *The Tory Islanders: A People on the Celtic Fringe* in 1978 and he underlined the lack of deference towards the priests but also gave a nuanced and credible assessment of why this was the case, explaining the degree to which, on certain islands, the parameters between priest and people operated differently than they sometimes did on the mainland:

> They are a pious people, but pragmatic. Priests sit lightly upon them. They did without for centuries and are not much awed by formal religion. They feel proprietary about 'their' priest and take good care of him, but they know he will not last. Should he go against 'the custom of the island' he can expect quiet non co-operation and even open defiance. A priest from Malin [in northern Donegal] tried to stop all night dancing but he was told the church hall was built by Tory men not Malin men and the Tory men would make their own rules about it.

While they humoured him and listened to him, they were often apt to 'politely disagree'.[136]

But Tory also had quite a troubled history when it came to the intermittency of priestly presence. For all those who wanted passionately to stay, there were others who could not wait to get off. Fr Hugh Strain lived up to his name in 1967 when he wrote to his bishop, Anthony McFeely:

> I wonder would you find it suitable to change me from Tory please? The reason I ask is that seasickness makes the journey to and from Tory a bit of an ordeal. As a result I have been on the mainland once between October 1st and April 1st. I thought that the seasickness would gradually disappear but instead it gets worse. For a place like Tory I think it is almost essential that the priest gets ashore at least monthly. The lighthouse keepers get a fortnight after every four weeks duty. My sea sickness is a family heirloom and it is not due to my being afraid (I hope so).

The bishop's curt response was 'no promise'.[137] Others found it difficult to leave islands: Fr Thomas Killeen, who spent twelve years on Aran from the 1930s, told Ciarán Bairéad, collector with the Irish Folklore Commission in 1966, that he was 'an Oileánach [islander] when I left it. I was out of touch with everything; indeed I'm still a bit of an Oileánach. I found it a bit hard to get used to the mainland again.'[138]

Island priests devoted much time to adjudicating. On Rathlin Island, those speaking to the collector from the IFC in 1954 remembered 'trouble and fights' over the Rundale system of land division (see chapter 1) and 'Fr McKinley had to go to make peace between them many's the time, with the horses tramping over the end of the land ... and he done a good job, I'll warrant you'. One respondent noted pointedly that she remembered with fondness Fr Lavery, who was 'a long time here and got on well. He used to visit the people, not like the priests now'; he also had the 'first gramophone ever to come to the island'. It was not all deference, however, and the islanders were quite 'capable of backchatting him' and some 'dinna trust him'. Another island priest, recalled Rose McCurdy, who had been resident on the island since 1899, 'made all on the island go over to Ballycastle [the nearest mainland town] and vote. All went but two. Well, them that went against Fr McGowan – some sudden calamity happened them all'. House visiting on New Year's Eve was traditionally organised for collections for the poor, but when the pensions were introduced 'they started to collect money and drink it so the priest put a stop to it'.[139] Rathlin islanders had a sharp wit and the priests were not spared; Fr McKinley censured an islander for beating his donkey and told him 'the Holy family rode on an ass escaping to Egypt', to which the reply came 'they wouldn't have got far if had been this ass then'.[140]

Elemental island forces, however, could render the priests mere spectators. A bitter row raged on Achill in the late 1930s that had its roots in civil-war politics. A contract for supplying school milk and food had rested with a supporter of Fine Gael, but seems to have been taken over by a Fianna Fáil supporter; it led to a school strike with accusations that Fr James Campbell had urged a boycott of the school. A statement had been read from the altars in November 1936 stating that 'a few in this parish say that the PP controls the liberty of the teachers. This is an untruth.' A few years later Fr Campbell wrote to Archbishop Gilmartin with the highly dubious claim that 'we, the priests, kept our opinions to ourselves. It was wise, otherwise there will be another storm in Achill. If every priest in Achill stands aloof from factions, religion is sure not to suffer.'[141] Standing aloof from factions on islands was hardly the stance adopted by most priests, though perhaps priests on Achill had the advantage of greater numbers, given the size of the island, which was by far the largest.

Fr Thomas Killea was a horrified spectator in 1947 when the *Dún Aengus* steamer that sailed to the Aran Islands was involved in an accident and temporarily became a stranded wreck; what transpired then left Killea incensed, as he explained to Archbishop Walsh:

> the old steamer is wrecked but the aftermath is worse than any wreck. The Inishmaan people, acting on the assumption that anything wrecked is for the first who can grab it have looted the cargo of the boat and even the boat itself. Some porter came ashore and led to orgies of sin. The guards are there but there is very little respect for them because the people know they will not be persecuted because the District Justice will not come out to hold a court. We must do something to bring home to the criminals that they cannot steal with impunity. I would suggest that your Grace give me permission to remove the blessed sacrament from the island and that no mass be celebrated there until restitution be made ... something drastic is required ... the whole life of the island is in jeopardy.[142]

Walsh subsequently contacted senior Fianna Fáil minister Seán Lemass; the boat was brought off the rocks and towed to Kilronan and plans were made for its repair.[143]

The following decade, an employee of the Office of Public Works, the resident engineer for the extension of the pier at Inisheer, complained bitterly to Archbishop Walsh about interference from the island's curate, Fr Moran, whom he maintained was distracting the foreman by 'smoking and talking ... this man's daughter is Fr Moran's housekeeper ... he stands over me every day on the job ... and told me the job has been a scandalous waste of tax payer's money'.[144] Fr Moran subsequently went to the OPW head office in Dublin with a ten-page typed memo that the engineer maintained had 'torn to shreds' his professional reputation, not unreasonably pointing out, 'I am a qualified engineer, Fr Moran is not ... he has held me up to public odium on the island' and had 'a lack of charity which I find difficult to understand in a priest'.[145]

Fr Moran defended his actions on the grounds that the foreman said he 'had never seen anything as bad' as the job being done but could not complain so there was an onus on the priest to do so.[146] The parish priest, Fr Tom Varley, then weighed in, suggesting it was 'hard to attach much weight' to Coughlan; that he was paranoid and did not appreciate island power hierarchies: 'I feel sure that Mr Coughlan does not realise that were it not for the interference of the priest there would be no pier there at all'. Varley boasted that he had persuaded the minister for finance, Gerard Sweetman, to come to the island and see the need for the pier himself; it was a sizeable grant and Fr Moran 'undertook to keep an eye on it', suggesting the minister expressed approval of such an arrangement, which was far-fetched. Coughlan was surely correct in writing to the archbishop: 'I do not believe that Mr Sweetman intended that he [Fr Moran] should supervise an engineer.'[147]

At the same time, Varley revealed in his correspondence the ongoing, all-pervasive engagement of the parish priest in island affairs. He wanted permission to give evidence in the circuit court in Galway regarding a disputed will on the island as the deceased had left all his property to his wife's relatives and his own relatives were challenging the will: 'unfortunately one has to become involved in these matters in Aran'. The tradition on the island was that the priests would preside over the drawing of a will as 'a solicitor would not come to Aran for that purpose'.[148]

Schemes to modernise the islands were also more likely to progress with priestly engagement. Achill was connected to electricity in 1952 and the parish priest, Fr John Godfrey, played a major role in encouraging the islanders to embrace it, with 1,500 homes connected; he had also been involved in 'much correspondence and agitation' concerning the building of more schools on Achill.[149]

Another priest determined to make an impact was Fr James Enright on Valentia in the 1950s, who was vocal about the demand of islanders for a bridge to the mainland. The question of improving communications between Valentia and the mainland had been considered since the second decade of the twentieth century and Kerry County Council had been considering the viability of a bridge since 1948, but the issue of where a grant would come from was a serious impediment, as was the fact that estimates of the cost ranged from £80,000 to £200,000. In 1952, Fr Enright presided over the Valentia Island Bridge Committee, emphasising that the island had valuable resources of slate and copper, which were not being exploited effectively because of the absence of a bridge, and the island was also missing out on tourism. The committee also made the argument that the island could be an important military post 'should war come', but ultimately this was about 'deliverance from isolation' at a time when there were 360 houses and 200 farm holdings; the population had declined in thirty years from 3,000 to 1,100.[150]

Fr Enright in his direct and personal correspondence (in English) with de Valera sought to emphasise the importance of the island as a repository of native language and culture. While 'foreign installations' such as cable and wireless had 'tended to anglicise the island somewhat', the 'native stock still act on the strongest Gaelic traditions and culture … the Seanchas [traditional Irish storytelling] and the purist native speakers still survive here'. Nor was he averse to a slice of moral blackmail: 'many old people in Valentia Island, who, all their lives have been hoping to see their bridge built, will be very glad to see its construction now competed before they die'.[151] John Garvin, secretary of the Department of Local Government, however, had a different take on the island, pointing out that it had three churches (two Catholic and one Protestant), shops, and a cottage hospital and therefore 'enjoys better public services, amenities and facilities than any other island off the Irish coast'. What it needed, he concluded, was a better ferry service, but the minister for industry and commerce, Seán Lemass, was backing the bid for a bridge so it was recommended to the Department of Finance for a special national development fund grant.[152]

There was also a full public inquiry into the matter the following year. Fr Enright told Taoiseach John A. Costello (ironically, given the complaints about isolation), 'we are ready to go to Dublin at a <u>moment's notice</u>' to talk about the bridge. The priest's tone the following month grew more irate and irascible. He insisted it would be 'extremely foolish' of the government to delay publishing the report of the inquiry as 'so much suffering and incessant hardship are involved', and he was extremely dismissive of 'other government sponsored schemes'. His stridency was undoubtedly prompted by the feeling, aptly summed up in a Department of the Taoiseach note, that the Taoiseach 'did not appear to have taken a particularly active part in the consideration of the proposal'.[153] A memorandum for the government insisted the bridge was not affordable, but in January 1959 minister for local government Neil Blaney announced its construction would go ahead as a partnership between the state and Kerry County Council. By 1964, however, islanders considered withholding their rates and taxes because of procrastination, and in November 1966 a deputation led by parish priest Revd John Beasley appeared before a special meeting of Kerry County Council complaining of delays with regard to tenders for the job.[154] As seen earlier, the 1,300-foot bridge was eventually erected in 1970 and formally opened in 1971 at a cost of £500,000.[155]

Another high-profile island priest was Fr Tomás Ó Murchú, who served on Cape Clear from 1965 to 1977 and became a militant defender of the Irish language of which the island was such an important repository. He was involved in a 'raid' on Gaeltarra Éireann headquarters in Galway and also had his telephone service cut off when he refused to pay his account as it was in English and he referred to the 'victimisation' of those who wanted to do business in Irish. When he left the island he suggested he was 'leaving part of myself behind' and according to contemporary reports 'his greatest gift to the island was a resurgence of spirit'. With that spirit came practical and far-reaching changes including piped water, electricity and a housing scheme as well as a twenty-four-hour phone service and a seven-day ferry service as well as the innovative island co-operative.[156] He also kept extraordinarily detailed notebooks – *leabhar na pfograí* or books of notices – which revealed the extent to which he had his pulse on island life and documented everything in detail.[157]

As chairman of the island co-operative, Ó Murchú was 'bitter' about the lack of a bigger generator and 'sour' about the absence of a decent factory for a new wrought-iron venture in 1972 and maintained that those managing Gaeltarra Éireann 'have the vision of sparrows'.[158] In 1966, in advance of the fiftieth anniversary of the 1916 Rising, he published a newsletter in Irish circulated to 'Cape Clear folk at home and abroad' in which he made a plea 'for loyalty to the ideals of the men of 1916'. He also launched a campaign to prevent land on the island 'falling into the hands of foreigners'.[159]

Ó Murchú was one of a number of island priests at the heart of modernisation thrusts in the 1960s and 1970s. One opportunity lay in the use of islands for summer schools in the Irish language, continuing a long tradition, given that the islands had historically been seen as intrinsic to the Irish language revival. The schools were now conceived on a grander scale but also had to contend with limited infrastructure on the islands. Fr Eamon Concannon, the curate on Inisheer from 1960 to 1967, remembered that an Irish-language summer school had been held in 'an old abandoned boat house with no facilities of any kind'. Efforts were then made to get running water and a community centre, which was the 'big breakthrough'. A bigger summer school also allowed for a stream of revenue for the islanders as they provided accommodation for the students.[160]

These developments also heralded the arrival to the island of television and some Aran islanders as a result managed to see Neil Armstrong land on the moon in 1969. Fr Paddy Gilligan, curate on Inisheer on that occasion, remembered that a television had arrived the same week and 'the battery just held out', but there was still no electricity 'other than that provided by a diesel generator on the island hall'. Gilligan later reflected on the lot of the island priest: 'I had a sense that my role as a priest was not confined to the altar or the pulpit but also to be involved in the social life of the parish, to build up a community to take responsibility for its own welfare'.

This was also relevant to the issue of electricity. There was opposition on the island to its introduction from some who baulked at the cost and 'how it would be dangerous in thatched houses ... an added element in Inisheer was that the business of the supplier of gas bottles was threatened'. Gilligan was adamant that self-help was needed to avoid 'going cap in hand to county councillors they did not know who were living on the mainland'. In the case of piped water, 'a community approach to state authorities was the proper way to make progress rather than waiting for politicians to claim credit for crumbs from the table'.

Island priests certainly ended up doing jobs they would hardly have performed on the mainland. As recalled by Gilligan, with the construction of the airstrip on Aran 'big earth moving equipment was brought in from Rossaveal on pontoons that were used in the Normandy landings. I spent several nights doing a few hours driving one of the machines as they operated twenty-four hours with three shifts.' But gradually co-ops were evolving into development agencies, including on Inisheer, and 'instead of the priest running affairs from his sitting room a full time manager was employed'. This, Gilligan saw as 'the beginning of local government' for the island.[161]

Nonetheless, some of the island disadvantages proved remarkably durable. Fr Joseph Cooney, curate at Kilronan on Aran from 1962 to 1967, became involved in the fishermen's co-op and was elected chairman, and soon 'realised that they were being ripped off by the prices they were paying for oil on the mainland. As chairman I went to Galway and negotiated a deal with an oil company for an agreed price for diesel,' which worked for a time, though there were 'dissenting voices'. He also went to Dublin to visit the Department of the Gaeltacht looking for support for a generator and film projector. It was also necessary to blast the rock on the site of the old school in order to build a new hall in 1966 which cost £7,000: 'I visited the premises of Roadstone outside Galway and succeeded in purchasing a small case load of gelignite. They assured me it was safe as long as I kept the detonators away from the gelignite. I filled my pockets with detonators and hoped for the best.'[162]

While accounts remain of 'red-faced, over fed' killjoy island priests in the 1970s cutting the ceilidhí (Irish dances) short,[163] the reality of power play on the islands was more layered. The priest on Inishbofin in Deborah Tall's *The Island of the White Cow* (1986) based on her time there from 1970 to 1975, has no real presence and was hardly generating fear. The 'most controversial' thing he managed to do 'was to let sheep into the graveyard one summer to trim the graveyard'. His successor was young and open-minded, but that in itself created suspicions. Tall was somewhat contradictory about the priest's role and status; he found the islanders' 'back-stabbing wearying' and yet they were more comfortable with a priest who was 'iron-handed'. He was 'treated lavishly' because 'the entire bureaucracy of the island resides in his single being'. And yet, the easygoing priest 'succumbed to the treachery of island politics and fled, battered', concluding in a letter to Tall that the 'terrible fascination' the island held for non-natives had 'an element of fantasy to its hold on one'.[164] It was a reminder that priests were not immune to delusions that afflicted their lay counterparts about islands representing a calm sanctuary.

Some Tory Island priests continued to run into trouble with their bishops. In 1969 Fr Séamus Meehan wrote to Bishop McFeely to express regret at 'the concern caused by my absence from Tory ... priests have been absent from Tory even in recent times and like me felt no obligation to inform the bishop. I can assure you my Lord that being overdue on the mainland can be a greater strain than being on the island.'[165] But his absences remained problematic. McFeely wrote to him to explain that his disappearance 'gives me great cause for concern'; he had been absent on holy days, some Sundays and a 'considerable number of occasions'. He insisted the curate had an obligation 'in charity and justice' to the islanders and 'I appeal to your conscience to look straight at what you consider your priestly commitment to be'. What was also interesting about this fraught correspondence was the extent to which the islanders were deemed to be a special case. Bishop McFeely wrote:

> From inquiries that I have made I learn that previous priests have not failed to give their flock the service they were rightly entitled to and seldom, if ever, ran the risk of being left on the mainland over the weekend or over a number of days. Neither were they in the habit of leaving the island frequently and depriving the islanders of the opportunity for weekday mass and these were priests who were more advanced in years and who spent a number of years on the island. I cannot but see your absence on these occasions as an expression of indifference to the spiritual welfare of people who have little else to comfort them not to mention the lack of priestly zeal that it indicates.[166]

But there was to be no cowering deference from the recalcitrant priest:

> the Church herself now allows people to fulfil their Sunday obligations on weekdays. If this is applicable anywhere surely it applies on Tory ... my inquiries find priests in the past were absent even nine weeks running but the priestly zeal and integrity of those men were never questioned ... I am in order in following the practice of former priests as regards coming and going.

The bishop's letter was 'a cause of annoyance to me'.[167]

There was also one last salvo from the bishop: 'your letter leaves me in no doubt about your attitude to your bishop, your parish priest and the people under your spiritual care. It is something I must bear in mind.'[168]

A few years later, Fr Bonar on Tory responded to a query about a planned visit by the bishop at a time when the island had a population of 310. He referred to attendance at Mass as being 'incredibly bad at times and not necessarily due to inclement weather'. He had to engage in 'unsavoury drudgery in confronting the backsliders to shame them into attending', as the 'group of pious parishioners' was only 'six to eight!' He also noted that the island was financially viable as a church concern 'only because I do not take any of my proportion of salary from the church account. This is entirely my own choice, necessitated by the commitments I have undertaken regarding projects on the church, presbytery and school.' He hoped 'I'll get my head above water – eventually.'[169]

This raised the intriguing question of just how religious islanders were. It was common to refer to islanders as a 'spiritual people'.[170] But historically, with regard to the Blasket islanders, for example, 'it was not felt there would be any great advantage to sending a priest to live among them. As a result of this, the clergy had no great hold on the islanders. Indeed, there was never any great need for one. Even if they were regularly at each other's throats and given to every sin worse than the other, the community was too small to have a priest ... priest or no priest they were a people with a strong faith in God'. They were characterised as 'staunch Catholics' and it was maintained 'Catholicism ruled their lives' and they often came across the sea to Mass in Dunquin or to baptise their babies and to be married. But mostly, they managed their own piety, including by honouring the Blessed Virgin (a practice widespread among fishermen, who sprinkled holy water on their boats): 'there was no house that didn't recite the rosary'.[171]

Attributing excessive piety to island communities is problematic. Islanders may have had a certain acceptance of God's will, heightened by the degree to which the sea could be such a cruel and absolute ruler, but they did not resign themselves to such a will when seeking answers for neglect, as evidenced by their caustic criticisms of government, and a centuries-old pagan cast of mind was in the blood of some. Dorothy Therman, keen to transcribe folklore on Tory Island in the 1980s, referred to their devout Catholicism, 'although their roots seem, at times, still firmly planted in pagan soil'.[172] Pádraig O'Toole, who grew up on the Aran Islands and himself became a priest, noted in his memoir that 'the priest was respected, as much for the fact that he was educated as for what he represented. He was not fawned over. Only a few priests acted the Dia beag, the little God, but people overlooked that failing.'[173] Priests were also dependent on their flock on islands in ways that did not apply to the mainland; Fr John Flannery, who was parish priest on Inishbofin from 1959 to 1966, noted in relation to Inishark, the neighbouring island, that once a month 'weather permitting, Shark families took their turn to row the priest three miles each way'.[174]

American anthropologist John Messenger (see chapter 6) left a contradictory impression of the relationship between priests and people on Inis Beag, the fictional name he gave to Inisheer. He saw them as 'devoutly Catholic, despite the fact that they are extremely critical of their priests and retain and reinterpret pagan religious forms'. Yet he also insisted 'it is difficult to overestimate the degree of fear of the clergy'. He observed 'the folk feel too many priests have acted aloof and supercilious' and lacked commitment; referring to the comfort of the curate's house, one islander commented acidly 'the house indulgences built'.[175] He also insisted anti-clericalism was 'as strong or stronger than its anti-government counterpart' and a significant source of humour.[176]

The regularity with which priests came and went may also have been a factor. Linguist Reg Hindley researched the subject on Cape Clear in 1958 and commented: 'There had been twelve different curates since 1928, a clear enough indication of the church's own assessment of the desirability or tolerability of life on Cape Clear.'[177] But islanders also had their own ideas as to the desirability and tolerability of their priests; on a journalistic assignment on Tory in 1983, Colm Tóibín found there were no rules or police, little work, and plenty of singing and drinking ('it is what I supposed heaven would be like'). The priest attempted to spoil the fun by coming into the bar; he 'told everyone to go to bed', but he only interrupted not finished the entertainment and one of the islanders imitated his limp: 'nothing which the priest did or said succeeded in making the islanders follow mainland hours'.[178]

That was a few years after the arrival to Tory of Jesuit and Dubliner Fr Diarmuid Ó Péicín, another remarkable priest who energetically earned an elevated place in the pantheon of clerical island champions. Frequently referred to as 'turbulent', he was also boastful, or, in the more diplomatic language of obituarists, 'knew his standing in the world'. For a decade, that world became Tory and his mission was to get attention focused on it and also imbue the islanders with the zeal to ensure their island remained populated.

Tory was, in fact, a retirement project for Ó Péicín; having worked and taught abroad as a missionary in Africa, he arrived on the island in 1980 to learn Irish and was angered by what appeared to be official disinterest and a seeming determination to get families to move to the mainland. This suspicion was heightened when journalist Gerry Moriarty unearthed evidence of a local authority plan from 1978 suggesting the 150 people on the island could be relocated, with various suggestions as to what new use the island could be put to: 'a holiday home for American tourists. A high security prison, a quarantine centre or a firing range for the army ... this astonishing official mindset triggered a ruthless, single minded old testament fury and zeal in Fr Ó Péicín who had a simple biblical take on his mission: if you weren't for Tory you were against Tory.'[179]

In December 1981 he handed journalists two pamphlets, *Tory's Horror* and *The Scandal of Donegal County Council*, focusing on the supposed three-point plan for the 'speedy elimination of Tory': cutting off essential services, refusing to develop the island and coaxing people into new houses on the mainland. He asserted that the council was 'determined to destroy one of the most independent-minded living Gaeltachts in the country ... brushing the human beings aside as if they were just rocks and stones ... Genocide is the name of this act and that is an ugly word.'[180] With a tongue as sharp as a knife, he was appointed curate and he found an ally in Ian Paisley, who lobbied on his behalf in Brussels ('Europe must look after its island people'), but Charles Haughey privately growled 'you know, he's mad'.

In 1984, Bishop Séamus Hegarty instructed him to leave the diocese, as he was too divisive. Ó Péicín's crusade prompted documentaries and books, including his own in which he excoriated the large gallery of rogues he deemed responsible for a general island neglect, leaving a Tory population not only without sealed roads, fuel or piped water but also 'haunted by rumours from the mainland'.[181] He was aghast at the 'faceless bureaucrats' but also, as seen in chapter 3, castigated the lack of action from the Catholic Church, especially from his vantage point as a Jesuit with a strong commitment to justice: 'why was the Church not openly condemning the Council?'[182] He encouraged the islanders to assert themselves (you are not 'beings for others') and secured grants from the Department of the Gaeltacht.

Ó Péicín was adept at using the media and became a bombastic practitioner of adversarial and emotive politics. It certainly worked to a point; he arranged travelling exhibitions, invited television crews to the island, got voluntary labour to connect houses to the water mains being laid and encouraged a knitting factory. His 16,000-signature petition for work on an airstrip, however, was 'in vain' and some islanders continued with their plans to leave, while other priests who had served there were angry with his denunciation of historic neglect and the accusations of a 'shameful' church that deliberately 'marginalised'.[183] After he was removed from the island against his will he was 'skewered by fear and rage'. But enough had been done – including a new hotel and harbour – to stabilise Tory and to encourage more solidarity amongst islanders, and Ó Péicín was subsequently involved in the establishment of the Irish Islands Federation (Comhdháil nOileáin na hÉireann).[184]

Also at the meeting to form the Islands Federation was Fr Eugene McDermott. He had argued for optional celibacy when a curate on Aran and attempts were made to shunt him off the island but he stayed there for eleven years.[185] Other, even more dissident priests found a haven on the islands as the ideal location to reach for a more liberating form of spiritual or religious practice. In 1996 Fr Dara Molloy severed his ties with Rome and established his own 'Celtic church' on Inishmore. His authority to administer was withdrawn by his bishop but he continued to celebrate Mass and the sacraments 'in the ancient pre-papal tradition'. He also asserted that celibacy should be optional and said he would continue to administer 'as a priest of the Celtic church ... mass will be said in Celtic churches without roofs ... put simply, Fr Molloy believes that a church run along traditional Celtic lines would tap deeper into the Irish spiritual psyche than any Rome controlled church could.'[186]

Islands continued to be associated with banishment in popular culture, none more famous in the late twentieth century than the fictional Craggy Island where the star of Channel 4's *Father Ted*, Fr Ted Crilly (Dermot Morgan), had been sent, or rather exiled, after an incident referred to mysteriously as 'that Lourdes thing' in which he allegedly stole charity money supposed to fund a poor child's pilgrimage. Fr Crilly always insisted that he did not, as alleged, use the money to fly to Las Vegas, but that the money was just 'resting' in his bank account. The aerial shot at the beginning of each episode was Inisheer Island, though the *Father Ted* filming locations were actually on the mainland in Clare. Such was the enduring popularity of the series that it inspired annual Craggy Island festivals on the Aran Islands with costumed priests, nuns, bishops and tea makers along with stand-up comedy.[187]

FIVE

ISLAND VISITORS:
THE FIRST WAVE

'What a strange lot to live in that bare, bleak place!'

In July 1895 Norah Workman from Belfast kept a diary of an Irish voyage, an antiquarian society cruise, in twenty-nine pages of impeccable handwriting, under the title 'A Summer Trip to the Isles of the West'. The visitors were on board a steamship, 'plunging up and down gaily in the waves', though there was awareness that 'uncertain and dangerous' currents could make landing and departure from the islands problematic. As they approached Tory Island, fishermen came out in boats to row them in:

> They speak Irish, some do not know any English at all and are a rough, wild-looking people. As they had been told of our visit, they gave us a kindly welcome, not like that accorded to the government boats which in being sent to Tory to collect rents were driven out to sea again by the natives – and quite right they were to refuse to pay rents, for how could those poor creatures make or save money on their bare island?[1]

Workman also described, in considerable detail, the 'strange scene' of the house they entered:

> The door was in the centre and the house consisted of a long room. At one end a mother and her three little children sat round a turf

fire on the earthen floor, the old grandmother talked at a great rate in Irish which unfortunately we could not understand. Excepting a huge four poster there was little furniture in the house. As we bade the inmates adieu, we heard a clanking of chains at the opposite end of the room where it was dark. Looking closer, we found that this house was also the home of two cows! What a strange lot to live in that bare, bleak place!

The touring party subsequently made their way to Inishmurray, off the coast of Sligo, where the 'King' of the island, Michael Waters, acted as guide; she found a kind and friendly people, 'more gentle looking than those on Tory'. They were told by a young girl what a dreary place it was in winter, that she could speak English as well as Irish and that she must go to America as a servant in the spring. She did not want to go '"But some of us go every year from Inishmurray as there is not food enough for all and whoever goes away is always homesick for the old home".[2] The antiquarians were also warned by an old man ('looked like an aged prophet'), not to interfere with ancient stones that were used to 'curse enemies'. Two members of the Royal Irish Constabulary were conspicuous at the pier, a reminder that poitín was made on the island 'in five places ... and openly too'.

It was then on to Mayo's Clew Bay, where they 'came in to what seemed to some of us, a new world ... with changing lines of blue, purple and green'. They landed on Clare Island and were rowed to the sandy beach, where they were 'much astonished to observe a fashionable white parasol moving along the beach' which 'contrasted oddly with the wild, romantic scenery of the place'. There was more hospitality enjoyed, 'tall, dark-haired and eyed, good looking girls' who offered the visitors 'a good drink of fresh milk, tasting strongly of turf fire ... they wished us God's blessings and that we could come everyday'.

The next stop was the Aran Islands, where 'everything around us was grey' and 'what we could see of it was not attractive, the grey, carboniferous limestone rocks shelved down in layers on terraces to our side of the island, bare, bleak rocks with not a vestige of green either of fields or trees to be seen. What a strange place for anyone to call home.'

Aran men moved swiftly in their pampooties (light, animal-skin shoes), springing over the stone walls 'like mountain goats'. The visitors also experienced some island entertainment with a young man singing several Irish songs, 'pathetic and mournful but still with a charm all their own' and there was a demonstration of dancing 'gravely as most Irishmen do'. Some of the women followed them all day, a number keeping up a cry of 'give me a penny please', though one particularly cheeky boy was more demanding in asking for 'a shilling please'. She also observed 'there are but few Protestants on Aran, the natives are Roman Catholics and Irish speaking, though English is now taught in the schools to all and in time the old language must die out'. The visit to Aran brought the trip to an end 'on those bare, interesting but little known rocks in the old sea'.[3]

Workman's diary was a reminder that the 'rocks' were becoming better known, her trip part of a wider 'discovery' of the islands in the latter part of the nineteenth century and the wonderment they created, not just in relation to the antiquities they held, but also regarding a lifestyle, customs, language and environment few comfortable urbanites had any knowledge of. The diary entries are striking in how they express incredulity at some of the primitivism and desolation, but also an appreciation of the hospitality and the natural beauty as well as a sense of the islanders as a breed apart with their own customs, practices and beliefs that ultimately could not remain completely immune from wider social and commercial forces. Workman had received quite an education during this short summer trip; it is noticeable that, despite the group under whose auspices the trip was organised, she spent precious little of her diary describing the island antiquities, being much more absorbed with the island people.

It was initially ordnance survey that brought official visitors to some of the islands for the first time. The decision by the British Parliament in 1824 to institute an Ordnance Survey mapping of Ireland played 'a decisive part in ending the isolation of the islands and opening them up to the world.[4] In 1839, artist and draughtsman William Wakeman, just nineteen years old, and assistant in the topographical division of the Ordnance Survey, accompanied to numerous sites John O'Donovan, a man with a profound knowledge of the Irish scholarly tradition. O'Donovan was employed by the Ordnance Survey as orthographer and etymologist to establish by reference to authoritative sources, a standard of orthography in English for Irish place names countrywide. It was an extraordinary undertaking, in all weathers and often on foot, and as Wakeman saw it in relation to Aran, 'these islands were as yet almost a terra incognita'. On seeing Dún Aengus, the prehistoric fort on Aran, O'Donovan 'literally shouted with delight'.[5] This fort was described in 1843 by George Petrie, a champion of the Royal Irish Academy (established in 1785 to promote science, literature and antiquities) who had also been appointed to the topographical department of the Ordnance Survey in 1833 as 'the most magnificent barbaric monument now extant in Europe' and was thereafter frequently described as an 'astounding structure', its defences 'built up against the vertical sea cliff almost a hundred metres above the boiling Atlantic'.[6]

But the euphoria could also be accompanied by fear. Notable Cork antiquarian and collector John Windele was another island hopper, who, with members of antiquarian societies, made journeys, usually by foot, throughout Cork and Kerry and to the Dingle peninsula. He also made the arduous journey to Skellig Michael, eight miles off the coast of southwest Kerry, in 1851, where, on ascent, he 'gradually became alarmed and nervous as I looked down upon the vast and frightful depths below and the total want of protection, and I found my best course was to shut out the view in that quarter by closing my seaward eye and looking only at the rock [to the] inside … and the steps before [me]'.[7] The monastery on Skelligs was in existence at the beginning of the ninth century and was 'one of the most dramatic monuments of early Christianity in Western Europe, but by the very extravagance of its situation, it is not fully typical of the monastic communities of its day' making it even more intriguing.[8]

Samuel Ferguson, deputy keeper of the public records in Dublin, was another antiquarian visitor to Aran in 1853, while in 1857, William Wilde, surgeon, polymath and antiquary as well as a naturalist, topographer, folklorist (and father of Oscar) brought seventy ethnologists and antiquaries from the British Association for the Advancement of Science to Aran, where a banquet was held inside the walls of Dún Aengus.

Thomas Westropp, another to distinguish himself in the antiquarian field, was also an Aran visitor when aged eighteen in 1878.

Antiquarians were also apt, in parallel with their comments on antiquities, to describe the lives and practices of the islanders 'thus establishing a strong sense of continuity with the distant past'. In this sense the antiquarians often seemed to view the islands as 'living museums'.[9] Wakeman's survey of the antiquities on Inishmurray was published in 1887 and he described it as 'a museum of antiquities' and the island people as a 'fair-headed, comely, well-built race, probably Tuatha de Danann'.[10] This referred to the people of the Goddess Danu, reputed to have landed in the west of Ireland thousands of years previously, believed to be half god and half human with mythical powers. There was nothing mythical, however, about the site of an early religious establishment on Inishmurray, probably dating from the sixth century. It was one of the best preserved early medieval religious sites with complex and extensive remains including three churches, three burial grounds, at least four *clochans* (beehive huts) and several possible altar cairns, holy wells and carved stones 'with several bearing written inscriptions'. It was clearly an important pilgrimage destination focused on the shrine of St Molaise, a saint of regional importance in the north-west of Ireland. All told, the archaeological treasures on Inishmurray were among 'the best preserved examples of early medieval ecclesiastical architecture in Atlantic Europe'.[11]

From the 1860s onwards something of a 'revolution' was clearly taking place in the study of Irish natural history and antiquarians. Another of the chief exponents was Robert Lloyd Praeger, a native of Down and founder of the *Irish Naturalist*, who began to focus on the study of specific areas by organised groups of specialists and was a member of the Belfast Naturalists Field Club. In 1893 he moved to Dublin to work in the National Library of Ireland and in 1895 he organised a trip to Inishmore by members of the Irish Field Club and referred to the islanders as 'stalwart', not least because he observed a fisherman who 'sat on the overhanging edge of the cliff, his feet dangling over the abyss and his line descending vertically into the ocean some 200 feet below'.[12] Praeger's *The Botanist in Ireland* was published in 1934 and referred to three days he had spent on Rathlin to study the flora and fauna in the late 1880s; what was remarkable was the variety of plants on islands off the west coast, as they could 'offer refuge for some plants very sparsely distributed in Ireland'.[13]

Cambridge's A. C. Haddon, a pivotal figure in the development of anthropology and ethnography as scientific disciplines, first acquired a taste for poitín on the island of Achill: 'it is rather amusing to find nearly everyone with some in the house when not only the making of it but the possession of it is illegal. Everyone knows where and by whom it is made but the difficulty is to catch the maker in the act.' These professionals were no antiquarian angels. Haddon had no qualms about plundering island graveyards and openly admitted his theft. He wrote in 1896 about thirteen crania from the island of Inishbofin that formed part of a collection of crania he gave to the anthropological museum of Trinity College Dublin in 1890: 'so far as I am aware they are the only specimens from that island, or indeed from that district of Ireland to be found in any museum'.[14] He had earned the nickname 'the Headhunter' because of his collection of cranium specimens from the Pacific.

Also crucial to awareness of the islands and the islanders was the work of Charles R. Browne, a GP and anthropologist from Dublin. The most comprehensive survey of island life in Ireland to which he contributed so much – the Irish Ethnographic Survey – documented the lives of people on the west coast between 1891 and 1903. The photographic results of the survey are held in six albums in the library of Trinity College Dublin and in various reports (ethnographies) published in the *Proceedings of the Royal Irish Academy* during those years. His trips included the Aran Islands, Inishbofin and Inishark in County Galway as well as Gorumna, Lettermullen, Carna and Mweenish in Connemara, the Inishkea Islands, Portnacloy, Ballycroy, Clare Island and Inishturk in Mayo and the Blasket Islands in Kerry. He recorded a multitude; coastline and surface, antiquities, lifestyle, housing and health, and especially the islanders' physical appearances, in minute detail.

In 1893 Browne and A. C. Haddon, 'pitched their tent' in Aran and began recording eye colour, skin pigmentation and cranial capacity of those who could be persuaded. Photographs were essential to all this, the camera by then being regarded as an indispensable part of the anthropometrics kit.[15] One of the most striking photographs – indeed a photograph that does much to sum up 'the complex origins of Irish anthropology' – was one taken by Browne in 1894 of the King of North Inishkea island, Philip Lavelle. Did his defiant look underline some of the tensions bordering the relationship between 'native' and anthropologist? (Browne also took the first photographs of the Blasket islanders.) More troubling, perhaps, was a photograph of Browne taking the physical measurements of islanders on Inishbofin in the presence of RIC officers, underlining 'the complex social, cultural and political situation that Browne had to deal with'.[16] There was interest too in the idea that the islanders might be descended from an ancient race. Part of the mission was to figure out the origins of the Irish 'primitives' inhabiting the western fringes of the UK; in the words of Browne and Haddon, to 'unravel the tangled Skein of the so-called Irish race', the idea of the prognathic 'Black Irishman' or Irish aboriginal.[17]

A particular preoccupation was the notion of the Aran islanders as descendants of the Firbolgs, an ancient race said to have ruled Ireland before the Tuatha de Danann. As observed by William Wilde, these were sometimes referred to as the Belgae, 'so called for their assumed Belgic origin', who had established 'kingly pentarchy' and who when challenged by newer settlers 'fled for security westwards and entrenched themselves in those stupendous fastnesses of Arran, in Galway Bay, so that even then we can see that the destiny of the Celt was westward'.[18] Browne, however, was unconvinced: 'to what race or races the Aranites belong, we do not pretend to say, but it is pretty evident that they cannot be Firbolgs if the latter are correctly described as "small, dark-haired and swarthy"'.[19] Wilde, however, noted that the Firbolgs did not all go west; this 'is manifest from the very marked characteristics of the two races, the dark and the fair, still remaining in the west'.[20]

Just how voluntary was the participation of the islanders in this research? Was there a perception that these were 'British scientists' inflicting anthropology in a racially inspired colonial project? The level of intrusion was certainly extensive ('the wrinkles on the face are very deep, most so about the eyes and at the "root" of the nose, where there is often a raised fold of skin between two deep furrows'[21]), but Browne was, in fact, Irish, born in Tipperary and educated at Trinity College Dublin, where he studied under the Darwinist Daniel J. Cunningham, who was also a member of the anthropological committee of the RIA. There were problems with the size of the samples (in the Mullet, a peninsula in north-west Mayo, and Inishkea Islands survey, there were 494 individuals 'of whom the full series of measurements and observations were made'.[22]) and it is clear that conclusions were qualified. Browne asserted that the inhabitants of Inishkea, for example, had different characteristics, physically and otherwise, from mainlanders: 'They have no traditions as to their origin but may be looked upon as *probably* the most unmixed representatives of the original inhabitants of the district.'[23]

Browne certainly left no shortage of material for the chroniclers of the islands; he also came to his surveys at a time when it was a 'race against time' as the traditional isolationism of the islands was being challenged by modernity or what has been termed 'the beginning of the end of the nineteenth century in the west of Ireland'.[24] The limitations of Browne and Haddon's endeavours are apparent – overall, on Aran, a 'fairly accurate, though somewhat imperfect presentment of the anthropography' and on folklore, 'we regret that our information is so scanty'. They had, nonetheless, 'far exceeded the lines of research' as they believed that ethnical characteristics were found not just in physical characteristics, but also in 'arts, habits, language and beliefs' and provided much information on these. They also emphasised urgency: 'no time should be lost in recording the vanishing customs and beliefs of old times'.[25]

Because of the growing extent to which the creative Irish were being 'possessed by place', writers also began to 'lavish' attention on geographic location and topography with a specific focus on Connemara and Aran and other 'lonely and barren spaces to which the Irish literary imagination has had frequent recourse'. This was also an Irish manifestation of an international development; playwright J. M. Synge, for example, was heavily influenced by Anatole le Braz, the Breton writer whose work he was immersed in before he first travelled to the Aran Islands in 1898. Le Braz celebrated 'a rather medieval peasantry' akin to the Aran islanders and there was a concomitant fear of the dilution or eradication of ancient customs and communities in the march towards 'bourgeois civilisation'.[26]

Dún Aonghasa (Dún Aengus) the stone fort on Inishmore, the largest of the Aran Islands, and set on 300-foot cliffs. An 'archaeological wonder', but had it been used in the ancient past more as a temple than as a fortress?

Aran Island people, May 1939, living on what the impressionist writer Arthur Symons decades earlier had called 'the last shivering remnant of Europe'.

Girls wearing First Holy Communion dresses on Inishmore during the Corpus Christi procession, August 2016. There were 762 people living on the island in 2016. St Enda, an early monastic founder of the Irish church, established a monastery on the island in the late fifth century.

On the road to the Steamer, Inishmore, Aran Islands, early 1930s. From 1912, fish were shipped from the island to Galway City on the steamboat *Dún Aengus*.

Loading the seaweed for manure on Aran, 1930s. There were occasional disputes on Aran over ownership of seaweed, harvested for both food and fertilising purposes.

Steps on Skellig Michael. In 1851 antiquarian John Windele 'gradually became alarmed and nervous as I looked down upon the vast and frightful depths below and the total want of protection'.

A restored cottage alongside abandoned homes on the Great Blasket Island, evacuated in 1953. 'A social system which could let such a culture die must be rotten.' (George Thomson)

Illegal poitín (poteen) stills. Inishmurray Island in Sligo Bay became notorious for its poitín making; John Wynne, who held the lease for the island, maintained in 1846, 'their great evil is their habit of illicit distillation which they carry on now for the purpose of providing their cattle with food in winter ... but the practice is very demoralising.'

A bullock being taken from Inisheer to the *Dún Aengus* steamer in 1939. From 1936 onwards there were numerous disputes over the state-subsidised steamer service from Galway to the Aran Islands.

David O'Callaghan, teacher at the Oatquarter School on Inishmore with his pupils. He was hounded off the island by Fr Murtagh Farragher and lost a slander trial after Farragher told islanders from the altar in 1911 he was 'not telling you not to send them' to O'Callaghan's school 'but if you take my advice you won't'.

Funeral service from church to graveside, following the Arranmore Island boating tragedy in Donegal in November 1935. Nineteen people drowned; there was one survivor, Patrick Gallagher. 'The world says it was a rock ... and the world says it was a fog. But it was not a rock. It was society. The world has spelled out one of its crimes in corpses.' (Peadar O'Donnell)

Early Celtic Christian Ring Fort and monastic settlement on Inishmurray Island, Sligo. William Wakeman's survey of the island was published in 1887 and he described it as a 'museum of antiquities'.

Dublin Opinion magazine, June 1933. The magazine had been satirising Irish pretensions since 1922, and here took aim at the island memoirs. The sparse style of Blasket islander Tomás O Crohan's *An tOileánach* (The Islandman) (1929) was much admired later by novelist John McGahern.

THE LITERARY WAVE
HITS THE ISLANDS

Liam O'Flaherty, a native of Inishmore, published his novel *Skerrett* in 1932, based on the feud between David O'Callaghan and Fr Murtagh Farragher. The instability of island life, suggested O'Flaherty, 'turns friends into foes and foes into friends with startling suddenness. It corrupts the dictionary of human qualities, making the stolid neurotic in their spleen.'

Gearóid O Catháin. By 1950 he was the only child left on the Blaskets and his status attracted an international spotlight: 'I felt that the rest of the islanders were as young as me and that I was as old as them.'
Photo: Donal MacMonagle
macmonagle.com

J. M. Synge's photograph of Aran men on the beach. He first visited the Aran Islands in 1898: 'the absence of the heavy boot of Europe has preserved to these people the agile walk of the wild animal.'

Painter Jack B. Yeats' frontispiece of Synge's *The Aran Islands* (1907). Poet W. B. Yeats was later to suggest that on Aran Synge had made it clear he loved 'all that had edge, all that is salt in the mouth, all that is rough to the hand, all that heightens the emotions by contest, all that stings into life the sense of tragedy.'

A still from the film *The Door Ajar* (2011) by Patrick Jolley which was based on the visit to Ireland of Antonin Artaud, the French poet and creator of the Theatre of the Absurd, who found himself on Inishmore in 1937 clinging to what he insisted was the cane of St Patrick. His controversial Irish sojourn 'belongs perhaps to the theatre of the absurd'.

Theodore Roethke, the American Pulitzer Prize winning poet and alcoholic who stayed on Inishbofin in Galway in July 1960 where he went berserk and was carted off to the mental hospital in Ballinasloe on the mainland. For the island publican, his visit 'was a nice diversion, dispelling the boredom of hearing the same old men of the sea repeating their stories night after night.'

The Back of Tory Island (1960). English portrait and landscape painter Derek Hill found Tory Island a creative sanctuary due to its 'out of the world quality'.

Tory Island aerial view. In 1922, the Catholic priest administering to the islanders noted 'the rock formation is granite, the soil is poor and shallow ... there is a population of 350, of whom two-thirds are said to be destitute.'

Island Voting 1992. Garda Jim Brennan, David Alcorn, the presiding officer and Donal Dufaigh, a radio reporter, return from Inishfree Island to Burtonport, Co Donegal, with the General Election ballot box, containing two votes, in November 1992. Islanders traditionally voted a day before the mainlanders in case adverse weather prevented them exercising their franchise.

Tim Robinson, cartographer and historian of the Aran Islands and the most majestic of the later Aran chroniclers. From 1972, he was transfixed with 'the immensities in which this little place is wrapped'.

Peadar O'Donnell, socialist republican and author of *Islanders* (1927) and *Proud Island* (1975): in the latter novel Mary Jim asks, 'What have we to do with Ireland? What notice did Ireland ever take of us?'

Charles Haughey, Taoiseach (prime minister) from 1979–82 and 1987–92. The most controversial politician of his generation, in 1974, for £25,000, he bought the island of Inishvickillane, one of the six that comprise the Blasket archipelago. The island acquisition allowed him to internalise 'the mystique of the Great Blasket Islands, in the process challenging the assumption that he was an effete dilettante'.

Gerard Dillon's *Island People* (1950). Dillon stayed on Inishlacken Island in Connemara for a year. The island priest, recalled Dillon 'was after me for months to go to mass' but Dillon fitted the island 'like a glove'.

Extolling the peasantry that Daniel O'Connell, the iconic nineteenth-century nationalist and Catholic leader, had labelled 'the greatest peasantry in the world' became quite an enterprise and ultimately part of the creation myth of the Irish state, 'with an aura of pre-history', the islands presented as representing some kind of mythic Irish unity before egregious conquest.

In John Wilson Foster's phrase, the islands were 'at once the vestige and the symbolic entirety of an undivided nation', even if the reality was that some of the islands were 'crumbling from the inside', as reflected in emigration and depopulation. By 1911 there were in Ireland about half as many people as in 1841. Less than half of that depopulation was as a result of the Great Famine itself; the rest was due to falling birth rates and high emigration rates; 4 million emigrated between 1851 and 1891. Kevin Martin points out, for example, that 'Many Aran islanders were more familiar with the operations of the transport system in downtown Boston than the ferocious beauty of the local seascapes.'[27]

But the idea that these islands were 'wells that could be drawn on to recreate Ireland' was a powerful and appealing one, helped by the work of the antiquarians and anthropologists but also in the 1890s by Jeremiah Curtin, who produced works examining ethnicity and folklore. Curtin was the son of an Irish emigrant to Detroit, educated at Harvard, and worked in the Bureau of Ethnology in Washington in the 1880s, where he liaised closely with the Native American peoples. He made three collecting trips to Ireland, the first in 1887. In his memoirs he explained: 'I hope that there might still remain in the minds of the people of the remote districts of Ireland many idioms useful in explaining the language of the manuscripts preserved in the Irish Academy, and myths that would supplement and strengthen recorded mythology.'[28] Curtin explored the links between the Irish language and folklore, and saw it as an urgent necessity to collect material from Irish speakers; as Maureen Murphy puts it 'His concern for the Irish language anticipated the founding of the Gaelic League in 1893'.[29] His books included *Hero Tales from Ireland* (1894) and his habit of recording texts verbatim from informants was highly influential.

In 1892, in Ireland in search of 'a few good myths', Curtin visited

Tory: 'the scene is one of wild grandeur ... the girls of Tory are fearless riders'. The weather turned – 'stupendous white capped waves threatened to engulf the island' – but he was still able to visit all the places 'mentioned in myth and story'.[30] On the Aran Islands he

> spent several days on the island talking with the people and studying the ruins ... I visited them all and the numerous holy wells as well. I took down what myths the old people knew. One aged man, afflicted with palsy, told me a number of 'true stories of the old time'. In relating them he got so enthusiastic that he rapped on my knees or nudged me continually. While we were on the island a policeman fell in love with Ellen, a Carrick [Carrick-on-Shannon in Leitrim] girl who was with us to cook.[31]

There was nothing romantic, pleasing or fruitful, however, about his Blasket Island trip:

> We climbed to the top of the cliff, and there was the village; perhaps twenty straw-thatched cabins, the thatch held in place by a network of straw ropes fastened down with stones. In front of each cabin was a pile of manure. Cattle are kept in the cabin nights. Each morning the earth floor is cleaned by shovelling out the straw, but it is not taken far from the house. It accumulates all winter, and in the spring is carried to the potato fields. The schoolhouse is the best building on the island. It has windows, and the outside walls were whitewashed. Kate, our faithful servant, found the cleanest house on the island and asked of its mistress the privilege of boiling a kettle of water to make tea. The wind blew so hard that a fire could not be built outside. She made the tea, but we could not sit inside to drink it; the house was too dirty. I asked a man on crutches if he knew any Gaelic myths. His answer was 'I care more about getting the price of a bottle of whiskey than about old stories.' Another man said, 'If you'll give me the price of a bottle of whiskey, I'll talk about stories.' I got no stories. Our return trip was not without danger. The boatmen had to row against a heavy

wind. Each time that a wave came toward us it looked as if the boat would fill and sink, but it rose, went down, and up on another wave. Mrs Curtin and Kate were seasick. Fitzgerald, pale from fear, repeated, time after time: 'God willing, this is my last trip in a canvas boat.' We were both thankful when we reached the little cove in safety.[32]

Others had more success, including folklorist and playwright Lady Augusta Gregory on the Aran Islands, who, even before she met poet W. B. Yeats in 1896, 'had begun looking for news of the Invisible world, for his stories were of Sligo and I felt jealous for Galway'. On his way to the Aran Islands in 1896 Yeats was 'fired by the sense of a dawning age' and his sensibilities 'were honed to a fine edge' by this visit. After it, he wrote giddily about fairies and 'new-old Celtic mysticism'. The islands also, as Roy Foster observes, held a special place in the imagination of that generation because the way of life and rhythm of the islanders suggested 'classical parallels to literary-minded visitors'.[33] In relation to the stories, Gregory cared less 'for the evidence given in them than for the beautiful rhythmic sentences in which they were told'. She had no theories 'or case to prove' but merely sought to 'hold up a clear mirror to tradition', for which was needed 'leisure, patience, reverence and a good memory'. As a result of her trip to the three Aran Islands, 'I give the sea stories first'; tales of sea horses and mermaids and an island 'as thick as grass' with spirits. On Inishmaan

> The men would sit in a half circle on the floor passing the lighted pipe from one to another; the women would find some work with yarn or wheel. The talk often turned on the fallen angels or the dead for the dwellers in those islands have not been moulded in that dogma which while making belief in the after life essential, makes belief in the shadow-visit of a spirit yearning after those it loved a vanity, a failing of the great, essential, common sense.[34]

In 1896 Arthur Symons also made the journey to the Aran Islands. Irish writer Padraic Colum regarded Symons as one of the most remarkable of the impressionist writers who had a 'most singular curios-ity' and he was a pivotal figure in British literature in the 1890s.[35] He was the only non-Irish member of a party of four, including W. B. Yeats, that travelled to Inishmore: 'we were nearly four hours in crossing and we had time to read all that needed reading of *Grania*, Emily Lawless's novel which is supposed to be the classic of the islands and to study our maps and to catch one mackerel.'[36] He asserted that 'noting is more mysteri-ous, more disquieting than one's first glimpse of an island'. He was also conscious of their primitivism and that they were 'venturing among an unknown people', but they were preceded by priests who had come on their holidays with bikes and 'a German philologist who was learning Irish'. The cabins, he found, were 'a little better built than those I had seen in Galway'. The islanders had a curiosity and shyness, 'an interest which was never quite eager', while the children were inquisitive and 'perfectly polite and neither resented our coming among them nor jeered at us for being foreign to their fashions ... a simple, dignified, self-sufficient, sturdy, primitive people to whom Browning's phrase "gentle islanders" might well be applied. They could be fierce on occasion as I knew' (a reference to the stoning of a rates collector).[37]

Symons recognised beauty and nobility of gesture and also the 'nar-row lives in which day follows day with the monotony of wave lapping on wave'. This island was 'the last shivering remnant of Europe', where a belief in fairies was paramount, but he was taken in: 'I have never believed less in the reality of the visible world, in the importance of all we are most serious about. One seems to wash off the dust of cities, the dust of beliefs, the dust of incredulities.'[38] He saw a civilisation similar to that of the Homeric poems; interestingly, the oldest man on the island, born in 1812, 'spoke the best English that we had heard there'. He wrote of a tale imparted to him by an islander that was to assume a great sig-nificance in the context of a visitor two years later: 'if any gentleman has committed a crime ... we'll hide him. There was a man killed his father and he came over here and we had him for two months and he got away safe to America.'[39]

That visitor, J. M. Synge, arrived in May 1898 and was eventually to use the tale of the father killer as the basis for his *Playboy of the Western*

World (1907), a play that generated much outrage for its earthy depiction of the west of Ireland and its inhabitants. Synge had met W. B. Yeats in Paris after Yeats had been on Inishmore, trying to gather material for his planned novel, 'The Speckled Bird', but due to his ignorance of Irish, Yeats's progress was stymied. Synge, Yeats suggested, could 'go to the Aran Islands and express a life that has never found expression'.[40] Struggling artistically and already in poor health – he was a chronic asthmatic with Hodgkin's disease – Synge's diaries reveal the calming effect the island had on him. After two weeks on Inishmore he moved to Inishmaan; he was so transfixed and enchanted by the experience he returned to the islands for the next four summers. Soon after he first arrived he found himself 'laid on the outstretched gable of a cliff ... great blue waves rhythm nimbly, from time to time a spray that rises to my face'. He found an old man who had guided the antiquaries George Petrie and William Wilde: 'he is one of the Aran islanders I read of in Petrie's notes when I was first touched with antiquarian passion', a man who has seen 'how the fairies were thrown from heaven and carry in themselves the pain of hell. He deplores continually my inability to follow his Celtic disquisition ... at times he recites poetry ... til he brings tears almost to my eyes though there is nothing I understand. He is unique.'[41] Synge also commented on an island woman who spoke of a bachelor who was seeking a wife and who 'criticised him for the inclination to choose riches before moral capacity omitting even all possibility of love', while, with another man, 'I have not found in him any belief in changelings [in folklore, fairy children, or fairies disguised as children]'.[42]

On Inishmaan,

> my hostess has both the baby and myself to tend, with a family of chickens that occupy a corner of the kitchen and the pigs that are always about the door ... my old storyteller has narrated at length his experiences with the fairies. They have often times interfered in his agriculture ... I did not fully understand but it seems they are all of a height about two feet and wear little caps like a policeman's pulled down upon their faces.[43]

He found great peace at one of the pagan forts which was

a stone's throw from my thatched home ... I shall up there after
my dinner to smoke drowsily in the stones in the shelter that the
round walls ensures ... the antiquarian treasures of the island are
not strictly within the scope of the scatters of ... my notes ... some,
however, possesses such conspicuous individual beauty.[44]

Synge made quite an impact on the islanders. The correspondence
sent to him by islander Martin McDonagh suggests almost a father–son
relationship: 'I was very lonesome after you ... the baits you send to us is
very good ... I am going to write to you some Irish and tell me will you
understand it ... please I want you when you go to France to send me
a small pocket knife.' In reading the letters Synge, who maintained his
apartment in Paris, wrote the English translation on top of some of the
Irish words.[45] He also received flirtatious letters from 'your little friend'
Barbara Connolly, thanking him for photos and looking forward to
dancing 'jigs and reels', but remarking that 'this place is not much in the
winter time; it's all fish ... the summer is near out always when you come
so come early this year'.[46]

By the end of 1898 Synge was publishing stories from Inishmaan
in the *New Ireland Review*, told 'by an old man'. Readers, he suggested
would 'recognise here two motives used by Shakespeare, one in the Merchant of Venice, the other in Cymbeline ... the story of the wager occurs
in Boccaccio ... in several French romances of early date and in a German
tale', but 'it is hard to assert at which date such stories as these reached
the west'. He was in no doubt about 'our heroic tales which show so often
their kinship with Grecian myths ... a comparison of all the versions will
show that we have here one of the rudest and therefore, it may be, most
ancient settings of the material'.[47]

Synge completed his Aran Islands book in 1901 but its publication
was not straightforward. In June 1903 publisher Brimley Johnson apologised for taking 'so long deciding about your manuscript, but the explanation is simply that I was very inclined to take it, from personal taste,
though I cannot see a definite prospect of a good market. I am afraid

that the latter considerations must outweigh the former.'[48] In contrast, English poet and writer John Masefield, in correspondence with Lady Gregory, thought the manuscript was 'excellent ... I have read some hundred and fifty books this year and Synge's is certainly among the best ... I don't know much about what is called the reading public but to me it is incomprehensible that such a book should not be wanted hungrily by the publishers. It is something new in addition to its merit as writing.' He also added waspishly, 'I am afraid its publication will send scores of tweeded beasts to the islands, but that cannot be helped, they will be going there anyhow now that there are motor cars to take them to the coast.'[49]

Some years later George Roberts from Maunsel publishers wrote to Lady Gregory suggesting that 'there are some very amateurish passages' in the book, but its strength lay 'in showing Synge moving about amongst the people'.[50] Synge had recognised the value of that himself; he recorded in his notebook, 'It is a great gain to have learned to wander'.[51] The book was eventually published in 1907, opening with Synge on Inishmore sitting over a turf fire 'listening to a murmur of Gaelic that is rising from a little public house under my room'.[52]

He characterised the islanders as a people of unique individuality but also idealised them to the point of unreality, by describing life on Inishmaan as 'perhaps the most primitive that is left in Europe' along with a warning that 'modern peasant Gaelic is full of rareness and beauty but if sophisticated by journalists and translators it would lose all freshness'. What was unique was the 'exquisite purity of intonation', while 'the absence of the heavy boot of Europe has preserved to these people the agile walk of the wild animal ... their grey poteen, which brings a shock of joy to the blood, seems predestined to keep sanity in men who live forgotten in these worlds of mist'. While they had Catholic beliefs, they also uttered cries of 'pagan desperation' and their claims of kinship were 'more sacred than the claims of abstract truth', while the women's 'red bodices and white taping legs make them as beautiful as tropical sea birds', alongside the island men who were 'as cool and fresh looking as the sea gulls'.[53]

In relation to personality he found both a 'strangely reticent temperament' but also, 'at odd moments only' a 'passionate spirit' that expressed itself 'with magnificent words and gestures'. They had a peace and dignity 'from which we are shut forever' and Synge was not at one with them; the islanders seemed 'strangely away from me'.[54] Synge had a great talent for translating dialect and depicting the dignity and wildness of the islanders. He did this in a way that was unparalleled and informed by direct experience. He made it clear that the community he had observed was full of sexual tension and coyness, interrupted by occasional frankness, such as the girl he encountered who 'told me with seriousness, as if speaking of a thing that surprised herself, and should surprise me, that she was very fond of the boys'.[55] Another character, 'Old Mourteen', wandered off into tedious matters of theology, repeating long prayers and sermons in Irish he had heard from priests, but when they came to a slate house and Synge asked him who was living in it, his tone and demeanour changed: 'a kind of schoolmistress' he said; then his old face puckered with a gleam of pagan malice. 'Ah, master,' he said 'Wouldn't it be fine to be in there, and to be kissing her.'[56]

Synge noticed many other things on the island; medleys of rude puns and jokes 'that meant more than they said', and an obsession with marriage or the lack of it: 'the women were over excited and when I tried to talk to them they crowded round me and began jeering and shrieking at me because I'm not married'. He concluded, in relation to the men,

> the greatest merit they see in a woman is that she should be fruitful and bring them many children. As no money can be earned by children on the island this one attitude shows the immense difference between these people and the people of Paris. The direct sexual instincts are not weak on the island, but they are so subordinated to the instincts of the family that they rarely lead to irregularity. The life here is still at an almost patriarchal stage, and the people are nearly as far from the romantic moods of love as they are from the impulsive life of the savage.[57]

Synge had also busied himself with other projects including the one-act play *Riders to the Sea*, completed in 1902 though not performed until 1904. Fellow playwright Padraic Colum wrote to him to applaud a 'perfect' play, remarking that 'even the few who were against the play began by admitting how impressive it was'.[58] Frank Fay, actor and producer with the Abbey Theatre, Ireland's national theatre established in 1904 'to bring upon the stage the deeper emotions of Ireland', also encouraged him, asking him for more such drama, 'showing what the peasantry had to endure'; not melodrama but the 'smaller tyrannies'.[59] In the case of *Riders to the Sea*, the tyranny was that of the sea and the hopeless struggle against it; it also underlined in the sorrow of the mother, the extent to which 'on these islands the women live only for their children ... the maternal feeling is as powerful on these islands that it gives a life of torment to the women'.[60] When a sea tragedy occurred the hope was for, in the words of Nora in the play, 'a clean burial by the Grace of God'; Cathleen points out that 'It's the life of a young man to be going out to sea', but it too often involved a reversal of the natural order, as Maurya lamented: 'In the big world the old people do be leaving things after them for their sons and children but in this place it is the young men do be leaving things behind for them that do be old'. The women are both impatient but accepting. A young priest suggests 'the almighty God won't leave her destitute with no son living', to which the response is, 'It's little the like of him knows of the sea.' Maurya's final thoughts are that 'they're all gone now and there isn't anything more the sea can do to me ... no man at all can be living forever and we must be satisfied'.[61]

C. P. Scott, editor of the *Manchester Guardian*, was also in touch with Synge in 1905 concerning articles on the congested districts of the west of Ireland 'to bring home to people here the life of those remote districts as it can hardly have been done before'.[62] That life, as recorded by Synge in his notebooks, included poetry, songs, stories and superstitions ('we don't like a cock or a hen to break anything in a house' he was told 'for when they break anything we know that someone will be going aways'), but there were also stories that showed 'the feeling of jealousy that is between the islands'.[63]

Synge also travelled to the Blasket Islands, where he found himself 'being thrown back on my Irish entirely' and enjoyed a 'magnificent air, which is like wine in one's teeth'. But his island engagements were not about unadulterated primitivism. In the acts of photographing, documenting and recording, he and other visitors were also engaged in 'part of the technocratic apparatus of modernity'. Synge even had a row with a boy on the Aran Islands who wanted to be photographed in his Sunday best clothes from Galway rather than the island homespuns that connected him to 'the primitive life of the island'.[64] Nor was Synge averse to violating the islanders' privacy, having to write to Lady Gregory at one stage to explain the islanders had 'forgiven me at last for my indiscretion' after he used without permission a letter of one of the inhabitants in an article.[65]

Another visitor, less artistic, more discreet and not quite as full of intense wonder as Synge as he had different priorities, was Eoin Mac-Neill. Reared in the Glens of Antrim, a Catholic enclave in a Protestant area where there was a long tradition of the Irish language, he subsequently became a clerk in Dublin's law courts and was a future university professor, chief of staff of the Irish Volunteers, in which role he famously countermanded the order to mobilise for the 1916 Rising, and the Free State's first minister for education from 1922.

MacNeill had started studying Irish in earnest in 1887 and he made annual visits to the Aran Islands from 1891 until 1908. During his first trip in July 1891 he wrote detailed letters from Inishmaan to his brother Charlie. Mid visit, he told him he had not yet looked at the antiquities

for the reason that I consider all the time I spend alone as time lost ... I have to go about where the people are at work during the day time ... after the accounts I got I was surprised to find that 90 per cent of the people here can understand and speak enough English for ordinary purposes, though among themselves they never use it.

He had been sent newspapers by a priest and was 'well up on external doings. I find that the people here are not so ignorant of the details of politics as I conveyed to you in my last letter' (see also chapter 1). He came across one man 'who professed himself a good nationalist but said he didn't know what material good home rule was going to do'; MacNeill tried to persuade him otherwise.[66]

MacNeill was fastidious about his finances and had a sociological bent as well as a prissy Victorian sense of righteousness and morality that he brought to his long-winded characterisation of the islanders. This was a far cry from the mixture of earthiness and nobility that Synge was to identify in the islanders later that decade; much of this had to do with the house in which MacNeill was staying. He did not want to take advantage of the hospitality of his hosts, the McDonaghs, and the 'debts of honour' he had contracted: 'I assure you it is easy to find creditors of that kind in this place'. Martin, the youngest of the family he was staying with was 'the best teacher of Irish I have come across yet as he has a grave and naïve way of jumping on my bad Irish which his elders politely overlook'. But MacNeill was in quite a state trying to figure out what to do about the women when it came to parting gifts: 'I don't know what [to do] about the girls. I don't want to give them anything out of consonance with the simple ideas of personal decoration that prevail here. Perhaps it is better to leave them out for this time.'[67]

Another letter saw him grappling with the social differences on the island. In general they were people of 'a high social standard', but the people of the house he was staying in

are much better than a fair average sample. I need not say how few of the people we move among could conveniently allow a stranger to enter so completely into their everyday life as I can do here. All this time I have not noticed an instance of correction or indulgence on part of the parents, nor of disobedience in the children, nor of a cross word between man and wife or among the young folks, nor of a disposition to shirk work or to deceive – faults falsely imparted to our national character – nor, need I say, of an act of civility or courtesy neglected when it could be done ... not one of the family smokes tobacco though nearly everybody else here does. Two faults I remarked, one of them common to all the simple folk in every place, the other, I am afraid Irish, but only accidentally Irish. The first is an extreme inquisitiveness which requires all the readiness one can command to meet without giving offence where no conscious offence is given. The other is that kind of respect for alcohol that destroys in the people's mind the moral force of all the arguments against intemperance. That feeling pervades, I believe, even a great part of the priesthood.

He suggested other countries 'not cursed with over fondness for drink' had faults that Ireland was still free from; in the south of Europe, for example, he maintained 'illicit lovemaking is glorified and prevalent. If we could deprive drinking of its glory here we should deprive it of its prevalence.' But he could not get the household to talk about payment for his stay. He was impressed with the food ('some very dainty meals of fresh bream') and the cleanliness; householder Paidín told him 'he has gone into houses in Galway for his dinner and has left the table without eating a bite'; but they did not know how to keep milk fresh. They had some 'curious customs' but he 'had not yet heard' any cursing or swearing.[68]

The following year, he was keen to introduce them to 'American wonder peas. These folk never even heard of peas and haven't a ghost of a notion of them', but he was doing well on the culinary front with a more varied diet than the previous year, including 'rabbit, ham, bacon and cabbage'. More importantly, he was 'much improving in the speaking of Irish' and one of the islanders was 'a treasure trove of pious recitals ... I find dictation a good exercise ... I took down the Resurrection, a piece of 150 verses and several smaller pieces from him'. He had also gone native in other ways and was 'becoming expert at fowling. The other day I shot four cormorants on the wing, killing two outright and disabling the other two, having only fired five shots.'[69]

MacNeill became something of a sage when it came to the intricacies of visiting Aran and in 1893 sent a memorandum to Joseph Henry Lloyd, among the first students to be sent to the Irish School of Learning in Dublin and now co-treasurer of the Gaelic League as well as a folklorist. The League had been established that year to revive spoken and written Irish, with MacNeill instrumental in its inauguration. Its successful spread involved much idealisation of the Gaeltacht. In 1891, 90 per cent of Irish speakers lived in Connacht and Munster, but the percentage of Irish speakers in southern Ireland was just 19.2. Lloyd sent MacNeill's memo the following year to a prospective visitor and in encouraging him to travel gave a good overview of the Gaelic League's use of the islands:

> Your pronunciation is very good. It is correct Connacht pronun-
> ciation ... what you should now pay particular attention to is the
> idiom or Irish method of expression ... no one should think that a
> literal or word for word translation of English is Irish. In ninety-
> nine out of a hundred cases the idiom differs. Be sure to take your
> notebook with you and write down these beautiful idioms that
> you hear the people use ... if you were to write down a few simple
> songs or stories from the dictation of the people you would also be
> helping to rescue Irish oral literature.[70]

MacNeill's memo was detailed and precise and his opening suggested the commitment to the language did not have to wait until arrival
on the islands: 'if you go 3rd class to Galway [on the train] especially after
a Dublin Cattle market, you have a good chance to meet Irish speaking
passengers'. He warned not 'to patronage' the Atlantic Hotel but to seek
out teacher David O'Callaghan, 'an earnest student teacher of Irish' (see
chapter 4). Inishmaan, where he had stayed, was 'the best of these islands
for an Irish student'. Once again, he also had firm thoughts on alcohol:

> Don't for goodness sake imitate some people in drawing the natives
> to talk by treating. They will talk to you without it, especially if
> they know you want to learn from them ... it was by hearing an
> old man read that I made most progress ... I broke in my ear to
> Irish conversation in this way ... I looked over his shoulder and
> by degrees I kept removing my eyes from the book as I got more
> familiar with the sounded words, only looking at the print where
> I failed to follow the words. In a short time I was able to under-
> stand the fluent speech without looking at the book at all. This is
> a method that I am most anxious to commend to all students.[71]

MacNeill's comments on drink and temperance were also indicative of a focus within some nationalist movements on the virtues of dissociating Irish identity with alcohol. By the last decade of the nineteenth century, some of the issues to be faced by temperance advocates were becoming more crystallised, and were dictating much wider social, political and religious agendas than hitherto. The Irish drink bill alone for 1891–2 had been an astounding £13,014,771, and this was accompanied by 100,528 arrests for drunkenness. The temperance question, it was felt, could be wedded to the wider cultural and spiritual ethos of Irish Catholicism, and in turn used to increase the potency and competence of the Irish national character. There was also a growing emphasis on the necessity of not repeating the mistakes of previous temperance campaigns, and this was done by stressing sobriety as a life-long commitment as opposed to a damage-limitation exercise undertaken in middle age. Thus, as Elizabeth Malcolm points out, by the 1890s 'the Catholic temperance movement, unlike its predecessors did not expect to convert the existing generation (except the most ardent Catholics) to abstinence: it looked rather to successive generations brought up without the taste of alcohol'.[72]

Some islanders were to get a blast of this temperance crusade as a result of the visits of Capuchins, an order of Friars in the Catholic Church who in 1905 were invited by the Catholic Hierarchy (the Irish bishops) to undertake a 'national crusade' against the evils of intoxicating liquor. Faithful and efficient record keepers, the Capuchins were also frank about moral failings in their reports. Their missions included morning and evening sermons together with the administering of the pledge, and also involved return visits and a 'renewal pledge'. There was a particular focus on women in this crusade; a need for 'Catholic women to the rescue' as 'no great reform has ever been effected without the intervention of women'. From the west of Ireland in 1908 came 'the most pleasing testimony' of 'constantly multiplying victories for temperance' while it was noted in 1912 that 'we have of course a percentage of lapsing sinners. It would be a miracle if we had not ... but the great body are staunch and true'.[73] Things were bleak, however, on Achill Island, according to Fr Benignus Brennan in November 1906. While the curate took the pledge

Ochone, Ochone, the memory of it is enough to make one laugh or weep. The people are moral but absolutely indifferent, if not worse. About 330 took the pledge in the district and most of the people didn't come near the church at all. To our exhortations to come to the retreat the old women would answer, 'Musha, may I would and may be wouldn't.' To give a triduum [three-day period of prayer] in Achill and thereby do good would require the eloquence of St Chrysostom [a fourth-century Church Father] the strength of a Jerome [a fourth-century confessor] and the support of the cat o' nine tails.[74]

That was not how the *Mayo News* reported it; the three friars, it maintained, 'came to preach temperance on Achill where it is much required. They attended the different churches for five days. Their mission was most successful. They gave the total abstinence pledge and medals to over 2,000 people.'[75]

But there seemed to be better news the following year from Achill, with a report that at the petty sessions court 'there was not a solitary case of drunkenness on the books, thanks to the good effect of the mission lately given by the great Capuchin fathers. It was the first time in the memory of the oldest inhabitant that there was such an edifying record.'[76] Fr J. P. Connelly, a parish priest on Achill, suggested that temperance work there was complicated by the fact that so many islanders went away for seasonal work; in September 1907 Fr Angelo was informed that any temperance mission at that stage would be a 'useless one' as 'we have at present only the children under 13 and the old people over 60'.[77]

A more perfunctory report for Clare Island in 1906 read 'we preached, gave pledge. Heard confessions during the short time we spent on the island.'[78] Writing from the island, James Campbell wrote to Capuchin Fr Paul that he was glad to learn that the island would be 'blessed with the presence' of the Capuchins 'as such a thing is very unusual here'. But the parish priest of Louisburgh, nearby on the mainland, in a common complaint, suggested 'a few paltry days' would hardly effect considerable change: 'I consider that anything shorter than one week at least is entirely too short to effect any reformation in the intemperate ... we are here in a very remote district, twenty years behind in temperance as well as everything else.'[79] Bere Island (where Fr Benignus, as the visitor, 'had to act as PP and manage the whole parish') and the Aran Islands were also visited by the Capuchins and they also targeted Donegal, another district where seasonal migration was a way of life; Fr James Scanlon in the Rosses noted that in relation to the two islands of Inishfree (with a population of 190) and Arranmore 'those people who migrate to Scotland don't like to bind themselves. The battle against drink is an uphill fight.'[80] Nonetheless, Arranmore was visited in February 1907.

Clare also received the mother of all visiting delegations as a result of the seminal Clare Island Survey. Following a survey by naturalists of Lambay Island, off the coast of North County Dublin, from 1905–6, encouraging results prompted them 'to develop a more ambitious island project', with Clare chosen for its accessibility, size and varied topography. It also had a small hotel, meaning those leading the charge during the 'golden age of Irish natural history studies' could be accommodated, fed and watered. It was the first major biological survey of a particular area and from 1909 to 1911 more than a hundred scientists from Britain, Denmark, Germany, Switzerland and Ireland were involved, incorporating both professionals and gifted amateurs; women also played a prominent part.[81] Naturalist Robert Lloyd Praeger was the organiser and co-ordinator and had the task subsequently of collating and editing sixty-seven separate papers: 'new to science were 109 in a total of 5269 animal species observed as well as eleven in a total of 3219 plant species'.[82]

Other visitors to islands were there for other new innovations. Tragedy struck when Edward Glanville, aged twenty-five, died on Rathlin. He had been lodging on the island for three weeks while working as an assistant to the pioneer of wireless telegraphy Guglielmo Marconi, who in 1898 had turned his attention to Ireland to set up a series of commercial ship-to-shore stations around the Irish coast, beginning with Rathlin and its nearest mainland village, Ballycastle. Granville was killed after falling from the cliffs at Ballycunningham. A witness at the inquest noted that 'there is no path down to the sea where the body was found'. He fell from a great height and the doctor concluded 'death must have been instantaneous'. His landlady on the island offered evidence that 'since he came to me he said he was very happy at being sent here ... he was accustomed to look for curiosities along the cliffs'.[83]

Along with language and Celtic scholars, antiquarians, naturalists and experimenters, those of an artistic bent continued to feel the island call, amongst them a number of female writers who added to the canon of island literature. Emily Lawless published her novel *Grania* in 1892; she had spent much of her childhood summers at a Galway castle. A keen sportswoman and outdoor painter, her depictions of Irish peasant life were hailed by some but resented by others, including nationalists who regarded them as exaggerated and patronising, but *Grania*, a romantic tragedy set on the Aran Islands, was hugely popular and also had interesting points to make about the status of women. Although Lawless was no feminist, she criticised Yeats 'for attaching more importance to the pursuit of literary perfection than to social responsibilities'. One of the points made about her relationship with the islands was that, unlike Synge, who lived for periods amongst the islanders, Lawless had a 'romanticised view based on distant observation'.[84]

But Lawless did tour the island while preparing the novel and her endeavours were also about the 'growing taste for the primitive', not just developing the symbolism of the islands but also reflecting on the tyranny of the sea. *Grania* was a product of her environment but also reflected her status as an outsider with 'a streak of Spanish blood' and she had a disregard for traditional gender divisions. Grania, the title character on an island where the natives were 'not particularly expert fishers' was 'the quickest to draw in the line at the right moment' and in her relationship with Murdough she breaks convention in relation to strictures against 'open demonstrativeness' and touches him, on an occasion where 'the witchery of the night was strong'.[85] What was also apparent was the idea of the volatile emotion of the Celt being aligned to changeable weather conditions in the conflation of landscape and national character; the relief and defiance after incessant bad weather is profound, ending a period of living 'in a sort of tomb – an open air one but still a tomb'.[86] Significantly, in relation to visitors, Grania experiences 'a vehement sense of annoyance' at gentry tourists who are surveying the land and 'enjoying the sense of discovery – for Inishmaan was all but untrodden ground'.

She had 'an angry sense that she was being stared at' and is then satisfied that 'her own fierce sea and sky ... had scared away these fine people so suddenly'.[87]

Caustic comment on the chasm between the visitor's view and the reality of island poverty was inevitable. An observer of Achill in 1890 had noted that 'the tourist may indeed rhapsodise in language fine on the feasts for the eye and soul which the island affords. The people of Achill would be very happy if they could live on such food.'[88] When nationalist MP and cultural revivalist Stephen Gwynn published *A Holiday in Connemara* in 1909 he acknowledged island poverty but concluded life was 'infinitely better' there than in the 'crowded slums' and contrasted the 'unspoilt beauty of coastal girls' with the factory girl, but he was still travelling around a part of the country 'that always lives on the brink of starvation'.[89]

On Inishbofin he observed a burial and the accompanying keening and saw it as 'part of nature's own music, just as the dresses of the men and women fall into tone with the grey and yellow of lichened rock ... everything was part of an unstudied pageant'. Such was the interaction of sky, light and water that a travelling companion's trip to Clare Island was akin to going to 'Fairyland'.[90] James Joyce was not so convinced, however, and had mixed feelings about the work of Synge. Unlike him, Joyce did not embrace the idea of finding inspiration in Irish folklore, but in his story 'The Dead', Miss Ivors tries to persuade Gabriel to go to Aran and when he refuses admonishes him for his lack of patriotism. For Gabriel, the west of Ireland is connected 'with a dark and rather painful primitivism, an aspect of the country he has already abjured by going off to the continent'.[91] In 1912 Joyce and his wife, Nora, did visit Galway and the Aran Islands and he wrote two articles about them, which did not display 'the contempt for Irish rural life and folklore he had evinced in 1902 and 1903 in talking with Yeats and Lady Gregory'. Rather, he depicted Aran 'with the affection of a tourist who has read Synge', noting the unique dialect, local customs and history, and the sixth-century sea voyager St Brendan, who according to some folklore accounts had made the voyage to America from Aran ('Christopher Columbus was the last to discover America').[92]

Another tragic island visitor was twenty-four-year-old Eileen Nicholls, daughter of a higher government official and a family with nationalist sympathies who was a brilliant student and had come first in Ireland in her BA degree in 1906. She was heavily involved in the Gaelic League and had been elected to its executive committee (the youngest to achieve that position). She was also a vocal feminist and article writer who greatly impressed Patrick Pearse. Keen to learn spoken Irish in the Gaeltacht, she had already spent time on the Aran Islands and in 1909 travelled to Kerry. Arriving in Dingle, 'the more she saw the more she wanted to go further west'. This brought her to the Blaskets as a visitor who was significant not just because she was regarded as 'a noble young woman' but also because 'few women visitors had gone alone, especially to stay overnight on the island'. She was known on the island as 'An Lady' ('The Lady') because of her fashionable clothes.[93] She was teaching the island girls to swim when she drowned, as did Donal Ó Crohan while he attempted to save her; Donal's father Tomás, later author of the renowned *The Islandman*, recalled him as 'a vigorous lad, and a good swimmer. He was eighteen years old ... he threw his spade away and took the shortest cuts down the beach until he came to the strand. He didn't take off a thing, his boots or anything else ... he went, and he and the lady were drowned together'.[94]

But it was Eileen's death that generated a national reaction, and those who have dug deep into this tragedy have unearthed associated evidence of class tensions and hierarchies. One account indicated that in relation to attempts at resuscitation Eileen, as 'the daughter of the gentleman', was given priority over the native islander Donal.[95] The island became better known as a result of the tragedy. In the aftermath, Eileen's mother wrote of her daughter's devotion to 'lofty ideals' and her time 'among the simple, loving, true-hearted peasants of Kerry'; she also regularly sent Tomás Ó Crohan money for the rest of his life.[96]

Other Gaelic Leaguers made similar pilgrimages to the islands, including Tomás MacDonagh and Patrick Pearse, both to be executed after the 1916 Rising. MacDonagh's 'extroversion had conquered Pearse's reserve when they met on visits to the Aran Islands'. They also chose Aran's patron saint, Enda, an early monastic founder of the Irish church whose monastery on Inishmore attracted a great number of disciples and who established other island monasteries, as the name for Pearse's school in County Dublin. MacDonagh had first visited the island in 1902 where he was said to have bonded with the locals. The mother of another future 1916 martyr, Joseph Mary Plunkett, sent five of her children to Achill for three months in the summer of 1909 to learn Irish, though its poverty 'had shocked the family and provoked Plunkett to more gloomy poetry'.[97]

Poet Austin Clarke also had an island experience. On Tory, he struggled to find lodgings; he went to a cottage and 'the woman could not give me a bed for she had ten sons in the house'. She put 'milk and large hunks of potato cake before me', but 'no one would take me in'. He found, however, that 'once the strangeness was broken they were a kindly generous people' and was struck by the extent to which 'the islanders rule themselves'. The island experience moved him to poetry:

> The Red Armada of the sun burned down
> From Magheroarty. Melodeons played
> The Waves of Tory and the young girls sat
> Upon the knees of men. I took my sup,
> I kissed the mouth beside me and forgot
> My sorrow and the cold dark tide.[98]

Carl Marstrander, a Celtic scholar from Norway, was encouraged by Oslo academics to travel to Kerry on a scholarship because of his flair for Old and Middle Irish. An outstanding athlete, he was prepared to forgo the Olympics for the Blaskets, where he achieved great competence in the language and was influential for Tomás Ó Crohan. He reminisced later, 'On this St Helena I lived for five months in voluntary jail ... they are rather unstable in their mind, like a lot of Celts,' but they had healthy scepticism about priests, were superstitious, prejudiced, jocular and their speech was 'like a big river flowing from the lips'. As one islander put it, Marstrander's mission 'was to get the fine flower of the speech' that was not to be found on the mainland. In some respects his was a visit that laid the ground for the future Blaskets literature as he convinced them of their uniqueness.

A few years later Robin Flower, a Gaelic scholar working in the

British Museum, who also studied under Marstrander, arrived aged twenty-eight: 'I lead the life of Tír na nÓg [land of youth – in Irish mythology, one of the names for the otherworld] here.'[99] He was followed in 1917 by nationalist and student of Irish Brian Kelly, who was even more important in influencing Ó Crohan and made him aware of international literature, including that by social realist Maxim Gorky, in order to emphasise that 'the lives of ordinary people, fishermen and Russian peasants could be the stuff of literature'.[100]

George Thomson, who read classics at Cambridge and took Gaelic League Irish classes, also travelled to the Blaskets on the advice of Robin Flower to deepen his understanding of Irish. He first visited in 1923 and again in 1926. He was a passionate man, who would 'write to his wife that Irish had thirty-nine ways to express "darling" and bestow on her a beautiful sampling of them'.[101] While he went for the language, he seems to have found the people more interesting and compelling and he connected with the younger islanders. According to his daughter, he would 'rather be in Ireland talking to a fisherman than gossiping in the common room' in Cambridge. He was also a mentor to Maurice O'Sullivan who produced the book *Fiche Bliain ag Fás* (*Twenty Years a Growing*, published in 1933) to add to the Blasket canon. E. M. Forster introduced the book, exaggeratedly, as 'an account of Neolithic civilisation from the inside'.[102]

O'Sullivan grew up without his mother, who died when he was six months old, but her loss is not evident in the book, partly because of a father who allowed him to experience the freedom of his environment ('getting the fun of the world', as Maurice described it) which in itself nurtured, developed and protected him; he was free from 'the oppression of the matrons ... for the women are the devil'.[103] While most reviewers gave themselves over 'to Maurice's exuberance', Ernest Boyd reviewed it more harshly in the US; Ireland, once again, as he saw it, was being saddled with a myth or the supposed 'charm of life without sanitation, adequate food and decent housing'.[104] Thomson had an alternative take; the strength of a simple culture, 'free from the rapacity and vulgarity that is destroying our own', or the idea of a society that was truly democratic and pre-capitalist.[105]

Painters were also attracted to the islands because of the grandeur of the landscapes. Paul Henry felt great pride in his adopted island home on Achill after his first visit there in 1910, and it came to mean as much to him 'as Paris had in my younger days' (he was in France from 1898–1900); the desire to stay on Achill was 'overpowering'.[106] His short holiday turned into a stay of nearly a year, and from 1912 he stayed for another seven years, and underpinned his excellence as a painter of western Ireland and its people. He subtly, if not surreptitiously, sketched the islanders at work and play in the fields and his drawings were strong, simple and full of pathos and were also influenced by the work of Jean-François Millet, whose paintings of the peasant life and nature he had studied closely at the Louvre in Paris.

The desire to live in Achill was also 'a purely emotional one. I wanted to live there, not as a visitor but to identify myself with its life', but 'my making drawings of the people was bitterly resented', especially by the older women, though more sympathetic islanders introduced him to the shier types. He was effusive about the beautiful women and children, who had a 'wild picturesque grace'; he tried to persuade them 'they were much more attractive when they did not try to "dress up"', but they were not for turning.[107] Nor were the men to be ignored, including one with 'a refined, ascetic face, a beautifully modelled aristocratic nose and gentle brooding green eyes'. The life there he found 'wild, often grim, but it was my life'.[108]

In August 1909 Harry Clarke, who achieved renown as a stained glass artist, went to Inisheer with a fellow student from the Metropolitan School of Art in Dublin and 'filled several sketch books'. It was the first of a succession of annual trips that produced drawings of harbour and fishing scenes and oil portraits of the island people in a manner similar to Patrick Touhy's *Aran Fisherboy* (1910). Clarke saw it as 'a very primitive place but very charming for a rest holiday'; he also honeymooned there.[109] Seán Keating's preoccupation with cultural nationalism also became apparent in his paintings during and after 1914, influenced by the Aran Islands, which he too visited with Clarke in 1913. This was also about aversion to the First World War, 'from which he wanted to get away as far as possible', and after 1916 the islands came to represent 'the concept of

Irishness' and a place 'from which a new school of art could be wrought'. One of the results was Keating's iconic *Men of the West* (1915) and *Aran Man and His Wife* (1914). Artists, as he saw it, had to develop their own culture based on their own surroundings and needed to return to their own 'place' and that was 'the Aran Islands in particular'.[110] Jack Yeats also produced *The Man from Aranmore* (1905) to accompany Synge's articles on the west of Ireland for the *Manchester Guardian*. Charles Lamb was similarly influenced, built a house in Connemara and painted on Aran. These painters were ultimately 'to present a coherent image of rural Ireland which was promoted by successive Irish governments at home and abroad'.

There were, however, different layers to this enterprise; the idea of an independent, unromantic hard-working race 'that would help to form a new nation' but also, with Lamb, for example, the interest in illustrating 'the harsh lifestyle'.[111] As with French artists' preoccupation with Brittany and English artists' fixation on Cornwall, it was also about the western Irish island dwellers being 'largely removed from progress and from political turmoil through lack of resources and distance from Dublin respectively'.[112]

Others were drawn to the flowers and fauna, including Terence Ingold, later a botany professor in London and president of the British Mycological Society, who first visited Rathlin in the mid 1920s as a place 'densely populated by noisy seabirds, fulmars, kittiwakes, guillemots and razor bills ... so many seabirds, so massed together'. He also holidayed on Achill, where 'often we were watched by an inquisitive seal', and his interest in mountain ecology could be pursued at a time when 'ecology had only recently entered the vocabulary of biology, the word being virtually unknown outside of academic circles'.[113]

Nor were the islands safe from actors. Orson Welles found himself dancing on the Aran Islands with 'Erin men in Indigo and homespun and beautiful and smiling colleens in nice red skirts ... stamping their leathern slippers on the flagging as the orchestra lays into the night ... and a long walk across the moonlit strand'. Welles was only a teenager in Dublin in 1931 when he launched his professional career at the Gate Theatre. A journal he kept of his trip to Galway was full of 'youthful exuberance' and high-flown prose. He described the west coast of Ireland as 'unknown and unbelievable ... the last frontier of romance' and depicted Inisheer as 'the most primitive spot in Europe, where an intelligent aristocratic people live in archaic simplicity, surpassing anything in Homer'. According to one of his biographers, Simon Callow, this was illustrative of how he polarised life in general into the innocent and the corrupt.[114]

It was left to the redoubtable Liam O'Flaherty, a native of the Aran Islands, to ferociously cut through the piety and the rhapsodies in his *Tourist's Guide to Ireland* (1929). He railed against

> Those literary hirelings that still dishonour our country by trying to persuade us that the peasant is a babbling child of God, who is innocent of all ambition, ignorant of guile, medium between heaven and earth, enveloped in a cloud of mystical adoration of the priests and of Caitlin ni Houlihan [Ireland as a personified woman] the raparee [guerrilla fighter] with a pike in his thatch ... a violent primitive who runs wild, naked and raving mad, once the gentle hand of the priest is raised from his back, a cold sexless ascetic whose loins never cry out for the pleasure of love, a quantity as fixed and unchangeable as the infallibility of the pope.[115]

SIX

ISLAND VISITORS: THE
SECOND WAVE

'heather and seaweed growing out of their ears so to speak'

Liam O'Flaherty upbraided distorted representations of life in western Ireland around the same time as one of the most powerful and enduring depictions of heroic island peasantry was gestating in the mind of the filmmaker Robert Flaherty, who first visited the Aran Islands in 1931. His *Man of Aran* won best film at the Venice Film Festival in 1935. It had been preceded by *Nanook of the North* (1922), Flaherty employing 'considerable sleight of hand' and going 'to great lengths to keep the modern world – with which the Inuit were very familiar – literally out of the picture' while filming in northern Quebec. What he framed as contemporary Inuit life 'was that of previous generations', an example being the use of harpoons to hunt walruses when guns were at that stage the norm.[1]

Flaherty – whose father had emigrated from Ireland and who was familiar with the work of Synge – remained on the main Aran island for two years while making *Man of Aran*, shooting thirty-seven hours for a seventy-four-minute film. He lived regally while the islander subjects endured the full extent of the elements. As with *Nanook*, however, Flaherty had a template that was effective in dramatic terms: an indigenous people struggling heroically for existence against harsh nature, and in *Man of Aran* he continued to bend the truth considerably, as was suggested by the staging of a climactic shark hunt the likes of which had long been abandoned by the Aranites. In bringing such drama to life 'he also continued to indulge in an appalling willingness to endanger the lives of his cast as he sought to frame their existence against the grandeur of the elements'.

Some critics defended Flaherty's taking of such liberties in not distinguishing clearly between reality and reconstructions, on the grounds that such practice was a legitimate tool of his business. As he saw it, he was involved in 'natural drama', not 'naturalism', and, given that some definitions of myth suggest that part of their purpose is to convey an essential truth, 'Flaherty may have gotten some things right along the way'.[2] He was certainly securing his reputation as a pioneer of modern documentary making; he was also drawn to the idea that Inishmore was 'a kind of little oasis ... on the fringe of modern industrial Europe, in which both nature and man have managed to preserve an aristocratic indifference to the unruly passage of time', but ultimately his film was 'not altogether faithful to man or Aran'.[3] As one of the islanders put it when asked if their fame arising out of the film had disturbed their lives: 'they were glad to earn a few extra pounds by showing themselves off, but they saw no sense to it at all'.[4] It was also mostly boring work for the islanders; as was reported in 1934, 'there were people who complained of monotony in this film story of eleven months of work and months of waiting'.[5]

The film nonetheless created a big impact in Ireland and beyond and there were rewarding spin-offs for some of those involved. By the end of 1934, for example, the book *Man of Aran*, by Pat Mullen, who was Flaherty's bridge to the islanders, and *Aranmen All*, by Tom O'Flaherty, another native good at spinning yarns, were in the top ten list of books most in demand from booksellers and libraries in Dublin.[6]

Mullen's father, Johnny, had been the self-styled 'King' of Inishmore and Pat had laboured in Boston, where he had been an active trade unionist; he had returned home in 1921 after the death of two of his brothers to help with the farm; his wife remained in the US and they became estranged. He formed a bond with Flaherty when the filmmaker first visited and when he returned in January 1932 to begin filming Mullen was crucial to the success of the project by persuading the islanders to embrace it; he also appeared in the film as one of the shark hunters.

While Mullen did not shy away from some of the social difficulties of island living, Tom O'Flaherty's books were cosier, with sketches, anecdotes and yarns. He followed *Aranmen All* with *Cliffmen of the West* (1935), which was regarded as encapsulating 'that homely outlook' with its depictions of cliff climbers and fishermen dodging coastguards and catching guillemots, his prose wrapped in bows of comedy, tragedy, piety and rebellion. As one of his characters, Black Coleman, attests:

> It seems to be the will of God that we will pull and tear at life from the time we are old enough to work until we are too feeble to rise out of the corner without getting any joy or comfort except enough to keep life in our bodies. Sure we might as well do the things we enjoy doing even though there isn't much profit in them as to be doing the things we don't like when there isn't much profit in them either.[7]

The Irish premiere of *Man of Aran* in May 1934 was notable for the strong presence of politicians and government members. Bridget Hourican points out it was

> attended by Éamon de Valera, W. B. Yeats, Eoin MacNeill and other luminaries. The nationalist historian and de Valera's close friend, Dorothy Macardle led the chorus of approval with a glowing review in the *Irish Press* praising Flaherty for capturing the reality of the Irish experience. The film accorded with de Valera's ascetic vision of an Ireland of frugal self-sufficiency, but outside Ireland the critical reaction was mixed. The *New Statesman* reviewer was first to question the anachronisms and idealism and the failure to deal with the social situation of the islanders – it was 'man's struggle with nature rather than man's struggle with man ... No less than Hollywood, Flaherty is busy turning reality into romance.'[8]

One acerbic Irish reviewer suggested 'it is quite free of stage Irishmen but only at the cost of being quite free from Irishmen of any kind'.[9] As the most majestic of the later Aran chroniclers, Tim Robinson, concluded, the film caused some tension as 'the way of life it recreated was still too salt in the memory for nostalgia and the simplicities it heroised were seen as brands of poverty'.[10]

But the film endured and, arguably, Flaherty's sojourn heightened political consciousness about the islands which Pat Mullen sought to prick at the time and after, insisting in 1952, 'the islands can be a vital national asset instead of a decaying liability – they can win a world market for Ireland into the bargain'. Mullen was heralded as the man who put the islands 'on the map'. He also gave broadcasts to the BBC and traded on his physical strength – 'physique was his principal marketable asset'[11] – and his ego; he had 'an incurable habit of dramatising almost every incident with himself in the role of hero'.[12] He also traded on the idea, which had a basis in truth, that despite all the razzmatazz and film opening nights in London and New York, 'none of us could live anywhere else',[13] though he spent the last twenty years of his life in Wales. His daughter Barbara, who had remained in the US, also became a performer and dancer and, 'dressed in his fisherman's jersey and rough homespuns, Pat Mullen mingled with a fashionable first night audience to see his young daughter Barbara become a west end star'.[14]

A visitor to the Aran Islands a few years after Flaherty was in another league altogether and, as he arrived, so began one of the most bizarre island episodes that could hardly have been conceived even as fiction. Antonin Artaud, the French poet and creator of the 'Theatre of the Absurd', had inquired via the Irish embassy in Paris of sources '*d'antiques tradition*' in Ireland and 'the Irish diplomats concerned with the case enacted a ... controversy that belongs perhaps to the theatre of the absurd'.[15] Artaud arrived in Ireland in August 1937 on his ill-fated mission and was eventually deported the following month as an undesirable alien. He entered Ireland without a visa but had a letter of introduction from Art Ua Briain, the Irish minister at the Free State legation in Paris, to whom the opium-addicted Artaud had told of his 'personal need' to reach the 'living sources' of the country.

Artaud travelled to Galway and was put in touch with the parish priest of Kilronan on Inishmore, Fr O'Cillín, who found lodgings for him on the island in the house of Seán Ó Milleáin. He stayed for two weeks and held tightly to his strange walking stick, which for him 'was nothing less than the prophetic canne de St Patrick' which had hung in Christ Church in Dublin until 1538. He believed he had repossessed it and was on a mission to return it to the 'sources of a very ancient tradition'. He was remembered on the island as 'a solitary, sick man, a duine le Dia' ('a person with God' – an Irish phrase to describe someone with mental illness) and he left a £1 17s 6d debt after his stay that the Department of External Affairs (DEA) requested Ua Briain to pay back, which he refused. Artaud found his way to Dublin, where a Department of Education translator considered him to be 'travelling light in the upper storey'. He ended up in a charity homeless shelter and then was refused access to a Jesuit building in a Dublin suburb before being arrested, hysterical and starving. He spent six days in Mountjoy Prison before being deported to Le Havre and then interned as mentally ill.[16] Artaud had the disadvantage, if more were needed, of knowing no Irish or English.

Ua Briain reacted angrily to a dressing down by Seán Murphy in the DEA for providing a letter of introduction; he disputed it was any such thing. True, Artaud seemed peculiar, 'but that generally speaking he left the impression of an absent-minded person of the student type'. Another big loser was Seán Ó Milleáin, the owner of the island house he lodged in, as pointed out by the island priest: 'He stayed a fortnight but he had paid only 7/6d in all. He also received 5/- to send a cable to Paris requesting money which never came ... I saw the letter from Art Ua Briain myself and it was my opinion that we were honour bound to heartily welcome Antonin. A lot of people were led astray and poor Seán lost his money to him.'[17]

Ua Briain sneered at the priest's letter, and expressed surprise that 'an educated man such as a parish priest, and one no doubt with some knowledge of the world, should write a letter of this sort'. He thought it a 'preposterous theory' that he should be liable for the debt. Ua Briain also received a deranged letter form Artaud insisting he was a Greek subject and blaming Irish police as 'partly responsible for my current misadventure'. Artaud's mother was approached for the debt but would not agree. Fr O'Cillín also wrote that Ó Milleáin was 'raging, which was no wonder and he vented his spleen on myself, especially when the neighbours started mocking him. And Artaud himself wouldn't let anyone handle his wonderful stick for the gold of the world'. The stick was lost in Dublin and 'exhaustive enquiries' failed to trace it.[18]

Much more punctilious about accounts and island business was Françoise Henry, a French art historian and one of the most significant chroniclers of Irish art in the twentieth century, who taught at UCD, and was an expert on early forms of sculptural decoration in stone, metal and enamel. In 1937 she visited the abandoned island of North Inishkea in Mayo in advance of excavations in search of early medieval remains. She received permission from the Office of Public Works to conduct excavations on condition that any finds would go to the National Museum. She returned in 1938 and again in 1946 and 1950. She left a detailed journal of her earlier tarriances and all her struggles – there were many – with her workers, former islanders from whom she demanded much but who were superstitious, especially about the disturbance of sacred sites, largely illiterate and spoke only Irish. She was also on a tight budget.[19] Henry could be blunt and prone to exaggeration and caricature but her detailed descriptions are engrossing. In April 1937 she noted, 'these men of Inishkea are the first in Ireland that I have ever seen put fishing ahead of everything. And yet, shaking his head, red moustache declares: the young people don't care for it, going out to sea.'[20] Henry struggled with speaking Irish and was transfixed by the sea that 'has no bounds ... long breakers on the shore which roll in with crunching and foaming, as if the sand were being gnawed to exhaustion. Explosions on the rocks, dull, violent, a force coming from one knows not where, that seems the herald of distant dramas.'[21]

The weather drove her to despair many times; when, eventually, boats were able to travel, the men propelling them had 'middle-aged, stubborn, dumb faces' and there was one who 'stammers ... "I don't think we should touch the place where the saint is"'. When the excavations were underway, 'the youngest, who has the face of a Greek God, a face that cannot smile, takes passionately to the trowel ... the crew scratches the sand as rabbits would', and too many only made 'a few half-hearted attempts at digging'.[22] There were tensions, rows and shortages of food and cigarettes, and men behaving 'like spoilt children'. The housekeeper,

Ann, punctuated 'anecdotes and malicious gossip, sometimes coarse, sometimes childish' with pantomimes and sketches, but the bond between them grew: 'until now, I was the stranger whom, together with her people, she considered it rather her duty of exploit. Now there is a kind of unspoken pact between us – the two of us against the men ... in the worst Irish that was ever spoken I gave them a piece of my mind'.

Henry's subsequent visits were also an opportunity for her to underline the themes of both decay and modernisation and independentminded islanders. In August 1946 she wrote of 'this dying island. The sea gnaws at it, breaking the granite slabs, throwing them back on top of the cliffs, devouring the sand whenever it can reach it. The wind wears it away, little by little removing the dunes. The rabbits undermine it ... the sheep gnaw it away.' In her journal in June 1950 she referred to a South Inishkea islander, Pat Monaghan, whose daughter Kathleen lived in Dublin: 'slacks, lipstick, fake diamond earrings. Insists on talking English,' while the next month, once again, the workers were not content: 'Labour trouble! Labour trouble, heavens what trouble!'[23]

Photographers were also inevitably seduced by the islands. Thomas Holmes Mason led a family business in optical manufacturing in Dublin from the 1890s but also expanded it to establish a photographic materials department, 'taking advantage of the growing contemporary interest in photography'. Picture postcards became a staple of the business; a keen photographer himself, he was drawn towards the natural world and archaeology and travelled all over Ireland with his full plate camera, leading to a huge collection of pictures and the publication of *The Islands of Ireland: Their Scenery, People, Life and Antiquities* (1936).[24] Welsh ornithologist and naturalist Ronald M. Lockley, who was passionately prolific in his coverage of islands and who achieved fame for his writing on rabbits – his *The Private Life of the Rabbit*, published in 1964 inspired Richard Adams's 1972 book *Watership Down* – was also in pursuit of Irish island treasures in the 1930s.

Lockley found himself on the Blaskets, where he was told by the islanders that they paid no rent, taxes or rates 'because Dublin cherishes them for their good Irish', but 'they tell you ... that in twenty years there will not be a house occupied in the island' (which proved accurate indeed). He also made it to one of the smaller Blasket islands, Inishvick-illane, whose sole resident, Pat Daly, suggested 'there's no peace with the young folk – they will be tearing off to the fairs and the races and cinema of Dingle'. Another island fisherman was 'surprised to hear that a civil war was going on in Spain'.[25] Lockley was transfixed by the fishing for lobsters and 'the manoeuvring of the canoe ... unconsciously graceful and beautiful ... Blasket men have thick neck muscles, for their heads are forever twisted over their shoulders now to the left and now to the right, in order to watch where they are going'. He was able to feast on 'maize bread, roast Pollack, wrasse and bacon'.

Another islander noted that scholars were coming to the Blaskets 'like bees to the heather ... the trouble is that they have all their brains in their big heads and none in their boots' and were apt to get lost on walks or trapped on dangerous cliffs. An older islander was frank about the extent to which in the summer, the fishing and the visitors could pay dividends but that the unfinished new road, being funded by local authorities to help alleviate unemployment, would be left unfinished in the winter:

> who would blame the youth of today? Three shillings is little enough to get for standing up there in pitiless rain and wind for nine hours without ever drawing a mouthful of a smoke. My soul, there's many of us would rather pull up a notch to the belt and be stretched out in front of the fire eating a cold potato and salted mackerel in fine independence.[26]

References to the scholar bees to the island heather became more frequent and also generated sarcasm and satire; the humorous magazine *Dublin Opinion* had a cartoon on the cover of one edition in June 1933 under the title 'The Literary Wave Hits the Blaskets', a reminder of the fame the expanding Blasket library was generating (see chapter 7). Seán O'Faoláin, however, was not beguiled by the island sages when he went on his travels in the late 1930s with the artist Paul Henry; they wanted to 'rediscover that simpler, more racy Ireland of the people'.[27] What could be more racy than the islands and their people? They went out to Cape

Clear Island in Cork, where O'Faoláin had previously learned some Irish, but with this trip, 'all charm vanishes. There is nothing romantic about Cape'. The Crusoe fantasy had given way to reality; he had gone to Cape Clear when he was young and romantic; he remembered the hearth of the cottage he stayed in and the warmth and courageous spirit of the woman of the house, the kind of person who became for him symbolic 'of human conquest over nature, without which nature is meaningless'. He remembered the sea, the birds and the light that made

> a lovely idleness, but they were and would have been nothing without the ever-present reminders of the challenge they imply and of the acceptance of that challenge by the people ... in every house there are photos of sons and daughters lost in America ... photos of boys drowned at sea ... there is hardly a house without furniture from some wreck ... you feel that this must, after a while, be a cat's hell.[28]

O'Faoláin found Sherkin Island 'much more benign', but when he arrived in Dunquin in west Kerry he observed that a man there 'said the word "island" with contempt' and he was unimpressed with the Blaskets, which he found 'not altogether magic ... I heard no stories of Aristotle on the island ... on the contrary I was frequently bored'. He sat by the hearth with Tomás Ó Crohan and 'I thought he was a pompous old man and I contradicted all his proverbs'.[29] He enjoyed much more the conversation with the couple he was staying with who had been in the US for seven years and were 'shrewd and had detachment ... more free in their minds'. He was cynical about the 'professional Gaels' and their 'innocent elation' in feeling that in visiting the islands 'they had returned to the land of their fathers and were free of the base trammels of English civilisation'. Twenty years previously, he had felt the same sense of release ('like taking off one's clothes for a swim naked in some mountain pool') but now, 'I found I had been happier on the mainland, so I returned there. There was more a doing.'[30]

Welsh native Emyr Estyn Evans, who had the distinction of being Ireland's first professor of Geography, appointed to that position in Queen's

University Belfast in 1945, excelled at surveying historic monuments and prehistoric geography. He had a strong sense of the significance of the islands because of his explorations of the links between landscape, people and heritage, which he insisted could not be understood except in relation to each other (though his brand of anthrogeography, he noted without self-pity, by the early 1970s was 'currently out of fashion').[31] He was probably also drawn to the islands because, as his wife saw it, inside the academic 'was a poet struggling to break free'. In his musings about Rathlin, reputed to have been the first place in Ireland to have suffered from Viking attacks at the end of the eighth century, and where he observed the islanders' clinker rowing boats were of Viking descent, he noted the islanders used to refer to Ireland as a 'foreign kingdom' and offenders against the unwritten island laws were punished by 'banishment to Ireland'. Evans was no abstract academic; he took a party of 'elegantly dressed English schoolteachers' to Rathlin in 1933 to make a survey of the island and they were in for a rude awakening. Not only did they have to take the same boat as the cattle had shortly before them ('and there were obvious signs of their tenancy'), the sea was also too rough to take them back later and they had to spend the night lying on an island floor. He returned in the mid 1940s and the school was closed; an islander predicted that the island would not survive populated. Evans too could envisage it as 'a tenantless hulk, a larger wreck in the Western ocean'.[32]

Interest from visitors and writers continued into the 1940s and 1950s. Daphne Mould, who had been raised as a high church Anglican but converted to Catholicism and then toured Ireland, experienced a serenity on the Aran Islands when being subjected to the Latin liturgy: 'I began to understand how the Catholic Church combines an intimate homeliness with a universality that is above all natural and racial boundaries', and indeed language boundaries: 'I would have been completely lost if the mass ... had been said in Irish'.[33] Brendan Behan, the hard-drinking Dubliner and former republican prisoner who was beginning to make a name for himself with his verses in Irish and his journalism was drawn to the Blasket Islands and made a visit there in 1947. Like many writers and journalists of that era he wrote clichéd romantic pieces for the Irish tourist magazine *Ireland of the Welcomes*, the Bord Fáilte (Irish

Tourist Board) publication. Here, in 1952, Behan waxed about the Blaskets 'where the smoke rises from the last chimneys between here and America and the last of the fishermen sit at the turf fire of an evening, telling stories that Homer heard from his grandmother'.[34] Ten years later he milked it further, in an external and inauthentic way in the book *Brendan Behan's Island*. When he was lying in Mountjoy Prison, he had thought of the islanders and the 'free and independent if frugal lives they and their ancestors had ... their eras of quiet happiness there on the outermost fringe of Europe'. It moved him to lament the death of the islands (the Blaskets was by now evacuated):

> 'The great sea under the sun will lie like a mirror
> Not a boat sailing, not a living sign from a sinner
> The golden eagle aloft in the distance the last
> Vestige of life by the ruined abandoned Blaskets'.[35]

Other writers may have had notions about an island sanctuary but came nowhere near realising them. Brian O'Nolan (who wrote under the pseudonyms Myles na gCopaleen and Flann O'Brien) was struggling badly with his alcohol addiction in the mid 1950s and was keen to get off the drink and isolate himself to write. During a drinking session he spoke with his friend Anthony Cronin about possible escape routes, including Tory Island (O'Nolan was familiar with the Donegal Gaeltacht from childhood and adult trips). The idea to go to Tory seemed to Cronin 'an extraordinary suggestion. There we were drinking poitín of which I had no doubt there was plenty on Tory Island, so the likelihood seemed to me that he would drink himself to death if he went there'.[36] Perhaps it was doubly ironic that the author of *An Béal Bocht* who so mercilessly lampooned the romanticisation of the islands was not averse to seeing one as the solution to his addiction and a space for his writing to flourish.

Visiting representatives of the Irish Folklore Commission made much effort to break down barriers in order to collect precious island folklore and their tasks could be complicated by the sense that they were treating the islanders as museum pieces. Michael Murphy, a full-time collector in Antrim, travelled to Rathlin in 1954:

I think that, on a first meeting, I did exceptionally well over there. The people are grand anyway and I got along with them right away. There is an initial suspicion and even resentment, but I was prepared for this; they have been somewhat 'sensationally' written up by a few Belfast people of cross-channel origin who seem to have approached the people with preconceptions – heather and seaweed growing out of their ears so to speak.[37]

Radio broadcasters also found useful raw material on islands. Proinsias Ó Conluain, who had a distinguished career in Irish radio, wrote a diary of his week on the Aran Islands in November 1949 with Bertie Rodgers from the BBC to make a programme. As the rain squalled outside they danced and drank ('a keg of porter on the BBC's tab!') in a cottage. Rodgers made a remark about the sea as a 'halter around men's lives and the land a stone about their feet', but Ó Conluain saw the sea differently (and far too romantically) as 'a great plain of freedom and identity, the rocks beneath their feet securing them, rooting them to their heritage.'[38]

As for tourists, information was, according to Brendan Scally, who journeyed to Achill in 1947, 'given by word of mouth' at that stage. It took sixteen hours to reach Dooagh on the island after leaving Dublin. Much action centred on the pub of Sonny O'Malley, which was 'hectic ... his Da used to burst into the pub from the kitchen after closing time like a flaming dragon, larruping everyone with his stick to clear the house. He laid it heavily on backs and shoulders but avoided giving the visitors the same treatment.'[39] Contributors to *Ireland of the Welcomes* were not quite as earthy. Writer Francis MacManus extolled the wonders of 'Life at Europe's Edge', in his case on a visit to Cape Clear. His claim that 'there is no room on the Cape for people to be enemies' was as erroneous an assertion about islands as could be found. More credible was his contention that 'who tells the story of the island, also tells, in miniature, the story of Ireland, even down to the empty houses'. Writer and actor Walter Macken, in his *Ireland of the Welcomes* essay, eulogised the 'mists rolling down the mountains' of Achill, while for Kevin Danaher, a member of the IFC who had received training in Scandinavia and had recorded the last native Manx speakers in the Isle of Man, they were simply 'the magic islands of myth and folktale'.[40]

Some journalists were bemused by the tourist influxes, including Malachy Hynes, who wrote about the Aran Islands in 1943 and its people – 'a race within a race' – who through centuries had 'refused to surrender to all the man made deviltry bombarding it from ashore' and where, alone in the modern world, the inhabitants 'remain unpredictably human beings who have the spontaneity of the wind-tossed gulls'. What they were now faced with was tourists armed with cameras and spyglasses 'and festooned with codological-archaelogical tourist folders'. Because of the war, Aran was now a 'must' on the itinerary of 'the intelligent Irish vocationalist' and visitors included 'the long-haired men and short haired women of Dublin's cocktail bars, hangers on in the outermost confines of the capital's artistically lunatic fringe ... "Those shadows moving about – they must be living beings! Quick! – the glasses!"'[41]

Former Irish revolutionary Ernie O'Malley, author of the classic autobiography of the revolution, *On Another Man's Wound* (1936), was also a visitor to the Aran Islands in 1944, and what struck him most, according to one of his diary entries, was a native's inability to speak English. He had approached a 'merry faced man' to find out the make and tonnage of his boat,

> but he spoke no English. He was about forty-five or fifty. That came as a shock ... why it should be a shock I don't know, but it suddenly brings you up against a foreign language in your own country, the foreign language being the native language and your language being the foreign language. And you realise that there is another way of life close to you that you can barely plumb save you have a very good knowledge of this language and have lived amongst them.[42]

Also in 1944, author, illustrator and engraver Robert Gibbings wrote about the Connemara islands for the literary and social realist magazine *The Bell* (in 1917 he had been stationed as a member of the British army at Bere Island in Cork). By that stage he was also an established travel writer: On Inishark, he was struck by the 'grey sea, grey cliffs, grey mist that silvered everything' and an old woman of an island house who was 'so serene, so monumental. She seemed as much a part of the house as the dresser and its china that stood against the wall'. He also wrote admiringly of the rowers of the island currachs and moved on to High Island: 'ashore with our provisions. Whether we could get off again next morning was another matter.'[43]

A year later, English artist Elizabeth Rivers, part of the progressive 'twenties group' of artists in London in the 1920s who moved to the Aran Islands and lived there in the 1930s before moving back to the capital, published her limited edition book *Stranger in Aran* (1946). She admired their skills; islanders who 'use a spade with the dexterity of a carpenter with his chisel' and newly dug fields that were 'works of art'. She recorded the importance of dress, ritual and matchmaking ('the girl herself may not, and often has not, any choice on the matter'). Acute concentration was also emphasised ('seemed to be tireless'), as was the centrality of smoking: 'we don't have poteen any more, we've only the tobacco'.[44]

A young Edna O'Brien, future renowned novelist, wrote an article on the Aran Islands for the *Irish Press* newspaper in 1952: 'no, we weren't drifting from civilisation – we were meeting a newer and more respectful friendliness that Galway, or Cork, or Dublin could never even imitate'. She then waded into the mush so derided by Seán O'Faoláin: 'Aran is a place where wonder never dies ... the rich rolling rhythm of Gaelic tongues will stay like soft music always zithering in my ears and above all else the Aran people's warmth will be like the glow of a hearth fire shaming the stiff stinted friendships of central heated cities and suburban towns.'[45]

Another author who wrote, much more substantially, about the Aran Islands was Richard Power, who worked as a civil servant and in 1950 was awarded a scholarship from Comhdáil Náisiúnta, the central steering council for the Irish language community, to research the lives of the Aran islanders. He spent six months on Aran and another six months in Birmingham, where he laboured with island emigrants. His resultant novel, *Úll I mBarr an Ghéagáin* (1959), was translated by his brother Victor as *Apple on the Treetop* in 1980. It was a masterpiece and was followed with an English language novel *The Land of Youth*, set on the fictional island of Inishkeever but based on his experiences on Aran, detailing a doomed love affair between an island girl and a man preparing for priesthood. His first novel was regarded as presenting 'the real Aran'.[46] He was strong in depicting the relationship between the sexes; young men 'with too many tricks learned in Birmingham city' but also girls who were not afflicted with innocence: 'they already knew a good deal about life, better maybe than the girls that come here from other places', including one characterised as 'a whore, no modesty, no shame'.[47] Power was captivated by their potency and good looks ('young and virile with thoughtful eyes, a mocking grin on their lips') and their artistic use of language ('they weave it like they'd be knitting each incident and each nuance like a twist in the thread ... a cast of mind unique, a gifted vestigial way of thinking'). On discovering that some of the visitors are writers, the character Bartley responds scathingly: 'So you tell me, is it looking for material they were? Oh, mischief! Isn't it a dirty rotten pair they are to come here to make money out of decent poor people.'[48]

Power contrasted the physical beauty – 'I took pleasure in the marine green light playing on a large brown rock just under the surface ... with each wave that swelled, the rock would expose a small scabrous wound that opened up and spread like a flower opening to the sun' – with the material realities, including fishermen who complain 'about the government that let foreign trawlers scoop in and sweep away every single fish, no matter how small ... there's nothing in a grant but a palliative and a bribe'. Others maintained the islanders were 'prosperous unbeknownst to themselves'; unlike city people on the dole they had food a plenty.[49] Power was well versed in the politics of the Gaeltacht. A German engineer on the island wonders why the government will not entice islanders to move inland: 'the state is only wasting money and effort keeping the people here ... which would you prefer: to put an ideal like that into effect, so that you have a few old people here in forty years talking Irish or new bustling villages in the midlands cultivating the soil and bringing up large families?'[50]

Instead, many of them emigrated. Power tracked down his island friend in Birmingham – 'digging pathways in a new housing estate ... I'd be sort of ashamed to go home now' – and saw 'young boys, just after arriving for the first time, still wearing the white, western sweaters'.[51] Some emigrants had, however, returned in previous decades. Power's *The Land of Youth*, set in the early twentieth century, sees Barbara return after three years' 'freedom' in the US; she returns on impulse but for the first time thought of the island 'as a precarious place to live ... it was the tone of the island, tolerant, but with an underlying malevolence toward what was beyond its experience'.[52]

The Belfast artist Gerard Dillon, largely self-taught, found himself unexpectedly on the Connemara island of Inishlacken (with a population of just seventeen), about a quarter of a mile off the mainland and a few miles from Roundstone village. Dillon lived on the island for a year. It was both productive and liberating; the painting *Island People* (1950) was one of a series he produced while there. The Dublin art dealer Victor Waddington financed his stay. A gay, northern nationalist, there was much advantage as he saw it in escaping the suffocations of his era to what he regarded as a rural idyll and he integrated well.[53] His painting was notable for its almost childlike style; a seemingly naïve but vivid expressionism, but that was its strength and when he died in 1971 James White, director of the National Gallery, noted, 'He looked at the world wide-eyed and innocent. Fortunately he has retained this virtue ever since.'[54] At an art auction in 2007 one of his paintings of Inishlacken sold for over £180,000, more than double the guide price.[55]

Dillon was reluctant to leave the island, but had to in order to sell his paintings.[56] Crucially, however, he was not alone in the summer of 1951; two older artists, James MacIntyre and George Campbell, joined him. Dillon had told the other two, 'You'll love it ... a real peasant life.' MacIntyre characterised them as 'three mad eejits of artists living on Inishlacken' who were frequently 'flushed with Guinness'.[57] The island priest, according to Dillon, was 'after me for months to go to mass'; he eventually agreed. The artists used to row to Roundstone for provisions but that was not always possible, leading to nicotine withdrawal crises, but they also had calm mornings 'listening to the island's first stirrings'. Dillon was 'temperamentally more suited to island life than George, being blessed with patience'. One island man, in response to a query as to why he couldn't swim, answered "'Ach, that would only make ye a careless fishermen and you'd take chances with yourself and the currach.'" On trips to the mainland (sometimes they were 'scared witless' but also had beautiful silent nights that enfolded them) they enjoyed some lavish sandwich dinners with writer Kate O'Brien, who also bought some of their drawings.[58]

Dillon was regarded as fitting the island 'like a glove' due to his calmness and self-sufficiency, whereas for George it was 'all right in small doses' and for MacIntyre it was invigorating; he left it fitter, 'mentally stimulated, ready to attack my painting with renewed energy'.[59] But the island was struggling to keep its few inhabitants; the *Tuam Herald* reported in June 1963 that Galway County Council had been told 'all the islanders had been moved to the mainland during the past year', but there seems to have been an intermittent presence until 1975.[60]

The three artists were certainly better behaved on their island than the American poet and Pulitzer Prize winner Theodore Roethke, who was on Inishbofin in July 1960. Such was his egregious carry-on that he ended up in the county mental hospital in Ballinasloe, Galway. He had travelled to the island at the behest of another writer, Mayo native Richard Murphy, who had built a retreat on Omey, a tidal island on the western edge of Connemara, and subsequently bought High Island, three kilometres off the north-west coast of Connemara, which contained an ancient monastic settlement; it had no landing place and Murphy spent periods on his own there in a beehive cell. Murphy had hoped Roethke might help him find an American publisher. Both Roethke and his wife, Beatrice, were dressed in city clothes as they clambered on to Murphy's boat at Cleggan; his wife, a former New York model, looked at the vessel 'with unconcealed disdain', while Roethke sat in the boat 'his high forehead creased with anxiety, sweating alcohol. He groaned a little now and then.'[61]

Roethke was particularly drawn towards Miko's pub on the island. To the locals Roethke, who thirsted after not just alcohol but fame, appeared a 'big-mouthed Yank, flush with dollars and bravado', but for the publican it was a nice diversion, 'dispelling the boredom of hearing the same old men of the sea repeating their stories night after night'.

Roethke drove his wife to despair, keeping her awake with his ranting, after which he would 'redeem himself by writing at dawn a contrite lyric celebrating her beauty and his love'. The dawn, however, was also a time for some of his whiskey consumption.[62] Beatrice sent for a doctor, who signed a certificate of insanity committing him as a voluntary patient to St Brigid's hospital. While on the island he had sent letters to Dorothie Bowie, a secretary in the university where he had taught and well used to dealing with his mania, demanding that she send him – 'air express' – various writings: 'we're both splendid and will be permanently so'. In another letter he raved about not the island's beauty but the majesty of the fish and fowl: 'finest lobster in the world, fresh mackerel, curlew, brown trout, turkey, geese, wild duck etc'. His next letter to her was from the hospital: 'am resting here for ten more days'.[63]

He referred to the hospital as the 'bughouse'; decades later, Irish writer Kevin Barry framed a short story about the episode:

> On Inishbofin he looked to the sky and saw fires on the moon. He lay wrapped in his overcoat on the pier all night long and for a while a safe harbour it seemed. Yes there was a bottle and Mars was also visible ... Shall I ever be satisfied, he asked himself, quite harshly, on the pier at Inishbofin, his legs crossed at the ankles ... what he thinks is this: maybe I can make my own mythology still.[64]

Roethke was dead three years later. One of his biographers suggested at the time of his Inishbofin interlude that 'Ted realised he was getting ill and he wanted treatment'. He had notions of spending Christmas on the island but experiencing the rain on a brief visit in October may have dissuaded him; he did, however, return for another trip, which was a lot less dramatic, 'writing more and drinking less'. He found a balance and peace, and 'there was always someone to listen to'.[65]

Heinrich Böll, recipient of the Nobel prize for literature in 1972, first visited Ireland in 1954 and his impressions of the country, *Irisches Tagebuch* (*Irish Journal*) (1957) became a very influential and bestselling book on Ireland in Germany. Böll had been exposed to Irish fairytales in his youth and later explored the work of many Irish writers including Synge and some of the Blasket writers. He spent a lot of time on Achill, and what captivated him most was the weather: 'The rain here is absolute, magnificent, and frightening. To call this rain bad weather is as inappropriate as to call scorching sunshine fine weather.' He was also absorbed by the 'skeleton of a village' on Achill, the cottage he stayed in close to this deserted hamlet that had been ravaged by emigration.[66]

The English portrait and landscape painter Derek Hill found a productive solitude on Tory Island; the only other place he found its 'out-of-the-world quality' was in Mount Athos in northern Greece.[67] But outside of periods of artistic isolation, Hill embraced the island community with considerable gusto. He first went there in 1954 and was to make thirty annual visits (though not during winter); an exceptional group of paintings recorded this connection at a time when 'visitors were rare and returning visitors were seen as eccentric ... stubborn necessity made it a community. Derek's response in those early days was soon grounded in a compassionate understanding of the hardships faced by the island community'. Bruce Arnold notes that one of the first friends Hill took there was art critic John Berger, 'who said the islanders were like survivors from a wreck in the middle of the sea with no hope of ever getting ashore', an emphatic rejection of the romanticisation of island life.[68]

Hill rented a hut from the Commissioner for Irish Lights; a small, crude telegraph lookout post 'over 150 feet up at the top of a cliff' and 'the islanders left him undisturbed'. Although he was sociable, he 'followed a dedicated work routine governed by the light and the source of the sun's rays' but also the storms: 'the rougher the element the more paintable I find the island ... it is then that I feel most part of the island, marooned there by the elements'.[69] The image that Hill gave of himself was powerful: 'lying down on the grass and rock to paint, his face into the wind that was too strong to sit or stand in ... he once said that he found in the raw monotonous tumult of the people's lives on Tory a strange kind of peace'.[70] Hill also encouraged islanders to paint and they became a distinct painting 'school' that included John and James Dixon, James Rodgers and Patsy Dan Rodgers, while other painters such as Raymond Martinez by the mid 1960s were also consumed: 'I must return,' Martinez wrote to Hill in 1965, 'I never before realised the vast difference between the light here to England.'[71]

But there was some consternation when, in 1962, Hill arranged for potatoes to be delivered to the island after a poor crop, with resentment about public depictions of island impoverishment and exposure of divisions amongst the islanders about how to interact with the mainland. The *Donegal News* reported on this 'embarrassment' in August 1962 and, furthermore, that islander Paddy McGinty was 'heading a group of Tory men who had come ashore to have the stories of hardship on their island home repudiated'. While the early potato crop had failed, the subsequent one did not; as to the news that Hill had personally donated £50 and a further £100 had been raised, it was 'rumoured' that Tory would not agree to a scheme that 'set them down as a poor relation of the mainland'.[72]

Hill also clashed in the 1970s with a priest who was said to have favoured resettlement on the mainland. This was part of Hill 'gaining the trust of some on the island whose relationships with authority, convention, the institutions of church and state and with each other were of an unparalleled individuality. Tory was a fighting community.' That fighting could be debilitating, and Hill's correspondence about the island was by no means just about wondrous nature; D. Collum from the post office on Tory wrote to Hill from the late 1950s, 'recounting various punch-ups and rows on the island', while fellow islander Patsy Dan Rodgers also wrote letters, 'some of them voluminous', to Hill that 'deal with painting as well as all aspects of Tory life – much of it fairly turbulent'.[73]

Given the pace of modernisation, technological change, increased urbanisation and noise levels domestically and globally, along with the sense of both the vulnerability and value of a more traditional way of life, the islands attracted visitors looking for sanctuary but also material for academic theses or research, and such quests generated tensions. The most famous visitor to an Irish island in the twentieth century was John Lennon, during a period when he was preoccupied with his Irish roots (his grandfather Jack was born in Dublin in the 1850s). In November 1969 newspapers were filled with stories about this and the prediction, in the words of the *Connaught Telegraph*, that 'Hippies may live on Mayo Isle' as they had been offered Dorinish Island in Clew Bay by Lennon, who had bought it when it was offered for sale by the Westport Harbour Board in 1966 for a reputed £1,700.[74]

In 1971 Sid Rawle, known as the 'king of the hippies', and twenty-five of his fellow travellers, duly occupied the island, but quit it after eighteen months; later Rawle would say 'Dorinish was heaven and it was hell'. The hippies who set up an island camp called themselves the Diggers and lived in tents, but could not survive the weather and lack of good soil. Lennon himself visited it for the first time in the summer of 1967 and was taken out on a raft by a local, Paddy Quinn ('I didn't give a shite who he was ... I didn't know who they were'). Lennon spent less than two hours there and the next time, in the summer of 1968, he travelled by helicopter with Yoko Ono and plans for a house on the island were reputedly drawn up.[75] Kevin Barry's 2015 novel *Beatlebone* tried to get into the mind of Lennon in relation to his island venture; a tortured soul who wanted three days there alone for some primal scream therapy: 'that is all he asks. That he might scream his fucking lungs out and scream the days into nights and scream to the stars by night – if stars there are and the stars come through.'[76] But it was not easy, owing to the weather, to get to the island that was 'nineteen acres of rocks and bloody rabbit holes'. As Barry saw it, it was not surprising Lennon's idea of a house there came to naught; one imagines it was not long 'before the idyll of a new West was smeared by the great dreariness that Ireland attempts to stay quiet about. Imagine the near perpetual assault of rain.'[77] The island was sold by Ono after Lennon's death in 1980, with the proceeds donated to charity.[78]

Shortly after Lennon's island flirtation, John Messenger, from the University of Indiana, published his book *Inis Beag: Isle of Ireland* (1969) (the fictional name he gave to Inisheer, the smallest of the three Aran Islands) which, its editors suggested, would 'doubtless raise controversy among Irish journalists, particularly those of nativistic persuasion', as it depicted an island life that was at odds with 'romanticism and nativism'. Messenger and his wife spent nineteen months on the island between 1959 and 1960 and they 'participated exuberantly' in island life 'in the best tradition of anthropological field work'.[79] Messenger raised some hackles with his comments on 'Puritanism' and a 'Jansenist [emphasis on original sin and depraved humanity] denial of sexuality' and suggested that for Irish 'scientists' to acknowledge the impact of religion on sexuality 'would be to commit job suicide'.

Messenger had a fine welcome for himself and boasted that it was 'rumoured that I was responsible for the replacement of a curate by complaining of his opposition to my research'. Most 'Inis Beag' people, he concluded, 'believe themselves to be materially poor ... although they resent others agreeing publicly with this view'. There was hostility to 'visiting Yanks' and antagonism towards governments that initiated island projects 'without consulting the islanders' with visiting Gardaí 'subjected to frequent criticism and derision'.[80] Messenger's book was riddled with contradictions and he was not as clever as he thought. As seen earlier, he found the islanders 'devoutly Catholic' but also 'extremely critical of their priests and [they] retain and reinterpret pagan religious forms'. He detected 'fear of the clergy and anti-clericalism', and also singled out the 'unwillingness of many men to accept the responsibilities of marriage, particularly its sexual responsibilities'. Yet there were also women complaining 'of the sexual demands of their mates'.[81]

So who was telling him what? And what trust existed? At least he could acknowledge the difficulty of obtaining reliable information and the islanders 'long tradition of verbal skill ... My wife and I took great pains to disentangle real from ideal culture by substantiating interview data with observation wherever possible.'[82] In truth, however, most of this was stabbing in the island dark. Messenger fancied himself as a psychiatrist as much as an anthropologist and conflated their suspicion of him and his ilk with wider personality issues. He and his wife switched to 'peasant' Ireland after 'being trained as Africanists and doing our first research among a non-literate group in Nigeria'. Not only that, but another reason they undertook the project was because 'we shared brandy and cigars with this most charming and persuasive cleric' who had been posted on the island and persuaded them to record life there.

On the island, Messenger found 'a people whose basic personality features such traits as sexual repression, hypochondria, depression, masochism, secretiveness, envy, jealousy and feelings of inferiority and whose behaviour is obsessively governed by the fear of gossip, ridicule and opprobrium'. Yet they had a well-defined comic tradition and dislike of 'inquisitive ethnographers'.[83] He also referred to his 'robust manner' but did not seem capable or willing to join the dots in relation to his possible duping, given that he could assert with a straight face that the Irish possessed 'one of the oldest and richest oral art traditions in the world' and in weaving legend and anecdote also weaved 'wings of fancy ... honeyed words and obfuscation.'[84] There was also the nonsense Messenger pedalled about the 'many ways' he attempted to 'conceal' the identity of the island, as if that was remotely possible, given the accompanying maps, photographs and detailed descriptions in the book.[85]

Messenger suggested hostility to his work was based on feelings of inferiority, and that he got a boon to his research because islanders' inability 'to evaluate our intentions' meant their guard was down, but those who knew the islanders a lot better suggested the Messengers were 'spun all kind of yarns'. That too might have been exaggerated; another contention was that all of the interest in the islands from visitors encouraged a 'restrained narcissism', allowing them to find themselves especially interesting.[86]

Leading Irish journalist Michael Viney, who became renowned in the 1960s for shining lights on dark corners of Irish society, was well placed to assess the ethical implications of the methods of the 'Yank in the corner' or American social researcher in Irish rural communities, partly because much of it was based on what Messenger termed 'conversation monitoring' (eavesdropping) and given the extent to which it 'focuses invariably on dysfunction'. Viney noted that some of the inhabitants of Inisheer walked away from Messenger when he and his wife returned in 1975, six years after the book was published.[87] Nancy Scheper-Hughes was also to cause anger with her book on mental illness in rural Ireland, *Saints, Scholars, and Schizophrenics*, published in 1979 and suggesting conflicts abounded about nurturance, physicality and sexuality, the product, she asserted, of the 'ascetic Jansenist tradition of Irish Catholicism'.[88]

Viney himself had become an intrepid island explorer with more endurance than most in the 1960s; he camped alone for three weeks on Inishvickillane in the Blasket archipelago in 1965 and described the 'vivid intensities of solitude'. Two years later he spent another three weeks on the uninhabited island of Caher in County Mayo, but this time he brought his wife and was the better for it: 'Crusoe isn't complaining at having a girl Friday who doesn't mind washing her hair in a billycan.'[89]

Many visitors remained concerned about the impact of modernity. One traveller to the Aran Islands wrote in 1967 to Irish actor Arthur Shields, who had settled in California and whose last visit to Ireland was in 1964: 'the large island is changing rapidly but the others are as Synge saw them'.[90] Journalist John Healy had written about Achill Island two years earlier and referred to 'an every day scene in the month of August' with a Triumph sports car whizzing by: 'each year the island does better and better in the matter of tourism ... the island is jammed full ... big fat beer lorries come snaking in an Armada through Achill Sound'. But that also underlined the degree to which there was another Achill Island, 'the island of the grass widows and the men and women who sneak away into statistics of another kind in the early dawn when the carousing tourists are scarcely in their beds', including those who were still heading 'for the train to Dublin and the boat to England'.[91]

But there was still much to be found on the islands for those seeking an antidote to an invasive materialism and by the late 1960s and early 1970s, the tourist message had been honed to a succinct 'escape from the twentieth century'.[92] Welsh native Andrew McNeillie was in search of a 'sea, pastoral adventure' at the end of 1968 when he moved to Aran and stayed for nearly a year, a place where 'extremity of matter and of mind, at the edge of the world, go hand in hand'. Weather, of course, continued to have the habit of destroying utopian notions and left 'no chance to relish the romance of voyaging'.[93] There was however, the fulfilment of independent living and domesticity: 'my husbandry a satisfaction in itself'; learning how 'to nightline for a fish and how to net a rabbit through a dry stone wall ... I liked to turn things upside down, to fish and sleep as the seas permitted and tiredness demanded'. But the weather ultimately imposed a restricted existence: 'I scribble. I read much. I prowl, restlessly mooching from window to window, making observations or looking for anything to observe.'[94]

Any opportunity to break the ice with the natives was welcomed and McNeillie learned of the prospects for young men little older than himself 'with nothing you could call a creature comfort ... no wife for company, no hope of one upon the horizon, a father in the mental hospital in Ballinasloe, a mother ostracised for the love child she'd had by a visiting labourer'; and yet, their stoical lives 'seemed to chasten me and I wanted to live as they did'.[95] That did not include attending Mass: 'In the midst of the devout I was Inishmore's sinner in residence that year'. Nor did the islanders have much time for the idealisation; a local man told him 'never trust the sea ... even on dry land ... fuck the Man of Aran'.[96] Nor could McNeillie tolerate those whose visits were more temporary than his, 'the plastic mac'd folk you tended to come upon, limping about in the mist, religious types in new sweaters, pilgrims, poets, Irish, Yanks, Britons. I learned to resent them as if I was a native ... they had no idea what times I'd had, through November and December.'[97]

A few years later theatre director Joe Dowling brought a group of forty 'tough teenagers from one of Dublin's most socially deprived districts' to the Aran Islands to get them to work on dramatic improvisations on the subject of Inishmaan in Synge's time, including an enactment of the rent collector's autumn visit: 'He has got them to recreate the sounds of the island: sea, wind, waves, cows, dogs, a storm with thunder. He has got them to row imaginary currachs in smooth and stormy seas.' They also discussed the contemporary challenges facing the islanders; 'the boys talk with concern of the needs and rights of the people ... they wax romantic about the dignity of their poverty, worry about them being exploited for the sake of the tourist trade, suggest ways to encourage the young people to stay to work on the islands instead of leaving for England or Dublin.'[98]

Others continued to pursue deep engagements with the islands born of personal or creative quests and dilemmas. Experimental playwright Tom MacIntyre, whose nature was 'to be on the outside' and whose plays were, according to poet Michael Longley, 'strays, wandering in the margins of the dominant discourse', spent time on Inishbofin and was asked to referee a match between its natives and those of Inishturk in front of spectators who were 'venomously eloquent'.[99] But his move to Inishbofin to live in 'resonating isolation' was also part of a mid-life crisis; isolation and silence enabled him to 'write a play without words' which became *Jack be Nimble* (1976); it used mime and represented a 'cathartic sense of starting again'.[100]

A decade later, Denis Smith, a firefighter in New York, came to Aran ('I came as a romantic') and after his three-hour boat journey had to reassess some of his preconceptions: 'no traditional dress to be seen'; instead women 'with their firm young breasts clearly outlined and unharnessed beneath their cotton T shirts'. This was a steaminess that would 'probably have thrown Synge for a loss'[101] (or maybe not, given that Synge had created controversy due to sexual frankness, most notably in the line spoken by Christy Mahon in *The Playboy of the Western World* – that he would have no other woman but Pegeen Mike, even if offered 'a drift of Mayo girls standing in their shifts'[102]). Tourism, Smith suggested, had rendered the traditional Aran patriarch 'an adjunct of the woman', but not all were welcoming; the young islanders 'appeared xenophobic'. One girl who smiled at him 'went sour when she found out I was American'.

Some of the natives spoke Irish to exclude and Smith 'felt myself the intruder at the Ceilí in much the same way I've felt when going into a bar for cigarettes in the now largely black south Bronx'. They had, he admitted, justification for their aloofness given the extent to which they too were 'much discriminated' against in Galway city. Ironically, in his search for authenticity he found that Inishmaan 'was not big enough for one to escape the tourists'.[103] He enthused about the beauty of the women and found in the men both 'a unique servant-like gentleness and a repressed violence, an intimidating combination that shows very much in the intensity of their gaze'.[104]

Much more problematic in that decade, however, was Deborah Tall's book on her stay on Inishbofin in the early 1970s as recounted in *The Island of the White Cow: Memories of an Irish Island* (1986). Tall was a product of a sheltered upper-middle-class Philadelphia suburb and the book was powerfully written, if occasionally overwrought, and combined snobbery and virtuosity ('we feel righteous as we contribute to the island's survival'). The book suffered from an immature appreciation of the historical context of island living but contained acute, accurate and stinging personal observations. Tall eloped to the island, just weeks out of an American college, with an academic twenty years her senior to live cheaply 'at a remove from the commercial world ... we are beyond the pale, beyond the clutches of the world'.[105]

At that stage there were 230 people left on the island; a 'bitterly poor' people with a monotonous life, 'but they are still willing to be surprised ... the island is a poignant mixture of beauty and ruin' and too many inhabitants were malnourished as they were devoted to 'convenience foods with a passion only the long-deprived can muster ... all the island have badly decayed teeth'. A shopkeeper served the shop fare with 'a touch of bitterness tempered by her red-cheeked wholesomeness' but 'the island offers itself an answer to all my vague, frustrated longings'.[106] For all her focus on the island as a refuge for some artists ('a deeply felt gesture ... I'll learn to be a better writer here') she also decided not to spare details of a 'tinge of malevolence I've begun to recognise between islanders ... an itchy jealousy and disparagement fed by convoluted family histories, old crimes and rivalries ... bitchiness is an art' with 'past lives perpetually retold'. They were also depicted as wallowing in the age-old tales of disaster – wrecks, drownings, government neglect – drawn to tragedy 'like moths to a flame ... they long for ears to pour their secret grievances into'.

She detected an ambivalence towards the church, while at the same time the islanders were caught in the 'strait jacket of asexuality ... sex is dark and private'. There were also imbibing men,

> their faces flushed with drink or virginity holding fat pints of stout in their left hands as lovingly as they might the hands of women ... a people watching the fabric of their lives disintegrate around them ... the verses of the song are a lengthy catalogue of abuse of the island, a heap of insults at its crudeness, oddness and worthlessness. It's no place to go, everyone should leave, the song insists. No one knows how to do anything, the rain never stops, the houses leak, the chimneys smoke, there's nothing but spuds to eat. A terrible spot, the last place God made. While the song is hilarious, it's also, of course, sad because within its satire lie bitter truths and the man who's singing it left the island for England thirty years ago.[107]

Tall was well aware of islanders having previously been betrayed by 'cynical and high-sniffing pundits'. She perhaps did not see herself in that category, but she was prurient in focusing on intimate details, including the face of the postmistress – 'grey hairs spout from a mole on her cheek' – and tardy in her sweeping generalisations: 'ninety-nine per cent of the islanders lack energy and ambition'.[108] Tall was proud about 'how much of an island voice and sensibility I've absorbed', an assertion undermined by the deception and breach of trust she was engaged in. There was plenty of truth in some of her observations, but they were not hers to tell publicly, given that she did not let the islanders know she would be publishing details of their private lives.

While Tall concentrated relentlessly on the perceived dead-end lives of the islanders, she exulted in 'how tremendously altered I am ... we share a passion for the life the islanders have discarded ... makes us feel part of a large story we'd only read before ... our appetite for customs of which they're ashamed'.[109] She was dismissive of 'Yanks routinely showing up in plaid pants and Aran sweaters bought duty-free at Shannon' while she honed in on the admission of a woman on the island that 'there was hardly a woman married in the last ten years who didn't have a child six months later ... and those are the first ones ye see parading into mass every morning'. An out-of-wedlock pregnancy saw an official reaction that was 'hushed and condemning, but unofficially there's amusement and glee'.[110]

Tall's book of poems composed while there was accepted for publication ('a vindication of our being here. The book is a pure product of this experience') but she increasingly felt a 'contradiction between our daily life and the rhetoric of our life' as she became inept outside the island and 'afraid of the mainland', raising doubts as to whether her experiment was really fostering independence. Bonding and submergence were 'the great risk' on the island; their adventure rigidified 'into a series of habits and now into a dogma ... I move backward as they move forward' and there was backstabbing and children who on Wren day 'went pagan and mad ... none of the island's flexibility and openness with outsiders applies to their own'.[111]

Tall castigated vindictive family rifts and the dominance of one family that 'is not only the entire upper class but also the controllers of medical care, food, fuel and tourism' and the 'righteousness of complaint on which she and the others have come to depend ... perhaps in the end the island was no escape from reality at all, just a different reality with its own abominations ... I'm unable to reach conclusions.'[112] That admission summed up the experiences of a number of island visitors who assumed their isolation would be an escape and then had to unpick the reasons why it was not and could not be any such thing. Readers of the book, however, were able to reach conclusions; a sense that the island as dream became the island as prison: 'in the end the island defeats her'.[113]

One review of the book by a woman whose grandmother was buried on the island and was one of three generations of islanders, noted that an islander had referred to the book as 'cruel'. The crucial point was that all was identifiable – the pseudonyms she used were never going to conceal identities – and that she weaved in to her story 'scandals, gossip and secrets which she was able to glean by her very privileged position of having been befriended and trusted'. She treated gossip as fact and in her focus on alcoholism, sexual indiscretion and suicide was engaged in not just betrayal but also presumptuousness. As the reviewer put it, 'I know only enough to know that it takes more than five years to understand complexities of pride and dignity of these 2,000-year-old people'.[114]

In contrast, Yorkshire-born Tim Robinson set himself a very different island mission. Having taught maths and painted, he left London in 1972 and settled in Aran, which he had first been intrigued by after Flaherty's *Man of Aran* film. His original aim was to write a novel and in that first winter 'what captivated me was the immensities in which this little place is wrapped'. It was not enough, however, to fill a 'diary of intoxication' with Aran. He yearned for a way to contribute to the island and so began work on a map of it at the suggestion of the island postmistress to assist tourists visiting a simple bare place but with richness attached to even 'the tiniest fragment of reality'.[115]

Robinson found something 'compulsive in one's relationship to an island ... it is as if the surrounding ocean like a magnifying glass directs an intensified vision onto the narrow field of view. A little piece is cut out of the world, marked off in fact by its richness in significance.'[116] Robinson, often in partnership with his wife, Máiread, sought to do justice to that by unwrapping the immensities, researching in minute detail and seeking to answer questions, such as why did the wren flourish on one side of the island and the raven on the other? His books included *Stones of Aran: Pilgrimage* (1986), *Stones of Aran: Labyrinth* (1995) and *Connemara* (1990). Robinson's personal archive underlines the depth of his research and the scale of his achievement in seeking to map Aran and some of the other western islands, including Inishbofin and Inishark. He compiled seventy-one place name cards alone for Inishark; for Inishbofin it was 223; he referred to these modestly as 'my efficient record cards'.[117]

Robinson sought to deal in fact; the origins of place names, monuments and small island landmarks, with detailed map work and information from locals ('local man thought', or 'as Mrs McDonncha tells me now'). His densely packed local cards were supplemented with wider context that amounted to an extraordinarily dense official and unofficial history of Connemara and the islands. His research and reading material included topographical dictionaries, statistical surveys, histories of archdioceses long out of print, academic debates about Cromwellian fortifications, detailed correspondence about coastguard stations and signal towers, his archive a monument to a researcher par excellence. For him, it might have been 'tempting' to reach conclusions based on partial stories or fragments 'but only a contemporary record' would justify confirmation.[118] Aran had twenty-four 'quarters' with quite different histories. In his second Aran volume he sought to unwrap 'the geological and historical tangle of Aran's interior'; its crevices, bogs, ruins and relics with the goal of arriving at a 'coherence of mind'. As he saw it, the sequence of the terrain had an 'inbuilt directionality' but achieving the unity of thought was an immense challenge: 'even a pilgrimage narrow-mindedly devoted to one end is endlessly ambushed and seduced by the labyrinth it winds through'.[119]

He also wrote like a gifted novelist with a marvellous turn of phrase and mixed empathy with frankness. He did not shy away from social and class tensions – 'the sidelong glance of envy and malicious supposition' – and the implications of gender divisions. Some Aran women 'had to work at the seaweed until late in their pregnancies ... women live out lives even more straitened in spatial terms than do the males', including the women who 'set themselves like jugs on the shelf of their marriage'; those who 'folded away their silken youth with their wedding dresses'.[120] He frankly addressed the dangers of island life and wrote of the hazardous life of the cliff men of the islands, the 'cragmen' who descended the cliffs, lowered down on a cable around their middle held by four or five others, to hunt seabirds, the killing often done with bare hands: 'in the summer of 1816 two unfortunate men, engaged in this frightful occupation of cragman missed their footing and were instantly dashed to pieces'. In hearing stories over so many years 'I picked up my objective folkloristic ear'.[121] An atheist ('I trust prayer no more than whiskey'[122]), he nonetheless celebrated the earth with almost a religious fervour and saw his task as akin to that of a Catholic pilgrim with the features he highlighted taking the role of stations.[123]

Robinson also corresponded with Etienne Rynne, the ever-forthright professor of archaeology at University College Galway about the Dún Aengus fort on Inishmore and was willing to go back and reassess his own conclusions in light of Rynne's theories. The fort, insisted Rynne, had been more a temple than a fortress and should not be thought of as a 'place where desperate men held out against ferociously attacking enemies' but a location for 'druids, ollavs [learned leaders] bards, kings and nobles ... some to perform rituals'.[124] Such was Robinson's range that he could be described as historical geographer, ecologist, environmentalist, natural historian, botanist, geographer and translator.[125] As critic John Wilson Foster saw it, 'surely in Robinson is an astonishingly sophisticated afterlife of Irish revival nativism', the difference being he was not just focused on revival of the past. There were 'global and cosmic' aspirations to his thinking and the idea of 'living well on earth and finding our way back to the world'.[126]

Robinson's project on Aran ultimately became 'one of the most sustained, intensive and imaginative studies of a place that has ever been carried out'. He walked the island not at a 'penitential trudge but at an inquiring, digressive and wandering pace'.[127] He was able to capture the 'subtle actualities of Aran life' on an island inhabited for more than 4,000 years. It is also noteworthy how others tried the same on different islands, with a similar devotion to small spaces. Frank Mitchell, an outstanding naturalist, also wore a multitude of hats – geologist, botanist, archaeologist, ornithologist, geographer and social historian – and published *Man and Environment in Valencia Island* (he used that version of its name) in 1989, the product of 'ten years in Valencia Island, walking its hillsides and its bogs' (it is seven miles long) in order to trace its evolution from when Mesolithic hunter-fishers arrived 6,000 years ago, much of the record from the bogs.[128]

Other visitors, however, continued to display a capacity to infuriate natives with their tendency to treat them like museum pieces and otherworldly or devoid of normal impulses. Novelist Colm Tóibín recalls how in the 1980s a literary native of the Aran Islands argued with a filmmaker. The native pointed out that the fishermen may have appeared photogenic and to be part of an ancient tradition 'but most of them have lived in Boston and most of them were down there watching for the arrival of American girls from the boat and all of them have condoms in their pockets'. The Aran novelist went further and sarcastically suggested the filmmaker hire a ship and remove the population of the island so that he could film it empty.[129]

The following decade, the Druid Theatre company based in Galway engaged in a very different kind of exercise when it brought its plays to seven different islands for its twenty-first birthday and made these stagings a celebration of 'Europe's most western communities', from the Cork islands up to Rathlin in County Antrim and from Donegal down to Kerry. As Fintan O'Toole pointed out, 'Druid's sense of place has never been sentimental.'[130] It did the same in 2005 as part of its Synge cycle, a huge achievement in Irish theatre involving the company staging all six plays of Synge as part of a single production and included a final open air performance on Inishmaan, chosen because of the major role the island played in Synge's development as a writer. The six plays were performed at various venues throughout the island in one day and everything required had to be ferried over.[131]

The Cripple of Inishmaan, a play by Martin McDonagh, a young playwright born in London to Irish parents, was unveiled by Druid at the end of 1996, and is set at the time of the filming of Flaherty's *Man of Aran*. As a child McDonagh had visited the Aran Islands when on holidays in Connemara, and what stuck in his mind was their remoteness, loneliness, wildness and 'lunar quality'. The annotated copy of the play belonging to director Garry Hynes highlighted, in her own words in the margins, two of its central themes: 'getting away from the island' and for those who did not, the need to 'keep them in line'.[132] The play was a huge success and in 2011 a twenty-one week tour of it included, for the first time, the island of Inishmaan itself, which was not for the thin skinned, given its focus on pettiness, bloody mindedness, the crumbling of authority and the dismissal of the *Man of Aran* myth: 'I suppose you shouldn't peg stones at an oul fella's head, but didn't he drive me to it? ... the man of Aran me arsehole. The lass of Aran they could've had, and the pretty lass of Aran. Not some oul shite about thick fellas fecking fishing.'[133]

McDongah's work made it clear that by the end of the twentieth century, the islands were still providing a great stimulus to creative endeavour, but not without complication. English artist Neal MacGregor seems to have had his own artistic desires wrapped in the idea of island living but he died alone in 1990 aged forty-four in a stone shed where he lived alone without electricity or heating on Inis Bó Finne in Donegal. He left behind diaries and volumes of illustrated bird notebooks. There were various theories as to whether he was 'insane, traumatised, enlightened' with even more outlandish theories that he was a 'British spy recording gun-running shipping routes of the IRA'.[134] What islanders would not have been aware of was that he had studied art at a prestigious college outside London, had been musical and sociable and had become part of the art émigrés fleeing big cities in the 1970s, partying and making highly regarded jewellery.

A plausible theory was that he was in search of 'artistic purity and aesthetic unencumbered by technical trickery'. He carved on stones, built boats, caught rabbits and fish and told no one of his previous life, which included a wife as well as a father about whom he knew nothing.[135] Mac-Gregor became like the islands themselves: a blank canvas on to which all sorts of projections and theories could be drawn. Perhaps a tribute to his self-sufficiency and unobtrusiveness was that he was referred to in 2014 by a Donegal newspaper as an 'Inishbofin man'.[136] But all that those attempting to chronicle his experience could offer were 'glimpses of a life'. A friend suggested something had happened for him to lose his bonhomie and gregariousness; extracts from his diaries, it could be argued, made it quite clear why he chose an island:

> I think I have to take a far deeper search in myself ... like a grey-hound from the track we chase an impossible hare ... but there's nothing for a dog to win. From the day we are born we know nothing but competition to suckle the lips of life, but life is an indefinable beauty, an elixir to be tasted by the lucky dogs who overtake the hare ... living on your own doesn't make much sense but I can't live with anyone else ... I lost my power such a long time ago.

He did, however, have a friend on the island and that prompted a diary entry: 'I hope <u>we</u> can manage the winter months on our own'. In that sense, his story was not quite as it was billed after he died. He also spent periods staying in some islanders' homes. He died unexpectedly from a heart attack, which was likely to have been the result of a rare genetic condition. Perhaps the central reason he was on the island was summed up in another diary entry: 'Come, let us try and stumble on essence'.[137] Therein, lay, perhaps, an impossible quest; as Irish poet Jerome Kiely saw it, 'I doubt if there is anyone, apart from an islander himself, who can see an island, any island, from the inside'.[138]

SEVEN

ISLAND LIFE AND MENTALITY

'What have we to do with Ireland?'

Islanders were understandably wary of visitors wielding cameras in the late nineteenth century. Doctor and ethnographer Charles Browne had to face the fact that, on Inishbofin and Inishark, the islanders had a 'strong dislike to having their portraits taken'. He was able, nonetheless, to get a representative sample, his attention to detail evident in observations such as 'the face is long and scutiform, narrowing in rapidly in the bigonial region. The cheek-bones are not prominent ... the ears are small, outstanding and somewhat coarsely moulded.' After the photos came the psychological portraits and Browne had plenty of positive things to write of the islanders – they had a 'healthy, active life', were 'kindly, courteous and very communicative' and 'honest and fair' (though he added that mainlanders insisted they did not pay their debts) and did not indulge much in drunkenness. But he also included the observation that 'their wit is not of a very sparkling character ... they are thriftless and not too cleanly in many of their habits and have little regard for ordinary sanitary laws ... said to be capable of acts of ferocity when roused'.[1]

Some of the CDB inspectors compiling reports on the islands were also keen to characterise the islanders, their attitudes and lifestyles. Robert Ruttledge-Fair visited Inishbofin in August 1892, at which time there was a population of 997 and 215 families. As with Inishark, he was critical of their cutting of clay and peat sods from mountain commonage for use as fuel: 'acres upon acres of these islands have been rendered useless for any purpose by this process'. He characterised them as industrious 'when labour pays' but 'easily discouraged and have little perseverance'.[2]

This was just one of many judgements made about the character of the islanders in the inspectors' reports in the 1890s on the back of detail about several of their habits. The Inishkea islanders could be 'careless and unequal in their treatment of their children', argumentative and litigious about trespass, 'not very cleanly' and 'little can be said in their favour' in relation to industriousness but there had been 'little inducement to them to be so' (the surveyors did not always, it appears, give enough consideration to the impact of the seasons on what islanders could or could not do at different stages of the year).[3] On Achill Island, 'the people do not exert themselves to improve their holdings ... the cattle occupy one end of the kitchen and the family take their meals and some members sleep in the other end. The fowls roost on the rafters. I am told pigs are often kept in the same apartment.'[4] On Clare Island and Inishturk, 'the inhabitants of both islands have lost almost all habits of industry and self-reliance'.[5]

Overall, negative commentary was balanced by complimentary observance, sometimes expressed with surprise, as if it had been inconceivable to the visitors that in some respects the islanders could be superior to the mainlanders in how they handled their affairs. In relation to Clare, Charles Browne suggested the manner in which they worked when organised by the CDB, 'and when they had inducement to do so, leads one to think that they did not work on account of having no real interest in doing so'.[6] They were, however, 'hospitable and kindly ... much given to chaff and joking ... their sense of the ridiculous seems to be rather keen. In times of trouble or distress they are very kind, generous with what they have and helpful to one another.'[7] On the Aran Islands, the population was 'an unusually healthy one'. Idiocy and imbecility were uncommon; they had the character of being 'exceptionally honest, straightforward and upright', but on the other hand 'we have been told that the men have no unity or organisation, that they are cunning, untrustworthy and certainly are very boastful when in liquor. They rarely fight, but will throw stones at one another.'[8] On Arranmore in Donegal, 'the women dress on the whole better than in many other parts. They often wear hats on Sundays and many wear boots on weekdays.'[9]

Inishbofin and Inishark fishermen were praised for their fishing prowess.[10] On Tory, the methods of cultivation of the land 'are in some respects more advanced than the mainland'; while the men did the ploughing, 'the women do the harrowing and indeed most of the other farm work'. CDB inspector F. G. Townsend Gahan was also particularly transfixed on the dexterity of the women during the kelp-making season, praising 'the clever way in which the girls ride the ponies up and down the steep banks ... there are no paths yet they gallop down without the smallest hesitation ... the men are not able to ride at all so well'.[11] Cape Clear islanders were also 'reputed for industry and bear a high character as intrepid and skilful fishermen'.[12]

Clearly, islanders could be characterised in numerous ways depending on the perspective or prejudices of the observers. They were certainly regarded as different from mainlanders, but there were also numerous differences between islands. The weather, island resources and the capabilities of the land dictated so much and each island had a unique mix of circumstances and practices in relation to agriculture, fishing, diet and housing, as underlined by the reports of the CDB inspectors. It was noted of Tory in 1897 that there was 'practically no meadow or grass', while the seaweed made the potatoes damp and spongy. While there was 'extensive' stock of 90 cattle, 200 sheep ('scraggy and diet extensively on seaweed'), there was a need for good rams and bulls and there were no pigs. Steamers to Liverpool, Glasgow and Sligo passed every week, 'by which food supplies were received and eggs and lobsters shipped', and, as with some other islands, the CDB inspector criticised the 'pernicious habit of cutting up their arable land to burn or skinning the sod off their pasture, leaving nothing but the bare gravel'. Fishing at that stage was in a healthy state because of the curing station on Tory and breakfast consisted of fish and potatoes but

> the women are for a great part of the time idle and except for the fishing there is nothing for the men to do ... they work very well in spurts ... but find continuous hard work at first very distasteful ...

the only custom peculiar to the island is that of dividing the shore for the purpose of collecting seaweed.[13]

There was also a detailed report for a part of Achill in April 1892. The area examined contained 276 families of which 73 were in 'very poor' circumstances. The cattle and sheep were 'of the most inferior description that can be imagined' and island pigs 'nearly always die' but the hens were 'splendid layers, the people deriving more profit from the sale of eggs than any other industry, except migratory labour'. These migratory labourers numbered 1,318. There was excellent turf from bogs that were 'practically inexhaustible' but no kelp industry or lobster fishing; indeed, other fishermen, including those from the Inishkea Islands 'take them in hundreds almost from the very doors of the people'. There were simply no facilities for the sale of fresh fish or knowledge about fish curing or shelter for boats ('the entire coast of Achill is singularly deficient in this respect').

Fifteen per cent was charged by traders for long credit, much lower than other rates prevalent at that time, probably because returning migrant labourers would have the wherewithal to pay. A measure of the differences in living standards was that a family in 'fairly comfortable' circumstances had a cash income of £33 while those in poor circumstances just £17.[14] Clothing was principally bought in Scotland. Most houses were stone though there were still a few 'sod huts'.

On the Aran Islands, the CDB inspector noted that there were better breeds of both cattle and sheep; flannel and frieze were still 'a great deal worn' but 'young people purchase considerable quantities of tweed and other shop goods' while more than two-thirds of the islanders burned kelp, generating almost £1,500 annually. There was no turf on the island, little lobster fishing ('the islanders hitherto could not be considered as fishermen' though recent efforts were bearing fruit) and owing to the bad weather 'much time is lost in enforced idleness'. There were 116 currachs, twelve small sailing boats ('third class') and four larger trading boats, but the pier at Kilronan was too inaccessible. There was potential for market gardening, given the mildness of the climate and the services of a steamer now available three times a week. Some islanders depended on credit: 'as a rule from three to six months to reliable customers is generally allowed. Shopkeeper charges from 20 to 25 per cent on all goods sold on credit.'[15]

On Arranmore, it was observed in 1896 that there was practically no weaving or spinning; kelp manufacture was the most lucrative business after fishing with up to 250 tons made annually and about sixty boats were engaged in herring fishing. Salmon fishing the previous year had been very profitable. The average family spent £43 a year on clothing ('almost entirely bought, even their underwear ... the women dress on the whole better than in many other parts ... Their dresses are generally made of shop bought goods'), fishing gear, meal and food (the staple foods were fish, tea, bread, stirabout and potatoes). They also needed a curing station to save them the trip to Burtonport on the mainland and 'from a moral point of view it would be a great advantage as the amount spent on drink at Burtonport during the fishing is enormous'.[16]

Concerns that the supposed 'purity' of islanders could be contaminated were long expressed and there was often an island 'notable' who would correspond with the mainland about island affairs. In 1912 and 1913 James Ward, a trader and publican on Tory, wrote regular letters to Archbishop Patrick O'Donnell: 'we are inclined to discontinue the sale of intoxicating drink if we know that it should not be stocked or sold by any other person or persons here'. He regarded it as 'the most depraving business anyone can be engaged in'. Despite being strict, 'we cannot manage to keep the fishermen always right ... Tory men are generally speaking inoffensive, retiring, altogether peaceable people sober, none more coarse, pugnacious, boisterous and quarrelsome in drink. Isn't it a pity they should have drink so?' Full of his own importance and righteousness, he piously asserted, 'It is only once in an age, I think, that a publican is willing to give up the trade.'[17]

The following year, he had yet to make progress in getting rid of the pub, noting pointedly that the fishermen on Inishbofin 'get on very well without one. So would Tory.'[18] Ward then decided, in collaboration with the priest, on the dramatic step of closing the pub on Sunday:

> the islanders looked on it as a calamity of some magnitude. It was, oh, a very arbitrary proceeding on the part of the Tory priest ...

after a few Sundays the lonely woe-begone look that many of them couldn't disguise gradually wore off ... they took to handballing and stone throwing ... it was I (unknown to my Tory customers of course) got the priest to have the pub closed on Sunday.[19]

The following winter he suggested in another letter to the bishop 'not one of all the fishermen seems to miss the drink'. Those who had taken pledges in the past only to break them after a week or two had now, as a result of temperance missions, kept it 'most religiously ... the present writer just cheated once by having a "half one" of Hennessy in his plum pudding sauce at Xmas, but that was no harm'. The islanders had even had a few sober dances at the school and

found they could get on as happily as if they had each his bottle carefully hidden away in some hole on a fence outside the dance hall. They used to have a swig now and again just to keep up their spirits and as the bottle was getting low, natural normal manners and descriptions changing to coarseness and boisterousness and irritableness and their tempers getting like wasps and nettles. Now, haven't we changed, thank Goodness.[20]

Decades later, poet Austin Clarke was to write about this in his memoir *A Penny in the Clouds* (1968). He stayed on Tory as a young traveller and noted 'there is no liquor on the island'. The trader, or 'King', he wryly observed, 'with a magnificent gesture put the shutters up – incidentally having made his money. As a result the islanders, who are a logical people, come over to the mainland when the fishing has been good and get glorious until the money runs out.'[21]

But just how disputatious were the islanders? Did their proximity to each other inevitably foment tensions and rows? Michael Carney, who grew up on the Blasket Islands suggested 'the islanders seldom got into an argument amongst themselves ... you couldn't carry a grudge because you would need others'.[22] This seems far-fetched. Fractiousness was a common aspect of island life, perhaps more so than the mainland, given the proximity in which the islanders lived and laboured. Despite the size of the islands there were also obvious social divides and tensions about property, land and boats and hostility towards authority.[23]

In 1911 *The Connacht Tribune* reported on an 'Aran tragedy' after a 'family quarrel' due to a 'bad feeling that had hitherto existed' between two families on the island of Inishmore: 'During the struggle that ensued a peasant named Patrick Conneally was struck on the head with a stone' and died.[24] There was also a legal case the same year arising out of a dispute between two island families, the Flahertys and O'Donnells, over land :'John O'Donnell had no stock at all. He was in America and after coming home was fond of drink ... the old man said he could not stand his son.'[25] When Brian McLoughlin visited Inishark and Inishbofin in the summer of 1942 to collect material for the Irish Folklore Commission he was able to record the memories of Inishbofin native Patrick Cunnane, who was born in the 1860s:

> In former days when any altercation arose between two neighbours, the dispute always ended in a bitter melee, which was always waged outside the chapel wall as soon as mass was over. Each disputant had informed his own friends of the possibility of such a clash and in this way both factions clashed. Not alone was that dispute settled in this manner, but all other disputes that might otherwise have gone into oblivion were given a rebirth and made the situation more spiteful. Sticks, known as 'clubs' were used in such melees. This custom [is] now completely vanished. Sunday of course was chosen because of the likelihood that each faction would be there as soon as mass was over.[26]

Similarly, on Clare Island, an IFC informant's grandfather had said 'that in his days every man took a blackthorn stick to mass with him because the faction fights were generally started after mass ... at one of the fights a man was killed once'.[27] On Rathlin one particular individual was 'a wild carnaptious man and was always having falling outs', so his fellow islanders built him a house on a patch up the mountain to isolate him. There were also obvious divides between the upper and lower ends of the island with fights between them at Christmas: 'there used to be great spite between them'. The observation of eighty-three-year-old Rathlin native Rose McCurdy in 1954 was that 'It's like a border', and yet, there were also stories of 'staunch' Protestants on the island who defended their Catholic counterparts, and it was frequently asserted 'there was no Sectarianism on Rathlin'.[28] Likewise on Valentia, with its minority Protestant population (100 out of 2,500 in 1868) it was maintained it was 'ecumenical before its time'.[29]

Pádraig O'Toole was explicit about Aran Island social divides: 'For us from Bung Abhla, the Gaelic-speaking west end of the island, the people of Kilronan were very foreign. They spoke their own brand of the English language and they made no secret of looking down on us and our Gaelic. They referred to us as the "westwards" or less complimentarily "Asail an Chinnthiar" (the donkeys of the west-end).'[30]

In 1939 Denis Healy from Dursey sued three island brothers – the Harrington family – and Jeremiah O'Leary, another islander, for £100 damages for assault. Those charged pleaded self-defence. Healy, aged thirty-two, had his teeth knocked out and had spent nine days in hospital on the mainland; he 'denied that he was fond of fighting but admitted that he had beaten a man named Sullivan'. The dispute arose because there was a suggestion Healy, 'should not be allowed to play the accordion as he had not contributed towards the cost of the accordion. He also admitted that he might have knocked James Harrington on the ground but he did not remember jumping on Harrington when he was on the ground. Healy admitted he was known on the island as "The Slasher" ... he denied that he had got the name because he was fond of fighting.' One of the defendants was cross-examined and maintained, 'The accordion started it all,' to which a barrister responded: 'So it was not an instrument of harmony?' The judge decided the plaintiff 'had to go to hospital largely through his own misconduct' and gave a decree against the defendants for twenty shillings.[31]

As seen in chapter 4, there was also much tension on Achill over the supply of school milk, which led to boycotts and school closures, and peace overtures did not initially have the desired effect. The *Irish Press* reported in March 1937: 'Women raid Achill School: Teacher and Pupils evicted: Bags of lime used as bombs'. Four women attacked the female assistant teacher in Dooega, the last of the affected schools remaining open. Apparently a compromise had been reached whereby the teachers 'agreed to accept the milk on condition that the parents would take it in turn to distribute it daily'. But the lime-bomb stormtroopers burst into the school to confront the teacher and 'an ugly scene developed and the women coming to grips ... quantities of lime were hurled ... the incident marks the breaking of a truce which it was hoped would become general'.[32] A few days later a 'mass meeting of islanders' ratified an unofficial and temporary pact 'in deference to the request of Mgr Walsh ... the parties shook hands and parted on very cordial terms'.[33]

Alongside fighting, how islanders amused themselves was paramount given the lack of social options available to them in contrast to mainlanders. There were strong musical and dance histories associated with some of the islands (the Blasket islanders had a tradition of fiddle making that stretched back 200 years) and until the early twentieth century an itinerant fiddler visited Inishbofin. When J. M. Synge played his fiddle on the Aran Islands,

> a tall man bounded out from his stool under the chimney and began flying around the kitchen with peculiarly sure and graceful bravado. The lightness of the pampooties seems to make the dancing on this island lighter and swifter than anything I have seen on the mainland, and the simplicity of the men enables them to throw a naïve extravagance into their steps that is impossible in places where people are self-conscious.[34]

In the 1950s, Micky Joe Anderson of Rathlin referred to the last piper on the island, 'Neal the piper'; his pipes still resided on the island 'but there's no one fit to play them on the island any more.'[35]

Irish traditional singing had deep roots, with the *Sean-nós* (old style singing) particularly strong in the west; the Galway version of this was regarded by some as the 'jewel in the crown' of such singing, but what was interesting was the extent to which the islands had their own approaches, including on Tory, where singers such as Jimmy Duggan (born in 1928) had a distinctive repertoire and style with different airs and interpretations of songs sung elsewhere. Styles evolved in response to the nature of island company and gatherings and Duggan was later to make an impact at An tOireachtas, the annual Gaelic League festival for Gaelic verbal and musical arts.[36]

There was also a tradition of island cake dances, including on Omey, off Clifden in County Galway, where a cake dance was held on St Patrick's Day 'organised by a woman who would always have a few gallons of poitín for sale' and a huge currant cake and piper. A young man who might think 'much of his fiancée' bought the cake and presented it to her and then he had to buy poitín and leave it on the table 'to be drunk free and freely by all who wished to drink it'. These cake dances were popular until the 1860s; a hurling dance was also held on St Patrick's Day: 'as the match was in progress the men and women danced to the piper's music on the hillside and the cake was displayed in the green'.[37]

For children, some pastimes could be as simple as seeing 'who could pee furthest against the wind'.[38] When Brian McLoughlin visited Inishark and Inishbofin in the summer of 1942 he recorded details of games of memory played in Inishark, including those played by a younger generation at wakes.[39] A game played on Clare Island involved one man stooped in the middle of the floor while another jumped over him: 'should the former happen to touch him while jumping he had to kiss a certain girl in the house'.[40] The islanders were also athletic; on Inishbofin hurling matches were played followed by *rince baire* (hurling dance), with hurling sticks made of elder branches and balls made from cow hair. Football was also introduced to the island; when the first football appeared 'every man, woman and child collected on the beach at the east end to see the newly introduced type of game'.[41]

Beach football was also common on the Blaskets, with 'a well trained dog' to retrieve the ball when it went into the sea.[42] On Omey, a seventy-two-year-old informant in 1942 remembered 'seeing as many as forty young men on each side hurling on the beach every bonfire night'.[43] Islanders were also renowned for their rowing skills as demonstrated by their success in the All-Ireland Gaeltacht Rowing Championships.[44] Martin Joyce, by the 1980s the sole inhabitant of the island of Inis Bearachain off Lettermore, was one of three cousins who won the

All-Ireland Currach Rowing Championships known as the 'Tóstal', three years in a row in 1956, 1957 and 1958. Other islanders were celebrated as both oarsmen and helmsmen.[45]

Games or contests between different parts of the same island were also common, as on Rathlin, where, at Christmas, games were played between the upper and lower ends of the island 'and after the drinking there'd be a dance the whole night'. All-night dancing was a regular theme to emerge in the testimonies of islanders as well as 'fireside games', which included balancing tricks, games of elimination and the use of blindfolds. As Micky Joe Anderson of Rathlin recalled 'if you only heard the laughing over that game on the island winter's night around the fire'.[46]

On Inishturk, dances were held on Sunday nights throughout the winter 'but in summer they retire to bed at a timely hour. There are few forms of pastime' but they did invent their own games, including money pitching and a rope game: 'part of the game [is] to slash him severely with it whenever the holder of the *bróg* (rope) gets his back turned towards him'. A game of Quoit involved flat stones pitched towards an upright stone; a quoit nearest the upright stone was worth an ace and twenty-one aces were required to win: 'this game occupies the long summer evenings and the whole of Sunday'.[47]

On 1 February, St Brigid's Day (Brigid was one of Ireland's first recorded saints), young women on Inishbofin carried a Brigid doll from house to house and were given foodstuff with which they prepared a feast.[48]

A Halloween custom, extinct by the 1940s on Inishturk, involved two young men being sent to the cabbage garden 'and each bring a head of cabbage to the house. Whoever brought a nice head would afterwards marry a nice girl and he who brought an ugly head, an ugly girl.'[49] Another tradition involved making a cake in which was put 'a thimble, button, rag and a match, or any bit of wood. When baked the cake is cut up ... he who happens to get the thimble will marry a tailor, he who gets the button will remain a bachelor, he who gets the rag will be a widower and the match portends an early death.'[50] On Inishturk, blood was drawn in honour of St Martin (of Tours, a particularly popular saint in Ireland). Then every member of the house puts the sign of the cross on his forehead with the blood; the blood is not then thrown away but is salted and put into a bag and tied and is kept safely in some secluded place on the house for the rest of the year. It is believed that this blood has the effect of curing certain ailments.[51]

In some cowsheds, noted McLoughlin, 'I have noticed a tiny bottle of holy water hanging on the wall above the cow's heads. A tiny bottle of holy water is also placed in the stem of each canoe and boat.'[52]

Other superstitions dictated that, on Omey, 'if a beast died no milk was given to neighbours on any Monday or Friday for the remainder of the year',[53] or, on Inishturk, a live fire ember be placed under the churn before churning. The pilgrimage to the abandoned Caher Island was also important for the residents of Inishturk, who said 'that several miraculous cures have been effected as a result of performing the pilgrimage ... in all, the pilgrims have to visit fourteen stone monuments, the chapel and the holy well'.[54] Inishark was also full of shrines, including St Leo's (the island's patron saint) and on Omey Island, St Festy's Day (a derivative of St Féichín, who established a monastic settlement on the island in the seventh century) in January was associated with St Festy's holy well and it was recorded in 1942 that 'some fifty years ago scores of people came from all parts of North Connemara to do the stations with the result that every house on the island was overcrowded with strangers ... the station is not fully performed unless the pilgrim sleeps at the well'.[55]

On Heir Island on Christmas morning 'the islanders rose at 6 a.m. in darkness. Each family carried a lantern and the moving pin points of light, as they walked through the island on their way to the slip to cross over to the mainland for mass, was a beautiful sight.'[56] There was also a welfare dimension to some of the customs, including, as was recorded on Clare Island, the 'widow's tillage ... the young men of every village in which there happened to be a helpless widow came together on an appointed Sunday and saved the widow's crops that day'.[57] On Rathlin at Hallow Eve 'they would hit the door with a Kale stalk and maybe throw a turnip or a cabbage in'.[58]

The tradition of storytelling and house visits (*scoruíocht*) was also intrinsic to island life; this was brought to prominence by the work of Lady Gregory and Synge and the literature of the Blasket islanders, but existed in all parts of rural Ireland, where traditional storytellers could 'tell stories for months – long stories that would sometimes take two nights to tell one of them'.[59] In Richard Power's novel *Apple on the Treetop* based on his experiences on the Aran Islands, a long story of the fishermen was recounted that was then revealed as a lie: '"The curse of hell on you" said I, "but you're the biggest liar I ever came across". "Didn't it put down the evening?" he asked rhetorically'.[60] The storytellers could, according to a description in the novel *Proud Island*, by Peadar O'Donnell, 'make a wonder out of the chirping of a cricket'.[61]

On Valentia, Nóra Ní Shúillobháin, born there in 1909, recalled the house visits when she was a child:

> a nucleus of six men came regularly. They had comfortable allusive jokes, knew from boyhood each other's foibles, railed, spoke in Irish in devoted voices of personal affairs, turned to English for the newspaper and wide-ranging conversation. The visitors wore their hats, kept walking sticks in hand, smoked pipes or chewed tobacco, begetting a flood of saliva with which they would some- times pattern the floor with their sticks, outlining face, map or diagram ... only island tragedy would make them mute.[62]

Poet Richard Murphy was drawn to Inishbofin because of the seafar- ing and the storytelling: 'I had been trying for more than a year to reach a mythical island in a poem based on a legend. Now I had really landed on an island where men had turned their seafaring lives into legends they recounted to each other in the island's only pub'. Pat Concannon, the stout fishermen who had survived the Cleggan disaster of 1927 (see chap- ter 2) began to 'draw me into his legend' which led to his poem *Sailing to an Island* in 1963:

> The breeze as we plunge slowly stiffens:
> There are hills of sea between us and land,
> Between our hopes and the island harbour.

A child vomits. The boat veers and bucks.
There is no refuge on the gannet's cliff.
We are far, far out: the hull is rotten,
The spars are splitting, the rigging is frayed,
And our helmsman laughs uncautiously.

What of those who must earn their living
On the ribald face of a mad mistress?
We in holiday fashion know
This is the boat that belched its crew
Dead on the shingle in the Cleggan disaster.[63]

On Heir Island, as well as wintertime social nights in houses, the men gathered in an old outhouse where they talked about current affairs, boats and weather: 'this was likened to the island's parliament'.[64] The notion of an island assembly or 'parliament' was also mentioned in relation to the Blaskets and there have been numerous references to island 'kings'. What this meant in practice varied, depending on the era, size of the island, literacy, seniority and who might have been equipped with the authority or experience of dealing with officialdom. The son of Michael Waters, who evacuated Inishmurray in 1948, suggested the title of island 'king' ascribed to his father was 'rather ludicrous' and to his father 'nothing more than an embarrassment, but I feel sure that his fellow islanders would agree that he was to them much more than an adviser'.[65]

The schools collection organised by the IFC and the Department of Education from 1937–8 to encourage children to document and collect folklore and local history generated many island giant stories.[66] One recounted

a giant who could start on the top of a hill near Croagh Patrick and speak to another giant in the island of Achill, asking him if the potatoes were boiled for his dinner. Then his sight was so strong that when the potatoes were strained he could see the steam rising from them as they lay on the basket. A hop, a step and a leap would then land him in Achill. The hop would bring him to Old Head, the step to a rock north of Clare Island and the leap to Achill head.[67]

Another story told of 'Balor of the mighty blows, a hairy giant remembered vividly in local tradition' in Donegal. He was king of a tribe of Fomorian pirates who 'about 1200 BC' had infested the northern coast:

Balor's headquarters was in Tory Island where a high, tower-like rock is called to this day Balor's Castle. He is also called Balor of the evil eye for he had one eye, with venomous properties, like a Basilisk. This eye would strike people dead or turn them into stone. So that Balor kept it covered, except when he wished to use it against his enemies.

In Irish mythology Balor represented 'the power of darkness'.[68] There was also much preoccupation with fairies. On Inishmurray a native recalled the island was 'infested' with fairies, 'but while you had the burnt coal in yer shawl or near the child, the good people, the fairies of the island, couldn't take or interfere with that child'.[69]

Brian O'Nolan (Flann O'Brien) mercilessly lampooned the storytelling tradition in *An Béal Bocht* with the character the Shanachee: 'He settled his body luxuriantly in the chair, fixed his backside carefully beneath him, shoved his two hooves into the ashes, reddened his pipe and, when he was at his ease, he cleared his windpipe and began to spew discourse upon us.'[70] O'Brien was also keen to satirise the focus in island accounts on death, poverty, bad weather and the language; all intrinsic to 'the destiny of the true Gaels ... we are all Gaelic Gaels of Gaelic lineage'.[71] He was reacting to the publication of Tomás Ó Crohan's *An tOileánach* (published in Irish in 1929 and later translated as *The Islandman* by Robin Flower). Born in the mid 1850s, Ó Crohan was largely self-taught and had a shrewd and vivid approach to writing about his island life, which he did with heavy doses of irony and humour.

The way in which O'Brien took the detail from the existing island accounts and exaggerated them is clear in his depiction of the homestead. A passage in *The Islandman* noted 'there used to be two cows in the house, the hens and their eggs and the rest of us'. In *An Béal Bocht* the house is even more crammed: 'two cows, a cart horse, a race horse, sheep, pigs and other lesser animals'. His mother

> spent her life cleaning out the house, sweeping cow dung and pig dung from in front of the door, churning butter and milking cows, weaving and carding wool and working the spinning wheel, praying, cursing and setting big fires to boil a houseful of potatoes to stave off the day of the famine ... her like will not be there again.[72]

In a letter to his publisher, O'Brien described the book as 'an enormous jeer at the Gaelic morons here with their bicycle clips and handball medals but in language and style, an ironical copy of a really fine autobiographical book', a reminder that his target was not Ó Crohan.[73] In a letter to playwright Seán O'Casey, who liked *An Béal Bocht* because it had 'the swish of Swift's scorn in it', O'Brien replied that he was trying 'to get under the skin of a certain type of "Gael" which I find the most nauseating phenomenon in Europe'. But the real argument he was making was that this approach to Gaeldom would scupper the prospect of reviving the Irish language. It was a crucial point; O'Brien argued that the Irish language had the power to transform English language. As he wrote elsewhere, 'there is scarcely a single word in Irish that is simple or explicit'; what the Irish language amounted to was 'a spectrum of graduated ambiguity'. But translations of the island autobiographies lost this, and this is what O'Brien was parodying; it was the literalness of the translation that robbed them of the 'graduated ambiguity' and humour and made them 'accidentally comic'.[74]

Decades later, novelist John McGahern was also grappling with the text of *The Islandman* and his private papers reveal the effort he put into translating the book because of his interest in the difference between the original and Robin Flower's translation.[75] Judging by his notes, he viewed Ó Crohan as having serious literary prowess, looking at fitting him in to a pantheon of great writers who took different approaches to landscape, sounds and words: Swift, Yeats, Beckett and Joyce as well as the extent to which *The Islandman* continued the 'older Homeric tradition' and the 'vulgar tradition of local colour. Easily identifiable symbols as a substitute for reality'. As McGahern saw it, the island in this book lay closer to 'Mount Olympus than it did to the Roman gate of heaven that we used to pray to in our youth'. The veneer throughout the book over the older reality was 'transparent'.[76]

These musings formed the basis for McGahern's 1987 essay on the book. He praised Ó Crohan for the absence of 'idle stretches' in his writing that lauded nature; he liked its sparseness and that 'people are presented only in their essential outline and that is only so far as their striking identities are visible to the eyes of those around them. Yet its pattern is punctuated by the changing of the seasons and the "continued breaking of new days"'. He was also taken by the idea that 'the rhythm of each individual human life can be seen as analogous to that of the sea tides'.[77] McGahern, too, was conscious of the limitations of literal translation. The phrases *rithe mo laethse* or *rithe mo bhearthain* were translated by Flower as 'in the running of my days', but McGahern saw it as much more; that it had the sense of a tide, ebbing and flowing.[78]

For many, however, it was the sheer bleakness of island life and the regularity of island deaths that was striking on reading these books, as well as the acceptance of premature demise ('we must endure it and be content') and a casualness about it: 'the rascal death carried off many a fine young ruffian'.[79] The relentless attrition was recorded succinctly by Ó Crohan:

> Ten children were born to us, but they had no good fortune, God help us! The very first of them that we christened was only seven or eight years old when he fell over the cliff and was killed. From that time on they went as quickly as they came. Two died of measles and every epidemic that came carried off one or other of them. Donal was drowned trying to save the lady off the White Strand. [Eileen Nicholls; see chapter 5] I had another fine lad helping me. Before long I lost him, too. All these things were a sore trouble to the poor mother, and she, too, was taken from me.[80]

Blasket islander Peig Sayers also achieved renown for her focus on loss; her book *Peig: A Scéal Féin* (*Her Own Story*), at the urging of island visitors, was published in 1936 having been dictated by her to her son as she could neither read nor write Irish but had a uniquely brilliant grasp of its spoken form. By mid life she had lost her husband and four children and, as she saw it, 'I used to think of Mary and the Lord – the hard life they had. I knew I had a duty to imitate them and bear my sorrow patiently.'[81]

Such were Peig's travails that her translator, Kerry writer Bryan MacMahon, whose English version appeared in 1970 ('I first read aloud a chapter in the original Irish, marked dubious words and phrases, pondered on them, switched on the little microphone of the cassette recorder and, still mimicking Peig's voice, but in English this time, began to translate') could summarise her life as 'forty tragic years as a member of the little community on that fearsome crag'.[82] As Liam Ó Murchú, a well-known Irish-language broadcaster, put it, the island women were 'gentle, imperilled women, living half in the eternity which was always close to them'.[83] The problem with such interpretations was that they placed the islands, in the words of Fintan O'Toole, as a 'place outside of history, a strange margin'.[84]

But it was also the case that the islanders were wary of giving away too much information. Ó Crohan's book might contain animated depictions of seal hunts, but contains precious few details of private, family or personal life.[85] Similarly, Conchúr Ó Siocháin's account of life on Cape Clear, *Seanchas Chléire* (*Cape Clear Lore*), published in 1940, is 'like a boat that brings you to the island but when you get there, there is much that you are never told'.[86] On Valentia, as observed by Daphne Mould 'the islanders have a great sense of the comic and a tendency to write songs on their own and their neighbour's foibles. It would, however, take a native or an Eric Cross living there indefinitely to get their real feelings behind the picturesque phrases.'[87] (Cross wrote *The Tailor and Ansty*, published in 1942 and based on encounters with a Cork tailor and storyteller and his wife; it was banned as 'indecent' because of its unvarnished references to animal reproduction.)

Neither was getting to the essence of the religiosity of island lives straightforward. True, much of Peig's life and attitude was rooted in religion – in historian Margaret Mac Curtain's words 'the springs of her humanity were nourished by an intense sense of the presence of God' – but she was also a convivial neighbour 'who enjoyed late nights of story-telling, a pipe of tobacco and the company of men'. Like other islanders, she had the capacity 'to confront their own isolation and to discover the truth behind the experience of living frugally and dangerously in such an exposed place'. But the spirituality, like so much else, had to be indepen-dent and instinctive. Peig's spirituality did not preoccupy her conscious-ness, nor fire her imagination 'to achieve any heroic goal of sanctity'. There was much that was left unsaid: 'she does not tell us of her moments of rebellion. She found relief by resorting to humour.'[88] Pride was intrin-sic to the island characters also; as Bryan MacMahon characterised it in 1976 when remembering Peig, she had a 'rareness of spirit, sprung from her conviction that she was one of the last of a noble line'. She once told him 'there will never again in Ireland be an old woman as Irish as me', in the sense of someone who had committed to rote such a storehouse of local lore. But that also indicated her preoccupation with performance; she was, simply, 'a superb natural actress'.[89]

Peig also, because so many students were forced to study her book for the state examinations, became an object of resentment and derision; a schoolroom illustration of a true Gael in the manner derided by Flann O'Brien, in order to emphasise an approach to Irish and tradition that suggested 'a past that would also be the future'.[90] What is better known now is the degree to which some of her stories were sanitised (so they could be, in Declan Kiberd's words, 'co-opted by state forces ... to stand sponsor over the baptismal font for De Valera's Ireland') which led some to later reclaim her as an independent and earthy woman, frank about sex, or even a pre-feminist.[91] To the young and innocent she was 'like a radio within herself'.[92] She was also remarkably media savvy; the IFC held 5,000 pages of recordings of her and when poet W. R. Rodgers vis-ited her in hospital in Dingle, she told him: 'I'll be talking after my death, my good gentleman', as indeed she was, with the 2010 book *I Will Speak to You All*.[93]

But was it true that the island women were more liberated than their mainstream counterparts? A conference in 1998 on the fortieth anniversary of Peig's death suggested her memories produced 'feminine literature', with much focus on not just her acceptances, but also her resentments. Patricia Coughlan did not herald her as a feminist but highlighted that she 'sharply resented the economic circumstances of her life and still felt strongly enough about this in her old age to communicate the feeling to her son'.[94] As Angela Bourke characterised it, Peig told stories that were full of 'anger, negativity and profanity though only those that suited the tastes of what was a repressive time were printed'.[95]

It was common for those compiling reports on the islands to highlight the degree to which women were reluctant to stay and in that sense their views held particular sway when it came to discussions of possible evacuation. Gearóid Ó Catháin, the last child on the Blasket Islands, suggested of his mother that she 'must have craved the company of people her own age' as the only young married woman on the island.[96]

The issue of marriage on the islands, or marrying into them, had long been a focus (one of the main issues here was finding a partner 'that was not too closely related'[97]), including in the work of J. M. Synge and Peadar O'Donnell, along with the fear that the women, who although not usually in the boats fishing, had to live with.

In Peadar O'Donnell's novel *Islanders* the desire of an outsider woman, Ruth, to live in the west is 'born of the Abbey Theatre' (which staged many plays set in western Ireland), and the lure of fisherman Charlie, 'my big, wild man of the sea'. But would she live and 'slave on an island? Would she starve on an island like his mother? He laughed, the bitterest laugh of life, the laugh of a man who mocks himself.'[98] As for the options for the women on the island in this book, they would emigrate, except Sally: 'poor Sally, she would remain to mother the brood and by the time that was done, her youth would be gone. She faced her task without thinking. Such was her stock and their code.'[99] On Achill, when the men were in Scotland, the women 'had to take over'; even when they were there, the men cut the seaweed, 'but the task of drawing it home from the shore in creels fell to the women'.[100]

Women had a degree of control over certain island matters. On the Blaskets, 'when it came to money matters especially, the women of the island called all the shots' and 'during the winter many of the men on the island slept a lot during the day'.[101] Another observation of the Blaskets was that 'the building of the house was the man's job but the defence of the island fell to the women.'[102] But island women also endured heavy labour to a more extensive degree than mainland women: on Aran in the early twentieth century, the district nurse observed 'it is not extraordinary to notice a woman holding a furious bull whilst a dozen of the men endeavour to drag him to the currach'.[103] On Sherkin, women 'carried pails of water and creels of butter on their heads'.[104] When he visited Achill in the late 1920s, botanist Terence Ingold noticed there were few 'able-bodied men between the ages of eighteen and sixty to be seen' because most were working in Britain. He observed an old woman 'bent and gnarled ... carrying, slung over her back, a huge sack of seaweed which she had collected. So I offered to carry it for her. Reluctantly she agreed. I just about managed to heave it on to my back and staggered the half mile home, arriving in an exhausted condition.'[105] On another occasion he noticed that her husband 'was a bent and wizened old man who did little but look after a few old cows leaving the hard work to his wife'.[106]

Pádraig O'Toole's mother on Aran Island in the 1930s and 1940s was 'no great respecter of tradition, did what needed to be done regardless of expectation' including the repairing of the roof.[107] While he was living and painting on Achill, Paul Henry was full of admiration for the amount of work women did and 'always astonished at their cheerful acceptance of life'.[108] When Andrew McNeillie was with a group of island women returning to the island after a shopping trip in 1968, the boat had to turn back owing to the gales and the women were not impressed: they 'demanded to see the captain. They called his manhood into question. They railed and mocked and jeered, scolding like fishwives, stranded with their shopping on Galway pier.'[109]

Matchmaking on the islands was common and commercial. As described by Richard Power in his novel *The Land of Youth*, where 'the women brush their hair, their only vanity', the matchmaker based himself in the pub, 'where shy clients whispered with him and did complicated sums on the counter with fingers dipped in stout. Kate's match was no trouble to him. Although she was rising thirty, her years in New York had earned her a sizeable dowry which almost compensated for the loss of childbearing years.'[110]

And what of the island children? Paul Henry, on Achill at various stages from 1910 to 1919, found the children there 'naturally self-possessed' on the stage for amateur dramatics, if lacking the 'graciousness of manner' of their elders. On the Blaskets, the motherless Maurice O'Sullivan had a childhood untrammelled and with much adult company; he could be found at wakes 'talking and conversing of the affairs of the world'.[111] Gearóid Ó Catháin's account of his Blasket childhood portrays it as idyllic and liberating 'roaming the island from house to house ... I felt that the rest of the islanders were as young as me and that I was as old as them ... I was always used to doing what I wanted', whereas children on the mainland were 'more disciplined and confined'.[112]

An account of childhood on Cape Clear in the 1930s recalled that 'although there was poverty and hardship around us we didn't seem to realise it. The shoes were discarded on 1 May and we walked on the grass margins until our feet got accustomed to the roads.' The regattas were the highlight of the summer with games of cards in the winter and very few radios: 'at the Scoruíocht (house visiting) people talked about fishing, the Great War and the civil war'. Irish was spoken by the older generation 'among themselves' though they 'often spoke English to the children'. The radio and the news of the war were particularly eagerly awaited on Cape Clear because of its tradition of marine service. There were more radios by 1939:

> It was very difficult to get Radio Éireann so we had to listen to the BBC home service and we often listened to Lord Haw Haw [William Joyce, broadcasting as a Nazi propagandist] as the people of the island were gravely concerned about the well-being of their relatives who were serving in the navy as they were all aware of the ships in which they were serving.[113]

Frances Daly also grew up on Cape Clear in the 1930s; her father was an avid reader and 'much in demand' as a letter writer 'especially important letters to government departments'. She also remembered tourists who were 'for the most part, day trippers of the affluent brigade. They bought picnic baskets and all kind of exotic fruits and foods.'[114] On the Aran Islands, for Pádraig O'Toole, the eldest of seven born on Inishmore in 1938, his 'first memories are of constant gales'. Like others, he recalled religion and the annual pilgrimage to honour various saints and maintained 'I never knew want … we were poor and didn't know it … I do not remember having any toys when I was very young.' He too recalled the impact of the radio: 'my mother bought a radio that worked with a big wet battery which had to be charged every two weeks. Generally it was my task to bring the battery the eight miles to Kilronan on my bike,' where the local policeman had a generator.[115] Young visitors to the islands sometimes found a freedom unavailable on the mainland; Sighle Humphreys, for example, devoted to the language and an ardent activist in the republican cause, found freedom on the Blasket Islands as well as cultural and linguistic purity: 'Here she had been able to slip from the reins of decorum that her family had tried (unsuccessfully) to impose on her and lead a wild, rampant life of dances, high-jinks and outdoor adventure.'[116]

But a child's time on the island was complicated by schooling or economic prospects. Before the national school system providing state-funded elementary education was introduced in the 1830s, on Inishbofin itinerant teachers known as 'poor scholars' sometimes visited and were paid in money or potatoes.[117] As Pádraig O'Toole saw it on the Aran Islands, his aim and that of his island peers was to grow up, emigrate and send money home.[118] This was hardly surprising, given what many of them grew up with: Michael Carney, who left the Blasket Islands aged sixteen in 1937, had a father who emigrated to America 'not once but twice and moving back to the island both times'. Carney remembered islanders saying 'you can't eat the view', but he was another who recorded 'they did not think of themselves as being poor either'. Yet it was revealing that 'the young people of the island were never taught about its history as we were growing up'. For O'Toole and his fellow islanders, there was always a 'thirst for information. But of course it was always old news by the time it got to the island.'[119]

In O'Donnell's *Islanders*, education is a priority: 'the school books were made the first call on the price of the eggs'.[120] Cape Clear school was inspected in 1854, when the teacher was 'untrained and a probationer'; the school was 'a very indifferent thatched cabin containing two rooms with a wooden partition between to separate the boys from the girls'. With the boys,

> the answering of the classes was in most particulars fair, and, under the circumstances, might be termed good. The island is about ten miles from the mainland, the channel often dangerous and the means of communication bad. It was gratifying to find that in so remote a locality so much progress had been made. Irish is the vernacular but even here it is becoming obsolete with the rising generation. I was informed that all the children were related as the islanders all intermarry. The children were not deficient in natural intelligence. Idiocy is rare in the island which contains about 819 inhabitants.

The girls' school, however, was not faring so well and was deemed to be in

> a very ineffective state and I believe, chiefly owing to the inattention of the teacher who seems to be occupied entirely with her domestic affairs to the neglect of her school ... as specimens of the pupils' ignorance I may mention that the most advanced said 'Ireland belonged to America' and that 'England was the capital of Ireland'.[121]

On a visit to Cape Clear in August 1920 the school inspector noted 'the speech of the pupils needs to be improved. They should be trained to speak readily, audibly and with a reasonable degree of correctness. Simultaneous reading and especially simultaneous speaking, serve little purpose here.'[122] The following year another inspector reported some progress and 'a fluent knowledge of the English and Irish language', but he was unimpressed with the lack of individuality and 'chorus answering'.[123] This remained a consistent complaint and was perhaps a particular issue on those islands where visits from officialdom were infrequent: 'The outstanding defect in the school still is that the pupils will not speak. They are not trained to use their vocal organs. This defect persists in Irish and in English.'[124]

There were more positive reports on the schoolchildren on Rathlin, it being observed in 1923 that 'there is a bright and progressive spirit in this island school at present. The children rally well and evidently appreciate their school business,' though three years later it was declared that 'infants are not well enough trained'.[125] Michael McLaverty in his novel *Call my Brother Back* (1939) depicts thirteen-year-old Colm MacNeill fishing idyllically with his father on Rathlin, but the teacher is frustrated: 'they say fish is good for the brain – the fool that said that never taught in an island'; the kids' stomachs were full of fish and their 'brains full of blackguardism'.[126]

Of course, many island teachers were also visitors, but native teachers too could make an impact, none more so than Myles Joyce. When Brian McLoughlin visited some of the western islands for the IFC in the summer of 1942 he travelled to Inishbofin and made the following robust assertion:

> I have never met in any single district, people as well educated as the elderly folk of this island. This they themselves attribute to the teaching ability of one Myles Joyce, who, being a native of the island was the first national teacher appointed by the government to teach in his native island. He is remembered by the older generation as having been a man of incomparable capabilities.[127]

The government's stance on the question of the feasibility of island schools was outlined by the Department of Education in early 1960 (see also chapter 3): 'if the number of pupils on an island is too small to justify a school there the department either pays in whole or in part for the cost of a boat service to bring the children to the mainland or gives a grant to enable them to be boarded out there'.[128] At that stage an average daily attendance of ten pupils was required, or in officialese, ten 'units'. But there were complaints in 1953 that the boarding-out grant for island children to be educated on the mainland was 'meagre' at only 1s 10d in the early 1950s: 'it wouldn't buy butter for their bread'.[129]

Numerous references to the Irish language in the context of island schooling were indicative of a wider concern about the demise of the native tongue. Irish-language island communities were often deemed to have a unique status as the purest keepers of the linguistic flame, but the islands were not immune from wider economic, social and cultural forces that impinged on the status and use of the language, though some islands remained resolutely Irish speaking. Rathlin was linguistically interesting because there was a good deal of Scots Gaelic intermixed with Irish, as recorded by Swedish language specialist Nils Holmer in 1937–8.[130]

In correspondence with some of the natives of Inishmaan, where he had stayed, Synge was told 'let you write the next letter in Irish, if you don't I won't look upon it'.[131] When his correspondent Martin McDonagh wrote in Irish, Synge sometimes struggled to translate; McDonagh was not comfortable writing in either language: 'excuse the writer for not writing good Irish or good English'.[132] The following year, however, he was able to report that 'we have a branch of the Gaelic League in Inishmaan now and the people is going on well with writing Irish and reading'.[133] Ultimately, Synge was to make the Aran Islands famous by writing about them in the English language, and his one-act play *Riders to the Sea* was also in English, though it was translated into Irish by a teacher at St Endas, Tomás Mac Domhnaill; like many Gaelic League activists Mac Domhnaill was concerned about the paucity of quality Irish-language drama.[134] The play was also translated into Russian and French: 'In French, it loses a good deal', was Synge's verdict.[135]

When giving evidence to the Commission on the Gaeltacht in 1925, the curate on Arranmore, Fr Duggan observed that the island children used Irish when playing but that 'there is one little section English speaking, the section of the police barrack and the landlord garrison character. The people who know a little English like to parade it on all possible occasions to show they are a little superior to the rest. Then in the homes these people themselves would speak Irish.'

Seasonal migration was a central part of the islanders' lives, as was emigration. Arranmore produced some of the best miners and tunnellers

working in England, who were later to be credited with making a significant contribution to the expansion of the London underground railway
network.[136] When aboard, noted Fr Duggan, 'they speak Irish exclusively
amongst themselves', while on the island, school attendance was irregular
and a place where 'English has got to be taught as a foreign language'.[137]
Yet there were also those 'Gaelic people who think themselves superior
to those who have lost the language. They sneer at people who threw up
Irish for English ... a sort of feeling that they themselves have preserved
some higher attitude to life than those who have lost the language ... it is
a sort of spiritual attitude – the other is material.'

One of the members of the Commission who questioned Fr Duggan was unequivocal in seizing on that remark: 'The inhabitants of
Arranmore are certainly a great asset to the nation if they keep the island
in that way with that spirit alive among them'.[138] Fr S. J. Walsh, the parish priest of the Aran Islands, also gave evidence to the Gaeltacht Commission and noted 'there are very few who do not understand English
fairly well. Most of them understand it quite well', and that school work
was done 'in almost every case' through Irish but due to the economic
realities and emigration young intending emigrants were 'most anxious
to know English and are urged to it by their older brothers or sisters or
friends in America or by their parents, who, in many cases have been to
America themselves'. Revealingly, however, the priest's main priority was
to speak about economic rather than linguistic matters.[139]

Collectors for the IFC also had many observations to make about
the status and use of the Irish language on the islands. Brian McLoughlin
went to great lengths to record the Irish words used to describe boat parts
and fish and the mood of the sea on Inishark and how descriptions of it
were colloquially expressed (*tá rit sa fairrige* – 'there's a run in the sea')
or a single word, such as *saigdú* ('the thrusting of oars perpendicularly in
the water between the two ends of a net circularly set so as to prevent the
escape of the surrounded fish') or *talta*: 'This is the name applied to the
improvised "tent" which is constructed by placing the sail of a boat across
the gunwales so as to provide shelter and protection against rain for the
members of the crew while sleeping.'[140]

On Inishbofin, McLoughlin recorded that the English language is that which is entirely spoken by the islanders. In the whole island of 500 persons there are only about ten people who could converse in the Irish language ... I have been told that the natives preferred to imitate their landlord Mr Allies and speak his vernacular ... for the past eighty years the Irish language has not been an everyday tongue amongst the natives.

Also relevant was the language of commerce – English – as practised at the ports of Westport, Galway and Clifden.[141] On Inishturk in County Mayo only English was spoken with 'only five or six elderly people capable of conducting a conversation through Irish. I have even met a man of ninety years who was unable to continue a conversation in Irish. He admitted his inability to do so, though he understands the language very well.' The younger generation, however, had no interest.[142]

On Clare Island, McLoughlin discovered

there are only half a score of people ... capable of conducting a conversation through the medium of Irish. Two generations ago however, the Irish language was widely spoken here. The only excuse offered for its disappearance is that the people became disinterested ... the fact that the police were ever stationed here may have had something to do with the sudden decay of the language here.[143]

Folklore collectors were ultimately reliant on a dwindling group; as Brian McLoughlin saw it on Inishark: 'I had in view one man in particular whose knowledge of Irish seems to be inexhaustible and I knew if I should get even one Fenian tale from him, the Commission should have a fair idea of the language as spoken in this island.'[144]

Michael Murphy was a full-time collector for the IFC in Antrim and went to Rathlin in 1954; he was told that 'when Rathlin folk went to Ballycastle the people there used to mock them for speaking Irish and that the people tried to learn as much English as they could. It was the Ballycastle people who helped to kill the Irish here on Rathlin.'[145] Reg Hindley studied the linguistic tradition of Cape Clear in 1958, at a time when it had 253 residents, but did not publish his results until 1994 owing

to 'assurances of confidentiality' and 'dependence on Gaeltacht grants'.
He did find elderly *Gaeilgeoiri* (Irish speakers) who were cynical about
the usefulness of the language. The appearance of the lighthouse in the
early nineteenth century had brought to the island the first known resident non-Irish speakers, while English was used by the post office service
from the 1870s and there was an increasing awareness of the economic
importance of English. But the language survived; by 1926 the population was still one of native speakers as Irish remained the home and community language 'but with a marked loss of confidence in its sufficiency
for a full and prosperous life'. Between 1925 and 1957, 90 per cent of the
island's youth had emigrated.[146]

The Cape Clear Island Irish dialect was rich and individual, but with
schooling came the teaching of 'correct standard Irish', which also shook
confidence in the local language. Conchúr Ó Siocháin commented in his
memoir of life on Cape that 'it used to gladden our hearts to be outside
the walls of the school and to be free to speak Irish to one another'.[147]
In any case, he left school before he was literate 'to stay at home to do
a little bit of work and be of general use'. The teacher was said to have
switched to teaching religion in English so that returned emigrants could
understand the language and because, in the words of native schoolmaster Joseph O'Driscoll, with the backing of the curate, 'the saving of one's
soul was by far more important than saving the language'. Hindley was
unambiguous; in his view, the fact 'that Irish has survived at all on Clear
Island may be regarded as a success for the state's language policies', a reference to the use of grants to sustain Gaeltacht areas (see chapter 3).[148]
Ó Siocháin was positive in his book in 1940 about the fate of the Irish
language; it was an excellent idea, he believed, to send children to the
Gaeltacht to learn Irish, but 'they should be a year among the old people
talking and listening to them ... I will not hold back as much as a single
word of the ancient heritage of the speech that I inherited from the old
people.'[149]

Cape Clear's poet and language scholar, Donnchadh Ó Drisceoil,
wrote extensively on aspects of the island's life and customs. He was
described as 'a philosopher who had a resource of humour and language'
with 'a creative and imaginative use of Irish'. In one of his essays he

expressed a meaning for fifteen different uses of one word. He possessed by nature the same characteristics he attributed to the old people whom he knew. They, he wrote, had fluency and accuracy of language that left poetry in their speech as a background to their conversation, the same as blood in a living body. Donnchadh was a teacher to many academics who came to visit him in his island home.

One observer suggested 'the heroic age comes to life again when Donnchadh speaks'.[150]

It was consistently maintained over decades that islanders needed to be better educated about health. On Tory in 1897, the inspector compiling a report for the CDB elaborated, with some surprise, on the health of the natives:

> This is the more surprising when one considers the conditions under which they live, conditions which, on the mainland are always conducive to weakness of intellect and insanity, viz: the intermarrying of persons related. There is not a family on Tory that is not connected in some way with another. Perhaps the large quantity of fish consumed by the islanders may account for this as that would keep the supply of phosphorous to the blood abnormally high.[151]

On Inishkea, Charles Browne found the hearing and sight of the fishermen 'very acute' but he also noted that 'disease is often ascribed to supernatural agencies and for this reason is often treated by charms and incantations'.[152] This was common on many islands. On Rathlin in the 1950s, Rose McCurdy noted that with regard to measles 'whiskey and sulphur was the remedy here' while asthma was treated with docken seed: 'they boiled it with dog-bane and drank the juice'. Cuts were treated with 'virgin moss and the leaves of sunflower'.[153] Traditional remedies infuriated the district nurse on Aran, B. N. Hedderman, a native of Clare who recalled her time on Aran from 1903 when she was 'cut off from all refined companionship, the counsel of superiors and the help of medical advice where scientific methods are unknown or ignored'.[154] Hedderman was one of the Jubilee Nurses who worked in remote districts from 1890 until the 1970s, their training financed by donations made to honour the golden jubilee of Queen Victoria. The poverty of the districts they covered and the sheer length of their working week complicated their lot.

Hedderman had to deal with an abundance of 'ignorant women' and men when it came to the rudiments of healthcare. She visited a very ill woman dying on a damp floor: '"Give her a drop of poteen" the woman's husband said. "No!" I replied.' Yet in recent years there had been some 'diminution of primeval customs' and they had a life span that was impressive: 'many can boast of having passed the allotted span ... what they eat is deprived of those culinary accessories and mixtures that bring disease to the rich and better fed and the diet they are obliged to subsist upon is better calculated to promote health.'[155]

In relation to dealing with maladies and injuries, however, Hedderman was aghast that the Aranites 'adopted ways as old-world and quackish as they were unscientific and some of the treatment applied for the ailments of children was really barbaric'; they also retained a boundless fatalism. There was a whooping cough epidemic in 1908 and the prevailing belief was that it was inevitable children would get this along with scarlet fever and measles, 'and the sooner the better', so that 'the diseased mingle indiscriminately with the healthy'. She was also unequivocal in asserting that their 'cures' were 'unmistakably responsible for a number of deaths amongst the children'.

Those deaths were seen as 'God's will', like so much else to do with island life, and any progress was often halted by women ('the men's conversion to modern methods is much more pronounced than the women's').[156] Hedderman lambasted 'absurd superstition', including the belief that 'the spell which is to bring about the cure is broken by the presence of either doctor or nurse'. An injured leg was treated with 'a compound of dock leaves blended with snails', and when one island man had a hernia, 'I went on a nine mile sea journey to procure him a truss, only to find on my next visit that he had not even tried it on.'[157]

A cradle for a newborn was a cast-off 'held together by whole colonies of crawling insects'. Before that, 'directly an infant is ushered into the world the first person entering the lying-in-chamber must spit upon the new born, then on the mother and finally on the nurse' (the 'saliva cure'). When a child was bitten by a dog the hair of the dog was 'rubbed swiftly across its mouth ... it is really sad that these relics of barbarism are still so strong in Aran.'[158] Hedderman was also concerned about excessive drinking; she lectured a man whose drinking was exacerbating his illness, to which he replied, 'If Solon and all the preachers had lived long in Aran, they'd want a pint.'[159] The attitudes and practices that appalled Hedderman were not exclusive to Aran. On Omey it was believed 'the juice of the boiled dog fish is very good for anyone suffering from asthma.'[160] On Inishmurray in Sligo, a cure for chest infections was 'an old style sugar bag of coarse brown paper impregnated with rendered goose fat pinned to the undershirt and worn next to the skin.'[161]

The absence of medical assistance on islands remained contentious for decades and was one reason for the evacuation of some of them; the death of Seán Carney on the Great Blasket Island in January 1947 was regarded by his brother Mike as an event that 'signalled the end for the island'. By the time Mike got back to the island from Dublin, Seán's body was still in the bed and 'decomposition had already started to set in'.[162] Seán had died of meningitis, 'but the islanders had no knowledge of this terrible disease'.[163]

But what difference would it have made if they had diagnosed it? Would aid have arrived in time? As his sister Kate recalled, Seán had complained of a headache:

> I did everything for him but he was not getting any better. He didn't want anyone to be walking on the floor he was so bad and the weather was bad outside and we couldn't send for a doctor or priest ... he had a very bad headache. We had done everything for him and we couldn't do any more. What did I do for him in the end? I put flour heating in the oven and I put it in a little flour bag and I put it across his head.[164]

Even in the 1960s Margaret Day, the public health nurse on Inishbofin, had to bring patients down to the ferry on a cart pulled by donkey;

she was one who 'cheerfully takes on the job of being nurse, health worker and chiropodist all rolled into one for the 247 islanders'. There was no doctor on the island but improvements came with a new medical centre and helicopter service.[165]

Islanders also had their own customs associated with death and burials that were much remarked upon by visitors. On Inishbofin the distribution of clay pipes and tobacco at wakes was the norm, the remnants of which were brought to the cemetery

> at a certain spot in which a fire was prepared and all the smoking population congregated around the fire; then the pipes and tobacco were distributed. In this manner was spent the interval during which the grave was being opened. Those who were looked upon as well-to-do people brought whiskey to the grave and distributed [it] but such practice would be strictly confined to the wealthy folk.[166]

On Inishturk in County Mayo coffins were made by a native free of charge and the keening over the dead body was

> generally begun by two old women who cry bitterly over the corpse. The keening is carried on at intervals – three times each night ... while the deceased is being waked a plate of tobacco is placed on the chest of the corpse. The grave is never dug until the corpse arrives at the cemetery. When the grave is closed the same plate which is placed on the corpse is again filled with tobacco and placed on the grave while all the smoking population sit around and smoke until satisfied.[167]

On Clare Island, old graves were 'reopened again and again', and at funerals 'if any tobacco and pipes remain over they are all piled in one heap on top of the grave and are left there'.[168] In 1942 the IFC's Brian McLoughlin, when visiting Omey, noted the waking of a corpse on a kitchen table with a plate of tobacco on feet or chest but the custom of bringing tobacco to the graveside was 'almost dead'.[169] An island widow was also one to be wary of: 'the widow woman's curse was the worst of all, except the priest'.[170] Tomás Ó Crohan devoted a chapter of his book to the Blasket Island wake; it was important to get 'goods for the wake' and such was the extent of the porter being purchased that he wondered 'if they were going to have both a wedding and a wake'. The corpse was carefully prepared 'for the journey to the other side'. Pipes of tobacco also featured strongly – 'so we spent a good part of the night; tobacco going in plenty; some of them sending their pipes three times to the tobacco place to be refilled; and all that before the day lightened' – as did drink:

> that was the wake that interested me most, and the reason was that there was drink at it – a thing I had never seen before. There have not been many wakes since without a cask or two, and I don't think much of the practice, for it's the usual thing that wherever there is drink there is horseplay and that's not a fit thing in a house of the kind.[171]

Ó Crohan recorded in his diary in 1921 that at another wake, 'Those with a fondness for drink had no interest whatever in the food.'[172] He also attributed the longevity of islanders to lack of food: 'the fact is that the eaters of good meat are in the grave this long time, while those who lived on starvation diet are still alive and kicking'.[173]

On Cape Clear at wakes in the 1930s

> the women stayed in the room [with the body] and the men went into the kitchen. Everyone was offered a cigarette or a smoke from a clay pipe. At night, about eleven o'clock, tea was served and the Rosary recited. There was another tea at about 4–5 a.m. for those who stayed up all night and a glass of whiskey for anyone who wanted it. In earlier times, the women used to keen over the remains before it was brought to the church but that custom had died out.[174]

On Inishmurray it was recorded for the IFC in 1938, 'when the cuckoo is heard on the island by a person on the mainland it is believed that someone on the mainland is going to die. There are separate burial places for males and females ... if a man were buried in a female place the corpse would be over the ground in the morning.'[175]

Many of these wakes and burials followed drownings; it was the sea that was the most savage force in the islanders' lives and it was unrelenting and unforgiving, creating a sound that, according to Darrell Figgis in *Children of Earth* (1918), 'was as complicated in its intimacies as it was terrifying in its vastness'.[176] Synge was being naïve and overly optimistic when he recorded in his diary in May 1898, just after he had arrived on Aran, that 'I feel before long I will know every secret of the sea'.[177] He did, however, capture aspects of its terror in *Riders to the Sea*. As Cathleen remarks, it is pitiful that what's left of 'a great rower and fisher' could just be a 'bit of old shirt and a plain stocking'.[178]

The islanders knew the sea like no others. Richard Power was entranced by watching a fisherman on Aran who was 'sort of drunk with the strength and marvel of the ocean. In moments like this I thought he wasn't Christian at all, but a pagan worshipping old nature Gods whose tyranny still held sway here,' but as the ocean became rougher, it became a 'merciless tyrant'.[179] Another novelist, Walter Macken, who achieved great success with *Rain on the Wind* (1950), was similar to Liam O'Flaherty in his direct, unflinching portrayal of the reality of the lives of the poor in the west and also focused some of his work on the Aran Islands, which, though born in Galway city, he regarded as 'on my own heath so to speak'. *Rain on the Wind* depicts the sea as

> a vicious enemy of land and it chewed its way in and out and in the middle and it scooped out Galway bay so that the bits that remain after its feats are the islands ... and it is obvious that they must be very tough land indeed when even the inexhaustible stomach of the Atlantic ocean could not digest them.[180]

German folklorist Heinrich Becker, who visited Aran for many years, was also transfixed with 'the constant anger of the jealous and hungry sea', while later, young poet Seamus Heaney was also enraptured, as seen in the poem 'Lovers on Aran':

Did sea define the land or land the sea?
Each drew meaning from the waves' collision
Sea broke on land to full identity.[181]

Stories, tales, myths and songs about the sea and fishing were a main-stay of island communication.[182] Proximity to and dependence on the sea also generated a preoccupation with mermaids. Lady Gregory was told 'there is no luck if you meet a mermaid and you are out at sea, but storms will come or some ill will happen'.[183] In 1939 Heinrich Becker travelled to Galway to research stories associated with the sea and collected a lot of material on the Aran Islands including audio-tapes, photographs and transcripts of stories:

> Oh yes, says I, I have seen the mermaid ... we caught her in the trammel net ... she had a fine pole of hair ... I caught her on the tail behind and sure it was no use for me to catch her on the tail; she was gone away, she was, right enough, she had a tail like a fish.

Mermaid stories from Aran from 1942 to 1944 included titles like 'Kilronan Boy Lives with Mermaid' and 'Man Marries Mermaid'.[184] Islanders also involved themselves in daring rescues:

> with a life line running from the cliff top to a sheep heeled over against the rocks, hounded there by the slavering storm, of the sailors carried up the very face of the cliffs to the warm safety of the islanders' homes and then, in the dawn, when the storm was spent, the islanders would climb the same cliff-face to carry up just as tenderly the precious wrack.[185]

The crew of the lifeboat on Arranmore rescued eighteen men from a Dutch steamer in 1940 in horrendous conditions; in an open boat, dur-ing a hurricane, they embarked on their four-hour rescue mission. The coxswain, John Boyle, was subsequently awarded a rare gold medal from the Royal National Lifeboat Institution; other crew members were hon-oured with silver and bronze medals for their 'courage, unselfishness and devotion to duty'. They were also honoured by medals awarded by Queen Wilhelmina of the Netherlands in 1942.[186]

Peadar O'Donnell was particularly familiar with the island of Arranmore (the islanders who only ever had 'dry bread an' tay, an' praties an' herrin' unlike the mainlanders with 'the bacon an' the eggs the beef an' the fowl') and was also able to capture in *Islanders* the impact of the decline of the fishing stock in the early twentieth century as the fishermen waited, too often in vain, for the appearance of fish. The excitement caused by the appearance of a herring shoal was dramatic: 'a week's frenzied reaping of a great harvest' as families suddenly leaped from naked poverty to comparative wealth and £23 for a week's fishing: 'tea, sugar, flour, tobacco were all available now' (before that 'Manus himself was smoking tea'). It was also a question of careful navigation: 'it's a question of bein' through the first breaker 'fore it bursts ... an' of no lettin' the next or the next catch ye with its broken top'.[187] In April 1922 Tomás Ó Crohan on the Blaskets noted that the weather was exceptionally poor: 'the islanders have been on holiday for almost the entire year. They cannot go fishing. They have nothing to do on land.'[188]

For some islanders everything, including their education, revolved around fishing. Tom Lacey, a native of Inishark, recalled learning how to mend fishing nets: 'that was the greatest lesson ... I never got anything out of the lessons that I learned going to school'. He noted that Michael Dillon from the Aran Islands 'came into the island to teach us how to mend nets ... he was there three months with us' (Dillon also went to the neighbouring islands of Inishbofin and Inishturk). But fishing also brought the most harrowing experiences including, for Lacey, 'the worst night ever ... what I thought of was how long would I be dying when I'd get out'.[189] On Inishbofin, the collector for the IFC found that the islanders were not 'nearly as hardy, cannot endure as much hardship and in dealing with the sea, are not as intrepid as the people of their sister isle, Inishark'.[190]

Micheál Ó Dálaigh, born in 1910 and who lived on Cape Clear and fished between the two world wars, remembered simply and starkly, 'we were often *fuar, fliuch, imníoch, ocrach, anróch*' ('cold, wet, anxious, hungry, miserable'). Ó Dálaigh's cousin John Daly was one of four islanders who saved forty-six sailors using a yawl in severe weather conditions when the SS *Nestorian* went aground south-west of the island in 1917; the following year Daly himself and five others were drowned. Islanders of Cape Clear had a long tradition and proud record of service in the US navy and merchant fleet, including during both world wars; twelve islanders lost their lives at sea during the Second World War.[191] Cape Clear fishermen often worked until 10 or 11 p.m. 'by the light of the Tilley lamps' and they had a hierarchy of fish: '*Is fearr craiceann an langa ná an trosc go léir*' ('the skin of the ling is better than a whole cod').[192]

Trying to read the sea required great precision. There was a saying of Aran boatmen, 'that a man must keep his tongue in the centre of his mouth when in a currach. Everything depends on a perfect balance.'[193] In Eilís Dillon's children's book *The Lost Island* (1952), 'the sea was too big to be inviting' and Mike, in search of his missing father, notes that 'very few of the island men can swim. They say the sea may be all right for the fishes but a Christian was meant to stay on dry land.'[194] This was a common attitude; on the Blasket Islands, Gearóid Ó Catháin noted that 'most of the fishermen never learned to swim, as they felt it would be better to drown quickly rather than put up a fight. Also, the sea was viewed as a place of work, not of leisure.'[195]

There were others, including on Inishturk, for example, who held the belief that 'when one is mysteriously saved from drowning he will at some future date when least expecting it become the victim of the sea ... "the sea must have its share" is a common phrase in all these islands.'[196] It was also believed unlucky on Inisheer 'to save a corpse from the sea'.[197] On Omey, the 'old people used say that if a dead body remained in the sea the weather would be bad ever until the corpse were removed from the tide'.[198] There were other superstitions about what was permissible on a boat: it was deemed unlucky to carry an empty coffin; whistling on board was also considered taboo – 'it was feared that it would cause the wind to rise' – as was spitting over the side of a boat.[199]

A measure of the toll the sea could take, when combined with other travails, was evident in a note compiled by a local priest on victims of the Inishbofin island tragedy in 1942 when four young island fishermen were drowned: 'Joseph Tierney (21). Single. His father gets £15 per year. Another brother Michael drowned in 1927. Two brothers away and working for themselves. Two sisters at home. Another brother died in the free state army ... very deserving.'[200] Tierney and three other island fishermen had come to Cleggan on the mainland to be paid for fish; there was a heavy mist as they prepared to return: Tierney 'tried hard without success to persuade his companions to delay their departure as they had no overcoats. There was a dance in the locality and he suggested that they should attend it for a few hours until the mist had lifted, but Cloherty was anxious to get home as there was nobody in the house with his aged, widowed mother.'[201]

There was also remarkable stoicism, acceptance and understatement in reacting to adversity. When, in 1990, Pat Reilly from the Inishkeas and a survivor of the 1927 Cleggan disaster was interviewed, he was asked, 'How did the families of the drowned lads get on?' and his response was, 'They got on all right, they had to bear it out.'[202] Sea tragedies also brought islanders together, or, as Peadar O'Donnell described it in *Proud island* (1975), 'one night of storm and the boats out made one heart of all its people ... no hope, no hope in the world for a boat further out ... they had come together in fear', but by spring 'young men willingly took to the spade ... the island was fighting back'.[203]

The sea was also relevant to the law of windfall, when wreckage came ashore on the islands. On Omey,

> he who first leaves his hand on the wreckage is he who becomes the owner of it, but should he have to solicit the aid of others to put the wreckage in a safe place it must then be divided equally among them. Or if one finds wreckage ashore one may make a small monument of stones – a few stones placed one over the other – in the shore beside it so that the next person to come that way will know that this windfall has been found by someone else. This law holds good at least on this island.[204]

In Maurice O'Sullivan's account of the Blaskets during the years of the First World War, one man could exclaim '"By God! ... War is good!"' with flour, meat, wine and clothes washed up (and also bodies). This was a time when the population was still growing. Island poet Micheál O'Guiheen recalled that after one vessel sank, 'there wasn't a morning for a month afterwards that you would not see some currach or other passing the Spur from the West, and it piled high with wreck.'[205]

On Achill, 'huge barrels of rum (unadulterated) containing about sixty gallons were washed up' during the same war. Salvage money offered by revenue commissioners was one-sixth of estimated value, which was deemed inadequate 'to compensate for the time and trouble spent in salvaging it', so instead such bounty was not reported.[206] While each tenant was deemed to own a portion of the shore there were also tensions over seaweed, understandable given the importance for so long of kelp. There were even disputes on Aran over ownership that resulted in court cases. This was a particularly difficult issue to adjudicate on as the names 'rambling weed' and 'drifting weed' would suggest ('Case dismissed' said the judge, hardly surprisingly). Stories were also recorded of fairies punishing the 'nocturnal seaweed gatherer' by beating him with sea rods.[207]

That was a reminder that there had to be order, method and systems for doing island work, including not just sea work but tasks performed on land. In this, much had to be made from so little. What poet Cathal Ó Searcaigh captured in verse about rural Donegal was applicable to many of the islands:

> Above and below, I see the holdings
> farmed from the mouth of wilderness
> This is the poem-book of my people,
> The manuscript they toiled at
> With the ink of their sweat
> Here every enclosed field is like a verse
> In the great poem of land reclamation.[208]

One observer of the Aran Islands suggested that 'much of the intelligence' of the islanders came from the absence of division of labour, which led to 'considerable activity of mind ... he is a skilled fisherman and can manage a currach with extraordinary nerve ... he can farm simply, burn kelp, cut out pampooties, mend nets, build and thatch a house and make a cradle or a coffin'.[209] Nóra Ní Shúillobháin, born on Valentia Island in 1909, recalled in 1976 that to be born there 'was to enter teeming, varied life', or as another Valentia native expressed it, 'there wasn't a man who hadn't a foot in the land and a foot in the sea'.[210]

Other islanders were doing completely different work and Aran native and writer Liam O'Flaherty found the island in general a good place to work, but it also drove him demented. He wrote to his agent, Edward Garnett, in 1924 after a spell on Aran: 'my visit home was very melancholy and the only way I could see my way out of going mad was by pretending to myself that nothing mattered to me in life but literature'.[211] He also decided to work there in the summer of 1931: 'I find it very invigorating and full of copy, together with being very cheap if one lives au naturel. Still, the weather is frightful.' The following summer he was, he wrote to fellow writer Francis Stuart, 'living a monastic life. No cigarettes, no drink, no women, nothing but work ... I was thinking of buying an old watchtower on the island ... I like it very much for work.' It was better for him to live like that and just 'be immoral now and again'.[212]

On Inishturk the people were found by the IFC collector to be 'very hardy'; at 122, the island had double the population of Inishark: 'this is due to the fact that each young man who becomes heir to his parents' property believes in getting married at a marriageable age and each couple rears a large family'.[213] This was an interesting observation, underlining again the variation of island patterns and different attitudes to marriage. On Tory, the findings of Robin Fox, who carried out fieldwork there from 1960 to 1965, yielded intriguing results on this subject. His 'most startling' discovery was the Tory pattern of separate residences for some husbands and wives: 'once predominant and even now prominent'. This was born of a reluctance to break up the original family unit, a situation 'both real and paradoxical'. In 1963, of fifty-one married couples, ten were not cohabiting. For some, a woman's first duty was to her 'own' people, and that was preferred to the alternative of creating extended households. Children would live with the mother, and as for carnal relations, '"there's always the fields, surely"' he was told, and '"who would want to be spending a long time at it anyway?"' ... intercourse on Tory is clothed and brief, nor is a horizontal position deemed essential ... immediate orgasm is the goal and the boast of sophisticates.' Fox was also told 'better an illegitimate child than an unsuitable marriage. This is not and was not a common attitude in Ireland.'[214]

The degree to which islanders were suspicious of outsiders continued to be commented on, but that was not the same as unfriendliness. As Francis MacManus saw it, 'the worst side the people could show you would be stolidly sullen faces, but they hardly ever show that unless some visiting fool is offensively patronising'.[215] It was perhaps no wonder that the question was asked: 'Don't we have the right to live unexamined lives?'[216] Islanders were well aware they were viewed with some hostility on the mainland, or, as Mike Carney of the Blaskets saw it, 'the people that lived on the mainland thought that the islanders were a different breed altogether; kind of wildish, I suppose'. They spoke a different Irish and walked 'single file ... like wild geese' due to narrow island paths; but they also 'took great pride in [their] appearance'.[217]

The wariness mainlanders and islanders had of each other boiled down to the idea that 'Ireland and the island are two quite different places'.[218] Rose McCurdy, an eighty-three-year-old woman living on Rathlin in 1954 told a collector from the IFC, 'I like the Irish people, that's what they call them from the mainland here. I'm one of the Irish myself. I was married to an islandman and they didn't like that. They weren't half satisfied and never are.'[219] Some islanders tended to say they were going 'out' rather than 'in' to the mainland, which Deborah Tall suggested indicated their disdain.[220]

Islanders were also capable of fierce criticism of the forces that marginalised them and dismissive of mainland life; as was said on Rathlin: 'wouldn't she be better at home on the island instead of living on the edge of the beam' (meaning 'with a precarious income or livelihood') on the mainland? Another expression there was 'when one leaves the island it's seldom a better'.[221] In Peadar O'Donnell's *Proud Island* Mary Jim asks, 'What have we to do with Ireland? What notice did Ireland ever take of us?' Another character wonders 'how would men from the inside of counters or teachers, or doctors know what an island needed?'[222] Islanders could also rejoice 'when a man from the island got the better of a know-all from outside'.[223] They resented being taken advantage of; T. H.

Mason recounted that a mainland doctor refused to travel to the island for a sick-call unless paid three guineas in cash, which was 'agreed angrily', but then the islanders refused to bring him back to the mainland for less than five pounds. He had no choice but to pay.[224]

On Cape Clear, Francis MacManus in 1950 refused to romanticise the inhabitants; the people were 'ordinary, respectable, matter-of-fact and solid ... there is none of the primitive colour and energy and deeply smouldering emotion that gives tourists the feeling they are in another land and even in another age ... they are emotionally stable'.[225] Likewise, in relation to the impending demise of Gola in Donegal in the late 1960s, the islanders were muted: 'to the outsider the situation appears highly dramatic, to the islanders it lacks all drama'.[226] Nor were the Aran island-ers, as folklorist Heinrich Becker discovered, ignorant of the affairs of the world; they were 'far wiser than visitors who come among them would imagine'.[227]

They were also occasionally boastful about the idea of exceptional autonomy; as noted earlier, Austin Clarke saw it simply: 'the islanders rule themselves'.[228] What did this mean for the island mindset? Moving to the mainland was undoubtedly regarded by some as a defeat. In Brian Friel's 1971 play *The Gentle Island* there is an exodus of the dwindling population of an offshore island apart from the one-armed King Manus Sweeney, his two sons and a daughter-in-law. Sweeney insists the exiles are on their way to slavery. An older gay man and his protégé then arrive, one enhanced by the island's tranquillity, the other cynical, while the king's stories of prowess are exposed as fraudulent. Violence ensues 'and the play ends with three frustrated and embittered people left in their several lonelinesses on the island paradise'.[229] There was little subtlety in this play but Friel was bravely exploring the theme of homosexual as outsider as well as the combination of humour, brutality and the chasm between rhetoric and reality that had been a mainstay in fictionalising the islands, and exposing the myth that the islanders were in any way 'innocent' or that they inhabited an idyll. The island is, in Fintan O'Toole's words, 'craggy, daunting and inhospitable but with a savage power that is always compelling'.[230]

As the decades progressed, modern amenities undoubtedly made island life somewhat easier, but many of the same troubling issues or versions of them remained, and modernisation and commercialisation brought new strains. Case studies of aspects of life on Cape Clear undertaken by third-level students in 1975 were critical of the 'nature of the people ... their inability to agree, their natural resistance to change and their lack of energy and confidence'. They predicted it could become deserted, 'sold piece by piece to weekenders'. One study suggested the islanders were a 'proud, independent people' but that 'it is only in the last few years the islanders are making practical efforts to survive'.[231] Another such study in the 1980s highlighted many tensions over the distribution of power on the island and the difficulties of co-operation. Of these observations, the island archivist looked askance in 2013; there were too many studies, he suggested 'by people who have no real knowledge of Cape Clear and some of these lack scientific investigation and sound judgement'.[232] It was the reiteration of a long-aired complaint about outsiders reaching judgement on the essences of island life and mentality.

POSTSCRIPT

'a working island, not a day tripper's theme park'

When he was interviewed in 1974 about his role as Island's Development Officer for Gaeltarra Éireann, the industrial development agency for the Gaeltacht, Tarlach de Blacam on Inishmaan talked at length about the potential of the islands. In particular he highlighted fishing, the co-operative spirit, tourism and quality of life: 'I believe that people who live on the islands can have as full a life as they can anywhere else, perhaps a fuller life in many respects.'[1] His assertion was central to how island issues were framed in the next few decades, but alongside the claims about potential, age-old concerns continued to generate pessimism. The challenges were summed up the following decade by a national newspaper that claimed islanders were 'a people under siege from the twentieth century ... battered by winter storms and the chill winds of a less than supportive government policy'.[2]

From the early 1970s the islands were being marketed in a limited way as ideal holiday locations. An advertisement for holiday accommodation on Galway's Inishbofin, for example, offered 'pure boredom, safe for children, no TV; nothing. Just peace, sandy beaches, sea, sleep, lakes, mountains, scenic views, donkeys.'[3]

But whatever about holidaymakers, could the native islanders survive on just peace? Or on the support of what Charles Haughey referred to in 1981 as an Irish people who were unique in their 'emotional' attachment to their inheritance and 'special link' with the 'immemorial past'? (Ironically, he was speaking about the Blasket Islands, abandoned decades before.)[4] Or on their 'unique ... cast of mind, a gifted, vestigial way of thinking'?[5]

One lesson being learned by the islanders by the 1980s was the need to 'hold and develop resources on the island rather than let them be developed totally by outside interests, and to make the most of their assets', including clean air and organic agriculture.[6] Exploiting opportunities required organisation and lobbying, and co-operatives were needed to ensure eligibility for grant aid and European Union support. There were efforts to form island development associations to participate in rural development pilot projects and to market island produce alongside increasing awareness of the environment and conservation.

Matt Murphy and his family moved to Sherkin in Cork in 1975 and began to self-finance a marine centre to study marine biology, which resulted in a flood of applications to do research there; 450 people volunteered in the twenty-five years following its foundation at a time when the total resident population was under a hundred. There were surveys of flora and fauna, both terrestrial and marine: 'on Sherkin Island alone, tiny though it is in area, there are an estimated six hundred species of beetle'. The island was, in effect, 'an incubator for marine scientists'. Murphy, who also published an environmental journal, was adamant that conservation of the environment could only be achieved through painstaking research and education.[7]

Organic salmon reared off Clare Island developed an outstanding reputation; the concept was introduced by island resident Dr Peter Gill. It provided employment, and the island's population rose by 28 per cent between the 2006 and 2011 censuses, with up to ten nationalities resident there. Gill suggested the farm had been 'the single most significant motor for communal regeneration that has ever occurred on an offshore island'. While Norway and Scotland had led the European way in farmed salmon production, the Clare Island project pioneered a niche market for Irish organically reared farmed fish, though Gill would have preferred it if the islanders had held the licence rather than just having a share.[8]

On the Blaskets, the island weaving tradition was revived as the islands were 'showing some life again', with Sue Redican living on the island intermittently.[9] Achill was described in 2001 as 'a thriving community' owing to tourism, but there was little interest shown by the islanders in an eco-labelling project.[10] Islanders were also heralded as innovators; Tory's waste management and recycling programme was showcased at a conference on how communities could reduce waste; the importance of the island as a haven for wildlife, and in particular corncrakes, was also noted.[11] Inishbofin received an international eco-tourism award ('islands like these must constantly innovate to remain vibrant places') and the unique potential for star gazing was also trumpeted.[12] Rathlin's future was also deemed to lie in environmental tourism; the islanders became adept at securing grants from various sources, national and European, with one resident adamant: 'this is a working island, not a day tripper's theme park.'[13]

The island pressure group Comhdháil nOileáin na hÉireann was not always that active but it did succeed in its aim of getting more government attention focused on the islands while also seeking to learn lessons from abroad, which included a trip to Denmark by five Irish islanders to look at its transport systems to small islands.[14] In 1998 an all-island Gaelic Athletic Association competition was also inaugurated while from the 1990s there were frequent assertions that islands were ideal places to bring up children with freedom, lack of crime and sense of community.[15]

Others persisted in claims of neglect. Dursey Island in Cork, for example, which could be accessed by a 'highly temperamental' cable car, was described in 2010 as 'like a part of the third world'. It had a population of just three people, and no shop, pub, church or post office, on the back of a history that included 'Vikings, Monks, mariners, pirates, bishops, soldiers, smugglers'. Now, it had no sustainable population, or 'community institutions' but 'superb opportunities for the diver and naturalist'.[16]

As minister for rural and Gaeltacht affairs from 2002 to 2010 with specific responsibility for the islands, Eamon Ó Cuív had cash to spend on the islands and they benefited considerably, part of an attempt to improve air access for both islanders and tourists, connected to the national development plan, giving some indication of how islands in the twenty-first century were being viewed.[17] There were other indications of regeneration; Gola had essentially been abandoned at the very end of the 1960s but former residents formed a development council for the island ('it has an abundance of fresh water supplies, adequate peat deposits and farmland') and some houses were being renovated as holiday homes, with grants for restoration offered by the Department of the Gaeltacht and plans to add more islands to the national electricity grid with a €1 million project by the ESB.[18]

There was also an insistence that islanders were entitled to a charter of rights; that they did not want to become a 'protected species' or receive tourists looking at them 'as if they were some type of strange people'.[19] It was not enough for urbanites to romanticise island life, the argument went and perhaps there was always something bogus or contrived about, in writer Deborah Tall's words, 'a passion for the life the islanders have discarded'.[20] But that romanticisation was repackaged in the early twenty-first century for profit, though not always of direct benefit to the islanders.

A hyperbolic chic mystique served the interests of those seeking to market products based on their connections – sometimes real, sometimes imagined – with islands.

Those using the services of Aer Lingus, Ireland's national airline, in the summer of 2017 could read rhapsodically of a company called Dúinn Designs that had 'invigorated the classic Celtic design with a contemporary twist that represents a modern Ireland', and perfect for 'any occasion' was the Skelligs Silk Scarf (€59), which for the wearer would be not only a fashion accessory but 'also a wonderful talking point at any party. This scarf represents the larger of the two Skellig islands off county Kerry, with a history dating back many centuries and just like the design itself Skellig Michael has re-emerged in a very modern form, being the location for the next Star Wars film, Episode VIII' (not without controversy as it was a UNESCO world heritage site). The scarf 'comprises of a mix of elements that elegantly reflect the Skellig Michael landscape with its grey and green colours and soft silk texture'.[21]

Traditional island garb was repackaged to suit style and sentimentality but alongside that, the continuities in the difficulties facing islanders continued to be aired in a media that was persistent – as it had been for decades – in highlighting island dilemmas. On two successive week-ends in December 2016, for example, the *Irish Times* magazine carried features relevant to the Irish islands. One was a fashion piece with sultry models promoting knitwear from one of the famed Aran Islands, Inish-maan: 'Knitwear collection mixes sturdy substance with sophistication', a reference to the most recent collection from the company established by Tarlach de Blacam and producing knitwear since 1976. It was a pre-view of the collection that would be debuted at Florence in 2017 and was a reminder of 'today's more luxurious updates aimed at sophisticated streets rather than rough seas'.

The Merino jacket 'is assembled by hand on the island and finished with Italian horn buttons'; the most expensive item, the 'storm jacket' was €520, while for half that price a 'linen/silk tunic with rolled trims' could be purchased. These would be on sale in Bergdorf Goodman in New York and Amin Kader in Paris. There would also be a new version of the traditional Aran man fisherman's sweater 'in collaboration with Lucy Downes's Sphere One collection for Winter 2017 at Pitti Uomo in Florence ... patterns introduced have names such as stone fence, wave, blackberry and floating moss'.[22]

Such fashions were characterised as involving the continued inter-play between tradition and innovation, and this was the bedrock of the remarkable success of de Blacam in finding sustainable employment for the islanders. From the early 1970s, when he settled on Inishmaan, he devoted himself to development projects to stem emigration and help build a co-operative spirit and self-sufficient community; his knitting company, established with his wife, Áine Ní Chongaíle, an Inishmaan native, began in a small factory with six domestic knitting machines, the knitters drawing on the depth of the Aran knitting tradition. Design orientated and of high quality, it was a product that soared, the factory eventually designing up to fifty different styles each season.[23]

The following week, the *Irish Times* magazine look a more prosaic look at the islands by examining the communities of Inishturk and Inish-bofin off the west coast, who were facing 'an uncertain future' as the com-bined population of the two islands had dwindled to about 220. There were eleven pupils in the school on Inishbofin, and on Inishturk, just three. While there were things to be positive about – the sense of community and a helicopter that could be a lifeline in time of crisis – there were also stark predictions: 'It will get to the point where nobody lives here in winter ... it will come to that.'[24] Islanders inhabiting the smaller islands also continued to face the problem that, even if their children could be educated at primary level on the islands, a move to the mainland was necessary for secondary education. The larger islands, including Arranmore, Achill and Inishmore, had secondary schools and on Tory a secondary school was established in 1999 as part of the state's island-development strategy.

During the period of the Celtic Tiger economy, before the economic crash in 2008, there were also inevitable tensions about holiday homes ('the developers gave them names like "Fishermen's Cottage"') when residents preferred the building of homes for permanent residents.[25] With economic recovery the thorny issue of the extent to which the islands were now playgrounds of the wealthy returned – 'a cottage on Boffin can go for up to €400,000 or can be rented out for up to €700 a week in summer'. This inevitably created difficulties for those wishing to live on the island by renting all year round.[26] Thanks to the continued flexing of Tarlach de Blacam's business mind, bare Inishmaan even became a destination for holiday suites designed for 'optimum luxury ... a custom Iroko kitchen housing everything needed to enjoy the delivered breakfast ... Philippe Starck bathrooms ... high thread cotton sheets'.[27]

The process of the 'gentrification' of some islands prompted an insistence that such augmentation inhibited the development of sustainable islands; almost 50 per cent of Clare Island's properties were holiday homes by 2016.[28] Some small islands were offered by estate agents as 'trophy buys' (singer Michael Jackson looked at a few, though did not purchase, unlike John Lennon), though more ambitious plans to turn them into luxury holiday destinations were complicated by practical infrastructural issues, the economic crash and planning problems. Sage advice was also offered to potential purchasers: 'look at it on a rainy day as well as a sunny day'.[29] Wiser natives were well aware that living an island life required 'an affinity with and a degree of humble abandonment to the elements'.[30]

Some island communities were also part of the technological

revolution, with broadband internet access on some of the western islands, though this was not to benefit many others.[31] In 2013 Shirley Gallagher, an environmental consultant, returned to her native Arranmore in Donegal, which had a population of 514, where she 'opened a café, introduced a local currency and galvanised the creation of a community council', but she was forced to leave because of the difficulty in getting high-speed internet, a reminder that there is no such thing as the seamless transfer of technological change and modern infrastructure to islands even in the twenty-first century.[32] There was community spirit and love of the way of life in abundance, manifold talents and creative endeavour, but rarely permanent solutions to the unemployment problem in many islands beyond emigration, and few prospects for the future for those seeking to fish in the manner of their ancestors owing to EU fishing policies and directives meekly accepted by Irish governments.

Artists continued to find creative havens on islands, including jazz singer Josephine Smyth O'Donnell on Sherkin: islanders, she found 'always let you stand in your own space'.[33] On Cape Clear, American-born writer and teacher Chuck Kruger settled on a sixty-acre farm in 1992. As soon as he first approached the island he had an 'ebullient sense that here, dead ahead, was a place where I could die'; he also began the Cape Clear Island storytelling festival in the mid 1990s.[34] Composer Bill Whelan composed *Inishlacken* because he always wanted to write a piece of music 'in praise of this island of contrasts and mood changes'.[35]

Annual island festivals were also experimented with ('Zebra Katz is a queer hip hop artist from New York who here [at the Aran Island cultural festival] works a stage with Dublin rapper Mythic Grim'[36]), as was island food ('home-grown herb pesto and Aran Goat cheese'[37]). There was an annual rock festival on Rathlin as well as the Valentia Isle festival, a 'boutique event par excellence'.[38] Fitness gurus designed island boot camps with week-long crash courses in diet and training for well over €1,000; in Cork, for example, this could buy a 'week on the island where they work out for eight or nine hours a day with a mixture of low and high intensity classes'.[39]

Islands also entered the fray as desired locations for civil wedding ceremonies in tandem with the decline in church weddings in the early twenty-first century, while the enactment of marriage equality legislation in 2015 also spiked numbers for civil ceremonies. Couples got more adventurous in choosing locations and weddings were performed at Clare Island lighthouse and Inishbeg island in Cork, while in 2014 the Office of Public Works approved the Great Blasket for wedding ceremonies, with a reminder that 'the national registrar will not conduct civil ceremonies on islands but humanist celebrants will'.[40] It was ironic, however, that such locations were being used to celebrate marriage, given the scale of population decline and the reluctance of people to stay there long term. Notwithstanding, there were clever and successful attempts to package the history of individual islands for tourists seeking dramatic, scenic locations and lessons in history and culture. In 2017 Spike Island in Cork, dominated by 200-year-old Fort Mitchel, a British artillery fortification, and incorporating a history that included monasteries and convicts, received the accolade of Europe's leading tourist attraction at the World Travel Awards for its Fortress Spike Island Visitor Centre run by Cork County Council: 'the former prison site beat off competition from Buckingham Palace, the Eiffel Tower, the Colosseum and the Acropolis'.[41]

It was also noted in March 2016 that 'for a brief moment earlier this year Inishturk was a viral sensation as a possible home for refugees from Donald Trump'.[42] Mary Heanue, development officer on Inishturk, remarked that her little island with a dwindling population of only fifty-eight would love to see Americans consider moving there in the event of a Donald Trump presidency. Her words went viral and a video, *Make Inishturk Great Again*, was made.

It continued to be maintained that the islands were where the 'soul' of Ireland was best preserved and that, in the words of Peter Somerville Large, 'each was home to a tribe that was really a small nation. There was a sense of nationhood, of absolute containment.'[43] Like so many other writers, Hubert Butler in 1987 was 'tempted to use the language of hyperbole' about the Aran Islands because they seemingly held on to a 'precarious beauty and simplicity' that the rest of the world 'is disastrously discarding'. He was convinced that the islands represented a tradition, and a pre-Christian one, that was about not just the Irish past but also the European past and the 'infancy of religion', but he also recognised that there was a significant gulf between life and scholarship.[44] Whatever about the ancient monks and saints, some of those who had approached the islands with a missionary zeal in more modern times had been frustrated, like George Thomson, who saw the Blaskets as containing a simple culture 'but free from the rapacity and vulgarity that is destroying our own', yet he lamented that he had 'failed ... to bring the people of the Gaeltacht into modern civilisation while retaining their own culture.'[45]

The appeal of the islands was also built, perhaps, on a paradox. Tommy Burke from Inishbofin summed up the essence of the attachment when he spoke of always feeling more in control on the island; a 'kind of comfort' that islanders could not feel on shore even though island life involved more precarious and vulnerable living. Journalist Rachel Donnelly suggested this was the 'freedom granted by the comfort of known borders ... while someone from the mainland might feel trapped by the surrounding ocean, islanders feel hemmed in by the expanse of unknown terrain on the mainland'.[46]

Given that the overall offshore island population was 34,219 in 1841 and in 1991 just 9,569, there is an obvious starkness about the decline over the centuries. By 2016, the census revealed that the numbers living on the inhabited offshore islands was 8,756, down from 9,029 in 2011.[47] The recent decline has been slight enough and the figures for the last quarter of a century stable enough to refute the idea that the future of Irish island life is unremittingly bleak, just as the history of the Irish islands suggests their past has been about much more than hardship and isolation.

NOTES

Introduction

1. National Archives of Ireland, Dublin (hereafter NAI), Dáil Éireann collection (DE) 2/413, March 1922.
2. Cole Moreton, *Hungry for Home: Leaving the Blaskets: A Journey from the Edge of Ireland* (London, 2000), pp. 75–95.
3. NAI Department of the Taoiseach (DT) S8670A, memorandum sent to Seán T. O'Kelly, Minister for Local Government and Public Health, by Dr Lester Klimm, 15 February 1936.
4. Stephen Royle and Derek Scott, 'Accessibility and the Irish Islands', *Irish Geography*, vol. 81, no. 2, 1986, pp. 111–19, and F. H. Aalen and H. Brody, *Gola: The Life and Last Days of an Island Community* (Cork, 1969), p. x.
5. Stephen Royle 'From Marginality to Resurgence: The Case of the Irish Islands', *Skima: The International Journal for Research into Island Cultures*, vol. 2, no. 2, 2008, pp. 42–54.
6. *Mayo News*, 30 August 2016.
7. Central Statistics Office, www.cso.ie, CNA35, Population of Offshore Islands Since 1841, accessed 31 January 2017 and 11 August 2017.
8. www.scotlandcensus.gov.uk, accessed 30 January 2017.
9. European Communities Economic and Social Committee, *Disadvantaged Island Regions* (Brussels, July 1988), p. 19.
10. Moreton, *Hungry for Home*, p. 5.
11. Reg Hindley, *The Death of the Irish Language: A Qualified Obituary* (London, 1990), p. 124.

12. Paul Henry, *An Irish Portrait: The Autobiography of Paul Henry* (London, 1951), p. 51.

13. Tim Robinson 'The Impossible Isles', *Ireland of the Welcomes*, vol. 30, no. 4, July–August 1981, pp. 18–19.

14. Paul Gosling, 'The Archaeology of Clare Island, Co. Mayo', *Archaeology Ireland*, vol. 4, no. 1, Spring 1990, pp. 7–12.

15. Paul Rainbird, 'Islands Out of Time: Towards a Critique of Island Archaeology', *Journal of Mediterranean Archaeology*, vol. 12, no. 2, 1999, pp. 216–34.

16. A phrase used by British historian E. P. Thompson in the *Times Literary Supplement* as far back as 1966, E. P. Thompson, 'History from Below', *Times Literary Supplement*, 7 April 1966, pp. 279–80; see also Diarmaid Ferriter, *The Transformation of Ireland* (London, 2004), pp. 23–6, and Brian Hanley, '"Moderates and Peacemakers": Irish Historians and the Revolutionary Centenary', *Irish Economic and Social History*, vol. 43, no. 1, 2016, pp. 113–30.

17. Godfrey Baldacchino and Stephen A. Royle, 'Postcolonialism and Islands: Introduction', *Space and Culture*, vol. 13, no. 2, 2010, pp. 140–43.

18. Rainbird, 'Islands Out of Time'.

19. NAI DT 16334, 'Islands off the West Coast', Bishop Cornelius Lucey to Eamon de Valera, 6 November 1957.

20. Moreton, *Hungry for Home*, p. 22 and p. 60.

21. Declan Kiberd, 'Inventing Irelands', *Crane Bag*, vol. 8, 1984, pp. 11–26.

22. Alice Curtayne, 1940, quoted in Diarmaid Ferriter, *Mothers, Maidens and Myths: A History of the Irish Countrywomen's Association* (Dublin, 1995), p. 3.

23. Fr Denis Meehan, 'The Island of Molaise', *Ireland of the Welcomes*, vol. 4, no. 1, May–June 1955, pp. 21–3.

24. Eric Luke, *Looking Back: The Changing Face of Ireland* (Dublin, 2016), p. 107.

25. Kevin Barry, *Beatlebone* (Edinburgh, 2015), p. 8, p. 105 and pp. 182–93.

26. Quoted in Ciarán Ó Coigligh, 'Cathair Synge agus Cathaoir Synge: J. M. Synge, Baile Átha Cliath agus Oileáin Arainn', *Journal of the Galway Archaeological and Historical Society*, vol. 64, 2012, pp. 153–69.

27. W. B. Yeats, *Synge and the Ireland of His Time* (Dublin, 1911), p. 20.

28. Colm Tóibín, 'The Mystery of Inis Meáin', *The Guardian*, 12 May 2007.

29. Peig Sayers, *Peig: The Autobiography of Peig Sayers of the Great Blasket Island*, trans. Bryan MacMahon (Dublin, 1974; first published 1936), p. 183.

30. Fintan O'Toole (ed.), *Modern Ireland in 100 Art Works* (Dublin, 2016), p. 40.

31. Ibid., p. 76.

32. Flann O'Brien, *The Poor Mouth*, trans. Patrick C. Power (London, 1993; first published Dublin, 1941), pp. 29–53.

33. Seán Ó Crohan, *A Day in Our Life*, trans. Tim Enright (Oxford, 1993), p. 41.

34. Tóibín, 'The Mystery of Inis Meáin'.

35. Quoted in James Morrissey and Brian Farrell, *Inishbofin* (Dublin, 1987), pp. 31ff.

36. Tuam Diocesan Archive, Tuam, County Galway (Hereafter TDA) P6/9/4, Box 13, Fr Murtagh Farragher to W. L. Micks, 5 April 1913.

37. Obituary of Fr Diarmuid Ó Péicín, *Irish Times*, 8 March 2008.

38. George Thomson, *Studies in Ancient Greek Society* (London, 1949), p. 540.

39. John Gibney, Review of *An tÉireannach Fáin*, *History Ireland*, vol. 19, no. 2, March–April 2011, pp. 50–51.

40. Sean O'Faoláin, 'The Gaelic Cult', *The Bell*, vol. 9, no. 3, December 1944, pp. 185–96.

41. Liam O'Flaherty, *Skerrett* (Dublin, 1977; first published London, 1932), pp. 135–6.

42. Michael McLaverty, *Call My Brother Back* (Belfast, 2003; first published London, 1939) introduction by Sophia Hillan, p. x.

43. *Irish Echo*, 28 August 2002; 'The Saturday Interview', *Irish Times*, 20 March 2010 and www.troublesarchive.com/artists/paul-brady, accessed 16 January 2017.

44. *Irish Times*, 9 February 2017.

45. R. T. Davies, *Samuel Johnson: Selected Writings* (London, 1965), pp. 301–16.

46. Ibid.

47. Ibid.

48. Ibid.

49. Public Record Office of Northern Ireland (hereafter PRONI) ED/13/2/427, Rathlin Island: Interdepartmental Review, 9 July 1975.

Chapter 1: *The Island Question in the Nineteenth and Early Twentieth Centuries*

1. Central Statistics Office, www.cso.ie, CNA35, Population of Offshore Islands Since 1841, accessed 31 January 2017 and 11 August 2017.

2. Kevin Whelan, 'Landscape and Society on Clare Island, 1700–1900', in Críostóir Mac Cárthaigh and Kevin Whelan (eds.), *New Survey of Clare Island*, vol. 1: *History and Cultural Landscape* (Dublin, 1999), pp. 73–99.

3. Mícheál de Mórdha, *An Island Community: The Ebb and Flow of the Great Blasket Island*, trans. Gabriel Fitzmaurice (Dublin 2015), pp. 167–211.

4. Kieran Concannon (ed.), *Inishbofin Through Time and Tide* (Galway, 1993), pp. 53–7.

5. Eamon Lankford, *Cape Clear Island: Its People and Landscape* (Cork, 1999), p. 69.

6. Ibid., pp. 25–7.

7. De Mórdha, *An Island Community*, p. 295.

8. J. M. Synge, *The Aran Islands*: ed. and intro. Tim Robinson (Harmondsworth, 1992), p. xiv.

9. Augustine McCurdy, *Rathlin's Rugged Story* (Ballycastle, 2000), pp. 35–45.

10. W. Forsythe, 'The Archaeology of the Kelp Industry in the Northern Islands of Ireland', *International Journal of Nautical Archaeology*, vol. 35, no. 2, October 2006, pp. 218–29.

11. Tim Robinson, 'Place/Person/Book', in Synge, *The Aran Islands*, p. xii.

12. National Archives of Ireland (NAI) Chief Secretary's Office Registered Papers (CSO/RP) 1822/2810, 17 June 1822.

13. NAI CSO/RP 1822/352, Alexander Nimmo to William H. Gregory, 19 June 1822, CSO/RP/1822/371 Alexander Nimmo to Alexander Mangin, 2 July 1822 and CSO/RP/1822/469, Arthur French to Gregory, 22 June 1822.

14. NAI CSO/RP/1822/509, Richard Thorpe to Richard Wellesley, 5 September 1822.

15. NAI CSO/RP/1822/3366, William Wrixon Beecher to William Gregory, 23 June 1822.

16. NAI CSO/RP/1819/596, 4 December 1819, CSO/RP/1819/152, 13 January 1819, CSO/RP/1818/639, 21 January 1818.

17. Bill Long, *Bright Light, White Water: The Story of Irish Lighthouses and Their People* (Dublin, 1993), p. 17.

18. NAI CSO/RP/1818/13, 12 January 1818, application from Denis Burke.

19. NAI SCO/RP/1820/224, 6 January – 13 November 1820.

20. National Folklore Commission (NFC), University College Dublin (UCD), Schools Collection, vol. 0475, p. 141, Waterville, County Kerry.

21. Patrick Long, 'George Halpin', in James McGuire and James Quinn (eds.), *Dictionary of Irish Biography: From the Earliest Times to the Year 2002* (Cambridge, 2009) (hereafter *DIB*), vol. 4, pp. 372–3.

22. Ibid.

23. www.skelligexperience.com/thelighthouses, accessed 7 April 2017.

24. Richard M. Taylor, *The Lighthouses of Ireland* (Cork, 2004), pp. 48–71.

25. Ibid., p. 120 and Commissioners of Irish Lights, *For the Safety of All: Image and Inspections of Irish Lighthouses* (Dublin, 2003), pp. 82–3.

26. Jim Hunter, *The Waves of Tory: The Story of an Atlantic Community* (Coleraine, 2006).

27. Forsythe, 'The Archaeology of the Kelp Industry'.

28. NAI CSO/RP/1821/418, Mary Walsh to LL, 3 March 1821.

29. McCurdy, *Rathlin's Rugged Story*, p. 50.

30. Ibid.

31. Ibid.

32. NAI CSO/RP/1821/266, Major Samson Carter to William Gregory, 19 March 1821 – 12 October 1821; CSO/RP/SC/1821/1455, George Warburton to Charles Grant, 12 January 1821.

33. Stephen Ball (ed.), *A Policeman's Ireland: Recollections of Samuel Waters, RIC* (Cork, 1999), pp. 34–5 and J. Anthony Gaughan, *Memoirs of Constable Jeremiah Mee, RIC* (Dublin, 1975), p. 54.

34. Joe McGowan, *Island Voices: Inishmurray* (Dublin, 2004), p. 165.

35. Ball (ed.), *A Policeman's Ireland*, pp. 34–5.

36. McGowan, *Inishmurray*, p. 46 and Gaughan, *Jeremiah Mee*, appendix.

37. Stephen A. Royle, 'Irish Famine Relief in the Early Nineteenth Century: The 1822 Famine on the Aran Islands', *Irish Economic and Social History*, vol. 11, 1984, pp. 44–59.

38. Ibid.

39. Ibid.

40. Jonathan Beaumont, *Achillbeg: The Life of an Island* (Usk, 2005), pp. 25–31.

41. Niall R. Branach, 'Edward Nangle and the Achill Island Mission', *History Ireland*, vol. 8, no. 3, Autumn 2000, pp. 35–9.

42. Tom Kelley and Linde Lunney, 'Edward Walter Nangle', *DIB*, vol. 6, pp. 854–6.

43. Ibid.

44. Branach, 'Edward Nangle and the Achill Island Mission'.

45. NAI Relief Commission Papers (RLFC) 3/1/1358, Edward Spring to Captain Shaw Kennedy, 8 April 1849.

46. Mac Cárthaigh and Whelan (eds.), *New Survey of Clare Island*, 1, p. 82.

47. De Mórdha, *An Island Community*, pp. 256–7.

48. McCurdy, *Rathlin's Rugged Story*, pp. 22–44.

49. Frank Mitchell, *Man and Environment in Valencia Island* (Dublin, 1989), pp. 117–20.

50. Royle, 'Irish Famine Relief'.

51. *Royal Commission on Congestion in Ireland: Final Report* (London, 1908), p. 187.

52. Cape Clear Archive (CCA) 5A/75 and 5A/12, 'Distress on Cape Clear', 31 May 1861 and *Hansard*, 5 June 1862.

53. CCA 5B/7, *Irish Times* report of 4 November 1879.

54. *Irish Times*, 8 November 1887.

55. *Irish Times*, 30 December 1887.

56. Morrissey and Farrell, *Inishbofin*, pp. 25–31.

57. Ibid.

58. National Library of Ireland (NLI), *The Irish Crisis of 1879–80: Proceedings of the Dublin Mansion House Relief Committee 1880* (Dublin, 1881), pp. 47–52.

59. Liam O'Regan, 'The Castle Island Evictions 1889–90', *Mizen Journal*, no. 6, 1998, pp. 116–29.

60. Eugene Daly, *Heir Island: Its History and People* (Cork, 2004), pp. 22–36.

61. Daphne D. C. Pochin Mould, *Valentia: Portrait of an Island* (Dublin, 1978), p. 1, and Mitchell, *Man and His Environment*, pp. 117–20.

62. Mould, *Valentia*, p. 88.

63. Michael Viney, 'Another Life', *Irish Times*, 20 January 2001, Maureen Keane, 'The Inishkeas: A Look at Life There Before the Islands Were Abandoned in 1937', *Cathair Na Mart*, Journal of the Westport Historical Society, vol. 11, 1991, pp. 66–74, and Brian Dornan, *Mayo's Lost Islands: The Inishkeas* (Dublin, 2000), pp. 147–50.

64. John Healy, 'A Pilgrimage to Inishmurray', *Irish Monthly*, vol. 5, July 1877, pp. 433–9.

65. P. J. Joyce, *John Healy, Archbishop of Tuam* (Dublin, 1931), pp. 30–31, and Patrick Maume, 'John Healy', *DIB*, vol. 4, pp. 561–4.

66. Henry Coulter, *The West of Ireland: Its Existing Condition, and Prospects.* (Dublin and London 1862), p. 1.

67. *Freeman's Journal*, 27 December 1871, quoted in Brian Harvey, 'The Emergence of the Western Problem in the Latter Part of the Nineteenth Century', MA Thesis, UCD, 1986, p. 12.

68. Eugene Daly, 'Heir Island', *Mizen Journal*, no. 8, 2000, pp. 34–56.

69. Siobhán Hawke, *A Social and Economic History of Bere Island, 1900–1920* (Cork, 2004), pp. 11–37.

70. *Royal Commission on Congestion*, p. 25.

71. Mitchell, *Man and Environment*, pp. 117–20.

72. James Coombe, 'The *Margaret Hughes* and the Maritime Tradition of Sherkin Island', *Mizen Journal*, no. 12, 2004, pp. 60–62; first published in 1974.

73. Breandán Ó hEithir 'The Birth, Death and Resurrection of the Aran Fishing Fleet', *Irish Times*, 27 May 1978.

74. NLI, OPIE R/23/1–7, *Coimisiún na Galetachta:*[Gaeltacht Commission] *Report and Evidence* (Dublin, 1926), p. 47.

75. Ó hEithir, 'The Birth Death and Resurrection'.

76. CCA 21C/11, Fr Charles Davis, 1827–1892.

77. CCA, Obituary of Fr Charles Davis, *Cork Examiner*, 18 October 1892.

78. National University of Ireland, Galway, Library Special Collections and Archives (NUIGA) LE11, Letter of appointment of Bailiff, 7 June 1844.

79. *Irish Times*, 12 October 1982 and 5 February 1997.

80. *Irish Times*, 25 September 1884.

81. *Irish Times*, 24 September 1884.

82. *Irish Times*, 26 September 1884.

83. Ibid.

84. *Irish Times*, 28 March 1973.

85. Mícheál Ó Dubhshláine, *A Dark Day on the Blaskets* (Kerry, 2003), p. 65.

86. Henry A. Robinson, *Further Memories of Irish Life* (London, 1924), p. 130.

87. NLI, *The Irish Crisis of 1879–80*.

88. De Mórdha, *An Island Community*, p. 280.

89. Ibid., pp. 284–6.

90. University College Dublin Archives (UCDA) Papers of Eoin MacNeill, LA1/G/1/282, Eoin MacNeill to Charlie MacNeill, 14 July 1891.

91. Raphoe Diocesan Archives (RDA), Letterkenny, Donegal, Tory Island Collection, 17, Fr D. E. Coyle to Patrick O'Donnell, 29 May 1889.

92. Ibid., O'Donnell to McFadden, 2 April 1889.

93. Michael Davitt, 'The Distress in Achill', reprinted in *Muintir Acla*, no. 6, Spring 1997, p. 20.

94. Quoted ibid.

95. NLI, *The Irish Crisis of 1879–80*, p. 48.

96. Harvey, 'The Emergence of the Western Problem', pp. 61–79.

97. David Murphy, 'James Hack Tuke', *DIB*, vol. 9, pp. 512–13; Ciara Breathnach, *Poverty and Development in the West of Ireland* (Dublin, 2005), pp. 43–51.

98. NFC, UCD, Congested Districts Board Local Reports (CDBLR), vol. 2, pp. 337–42, 'Achill Island', by Robert Ruttledge-Fair, 14 May 1892.

99. Henry A. Robinson, *Memories: Wise and Otherwise* (London, 1923), pp. 72–104.

100. James Quinn, 'James Arthur Balfour', *DIB*, vol. 1, pp. 239–42.

101. Breathnach, *Poverty and Development*, p. 30.

102. F. H. A. Aalen, Kevin Whelan and Matthew Stout (eds.), *Atlas of the Irish Rural Landscape* (Cork, 1997), p. 163.

103. NLI, *Coimisiún na Galetachta: Report and Evidence*, Evidence of Fr Duggan, 18 August 1925.

104. Tim Robinson, *Connemara: A Little Gaelic Kingdom* (London, 2011), pp. 192–3 and p. 342.

105. Mac Cárthaigh and Whelan (eds.), *New Survey of Clare Island*, 1, pp. 41–55.

106. Ibid.

107. Harvey, 'The Emergence of the Western Problem', p. 177.

108. Dornan, *Mayo's Lost Islands*, p. 170.

109. NFC, CDBLR, vol. 1, pp. 141–8, 'District of Arranmore', by Inspector F. G. Townshend Gahan, 13 September 1996.

110. Ibid.

111. Ibid.

112. Dáil Éireann Debates (Irish Parliamentary Debates) (DED), vol. 144, no. 7, 30 March 1955, CSO CNA35, Population of Offshore Islands Since 1841: Island Population 2006.

113. NFC, CDBLR, vol. 1, 'District of Arranmore'.

114. Ibid.

115. NFC, CDBLR, vol. 2, pp. 367–71, 'Clare Island', by Robert Ruttledge-Fair, 18 May 1892.

116. Ibid.

117. NFC, CDBLR, vol. 2, pp. 453–9, 'Inishbofin', by Robert Ruttledge-Fair, 26, August 1892.

118. Ibid.

119. Ibid., vol. 3, pp. 705–9, 'District of Baltimore', by Redmond Roche, 7 January 1893.

120. NFC, CDBLR, vol. 3, pp. 133–7, 'Aran Islands', by Robert Ruttledge-Fair, 31 March 1893.

121. Ibid.

122. Ibid., vol. 2, 'Achill Island'.

123. Kieran Clarke, 'The Clew Bay Boating Disaster', *Cathair Na Mart*, vol. 6, no. 1, 1986, pp. 5–24.

124. *Irish Weekly Independent*, 23 June 1894, quoted ibid.

125. Breathnach, *Poverty and Development*, p. 87.

126. Harvey 'The Emergence of the Western Problem', p. 242.

127. Breathnach, *Poverty and Development*, p. 163.

128. Mícheál Ó Fathartaigh, 'Cumann na nGaedheal, Sea Fishing and West Galway, 1923–32', *Irish Historical Studies*, vol. 36, no. 141, May 2008, pp. 72–90.

129. Breathnach, *Poverty and Development*, pp. 91–5.

130. Ibid., p. 99.

131. Aalen and Brody, *Gola*, pp. 44–8 and p. 76.

132. McGowan, *Inishmurray*, pp. 14–18.

133. PRONI COM 9/50, Rathlin Island, John McCuaig to Department of Agriculture, October 1900.

134. Ibid., Inspector's Report, WSO, 9 February 1901.

135. Ibid., COM 9/50, Fr Joseph McGlave to Mr Bryce, October 1906.
136. Ibid., 9 November 1906, from Under Secretary.
137. Ibid., 28 May 1907 and memorandum of 29 August 1908.
138. TDA P6/9/4, Box 13, Memorandum of Fr Farragher to L. M. Micks, 24 November 1910.
139. Ibid.
140. Ibid., Farragher to Micks, 5 April 1913.
141. Ibid., n.d., but 1913, Farragher to Micks, n.d., but 1913.
142. Ibid., Farragher's memorandum to CDB, 24 November 1910.
143. Ibid., Farragher to Micks, 30 March 1919.
144. Ibid., Farragher to Micks, 4 July 1916 and 9 January 1919.
145. Ibid., Micks to Farragher, 16 February 1917.
146. *Hansard*, Commons Sitting, oral answers to questions, 2 November 1911.
147. *Royal Commission on Congestion*, p. 156.
148. Ibid., p. 4.
149. Ibid., p. 6.
150. Ibid., Memorandum by Sir John Colomb, pp. 187–202.
151. Ibid., p. 11.
152. RDA, Tory Island Collection, 33, Michael Doogan to Bishop Patrick O'Donnell, 4 June 1908.
153. L. P. Curtis, 'Ireland in 1914', in W. E. Vaughan (ed.), *A New History of Ireland*, vol. 6: *Ireland Under the Union II, 1870–1921* (Oxford, 1996), pp. 145–88.
154. Patrick Bolger, *The Irish Co-Operative Movement: Its History and Development* (Dublin, 1977) and Diarmaid Ferriter, 'Patrick Gallagher', *DIB*, vol. 4, pp. 11–12.
155. RDA, Tory Island Collection, 35/36, James J. Ward to O'Donnell, 16 August 1913.
156. Ibid., 37, Fr John Boyle to Patrick O'Donnell, 21 December 1914.
157. *Connacht Tribune*, 4 September 1909.
158. *Connacht Tribune* and *Irish Times*, 13 June 1911.
159. Séamas Ó Siocháin, *Roger Casement: Imperialist, Rebel, Revolutionary* (Dublin, 2008), p. 339.
160. Angus Mitchell, 'An Irish Putumayo: Roger Casement's Humanitarian Relief Campaign Among the Connemara Islanders 1913–14', *Irish Economic and Social History*, vol. 31, 2004, pp. 41–61.
161. Ibid.
162. A. S. Green, H. Barbour, Douglas Hyde and Alec Wilson, 'The Connemara Islands', *Irish Review*, 4, March–November 1914, May 1914, pp. 113–27.
163. Ibid.

164. Ibid.
165. Irish Military Archives (IMA) Bureau of Military History (BMH), Witness Statement (WS) 1772, John Kiernan Cotter.
166. Richard Power, *The Land of Youth: A Novel* (New York, 1964), pp. 262–71.
167. IMA, BMH WS 807, Revd Patrick J. Doyle.
168. IMA, BMH WS 565, Liam Deasy.
169. www.census.nationalarchives.ie, 1911 Census, Myross, Rabbit Island, accessed 16 February 2017.
170. IMA, BMH WS 982, Alice Ginnell.
171. Reported in the *Limerick Leader*, 11 June 1920, quoted in Mary Kotsonouris, *Retreat from Revolution: The Dáil Courts, 1920–1924* (Dublin, 1994), p. 20.
172. William Murphy, *Political Imprisonment and the Irish, 1912–1921* (Oxford, 2014), pp. 195–7.
173. IMA, BMH WS 1582, James Sullivan.
174. Murphy, *Political Imprisonment*, p. 239.
175. IMA, BMH WS 1131, Patrick Burke.
176. IMA, BMH WS 1424, Michael Burke.
177. IMA, BMW WS 656, Richard Ó Connell.
178. IMA, BMH WS 827, Denis Collins.
179. IMA, BMH WS 838, Seán Moylan.
180. Murphy, *Political Imprisonment*, p. 205.
181. IMA, BMH WS 429, Thomas Flynn.
182. DED, vol. S, no. 4, 22 August 1921.
183. IMA, BMH WS 418, Una Stack.
184. DED, vol. T, no. 11, 4 January 1922.
185. Diarmaid Ferriter and Lawrence White, 'Francis Patrick Fahy', *DIB*, vol. 3, pp. 691–2.
186. DED, vol. T, no. 10, 3 January 1922.

Chapter 2: *The Islands and the Irish State, 1922–53*

1. Michael Collins, *The Path to Freedom* (Dublin, 1922), p. 99.
2. Jude McCarthy, 'State-Aided Island Migration, 1930–60', MA thesis, UCD, 1997, p. 3.
3. NAI DT S2478, 'Distress and Unemployment in Saorstát, Conditions on Achill', 19 December 1925.
4. NLI, *Coimisiún na Gaeltachta: Report and Evidence*, pp. 3–30.

5. Bulmer Hobson (ed.), *Saorstát Éireann: Irish Free State Official Handbook* (Dublin, 1932), p. 13 and pp. 134–6.

6. Ibid., p. 214.

7. Ibid., pp. 305–14.

8. McCarthy, 'State-Aided Migration', pp. 25ff.

9. Breathnach, *Poverty and Development*, p. 170.

10. Ibid.

11. DED, vol. 5, no. 12, 18 May 1922.

12. DED vol. 1, no. 29, 16 November 1922.

13. DED, vol. 6, no. 6, 18 January 1924.

14. *Freeman's Journal*, 22 July 1924.

15. *Manchester Guardian*, 2 February 1925, *Connacht Tribune*, 2 and 24 February 1925.

16. *Connacht Tribune*, 7 February 1925.

17. NLI, *Coimisiún na Gaeltachta: Report and Evidence*, p. 3.

18. Ibid., p. 30.

19. Ibid., 18 August 1925, pp. 4–8.

20. Ibid.

21. Ibid.

22. Ibid., Evidence in Galway on 20 August 1925 by Revd S. J. Walsh, PP Aran Islands.

23. Ibid.

24. Ibid.

25. DED, vol. 20, no. 7, 7 July 1927, quoted in Harvey, 'The Emergence of the Western Problem'.

26. Ó Fathartaigh, 'Cumann nGaedheal, Sea Fishing and West Galway'.

27. Ibid.

28. Breathnach, *Poverty and Development*, pp. 96–9 and p. 163.

29. Ó Fathartaigh, 'Cumann na nGaedheal, Sea Fishing and West Galway'.

30. DED, vol. 20, no. 7, 7 July 1927.

31. UCDA, Papers of Richard Mulcahy, P76/7C, National Insurance, November 1927.

32. Ibid., O'Grady to Mulcahy, 28 March 1926.

33. Ó Fathartaigh, 'Cumann na nGaedheal, Sea Fishing and West Galway'.

34. Jerome Toner, *Rural Ireland: Some of Its Problems* (Dublin, 1955).

35. Peadar O'Donnell, *Islanders* (Cork, 2005; first published London, 1927), p. 42.

36. Ibid., pp. 79–82.

37. Keane, 'The Inishkeas'.

38. Marie Feeney, *The Cleggan Bay Disaster* (Donegal, 2001), p. 63.

39. *Irish Times*, 31 October 1927.

40. *Irish Times*, 2 November 1927 and 31 October 1927.

41. Ibid.

42. Feeney, *Cleggan Bay Disaster*, pp. 50–53.

43. 'How dependants were helped: report of National Committee', *Irish Times*, 5 February 1929.

44. Ibid.

45. Feeney, *Cleggan Bay Disaster*, pp. 68–78.

46. Ibid., p. 85.

47. McCarthy, 'State-Aided Migration', p. 36 and *Irish Times*, 1 November 1927.

48. McCarthy, 'State-Aided Migration', p. 41.

49. NFC, The Schools Collection, Ballintra, Co. Donegal, vol. 1033, p. 132.

50. *Irish Press*, 11 November 1935.

51. *Irish Times*, 12 November 1935.

52. *Irish Press*, 11 and 12 November 1935.

53. *Irish Press*, 12 November 1935.

54. Ibid.

55. Donal Ó Drisceoil, *Peadar O'Donnell* (Cork, 2001), pp. 7–9, pp. 69–91, and 'Peadar O'Donnell', by Michael McInerney, *Irish Times*, 1 April 1968.

56. Sheila Kennedy 'Our Western Seaboard', *Ireland Today*, vol. 11, no. 12, December 1937, pp. 13–20.

57. NAI DT 8259, 'Arranmore Disaster', 9 November 1935, Eamon de Valera to Bishop William MacNeely, 23 November 1935.

58. Ibid.

59. Ibid., MacNeely to de Valera, 12 December 1935.

60. *Irish Times*, 28 July 1937.

61. NAI DT 8259, Patrick Gallagher, Arranmore, to Eamon de Valera, 20 July 1936.

62. Ibid., Response of 6 August 1936.

63. Ibid., Nellie Gallagher to de Valera, 31 July 1936.

64. Ibid., John Ward to de Valera, 5 August 1936.

65. *Irish Independent*, 8 December 1936.

66. *Irish Press*, 9 November 1985.

67. NAI DT 8670A, 'Western Islands: Communication with the Mainland', Report of Joseph Connolly, 19 November 1935.

68. Ibid., Memorandum from Department of Finance, 25 November 1935.

69. Ibid., 'Report of Interdepartmental Committee on Communication with the Islands', 5 February 1936.

70. Ibid., Observations of Department of Finance, 20 April 1936.

71. Ibid., DT and Department of Local Government and Public Health (DLG), notes of 29 April 1937 and 18 May 1937.

72. Ibid., Letter of Fr Killeen to Archbishop Thomas Gilmartin, 7 April 1937.

73. Ibid.

74. NAI DT 8670A, Department of Industry and Commerce, 25 March 1936 and DLG, 8 April 1936.

75. Ibid., Industry and Commerce to DT, 17 February 1938 and Posts and Telegraphs to DT, 21 February 1938.

76. Barry Sheppard, 'The Kirkintilloch Tragedy, 1937', www.theirishstory. com/2012/09/24/the-kirkintilloch-tragedy-1937/, accessed 28 February 2017.

77. Ibid.

78. *Report of the Committee on Seasonal Migration to Britain, 1937–8* (Dublin, 1938).

79. Peadar O'Donnell, 'Kirkintilloch', *Ireland Today*, vol. 2, no. 10, October 1937, pp. 45–52.

80. Cited in *Muintir Acla*, no. 6, Spring 1997.

81. Mícheál Briody, *The Irish Folklore Commission, 1935–1979* (Helsinki, 2008), pp. 20–21.

82. Ibid. and pp. 230–39.

83. PRONI CAB 9F/84/1, Memorandum by J. Milne Barbour, 1 December 1926.

84. PRONI CAB/9/B/20211, 'Rathlin Island', Seamus O'Neill to Lord FitzAlan, 18 June 1932; Craig to Charles Blackmore, 20 June 1932, FitzAlan to Craig, 18 June 1932.

85. Ibid., Craig to FitzAlan, 20 June 1932.

86. Ibid., Harold Barbour to Craig, 20 June 1932 and Craig's reply, 23 June 1932.

87. Ibid., Mrs Anna Barbour to Blakewell, 30 June 1932.

88. Ibid., D. H. Clarke to Blackmore, 22 July 1932.

89. Ibid., Craig to FitzAlan, 25 June 1932.

90. Ibid., Norah Gage to Craig, 9 August 1933; D. L. Clarke, Home Affairs, note of 31 August 1933; Gage to Craig, 7 September 1933.

91. Ibid., Blackmore to A. Robinson, Home Affairs, 14 October 1933.

92. Ibid., Robinson to Grandsen, 25 May 1934.

93. Ibid., Norah Gage to HRH the Duke of Gloucester, 22 February 1937.

94. Ibid., Governor of Northern Ireland to Blackmore, 1 April 1937.

95. PRONI CAB/9/B/20211, 'Rathlin Island', Memorandum of Ulster Sea and Fisheries Association to Craig, 1 December 1937.

96. Ibid., Minute from Ministry of Commerce, 8 December 1937.

97. Ibid., Rathlin Island telegram to Craig, 31 January 1938 and Stormont Press Release, 1 February 1938.

98. NAI DT 8670A, Telegram from Tory Island to de Valera, 10 February 1938.

99. Ibid., DT, note of 10 February 1938.

100. Ibid.

101. Ibid., DT, note containing information from Cormac Breslin TD, 16 June 1938.

102. Ibid., Memorandum on Tory Island by J. MacLysaght, DLG Inspector, 17 September 1938.

103. Ibid.

104. Ibid., *Daily Express*, 28 February 1939 and 1 March 1939.

105. Ibid., DT memorandum, 28 February 1939.

106. Ibid., Memorandum by MacLysaght, 19 May 1939 and questions of de Valera, 26 May 1939.

107. Ibid., Interdepartmental conference on food shortages on islands during storms, 27 June 1939.

108. Ibid.

109. Ibid.

110. Ibid.

111. NAI DT 8670B, 'Western Islands: Communication with the Mainland', 17 May 1944.

112. Ibid., Memorandum of Revd J. Cannery, Clare Island, 6 March 1941.

113. Ibid., Memorandum from Archbishop of Tuam, Dr Joseph Walsh, on Inishturk and Clare Islands, 17 April 1944.

114. Ibid., DLG memorandum, 13 September 1944.

115. Ibid., S. D. MacLoughlin to DLG, 3 July 1944.

116. NAI DT 8670B, 'Confidential Report on Supplies Position on Tory Island', 3 July 1944.

117. Ibid.

118. Ibid., Chief Superintendent W. Leen, Letterkenny, Donegal, 14 February 1944.

119. Ibid.

120. Ibid., 20 September 1944: 'Spotlight on Tory Island', 29 January 1944 and 5 February 1944.

121. *Irish Press*, 12 February 1949.

122. Ibid., 20 November 1945, and Industry and Commerce to DT, 15 October 1946.

123. *Irish Press*, 28 October 1946.

124. *Irish Independent*, 11 March 1939; *Irish Press*, 13 March 1939.

125. McCarthy, 'State-Aided Migration', p. 50.

126. Ibid., pp. 51–9.

127. McGowan, *Inishmurray*, p. 165.

128. Michelle Dowling, '"The Ireland that I would have": De Valera and the Creation of an Irish National Image', *History Ireland*, vol. 5, no. 2, Summer 1997, pp. 37–42.

129. UCDA, Papers of Eamon de Valera, P150/2743, schedule for 15 and 16 July.

130. *Connacht Tribune*, 19 July 1947.

131. Ibid., Telegram from Muiris Ó Concubair, Ballydavid and *Irish Press* 15 and 16 July 1947.

132. Ibid., Dr Bryan Alton to de Valera, n.d. but July 1947.

133. NAI DT 97/7/47, Letter of Patrick Gibbons to county manager, Castlebar, 11 June 1947.

134. UCDA, Papers of Eamon de Valera, P150/2743, Account of Visit to Clare Island, 18 July 1947.

135. Ibid. and *Irish Press*, 21 and 23 July 1947.

136. Ibid. and *Irish Independent*, 21 and 22 July 1947.

137. NAI DT 97/7/47, E. J. McLoughlin to Department of Finance, 28 August 1947.

138. *Irish Press*, 14 July 1943.

139. NAI DT 97/7/47, 15 September 1947 and 22 September 1947; Letter of minister for health regarding Clare Island, 6 January 1948.

140. Ibid., P. J. Dempsey, ESB to Kathleen Ó Connell, DT, 1 October 1947.

141. *The Kerryman*, 19 July 1947; *Sligo Champion*, 26 July 1947.

142. *Irish Press*, 19 July 1947.

143. NAI DT 8670C, 'Western Islands: Communication with the Mainland'. Transcript of Radio Éireann broadcast, 21 November 1948, and memorandum from DT, 7 December 1948.

144. Moreton, *Hungry for Home*, pp. 56–61.

145. Michael J. Carney with Gerald Hayes, *From the Great Blasket to America: The Last Memoir by an Islander* (Cork, 2013), pp. 121–3.

146. *The Kerryman*, 20 November 1953.

147. NAI DT 14122A, Michael Carney to de Valera, 26 January 1947.

148. DED, vol. 104, no. 9, 25 February 1947.

149. NAI DT 14122A, Telegram from Blaskets, 22 April 1947.

150. NAI DT 14122A DT, Memorandum on conditions on Blaskets, 6 August 1947.

151. Ibid., Account of meeting in Taoiseach's room, 6 August 1947.

152. Ibid., Letter from Blasket islanders to de Valera, 18 October 1947.

153. NAI DT 8670C, Report on Blaskets, 21 December 1948.

154. Ibid.

155. Ibid., Report of A. Ó Gallchobhair, 20 August 1947.
156. Ó Fathartaigh, 'Cumann na nGaedheal, Sea Fishing and West Galway'.
157. NAI DT 8670C, Report of A. Ó Gallchobhair, 20 August 1947.
158. Ibid., Report of J. F. Flynn, 26 August 1952.
159. *Irish Press*, 4 August 1951.
160. NAI DT 8670C, Memorandum from Department of Education, 5 November 1952.
161. Ibid. and *Irish Independent*, 17 September 1952.
162. NAI DT 8670C, Memorandum from Department of Lands, 8 July 1953.
163. McCarthy 'State-Aided Migration', p. 76.

Chapter 3: *The State and the Islands, 1953–2016*

1. DED, vol. 139, no. 10, 17 June 1953.
2. NAI DT 8670C, Minister for Posts and Telegraphs to Fr Varley, Aran Islands, 5 July 1955.
3. Ibid., Varley to John A. Costello and replies, 17 August 1955 and 8 September 1955.
4. Ibid., Revd John Walsh, Cape Clear, to Costello, 24 October 1956.
5. Ibid., *Sunday Press*, 17 February 1957.
6. NAI DT 8670C, DT, Memorandum of 6 February 1957 and note of John Garvin.
7. Ibid., Memorandum from Department of Justice, 11 February 1957.
8. NAI DT 16282, 'Statement of Families from Inishark Island', 26 August 1952.
9. Ibid., Fr Charles O'Malley, St Colman's Inishbofin, to Gerald Bartley, 22 June 1957.
10. Ibid., Bartley to Fr O'Malley, 25 June 1957, and Department of the Gaeltacht, note of 20 August 1957.
11. Ibid., Erskine Childers to Archbishop Walsh of Tuam, 12 August 1957.
12. Ibid., Department of Lands to DT, 27 August 1957.
13. Ibid., Special Employment Schemes Office, note of 30 August 1957.
14. Ibid., Minister for Local Government to DT, 10 September 1957.
15. Ibid., 'Report of the Interdepartmental Committee on Inishark Island, Co. Galway', 15 February 1958.
16. Ibid.
17. Ibid., Cabinet decision of 20 June 1958.
18. McCarthy 'State-Aided Migration', pp. 117–36.
19. *Irish Times*, 24 October 1957.

20. *Irish Times*, 28 and 29 October 1957.
21. NAI DT 8670C, Department of Industry and Commerce to DT, 8 May 1957.
22. NAI DT S8670C, *Irish Independent*, 16 December 1957.
23. Ibid., *Sunday Express*, 12 January 1958.
24. NAI DT 8790C, Memorandum from Department of Industry and Commerce regarding investment in Galway Aran Steamer service, 18 March 1949.
25. Ibid., Government decision 25 March 1949 and Memorandum of T. C. Courtney, 13 April 1953.
26. DED, vol. 123, no. 6, 16 November 1950.
27. NAI DT 8790D, *Sunday Independent*, 22 March 1953.
28. Ibid., *Sunday Independent*, 29 March 1953.
29. Ibid., *Sunday Independent*, 5 April 1953.
30. Ibid., T. C. Courtney to de Valera, 13 April 1953.
31. Ibid., T. Varley, PP Aran Islands, to John A. Costello, 15 November 1954.
32. Ibid., Industry and Commerce to DT, 10 February 1954, Costello to Varley and replies, 11 and 22 December 1954, and Costello to Varley, 3 January 1955.
33. Ibid., Varley to Costello, 8 January 1955.
34. Ibid., 20 September 1955.
35. Ibid., 10 February 1956.
36. Caoimhghin Ó Croidheáin, *Language from Below: The Irish Language, Ideology and Power in Twentieth Century Ireland* (Oxford, 2006), p. 243.
37. Pádraig Ó Riagáin, *Language Policy and Social Reproduction: Ireland, 1893–1993* (Oxford, 1997), pp. 15–52; Ó Croidheáin, *Language from Below*, p. 245; Gearóid Ó Tuathaigh, 'The State and the Irish Language: A Historical Perspective', in Caoilfhionn Nic Pháidín and Seán Ó Cearnaigh (eds.), *A New View of the Irish Language* (Dublin, 2008), pp. 26–43.
38. Bernard J. Canning, *Bishops of Ireland, 1870–1987* (Donegal, 1987), p. 270.
39. NAI DT S16334, Bishop Cornelius Lucey to de Valera, 6 November 1957.
40. NAI DT S16334, DLG Memorandum, 5 December 1957.
41. Ibid.
42. Ibid.
43. Ibid., Draft of letter to Bishop Lucey, 6 December 1957; de Valera note and de Valera to Lucey, 12 December 1958.
44. Ibid., *Irish Press*, 30 April 1958.
45. *Irish Times*, 15 May 1958 and 18 June 1958.
46. NAI DT S16925A, Islands off the Coast of Ireland, November 1959.
47. Ibid., 19 January 1960.
48. Ibid.

49. Ibid., Cabinet minutes, 6 September 1960.

50. NAI DT S16921, Cabinet minutes, 21 July 1961, Report of Interdepartmental Committee on Problems of the Islands, June 1961.

51. Barbara Brooks Walker, 'Achill Holiday', *Ireland of the Welcomes*, vol. 11, no. 1 May–June 1962.

52. 'Nomad', 'The Aran Islands', *Ireland of the Welcomes*, vol. 11, no. 2, July–August 1962.

53. *Cork Examiner*, 13 May 1962.

54. 'The Aran Islands', *Ireland of the Welcomes*, vol. 13, no. 2, July–August 1964, pp. 18–24.

55. John Reader, 'Shark Men', *Ireland of the Welcomes*, vol. 13, no. 5, January–February 1965, p. 10.

56. *Irish Independent*, 9 December 1963.

57. *Fermanagh Herald*, 29 November 1969.

58. Denis Coughlan, 'Cape Clear and Its People', *Irish Times*, 8 May 1968.

59. Ibid.

60. *Irish Independent*, 17 August 1964.

61. *Irish Independent*, 15 and 26 April 1967.

62. *Irish Independent*, 21 October 1968.

63. *Irish Independent*, 17 August 1970.

64. *Irish Times*, 31 July 2010.

65. *Irish Press*, 2 January 1971.

66. *Irish Times*, 7 January 1971.

67. *Census of Ireland, 1979* (Dublin, 1980), Population Table 14: Population of inhabited islands off the coast and CSO, CNA35, Population of Offshore Islands Since 1841.

68. 'Cape Clear Enters Age of Electricity', *Irish Times*, 1 November 1971.

69. NAI DT 2004/21/280, Liam Ó Rocháin, 'Manifesto for the Islands', c. March 1973.

70. Ibid., Islands off the Coast of Ireland: Living conditions, April 1973.

71. Ibid.

72. *Hibernia*, 12 April 1974.

73. NAI DT 2005/151/193, Islands Off the Coast of Ireland: Living Conditions, 29 April 1975.

74. Ibid., Peter Barry to Liam Cosgrave, 10 July 1975.

75. Ibid., Memorandum of 20 May 1975.

76. *Magill*, August 1979, p. 41.

77. NAI DT 2005/151/193, Peter Barry to Liam Cosgrave, 21 May 1975, and Robert Molloy to Cosgrave, 28 May 1975.

78. NAI DT 2009/135/127, Islands off the Coast of Ireland: Living Conditions, C. O'Grady to Cosgrave, 26 January 1977, and *Irish Press*, 23 September 1977.

79. Ibid., Memoranda of 20 October 1978, 1 November 1978 and Department of Taoiseach, note of 1 November 1978.

80. *Sunday Independent*, 2 January 2011.

81. *Irish Independent*, 8 and 9 January 1979.

82. NAI DT 2005/151/193, Islands Off the Coast of Ireland, 29 April 1975, and Department of Lands memorandum, 24 April 1975.

83. NAI DT 2009/135/127, Memorandum on Improvement of Conditions on Non-Gaeltacht Islands.

84. Ibid., Memorandum of V. Mulcahy, 1 November 1978.

85. Ibid., Minister for Industry and Commerce Memorandum, 2 February 1979.

86. Ibid., Response of Minister for Agriculture.

87. PRONI ED 13/2/427, 'Rathlin Island: Interdepartmental Review'; J. P. McGrath, Department of Housing, Planning and Local Government, to T. J. Sheehan, 6 June 1975.

88. Ibid., Memorandum of R. R. Johnston, 9 July 1975.

89. *Sligo Champion*, 9 May 1975.

90. Proinnsias Breathnach et al., 'Aspects of Rural Development in the Scottish Highlands and Islands: Report of a Study Visit', Geography Department, Maynooth University, February 1984, pp. 2–14.

91. *Irish Press*, 22 May 1974.

92. Stephen A. Royle, 'A Dispersed Pressure Group: Comhdháil na nOileán: The Federation of the Islands of Ireland', *Irish Geography*, vol. 19, 1986, pp. 92–5.

93. DED, vol. 392, no. 7, 7 November 1989.

94. European Communities Economic and Social Committee, *Disadvantaged Island Regions*, p. 3.

95. *Irish Independent*, 28 December 1982.

96. *Irish Independent*, 24 August 1982.

97. *Irish Press*, 6 January 1983.

98. PRONI ED/13/2/805A, 'Rathlin Island: Secondary Education', John Hume to Minister, Department of Environment, Stormont, 14 January 1982.

99. Ibid.

100. Ibid., Jill Heron, note regarding education on Rathlin, 12 February 1982; Minutes of Butler's meeting with John Hume, 14 April 1982.

101. 'Tory Island PP accuses Council of "Genocide"', *Donegal News*, 12 December 1981.

102. 'A People Under Siege from the Twentieth Century', *Irish Independent*, 9 January 1985.

103. Diarmuid Ó Péicín with Liam Nolan, *Islanders: The True Story of One Man's Fight to Save a Way of Life* (London, 1997), p. 60 and pp. 33–9.

104. Ibid., p. 57.

105. Ibid., pp. 107–16.

106. *Irish Times*, 3 November 1990.

107. Royle and Scott, 'Accessibility and the Irish Islands'.

108. Stephen Royle, 'Leaving the "Dreadful Rocks": Irish Island Emigration and Its Legacy', *History Ireland*, no. 4, Spring 1998, pp. 34–8.

109. DED, vol. 462, no. 7, 7 March 1996.

110. Patrick Maume, 'Charles James (C. J.) Haughey', *DIB*, online entry, revised February 2016, www.dib.cambridge.org, accessed 5 September 2017.

111. Bruce Arnold, *Haughey: His Life and Unlucky Deeds* (London, 1993), pp. 267–8.

112. *Irish Independent*, 11 February 2013.

113. Justin O'Brien, *The Modern Prince*, (Dublin, 2002), p. 6.

114. DED, vol. 462, no. 7, 7 March 1996.

115. *Irish Times*, 22 August 1931, quoted in McCarthy, 'State-Aided Migration', p. 139.

116. DED, vol. 462, no. 7, 7 March 1996.

117. McCarthy, 'State-Aided Migration', pp. 138–43.

118. DED, vol. 462, no. 7, 7 March 1996.

119. UCDA, Papers of Ernest Blythe, P24/304, 'Education and Language', July 1931.

120. DED, vol. 462, no. 7, 7 March 1996.

121. Ibid.

122. CCA 46/4, 'A Week in Cape Clear', 1993.

123. CCA 46/3, 'Case Study of Aspects of Island Life', 'A Social Study of Cape Clear, June–October 1995'.

124. CCA 29A/18, West Cork Island Study Draft, December 1994.

125. *Southern Star*, 24 April 1993.

126. *Irish Farmer's Journal*, 18 August 1990, and *Cork Examiner*, 12 March 1992.

127. PRONI DED/3/75/A, 'Rathlin Island Electrification', Jim Anderson to Northern Ireland Electricity, 7 November 1990.

128. Ibid., Department of Economic Development, note of 8 November 1990.

129. Ibid., Needham to R. L. Schierbeek, Chairman of NIE, 11 November 1990.

130. Ibid., W. Redpath to Robin McMinnis, 8 June 1990.

131. Ibid., *Belfast Telegraph*, 3 December 1990; *Ulster Newsletter*, 4 December 1990; *Belfast Telegraph*, 29 January 1991.

132. Ibid., R. McMinnis and Schierbeek to Needham, note of 14 December 1990.
133. Ibid., NIE papers, 7 February 1991, and Department of Economic Development, note of 30 August 1991.
134. Ibid., Rathlin Development and Community Association to Robin McMinnis, 18 November 1990.
135. DED, vol. 475, no. 2, 19 February 1997.
136. *Slí Na nOileán*, no. 1, Summer 2009, p. 8.
137. *Irish Times*, 29 July 2017.
138. *Irish Times*, 28 February 2004.
139. *Ireland: National Development Plan, 2007–2013* (Dublin, 2007), p. 45; *Irish Times*, 17 August 2001, 4 November 2008, 25 October 2007 and 4 March 2004.
140. DED, vol. 894, no. 3, 3 November 2015.
141. Statement posted by Sean Kyne TD, 13 October 2016, www.seankyne.ie, accessed, 22 August 2017.
142. *Irish Times*, 9 February 2016.
143. *Irish Times*, 10 March 2006.
144. Ibid.
145. *Irish Times*, 25 February 2016.
146. Ibid.
147. *Irish Times*, 4 October 2015, and Loïc Jourdain's film *In Éadan an Taoide* (*Against the Tide*) broadcast on TG4 May 2016.
148. *Irish Times*, 10 March 2006.
149. *Irish Times*, 5 September 2015.
150. *Irish Examiner*, 11 June 2015.
151. *Sunday Business Post*, 6 July 2008.
152. *Irish Times*, 29 October 2014.
153. *Irish Times*, 17 February 2015.
154. *Irish Times*, 27 September 2016.

Chapter 4: The Island Priest

1. Revd John Neary, 'History of Inishbofin and Inishark', *Irish Ecclesiastical Record*, 5th series, vol. 15, January–June 1920, pp. 216–28.
2. Ibid.
3. Concannon (ed.), *Inishbofin Through Time and Tide*, pp. 25–6.
4. Neary, 'History of Inishbofin'.

5. 'Rev. John Canon Neary PP', *Irish Independent*, 31 March 1951, and 'Death of Noted Priest Historian', *Tuam Herald*, 7 April 1951.

6. NFC CDBLR, vol. 3, 'District of Baltimore'.

7. CCA 21C/3–11, Fr Charles Davis, 1827–1892, and *Cork Examiner*, 18 October 1892.

8. *Irish Times*, 8 November 1880.

9. Ó hEithir, 'The Birth, Death and Resurrection'.

10. *The Tablet*, 12 July 1902.

11. Leo Daly, 'Hero Breed: Pat Mullen', in Proinsias Ó Conluain (ed.), *Islands and Authors: Pen-Pictures of Life Past and Present on the Islands of Ireland* (Cork, 1983), pp. 86–7; *Freeman's Journal*, 23 March 1886; *Irish Times*, 1 August 1892.

12. Tim Robinson, *Stones of Aran: Pilgrimage* (Dublin, 1986), p. 216.

13. Robinson, *Memories*, p. 112.

14. *Freeman's Journal*, 28 October 1882.

15. Robinson, *Memories*, pp. 74–6.

16. Marie Louise Legg, *Newspapers and Nationalism: The Irish Provincial Press, 1850–1892* (Dublin, 1999), p. 3.

17. Ó Péicín, *Islanders*, pp. 60–62.

18. *Freeman's Journal*, 28 October 1882; *Pall Mall Gazette*, 28 October 1882.

19. *Freeman's Journal*, 4 and 21 November 1882.

20. *The Tablet*, 12 July 1902.

21. Joyce, *John Healy*, pp. 37–8.

22. CCA, *Skibbereen Eagle*, 12 January 1918; *Cork Examiner*, 12 January 1918.

23. Letter from former curate Michael O'Donnell to John O'Donnell, Inishkea Islands, 13 November 1927, quoted in *Cathair Na Mart, Journal of the Westport Historical Society*, no. 28, 2010, p. 93.

24. Dornan, *Mayo's Lost Islands*, p. 11; Viney, 'Another Life'.

25. NFC MS 839, Brian McLoughlin, Clare Island, 14 August 1942, informant: 85 year old Michael O'Malley, pp. 134–5 and pp. 139–47.

26. Arminta Wallace, 'The Prodigious Sebastian Barry', *Irish Times*, 17 November 1990.

27. Sebastian Barry, *Prayers of Sherkin, Boss Grady's Boys: Two Plays* (London, 1991).

28. CCA 21G/1, Island and Coast Society Report for 1847.

29. CCA 21A/4/3, Income of Priests on Cape Clear.

30. CCA 21G/1, Revd Edward Spring, Cape Clear Mission, March 1851.

31. *Muintir Acla*, no. 11, Winter 1998, pp. 21ff.

32. Branach, 'Edward Nangle and the Achill Island Mission'.

33. NLI, *Missionary Progress of the Island and Coast Society* (Dublin, 1863), pp. 16–20.
34. CCA 21A/16, Visits of Bishops.
35. NLI, *Missionary Progress of the Island and Coast Society for Ireland* (Dublin, 1865), pp. 9–15.
36. NLI, *Missionary Progress of the Island and Coast Society for Ireland: Forty-Third Year* (Dublin, 1878), p. 9.
37. NLI, *Missionary Progress of the Island and Coast Society for Ireland: Forty-Sixth Year* (Dublin, 1881), p. 24.
38. NLI, *Missionary Progress of the Island and Coast Society for Ireland: Sixtieth Year* (Dublin 1894), pp. 24–7; *Missionary Progress of the Island and Coast Society for Ireland: Sixty-First Year* (Dublin, 1895), pp. 24–36.
39. NFC MS 838, Accounts of collector Brian McLoughlin, April–June 1942, pp. 428–73.
40. NFC MS 1738, p. 274 Galway Arranmore Seanchas, 4 November 1966, collector Ciarán Bairéad.
41. RDA, Letterkenny, Tory Island Collection, 5, Bishop James MacDevitt to Fr James McFadden, 8 October 1875 and McFadden to MacDevitt, 10 and 18 October 1875.
42. Ibid., 9, McFadden to Logue, 19 October 1879.
43. Ibid., 15, Fr D. E. Coyle, Tory Island, to Bishop Patrick O'Donnell, 19 May 1889.
44. Ibid., O'Donnell to McFadden, 2 April 1889.
45. Ibid., Fr D. E. Coyle to Bishop Patrick O'Donnell, 29 May 1889.
46. Ibid., 22, Memorandum by Fr James McFadden, 22 October 1901.
47. *Freeman's Journal*, 10 January 1908.
48. Micheál Ó Dálaigh, 'Memories of Fishing in Cape Clear Between the Two World Wars', *Mizen Journal*, no. 9, 2001, pp. 111–28.
49. *Irish Independent*, 10 November 1928; *Connacht Sentinel*, 13 November 1928.
50. Timothy G. McMahon, *Grand Opportunity: The Gaelic Revival and Irish Society 1893–1910* (New York, 2008), pp. 54–5.
51. Ibid., pp. 56–7.
52. UCDA, Papers of Eoin MacNeill, LA1/L/79, S. G. Barrett to MacNeill, 12 December 1901.
53. *Connacht Telegraph*, 27 February 1904.
54. Brian Hughes (ed.), *Eoin MacNeill: Memoir of a Revolutionary Scholar* (Dublin, 2016), pp. 8–19.
55. UCDA, Papers of Eoin MacNeill, LA1/6/284, Eoin MacNeill to Charlie MacNeill, 14 May 1892.
56. *Irish Examiner*, 23 July 1908.

57. *Irish Times*, 2 July 1908.
58. *Irish Times*, 3 and 23 July 1908.
59. *Irish Times*, 22 July 1908.
60. *Freeman's Journal*, 21 March 1912; Patrick F. Sheeran, *The Novels of Liam O'Flaherty: A Study in Romantic Realism* (Dublin, 1976), pp. 176ff.
61. *Freeman's Journal*, 23 March 1912.
62. *Galway Express*, 28 February 1914, quoted in Sheeran, *The Novels of Liam O'Flaherty*, pp. 176–80.
63. Peter Costello, *Liam O'Flaherty's Ireland* (Dublin, 1996), pp. 1–8.
64. Breandán Ó hEithir, '"Skerrett", by Liam O'Flaherty', in Ó Conluain (ed.), *Islands and Authors*, pp. 59–63.
65. A. A. Kelly (ed.), *The Letters of Liam O'Flaherty* (Dublin, 1996), p. 250; letter from O'Flaherty to A. D. Peters, 12 September 1931.
66. Costello, *Liam O'Flaherty's Ireland*, p. 15.
67. O'Flaherty, *Skerrett*, p. 41, p. 161 and p. 262.
68. Seán O'Faoláin, 'Don Quixote O'Flaherty', *The Bell*, vol. 2, no. 3, June 1941, pp. 28–37.
69. Ó hEithir, '"Skerrett"'.
70. *Freeman's Journal*, 22 July 1911.
71. Ibid.
72. *Sunday Independent*, 4 August 1907.
73. *Connacht Tribune*, 4 September 1909.
74. *Connacht Tribune*, 12 April 1913.
75. *Freeman's Journal*, 11 February 1915.
76. TDA P6/9/4, Box 13, Farragher to W. M. Micks, 4 July 1916.
77. Ibid., Farragher to Archbishop Thomas Gilmartin, 16 December 1918.
78. TDA P6/7/9 Box 12, P. H. Johnston to Archbishop John Healy, 29 January 1906.
79. Ibid., Archbishop Healy to Farragher, 15 April 1907, and Farragher to Healy, 19 April 1907.
80. TDA P6/9/4, Box 13, Farragher's memorandum to CDB, 24 November 2010.
81. Ibid., Farragher to Archbishop Gilmartin, 16 December 1918, and Thomas O'Dea, Galway, to Gilmartin, 5 December 1918.
82. Ibid.
83. *Connacht Sentinel*, 13 November 1928.
84. Ó hEithir, '"Skerrett"'.
85. Catherine Candy, *Priestly Fictions: Popular Irish Novelists of the Early Twentieth Century* (Dublin, 1995), p. 12.
86. Maurice Cronin, 'Joseph Guinan', *DIB*, vol. 4, pp. 310–11.

87. Candy, *Priestly Fictions*, p. 104.

88. Patrick Maume, 'A Pastoral Vision: The Novels of Canon Joseph Guinan', *New Hibernia Review*, vol. 9, no. 4, Winter 2005, pp. 79–98.

89. Joseph Guinan, *Island Parish* (Dublin, 1908), p. 244.

90. Ibid., pp. 171–2.

91. McCurdy, *Rathlin's Rugged Story*, p. 44.

92. O'Donnell, *Islanders*, pp. 106–7 and p. 42.

93. Quoted in Dornan, *Mayo's Lost Islands*, p. 11.

94. Robinson, *Further Memories*, pp. 133–5.

95. Dornan, *Mayo's Lost Islands*, pp. 246–7.

96. Power, *The Land of Youth*, p. 23.

97. Ibid., p. 230.

98. Ibid., p. 314.

99. TDA P6/9/4, Box 13, Fr Farragher to Archbishop Thomas Gilmartin, 10 June 1919.

100. NLI, *Coimisiún na Gaeltachta: Report and Evidence*, Evidence of Revd S. J. Walsh, Galway, 20 August 1925, pp. 1–4.

101. TDA P6/9/4, Box 13, Parish Priest of Achill to Archbishop Gilmartin, 30 December 1918.

102. TDA P4/9/1 Box 11, Anita Mac Mahon to Archbishop Gilmartin, 5 March 1919.

103. Ibid., P. J. Joyce, Keel Post Office, Achill, to Gilmartin, 6 August 1919.

104. Ibid., Fr John Keavy to Gilmartin, 28 July 1927 and 18 August 1927.

105. Ibid., Letter of 27 February 1928.

106. Ibid., Letter of 18 August 1927.

107. Ibid., Fr John Keavy to Gilmartin, 15 July 1928.

108. TDA P4/9/2, Box 11, Bishop MacNeely to Gilmartin, 28 July 1937; Bishop Browne to Gilmartin, 30 July 1938 and Archbishop Dignan to Gilmartin, 26 July 1938.

109. Ibid., John O'Malley to Gilmartin, 14 January 1939.

110. NAI DT 8670B, Memorandum of Revd J. Cannery, Clare Island, 6 March 1941; DT 8670A, Fr T. Killeen to Archbishop Gilmartin, 9 September 1937; DT 8670C, Fr T. Varley to John A. Costello, 22 December 1954; DT 97/9/310, Fr Cullane to DT, 15 December 1942.

111. NLI, *Coimisiún na Gaeltachta: Report and Evidence*, 18 August 1925, Evidence of Revd Dr Duggan, CC Arranmore, 18 August 1925.

112. Ibid.

113. *Strabane Chronicle*, 2 April 1938; *Irish Independent*, 13 September 1939.

114. *Irish Press*, 13 July 1962.

115. NAI DT S16282, Settlement of Families from Inishark Island, Fr Charles O'Malley to Gerald Bartley TD, 22 June 1957.

116. TDA P20/9/1, Fr James Heaney to Archbishop Walsh, 25 November 1955, and Fr Canning to Irish Land Commission, 28 August 1940.

117. M. Nic Craith, 'Primary Education on the Great Blasket Island, 1864–1940', *Journal of the Kerry Archaeological and Historical Society*, no, 28, 1995, pp. 77–138.

118. Beaumont, *Achillbeg*, pp. 147–57.

119. TDA P20/2/3, Box 28, T. O'Murghleasa to Gilmartin, 11 October 1935.

120. Ibid., Gilmartin to Walshe, 24 January 1936.

121. Ibid., P. O'D, Department of Education to Walshe, Department of Education, 20 May 1936.

122. TDA P20/9/1 Box 29, Fr Canning to Secretary, Archbishop Walsh, 23 April 1942; Fr T. Varley to Walsh, 1 February 1952; Fr Jennings to Walsh, 27 November 1944.

123. TDA P6/7/11 Box 12, Fr Martin O'Donnell to Gilmartin, 5 December 1933.

124. Ibid.

125. NFC MS 1738, Galway, Aran Mór Seanchas, interview with Bean Sheáin Sharry by Ciarán Bairéad, 21 June 1965.

126. RDA, Tory Island, 52, Paschal Robinson to Archbishop Mac Neely, 3 January 1942 and 23 January 1942.

127. Ibid., 59, Fr J. Cunningham to MacNeely, 11 January 1942.

128. Shaun Boylan, 'James McDyer', *DIB*, vol. 5, pp. 986–7; NAI DT 97/9/773, Taoiseach's Tour of Western Isles, E. J. McLoughlin to Department of Finance, 28 August 1947; DT note, 22 September 1947.

129. James McDyer, *Fr McDyer of Glencolumbkille: An Autobiography* (Kerry, 1982), p. 43.

130. 'Canon James McDyer: An Appreciation', *Irish Times*, 30 November 1987.

131. *Irish Press*, 26 November 1987; *Donegal News*, 8 September 1951.

132. McDyer, *Fr McDyer of Glencolumbkille*, pp. 41–2.

133. Ibid., pp. 44–5.

134. Quoted in Séamas Ó Catháin, 'Toraigh na dTonn', in Ó Conluain (ed.), *Islands and Authors*, pp. 106–9.

135. Ibid.

136. Robin Fox, *The Tory Islanders: A People of the Celtic Fringe* (Cambridge, 1978), p. 27.

137. RDA Tory Island, 69, Fr Hugh Strain to Bishop McFeely, 27 April 1967.

138. NFC MS 1738, p. 347, Ciaran Bairéad, interview with Revd Thomas Canon Killeen in Mayo, 13 January 1966.

139. NFC MS 1365, pp. 2–211, Rose McCurdy, interview with Michael J. Murphy, full-time collector in Antrim, Rathlin Island, August 1954.

140. Ibid.

141. TDA P4/9/2, Box 11, Fr James Campbell to Gilmartin, 16 January 1939.

142. TDA P6/9/8 Box 13, Fr Thomas Killea to Archbishop Walsh, 29 May 1947.

143. Ibid., Seán Lemass to Walsh, 7 June 1947.

144. TDA P6/7/7, Box 12, Eamon Coughlan, OPW, to Archbishop Walsh, 11 September 1956.

145. Ibid., Coughlan to Walsh, 24 September 1956.

146. Ibid., Fr Moran to Walsh, 5 October 1956.

147. Ibid., Fr T. Varley to Walsh, 5 October 1956, and Coughlan to Walsh, 14 November 1956.

148. Ibid., Varley to Walsh, 5 October 1956.

149. *Muintir Acla*, no. 6, Spring 1997, p. 32; *Muintir Acla*, no. 9, Spring 1998.

150. NAI DT S15093A, Valentia Island, Co. Kerry, Development Work on Bridge to Mainland, Cornelius Lune, Honorary Secretary, Valentia Bridge Committee, to de Valera, 19 February 1952.

151. Ibid., Fr James Enright to de Valera, 10 December 1953.

152. Ibid., Memorandum of John Garvin, Department of Local Government, 26 March 1954.

153. Ibid., Fr James Enright to John A. Costello, 14 December 1955 and 2 January 1956, and DT note of 27 April 1956.

154. *Irish Independent*, 21 January 1964 and 30 November 1966.

155. *The Kerryman*, 31 July 1971.

156. CCA 21H-F, Religious Figures and Events, notes on Fr Tomás Ó Murchú; *Cork Examiner*, 30 May 1977.

157. Ibid., 21H, 'Leabhar na pfograí' (books of notices).

158. *Irish Times*, 16 May 1972.

159. *Cork Examiner*, 31 March 1966.

160. TDA, Memoranda by priests serving in the islands, compiled by Fr Kieran Waldron, June 2016. Account of Fr Eamon Concannon, CC Inisheer, 1960–67.

161. Ibid., Account of Fr Paddy Gilligan, CC Inisheer,1969–71.

162. Ibid., Account of Fr Joseph Cooney, CC Kilronan, Inishmore, 1962–67.

163. Denis Smith, *Aran Islands: A Personal Journey* (New York, 1980), p. 14.

164. Deborah Tall, *The Island of the White Cow: Memories of an Irish Island* (London, 1986), pp. 195–6 and pp. 232–4.

165. RDA, Tory Island, 75, Fr Seamus Meehan to Archbishop McFeely, 20 February 1969.

166. Ibid., McFeely to Fr Meehan, 11 November 1969.

167. Ibid., Fr Meehan to McFeely, 15 January 1970.
168. Ibid., McFeely to Fr Meehan, 28 January 1970.
169. RDA, Tory Island, 100, Fr Joe McBreaty to Fr Bonar and reply, 2 July 1973.
170. De Mórdha, *An Island Community*, p. 24.
171. Ibid., pp. 24–5.
172. Dorothy Harrison Therman, *Stories from Tory Island* (Dublin, 1999, first published 1989), p. xiii.
173. Pádraig O'Toole, *Aran to Africa: An Irishman's Unique Odyssey* (Galway, 2013), p. 9.
174. *Irish Times* article on the evacuation of Inishark, 25 October 1960.
175. John C. Messenger, *Inis Beag: Isle of Ireland* (New York, 1969), pp. 59–68.
176. John C. Messenger, 'The Irish Comic Tradition of Inis Beag', *Journal of the Folklore Institute*, vol. 15, no. 3, September–December 1978, pp. 235–51.
177. Reg Hindley, 'Clear Island in 1958: A Study in Geolinguistic Transition', *Irish Geography*, 27, 2, 1994, pp. 97–106.
178. Agnès Pataux, *Ireland on the Edge of Europe* (Milan, 2003), Introduction by Colm Tóibín, p. 15.
179. Gerry Moriarty, 'Turbulent Priest Who Saved Tory Island', *Irish Times*, 8 March 2008.
180. *Donegal News*, 12 December 1981.
181. Ó Péicín, *Islanders*, p. 2.
182. Ibid., pp. 23–39.
183. Ibid., pp. 79–95.
184. Ibid., pp. 130–40.
185. Ibid.
186. *Cork Examiner*, 18 September 1996.
187. www.craggyislandfestival.com, accessed 21 April 2017; *Irish Independent*, 25 February 2012.

Chapter 5: Island Visitors: The First Wave

1. PRONI D3335/10/13, Diary of Norah Workman, Belfast, 'A Summer Trip to the Isles of the West', 2 July 1895.
2. Ibid.
3. Ibid.
4. J. W. O'Connell, 'The Rediscovery of Aran in the 19th Century', in John Feehan (ed.), *The Book of Aran* (Galway, 1994), pp. 182–94.
5. Ibid.

6. Barry Raftery, *Pagan and Celtic Ireland: The Enigma of the Irish Iron Age* (London, 1994), pp. 44–5.

7. Peter Harbison, 'John Windele's Visit to Skellig Michael in 1851', *Journal of the Kerry Archaeological and Historical Society*, vol. 9, 1976, pp. 125–6.

8. Michael Ryan (ed.), *Irish Archaeology* (Dublin, 1994), p. 56.

9. Aidan O'Sullivan, 'The Western Islands: Ireland's Atlantic Islands and the Forging of Gaelic Irish National Identities', in Gordon Noble (ed.), *Scottish Odysseys: The Archaeology of Islands* (London, 2008), pp. 172–90.

10. Ibid.

11. Jerry O'Sullivan and Tomás Ó Carragáin, *Inishmurray: Monks and Pilgrims in an Atlantic Landscape*, vol. 1: *Archaeological Survey and Excavations 1997–2000* (Cork, 2008), pp. 5–8 and pp. 346–9.

12. Timothy Collins, 'Praeger in the West: Naturalists and Antiquarians in Connemara and the Islands, 1894–1914', *Journal of the Galway Archaeology and Historical Society*, vol. 45, 1993, pp. 124–55.

13. Robert Lloyd Praeger, *The Botanist in Ireland* (Dublin, 1934), pp. 459–60 and pp. 64–6.

14. Ibid.

15. Trinity College Dublin (TCD) MS 10961, Browne and Haddon on Aran; the collection of Dr Charles R. Browne (186[7]–1918) consists of six albums of images from the western islands, as well as scenes of Dublin and Trinity College.

16. Ciarán Walsh, 'Charles R. Browne, the Irish "Headhunter"', *Irish Journal of Anthropology*, vol. 16, no. 1, 2013, pp. 16–23; TCD MS 10961/4/5v, Charles Browne Collection.

17. A. C. Haddon and C. R. Browne, 'On the Ethnography of the Aran Islands, Co. Galway', *Proceedings of the Royal Irish Academy* (*PRIA*) 3rd series, vol. 2, 1891–3, pp. 768–830.

18. William R. Wilde, 'On the Battle of Moytura', *PRIA*, 1836–1869, vol. 9, 1864–6, pp. 546–50.

19. Haddon and Browne, 'On the Ethnography of the Aran Islands'.

20. Wilde, 'On the Battle of Moytura'.

21. Charles R. Browne, 'Ethnography of the Mullet, Inishkea Islands, and Portacloy, County Mayo', *PRIA*, 3rd series, vol. 3, 1893–6, pp. 587–648.

22. Ibid.

23. Ibid.

24. Walsh, 'Charles R. Browne'.

25. Haddon and Browne, 'On the Ethnography of the Aran Islands'.

26. John Wilson Foster, *Colonial Consequences: Essays in Irish Literature and Culture* (Dublin, 1991), pp. 21–3 and p. 51.

27. Kevin Martin, 'How the West Was Wonderful: Some Historical Perspectives on Representations of the West of Ireland in Popular Culture', *Institute of Technology Blanchardstown Journal*, vol. 2, no. 2, 2001, pp. 89–94.

28. Joseph Schafer (ed.), *Memoirs of Jeremiah Curtin* (Madison, WI, 1940), p. 385.

29. Maureen Murphy, 'Jeremiah Curtin', *DIB*, vol. 2, pp. 1114–16.

30. Schafer (ed.), *Memoirs of Jeremiah Curtin*, pp. 462–3.

31. Ibid., p. 464.

32. Ibid., pp. 454–6.

33. R. F. Foster, *W. B. Yeats, a Life*, vol. 1: *Apprentice Mage, 1865–1914* (London, 1997), pp. 166–7.

34. Lady Gregory, *Visions and Beliefs in the West of Ireland* (London, 1920), Preface by Gregory, Coole, February 1916, pp. 3–4 and pp. 112–14.

35. Arthur Symons, *Cities and Sea Coasts and Islands* (Evanston, IL, 1998; first published New York, 1918), Preface.

36. Ibid., p. 305.

37. Ibid., pp. 309–11.

38. Ibid., p. 313.

39. Ibid., p. 319.

40. W. B. Yeats, *Essays and Introductions* (London, 1961), p. 299.

41. TCD MS 4385, Synge Notebook, May 1898, pp. 1–6.

42. Ibid., pp. 10–20.

43. Ibid., p. 29.

44. Ibid., pp. 29–53.

45. TCD MS 4424/73–80, Martin McDonagh, Inishmaan, to Synge, 23 July 1898, 10 October 1898 and 20 February 1899.

46. TCD MS 4424/105–110, Barbara Connolly to Synge, 16 November 1901 and 6 February 1902.

47. J. M. Synge, 'A Story from Inishmaan', *New Ireland Review*, vol. 10, September 1898–February 1899, pp. 153–7.

48. TCD MS 4424/127, Brimley Johnson to Synge, 9 June 1903.

49. TCD MS 4424/137, John Masefield to Lady Gregory, 2 December 1903.

50. TCD MS 4424/553, George Roberts, Maunsel, to Lady Gregory, 6 September 1910.

51. TCD MS 4385, Synge Notebook, May 1898, p. 42.

52. Synge, *The Aran Islands*, p. 5.

53. Ibid., pp. 13–14.

54. Ibid.

55. Ibid., p. 84.

56. Ibid., p. 31.

57. Ibid., pp. 114–17 and p. 122.
58. TCD MS 4424/142, Padraic Colum to Synge, 24 February 1904.
59. TCD MS 4424/145, Frank Fay to Synge, 5 April 1904.
60. Synge, *The Aran Islands*, pp. 107–13.
61. J. M. Synge, *Riders to the Sea*, in Ann Saddlemyer (ed.), *The Playboy of the Western World and Other Plays* (Oxford, 2008), pp. 1–13.
62. TCD MS 4424/178, C. P. Scott to Synge, 6 July 1905.
63. TCD MS 4387, Synge Notebooks, pp. 11–41.
64. Elaine Sisson, 'The Aran Islands and the Travel Essays', in P. J. Matthews (ed.), *The Cambridge Companion to J. M. Synge* (Cambridge, 2009), pp. 52–64.
65. Pataux, *Ireland on the Edge of Europe*, pp. 11–12.
66. UCDA, Papers of Eoin MacNeill, LAI/G/1/282, Eoin MacNeill to Charlie MacNeill, 14 July 1891.
67. Ibid., Eoin MacNeill to Charlie MacNeill, 17 July 1891.
68. Ibid., Eoin MacNeill to Charlie MacNeill, 18 July 1891.
69. Ibid., LAI/6/284, Eoin MacNeill to Charlie MacNeill, 14 May 1892.
70. NUIGA G3/111, Bairéad Collection, J. H. Lloyd to Mr Barrett, 4 July 1894.
71. NUIGA G3/664, Memorandum of John MacNeill, 3 June 1893.
72. Elizabeth Malcolm, 'Temperance and Irish Nationalism', in F. S. L. Lyons and R. A. J. Hawkins (eds.), *Ireland Under the Union: Varieties of Tension* (Oxford, 1980), pp. 69–115.
73. Capuchin Archives, Church Street, Dublin, Records of Missions Given by the Capuchin Fathers of Dublin, 1904–1947, and Record of the Working of the National Temperance Crusade, 1901–1904; Mission and Retreats Section 10/4, Report on Temperance Work compiled by Fr Thomas Dowling, 7 May 1912; *The Father Matthew Record*, vol. 1, no. 6, June 1908.
74. Ibid., Missions and Retreats, 1906, Reports by Fr Benignus Brennan, 9–12 November 1906.
75. Ibid., *Mayo News*, 17 November 1906.
76. Ibid., Report to Most Revd Father General by Fr Paul, 28 February 1907.
77. Ibid., Fr J. P. Connelly to Fr Paul, 26 June 1906, and Fr Colleran to Fr Angelo, 16 September 1907.
78. Ibid., Report of Missions, Fr Albert, Clare Island, October 1906.
79. Ibid., 10/4 Missions and Retreats, Fr J. P. Connelly to Fr Paul, 26 June 1906, and Fr Thomas Healy to Fr Paul, 5 October 1906.
80. Ibid., Record of Missions Given by Capuchin Fathers of Cork, 1906–7, remarks on Bere Island, 22 to, 6 September 1908; Fr James Scanlon to Fr Peter, 8 April 1906; Fr John Byrne to Fr Peter, 15 April 1906.
81. Mac Cárthaigh and Whelan (eds.), *New Survey of Clare Island*, 1, p. v.

82. Ibid.
83. PRONI ANT/6/1/1/18/317, Coroner's Inquest Relating to Death of Edward Glanville, Rathlin Island, 22 August 1898.
84. Frances Clarke and Patrick Maume, 'Emily Lawless', *DIB*, vol. 5, pp. 351–3.
85. Emily Lawless, *Grania: The Story of an Island* (London, 1892), pp. 214–23.
86. Ibid., p. 203.
87. Ibid., pp. 272–4.
88. Barbara Ó Connor and Michael Cronin (eds.), *Tourism in Ireland: A Critical Analysis* (Cork, 1993), p. 88.
89. Stephen Gwynn, *A Holiday in Connemara* (London, 1909), p. 123.
90. Ibid., p. 195.
91. Richard Ellmann, *James Joyce* (Oxford, 1982, first published 1959), pp. 245–8.
92. Ibid., p. 325.
93. Ó Dubhshláine, *A Dark Day on the Blaskets*, pp. 17–57 and pp. 70–79.
94. Tomás Ó Crohan, *The Islandman* (Oxford, 2000, first published Dublin, 1929), pp. 197–8.
95. Ó Dubhshláine, *A Dark Day on the Blaskets*, p. 101.
96. Ibid., p. 160.
97. Ruth Dudley Edwards, *The Seven: The Lives and Legacies of the Founding Fathers of the Irish Republic* (London, 2016), p. 133, p. 154, p. 186.
98. Austin Clarke, *A Penny in the Clouds: More Memories of Ireland and England* (London, 1968), pp. 133–45.
99. Robert Kanigel, *On an Irish Island* (New York, 2012), pp. 31–6.
100. Diarmuid Ó Giolláin, *Locating Irish Folklore: Tradition, Modernity, Identity* (Cork, 2000), p. 127.
101. Kanigel, *On an Irish Island*, p. 9.
102. Maurice O'Sullivan, *Twenty Years a Growing*, trans. George Thomson (Oxford, 1953), p. ii.
103. Ibid., pp. 18–32.
104. Ibid., p. 167.
105. Ibid., p. 250.
106. Henry, *An Irish Portrait*, p. 2.
107. Ibid., pp. 51–8.
108. Ibid., p. 66.
109. Nicola Gordon Bowe, *The Life and Work of Harry Clarke* (Dublin, 1989), pp. 16–18.
110. Eimear Ó Connor, *Seán Keating in Context: Responses to Culture and Politics in Post-Civil War Ireland* (Dublin, 2009), pp. 10–11 and p. 31.

111. Marie Bourke, 'Yeats, Henry and the Western Idyll', *History Ireland*, vol. 11, no. 2, Summer 2003, pp. 28–34.
112. Ibid.
113. NUIGA P93, Papers of Terence Ingold, Draft essays on Rathlin and Achill Island trips, from notes written in September 1997.
114. Simon Callow, *Orson Welles: The Road to Xanadu* (London, 1995), pp. 72–112.
115. Liam O'Flaherty, *A Tourist's Guide to Ireland* (London, 1929), pp. 109–11.

Chapter 6: Island Visitors: The Second Wave

1. Gibney, Review of *An tÉireannach Fáin*.
2. Ibid.
3. Richard Barsam, *The Vision of Robert Flaherty: The Artist as Myth and Film Maker* (Indianapolis, 1988), pp. 59–61.
4. Ó Conluain (ed.), *Islands and Authors*, p. 194.
5. *Irish Press*, 18 October 1934.
6. 'What Dublin is Reading', *Irish Times*, 17 November 1934.
7. Tom O'Flaherty, *Cliffmen of the West* (London, 1935), p. 53.
8. Bridget Hourican, 'Robert Flaherty', *DIB*, vol. 3, pp. 994–6.
9. Ibid.
10. Robinson, *Pilgrimage*, p. 189.
11. *Irish Independent*, 11 June 1940; *Cork Examiner*, 22 May 1952, *Irish Press*, 12 January 1938.
12. *Irish Independent*, 11 June 1940.
13. *Irish Press*, 13 November 1934.
14. *Irish Independent*, 5 April 1940.
15. Sylvie Kleinman-Batt and Elaine Garvey, 'An Absent Minded Person of the Student Type: Extracts from the Artaud File', *Dublin Review*, no. 1, Winter 2000–1, pp. 58–81.
16. 'Artaud on Aran', *Irish Times*, 14 August 1997.
17. Letters contained in NAI DFA Paris P34/119 and reprinted in Kleinman-Batt and Garvey, 'An Absent Minded Person'.
18. Ibid.
19. Janet T. Marquardt (ed.), *Françoise Henry in County Mayo: The Inishkea Journals* (Dublin, 2012), pp. 3–7.
20. Ibid., p. 19.
21. Ibid., p. 44.

22. Ibid., pp. 55–77.

23. Ibid., pp. 117–43.

24. Turlough Ó Riordan, 'Thomas Holmes Mason', *DIB*, vol. 6, pp. 410–11, and Rose Doyle, 'Saga of a Scientific Family by a Seventh Generation Son', *Irish Times*, 22 October 2003.

25. R. M. Lockley, *I Know an Island* (London, 1938), pp. 104–28.

26. Ibid.

27. Séan O'Faoláin, *An Irish Journey* (London, 1940), p. 3.

28. Ibid., pp. 110–11.

29. Ibid., pp. 141–3.

30. Ibid., pp. 143–4.

31. Emyr Estyn Evans, *The Personality of Ireland: Habitat, Heritage and History* (Dublin, 1992; first published 1973), p. 1.

32. Emyr Estyn Evans, *Ireland and the Atlantic Heritage: Selected Writings* (Dublin, 1996), pp. 121–3.

33. Daphne D. C. Pochin Mould, *The Rock of Truth* (London, 1953), p. 204.

34. Brendan Behan, 'In the Kingdom of Kerry', *Ireland of the Welcomes*, vol. 1, no. 2, July–August 1952, p. 15.

35. Brendan Behan, *Brendan Behan's Island* (London, 1962), p. 70.

36. Anthony Cronin, *No Laughing Matter: The Life and Times of Flann O'Brien* (London, 1989), p. 197.

37. NFC MS 1365, Michael J. Murphy to Séamus Ó Duilearga, 27 August 1954, p. 2.

38. Proinsias Ó Conluain, 'Cín lae Craoltóra', in Louis McRedmond (ed.), *Written on the Wind: Personal Memories of Irish Radio 1926–76* (Dublin, 1976), pp. 87–106. Translation by Deirdre Ní Chonghaile.

39. Brendan Scally, 'A Journey to Achill, 1947', *Cathair Na Mart*, vol. 8, no. 1, 1988, pp. 118–22.

40. Francis MacManus, 'Life at Europe's Edge', *Ireland of the Welcomes*, vol. 2, no. 5, January–February 1954, pp. 5–8; Walter Macken 'Achill Island', *Ireland of the Welcomes*, vol. 3, no. 5, January–February 1955; Caoimhín Ó Danachair [Kevin Danaher], 'The Magic Islands', *Ireland of the Welcomes*, vol. 5, no. 1 May–June 1956.

41. Malachy Hynes, article on Aran Islands, *Times Pictorial* (Dublin), 6 November 1943.

42. Archive of Irish America, New York University, Papers of Ernie O'Malley, Diary Entry on Aran Islands, 1944, p. 6, quoted in Cormac O'Malley, *Ernie O'Malley*, A booklet to accompany a symposium at Glucksman Ireland House, NYU, on Ernie O'Malley (New York, 2014), p. 8.

43. Robert Gibbings, 'The Connemara Islands', *The Bell*, vol. 8, no. 5, August 1944, pp. 427–40.
44. Elizabeth Rivers, *Stranger in Aran* (Dublin, 1946), pp. 20–47.
45. Edna O'Brien, article on Aran Islands, *Irish Press*, 12 June 1952.
46. Richard Power, *Apple on the Treetop*, trans. Victor Power (Dublin, 1980; first published 1958), p. 6.
47. Ibid., p. 45.
48. Ibid., p. 49.
49. Ibid., pp. 84–94.
50. Ibid., pp. 105–7.
51. Ibid., pp. 163–89.
52. Power, *The Land of Youth*, pp. 49–51.
53. *Irish Times*, 11 July 2015.
54. *Irish Times*, 8 April 1971.
55. *Irish Times*, 5 December 2007.
56. O'Toole (ed.), *Modern Ireland in 100 Art Works*, p. 103.
57. James MacIntyre, *Three Men on an Island* (Belfast, 1996), pp. 1–19.
58. Ibid., pp. 81–93.
59. Ibid., pp. 134–42.
60. *Tuam Herald*, 1 June 1963; MacIntyre, *Three Men on an Island*, p. 142.
61. Richard Murphy, *The Kick: A Memoir* (London, 2002), pp. 199–207.
62. Ibid.
63. Ralph J. Mills (ed.), *Selected Letters of Theodore Roethke* (Seattle, 1968), pp. 237–8.
64. Kevin Barry, 'Roethke in the Bughouse', short story published in the *Irish Times*, 29 December 2015.
65. Allan Seager, *The Glass House: The Life of Theodore Roethke* (Ann Arbor, MI, 2002; first published New York, 1968), pp. 267–9.
66. Heinrich Böll, *Irish Journal*, trans. Leila Vennewitz (New York and London, 1967; first published 1957), pp. 59–63.
67. PRONI D440/E/4, Catalogue of Derek Hill Papers; Hill's descriptions of Tory and Mount Athos.
68. Bruce Arnold, *Derek Hill* (London, 2010), p. 210.
69. Ibid., pp. 210–12.
70. Ibid., pp. 226–8.
71. PRONI D4400/C/9/18, Catalogue of Derek Hill Papers, Letters from Raymond Martinez to Hill, August 1965.
72. *Donegal News*, 25 August 1962.

73. PRONI D4400/D/14, Catalogue of Derek Hill Papers, Letters from D. Collum to Derek Hill, 1958–61, and D4400/D/1/10, Letters from Patsy Dan Rodgers to Hill, 1967–97.

74. *Connaught Telegraph*, 20 November 1969.

75. *Mayo News*, 6 November 1996; *Sunday Independent*, 9 October 2011; *Irish Independent*, 5 October 2012.

76. Kevin Barry, *Beatlebone* (Edinburgh, 2015), p. 6.

77. Ibid., pp. 182–3.

78. *Irish Independent*, 5 October 2012.

79. Messenger, *Inis Beag*.

80. Ibid., pp. 24–57.

81. Ibid., pp. 72–7.

82. Ibid., p. 84.

83. Messenger, 'The Irish Comic Tradition of Inis Beag'.

84. Ibid.

85. Michael Viney, 'The Yank in the Corner', *Irish Times*, 6 August 1983.

86. Ibid. and Breandán Ó hEithir and Ruairi Ó hEithir, *An Aran Reader* (Dublin, 1991), p. 3.

87. Viney, 'The Yank in the Corner'.

88. Nancy Scheper-Hughes, *Saints, Scholars and Schizophrenics: Mental Illness in Rural Ireland* (Berkeley, 1979), p. 133.

89. *Irish Times*, 15 September 1965 and 13 July 1967.

90. NUIGA T13/A/329, Papers of Shields Family, David Clarke to Arthur and Laurie Shields, 6 May 1967.

91. John Healy, 'The Largest Island' (1965), in John Horgan (ed.), *Great Irish Reportage* (Dublin, 2013), pp. 104–12.

92. *Ireland of the Welcomes*, vol. 20, no. 2, July–August 1971.

93. Andrew McNeillie, *An Aran Keening* (Dublin, 2001), pp. 5–24.

94. Ibid., p. 83.

95. Ibid., pp. 56–89.

96. Ibid., pp. 98–138.

97. Ibid., p. 201.

98. Ann Saddlemyer, 'J. M. Synge', *Ireland of the Welcomes*, vol. 19, no. 6, March–April 1971, pp. 6–13.

99. Tom MacIntyre, 'Men of the West', *Ireland of the Welcomes*, vol. 22, no. 4 November–December 1973, p. 31; Bernadette Sweeney and Marie Kelly (eds.), *The Theatre of Tom MacIntyre: Strays from the Ether* (Dublin, 2010), pp. 24–63.

100. Ibid., p. 71.

101. Smith, *Aran Islands*, pp. 8–9.

102. Christopher Morash, 'All Playboys Now: The Playboy of the Western World and the Audience', in Nicholas Grene (ed.), *J. M. Synge and Irish Theatre* (Dublin, 2000), pp. 131–51.

103. Smith, *Aran Islands*, pp. 22–5.

104. Ibid., p. 31.

105. Tall, *Island of the White Cow*, pp. 6–9.

106. Ibid., pp. 17–37.

107. Ibid., pp. 55–68 and pp. 128–9.

108. Ibid., p. 92.

109. Ibid., p. 132.

110. Ibid., pp. 139–45 and p. 179.

111. Ibid., pp. 196–203.

112. Ibid., pp. 205–34.

113. Vicki Freeman, Review of Tall, *Island of the White Cow*, New York Times, 16 March 1986.

114. Marguerite Mac Curtin, 'Deborah and the Island', *Irish Times*, 4 October 1986.

115. Robinson, 'The Impossible Isles'.

116. *Irish Times*, 2 September 1999.

117. NUIGA P120/1/12, Papers of Tim Robinson; Robinson, *Pilgrimage*, p. 9.

118. NUIGA P120/3/30/8–9, Papers of Tim Robinson, Robinson to Registrar, Commissioner of Irish Lights, 8 July 1987; Robinson to Paul Kerrigan, 31 March 1984; Kerrigan to Robinson, 11 July 1984; Robinson to 'Frank', 8 October 1989.

119. Tim Robinson, *Stones of Aran: Labyrinth* (New York, 2009; first published 1995), p. xi and pp. 593–603.

120. Ibid., p. 188 and pp. 419–20.

121. Robinson, *Pilgrimage*, pp. 63–70, and *Labyrinth*, pp. 419–20.

122. Robinson, *Labyrinth*, p. 11.

123. Ibid.

124. NUIGA, Etienne Rynne Papers (uncatalogued), Robinson to Rynne, 5 March 1984 and 17 January 1985.

125. Derek Gladwin and Christine Cusick (eds.), *Unfolding Irish Landscapes: Tim Robinson, Culture and Environment* (Manchester, 2016).

126. John Wilson Foster, review of Gladwin and Cusick, *Dublin Review of Books* online, 29 September 2016, www.drb.ie, accessed 7 September 2017; Robinson, *Pilgrimage*, p. xiv, and *Labyrinth*, p. 25.

127. Robinson *Pilgrimage*, p. xxiii.

128. Mitchell, *Man and Environment*, p. ix.

129. Pataux, *Ireland on the Edge of Europe*, pp. 7–11.

130. NUIGA T2, Druid Theatre Company, Druid Tour Schedule 1996; includes programme note by Fintan O'Toole, 'Changing Places'.

131. NUIGA T2/261, Druid Synge 2005: Media File, September and October 2005.

132. NUIGA T2/389–90, *Cripple of Inishmaan*, annotated copy of Garry Hynes.

133. Martin McDonagh, *The Cripple of Inishmaan* (London, 1997), pp. 23–49.

134. RTE Documentary *The Stranger*, broadcast on RTE One, 15 September 2016; *Donegal News*, 26 August 2016.

135. *The Stranger*.

136. *Donegal News*, 11 July 2014.

137. *The Stranger*.

138. Jerome Kiely, 'The Man from Cape Clear by Conchúr Ó Siocháin', in Ó Conluain (ed.), *Islands and Authors*, pp. 95ff.

Chapter 7: Island Life and Mentality

1. Charles Browne, 'The Ethnography of Inishbofin and Inishark Co. Galway', *Proceedings of the Royal Irish Academy*, 3rd series, vol. 17, 1894, pp. 317–70.

2. NFC CDBLR, vol. 2, 'Inishbofin'.

3. Browne, 'Ethnography of the Mullet'.

4. NFC CDBLR, vol. 2, 'Achill Island'.

5. NFC CDBLR, vol. 2, 'Clare Island'.

6. Charles R. Browne, 'The Ethnography of Clare Island and Inishturk, Co. Mayo', *PRIA*, vol. 5, June 1997, p. 58.

7. Browne, 'Ethnology of the Mullet'.

8. Haddon and Browne, 'On the Ethnography of the Aran Islands'.

9. NFC CDBLR, vol. 1, 'District of Arranmore'.

10. NFC CDBLR, vol. 2, pp. 533–7, 'District of Clifden', by Robert Ruttledge-Fair, 26 August 1892.

11. NFC CDBLR, vol. 2, 'Achill Island'.

12. NFC CDBLR, vol. 3, 'District of Baltimore'.

13. NFC CDBLR, vol. 1, pp. 109–16, 'Tory Island', by F. G. Townsend Gahan, 1 February 1897.

14. NFC CDBLR, vol. 2, 'Achill Island'.

15. NFC CDBLR, vol. 3, 'Aran Islands'.

16. NFC CDBLR, vol. 1, 'District of Arranmore'.

17. RDA, Tory Island, 34, James J. Ward to Archbishop Patrick O'Donnell, 28 November 1912.

18. Ibid., 36, Ward to O'Donnell, 16 August 1913.

19. Ibid.

20. Ibid., 38, Ward to O'Donnell, 18 January 1914.

21. Austin Clarke, *A Penny in the Clouds* (London, 1968), p. 139.

22. Carney, *From the Great Blasket to America*, p. 19 and pp. 46–7.

23. McNeillie, *An Aran Keening*, p. 5.

24. *Connacht Tribune*, 17 June 1911.

25. *Freeman's Journal*, 22 July 1911.

26. NFC MS 838, Inishark and Inishbofin, April–June 1942, p. 413.

27. NFC MS 839, Clare Island, p. 157.

28. Ó Conluain (ed.), *Islands and Authors*, p. 129.

29. Mould, *Valentia*, p. 119.

30. O'Toole, *Aran to Africa*, p. 28.

31. *Cork Examiner*, 10 November 1939.

32. *Irish Press*, 10 March 1937.

33. *Irish Press*, 15 March 1937.

34. Synge, *The Aran Islands*, p. 105.

35. NFC MS 1365, Rathlin Island, p. 56.

36. Lillis O'Laoire, 'Field Work in Common Places: An Ethnographer's Experiences in Tory Island', *British Journal of Ethnomusicology*, vol. 12, no. 1, 2003, pp. 113–36, and Lillis O'Laoire, *On a Rock in the Middle of the Ocean: Songs and Singers in Tory Island* (Galway, 2007).

37. NFC MS 839, Omey Island, p. 291.

38. Carney, *From the Great Blasket to America*, p. 31.

39. NFC MS 838, Inishark and Inishbofin, April–June 1942, pp. 340–1.

40. NFC MS 838, Clare Island, August 1942, p. 170.

41. NFC MS 838, Inishbofin, pp. 465–7.

42. Alf MacLochlainn, 'Blasket Island Life and Work', *Journal of Kerry Archaeological and Historical Society*, 2nd series, vol. 10, 2010, pp. 115–42.

43. NFC MS 839, Omey Island, 18 September 1942, p. 184.

44. *Donegal News*, 18 July 2008.

45. Bob Quinn and Liam Mac Con Iomaire, *Conamara: Tír Aineoil: The Unknown Country* (Galway, 1997), p. 15.

46. NFC MS 1365, Michael J. Murphy, collector in Antrim, August 1954, pp. 50–6, informant: Rose McGurdy.

47. NFC MS 839, Inishturk, June–September 1942, p. 55 and pp. 95–100.

48. NFC MS 838, p. 476.

49. Ibid., p. 89.

50. Ibid.

51. Ibid., p. 82.

52. NFC MS 838, pp. 55–82.

53. NFC MS 839, Omey Island, p. 291.

54. NFC MS 838, p. 102.

55. NFC MS 839, Omey Island, 18 September 1942.

56. Daly, 'Heir Island'.

57. NFC MS 839, Clare Island, pp. 172–3.

58. NFC MS 1365, Rathlin Island, p. 195.

59. NFC MS 990, Ballyshannon District, April 1946, pp. 626–7.

60. Power, *Apple on the Treetop*, p. 127.

61. Peadar O'Donnell, *Proud Island* (Dublin, 1975), p. 42.

62. Nóra Ní Shúillobháin, 'Valentia Fireside – Yesterday', *Capuchin Annual*, vol. 43, 1976, pp. 184–98.

63. Murphy, *The Kick*, pp. 141ff.

64. Daly, 'Heir Island'.

65. *Irish Press*, 11 March 1949.

66. NFC MS 593, Rathlin Island, p. 96 and p. 227, Stories of Jack MacCurdy, September 1937.

67. NFC Schools Collection, vol. 0138, p. 326, Taobh na Cruaiche school, County Mayo, informant Micheál McGreal.

68. Ibid., vol. 1119, p. 635, St Columb's, Moville, Co. Donegal.

69. McGowan, *Inishmurray*, pp. 29–30.

70. O'Brien, *The Poor Mouth*, p. 68.

71. Ibid., pp. 16–54.

72. Ibid., pp. 13–16.

73. Anne Clissmann, *Flann O'Brien: A Critical Introduction to His Writings* (Dublin, 1975), pp. 234–5.

74. Ibid., p. 236.

75. NUIGA P71, Papers of John McGahern, pp. 820–23.

76. Ibid.

77. Stanley van der Ziel, *John McGahern and the Imagination of Tradition* (Cork, 2016), pp. 82–92, p. 123 and pp. 178–211; John McGahern, 'What is My Language?', in Stanley van der Ziel (ed.), *Love of the World: Essays by John McGahern* (London, 2009), pp. 26–274.

78. Ibid.

79. Ó Crohan, *The Islandman*, p. 1.

80. Ibid., p. 147.

81. Sayers, *Peig*, pp. 183–93.

82. Mícheál de Mórdha, 'Bryan MacMahon, Peig Sayers and the Publication of *Peig* in English', in Gabriel Fitzmaurice (ed.), *The Worlds of Bryan MacMahon* (Cork, 2005), pp. 107–28.

83. *Ireland of the Welcomes*, vol. 23, no. 4, July–August 1974, pp. 19–26; vol. 30, no. 2, March–April 1981, pp. 18–21.

84. Fintan O'Toole, 'An Island Lightly Moored', *Irish Times*, 29 March 1997.

85. Ó Conluain (ed.), *Islands and Authors*, p. 47.

86. Ibid., pp. 95–6.

87. Ibid., p. 162.

88. Margaret Mac Curtain, 'Fullness of Life: Defining Female Spirituality in Twentieth Century Ireland', in Margaret Mac Curtain, *Ariadne's Thread* (Galway, 2008), pp. 175–211.

89. De Mórdha, 'Bryan MacMahon'.

90. O'Toole, 'An Island Lightly Moored'.

91. Fitzmaurice (ed.), *The Worlds of Bryan Mac Mahon*, p. 115.

92. Carney, *From the Great Blasket to America*, p. 75.

93. *Irish Times*, 14 April 1998 and Peig Sayers, *Labharfad Le Cách* (*I Will Speak to You All*), trans. Bo Almqvist and Pádraig Ó Héalaí (Dublin, 2009).

94. *Irish Times*, 14 April 1998.

95. *Irish Times*, 6 December 2008.

96. Gearóid Cheaist Ó Catháin, *The Loneliest Boy in the World: The Last Child of the Great Blasket Island* (Cork, 2014), p. xiii.

97. Carney, *From the Great Blasket to America*, p. 52.

98. O'Donnell, *Islanders*, p. 95.

99. Ibid., p. 110.

100. Joan Murray, 'One Woman's Life', *Muintir Acla*, no. 6, Spring 1997, pp. 29–31.

101. Ó Catháin, *Loneliest Boy in the World*, p. 79.

102. Ó Conluain (ed.), *Islands and Authors*, p. 47.

103. B. N. Hedderman, *Glimpses of My Life in Aran* (London, 1917), p. 72.

104. NFC MS 1669, Revd J. Coombes, Response to questionnaire, 27 April 1959.

105. NUIGA P93/1, Terence Ingold, Essay on Achill Island, September 1997.

106. Ibid.

107. O'Toole, *Aran to Africa*, pp. 16–17.

108. Henry, *An Irish Portrait*, pp. 60–108.

109. McNeillie, *An Aran Keening*, p. 134.

110. Power, *The Land of Youth*, pp. 19–20.

111. O'Sullivan, *Twenty Years a Growing*, pp. 18–32.

112. Ó Catháin, *Loneliest Boy in the World*, pp. 4–6 and p. 41.

113. CCA 34B/58, Cait Gibson, 'Life on the Island in the 1930s', September 1984.

114. Ibid., Frances Daly, 'Account of Growing Up on the Island in the 1930s', March 1984.

115. O'Toole, *Aran to Africa*, pp. 6–13.

116. As recalled by her grandson Manchán Magan in the *Irish Times*, 27 February 2012.

117. NFC MS 838, p. 458.

118. O'Toole, *Aran to Africa*, pp. 7–8.

119. Carney, *From the Great Blasket to America*, pp. 3–20 and pp. 40–52.

120. O'Donnell, *Islanders*, p. 25.

121. CCA 22/4, Appendix to 21st report of the Commissioners of National Education, 1854, pp. 133–4.

122. CCA 21G/1, District Inspector M. Franklin report, 4 August 1920.

123. Ibid., Report of Inspector A. E. Carter, 6 June 1921.

124. Ibid., Inspector's report of 17 June 1925.

125. PRONI ED/14A/250, Rathlin Island National School, General Reports, 9 August 1923 and 17 June 1926.

126. McLaverty, *Call My Brother Back*, pp. 17–18.

127. NFC MS 838, Notebook of Brian McLoughlin, April–June 1942, Inishbofin, pp. 397–492.

128. NAI DT S16925A, Islands Off the Coast of Ireland, Department of Education memorandum, 19 January 1960.

129. NAI DT 97/9/1283, Coney Island: National School, P. J. Normoyle to de Valera, 1 May 1953.

130. McCurdy, *Rathlin's Rugged Story*, pp. 72–7.

131. TCD MS 4424/74, Synge Papers, Martin McDonagh to Synge, 23 July 1898.

132. Ibid., 10 and 20 October 1898.

133. Ibid., 20 February 1899.

134. Declan Kiberd, *Synge and the Irish Language* (London, 1993), p. 245.

135. TCD MS 4424/149, Synge to 'K', June 1904.

136. *Irish Times*, 16 February 1989.

137. NLI, *Coimisiún na Gaeltachta: Report and Evidence*, Evidence of Fr Duggan, CC Arranmore, 18 August 1925, pp. 4–8.

138. Ibid.

139. Ibid., Evidence of Fr S. J. Walsh, 20 August 1925, pp. 1–2.

140. NFC MS 838, Inishark and Inishbofin, April–June 1942.

141. Ibid., pp. 397–492.

142. NFC MS 839, Inishturk, June–September 1942, pp. 51ff.

143. NFC MS 839, Clare Island, August 1942, pp. 139–45.

144. NFC MS 1375, Inishark, 1942, and notes on the dialect there, p. 366.

145. NFC MS 1365, Michael J. Murphy, Rathlin Island, August 1954, p. 62.

146. Hindley, 'Clear Island in 1958'.

147. Conchúr Ó Siocháin, *The Man from Cape Clear*, trans. Riobárd P. Breatnach (Dublin, 1975), p. 10.
148. Hindley 'Clear Island'.
149. Ó Siocháin, *The Man from Cape Clear*, p. 129.
150. CCA 35/41, Donnchadh Ó Drisceoil, 1912–84; *Cork Examiner*, 2 September 1966; *Irish Times*, 1 November 1982.
151. NFC CDBLR, vol. 1, 'Tory Island'.
152. Browne, 'Ethnography of the Mullet'.
153. NFC MS 1365, Rathlin Island, p. 11.
154. Hedderman, *Glimpses of My Life in Aran*, p. vi.
155. Ibid., pp. 58–72.
156. Ibid., pp. 80–82.
157. Ibid., pp. 94–7.
158. Ibid., p. 106.
159. Ibid., p. 94.
160. NFC MS 839, Omey Island, 18 September 1942, p. 324.
161. McGowan, *Inishmurray*, p. 85.
162. Carney, *From the Great Blasket to America*, pp. 121–3.
163. De Mórdha, *An Island Community*, p. 398.
164. Ibid., pp. 395–6.
165. *Irish Independent*, 24 July 1974.
166. NFC MS 838, pp. 463–5.
167. NFC MS 839, Inishturk, pp. 89–102.
168. Ibid., Clare Island, pp. 127–30.
169. Ibid., Omey Island, p. 332.
170. NFC MS 917, Tory Island, p. 170.
171. Ó Crohan *The Islandman*, pp. 208–13.
172. Tomás Ó Crohan, *Island Cross-Talk: Pages from a Blasket Island Diary*, trans. Tim Enright (Oxford, 2000; first published Dublin, 1928), p. 101.
173. Ó Crohan *The Islandman*, p. 101.
174. Lankford, *Cape Clear Island*, p. 113.
175. NFC Schools Collection, vol. 0155, p. 0493, Inishmurray Island by James Ó Connor Sligo, 16 May 1938.
176. Darrell Figgis, *Children of Earth* (London, 1918), p. 2.
177. TCD MS 4385, Synge Papers, Notebook, May 1898, p. 10.
178. Synge, *Riders to the Sea*, pp. 1–13.
179. Power, *Apple on the Treetop*, pp. 127–41.
180. Walter Macken, *Rain on the Wind* (London, 1950), p. 176; Ultan Macken, *Walter Macken: Dreams on Paper* (Cork, 2009), p. 244.

181. Heinrich Becker, *Seaweed Memories: In the Jaws of the Sea* (Dublin, 2000), p. 12, Seamus Heaney, 'Lovers on Aran', in Seamus Heaney, *Death of a Naturalist* (London, 1991; first published 1966), pp. 34–5.

182. Tall, *Island of the White Cow*, p. 37.

183. Gregory, *Visions and Beliefs*, p. 10.

184. NUIGA G22/200/2–6, Becker Collection, Mermaids.

185. Eilís Dillon, *The Lost Island* (London, 1976; first published London, 1952), p. 158.

186. *Irish Times*, 7 March 1942. A memorial to the lifeboat team was unveiled on Arranmore in August 2017.

187. O'Donnell, *Islanders*, pp. 50–74.

188. Ó Crohan, *Island Cross-Talk*, pp. 190–91.

189. NFC MS 1767, Tom Lacey, Inishark, 17 July 1969, p. 38.

190. Ibid., pp. 406ff.

191. CCA 15/15, 'Island Seamen'.

192. Ó Dálaigh 'Memories of Fishing in Cape Clear'.

193. Donal Ó Flanagan, 'Curraghs of Aran', *Ireland of the Welcomes*, vol. 5, no. 5, January–February 1957, pp. 27–36.

194. Dillon, *The Lost Island*, pp. 138–9.

195. Ó Catháin, *Loneliest Boy in the World*, p. 65.

196. NFC MS 839, Inishturk, p. 67.

197. Becker, *Seaweed Memories*, p. 53, Beaumont, *Achillbeg*, p. 177.

198. IFC MS 839, Omey Island, 18 September 1942.

199. Ó Dálaigh, 'Memories of Fishing in Cape Clear'; McGowan, *Inishmurray*, p. 95.

200. TDA P31/9/7, Box 41, Irish Red Cross to Archbishop Walsh, 15 July 1942.

201. *Irish Times*, 4 June 1942.

202. Keane, 'The Inishkeas'.

203. O'Donnell *Proud Island*, pp 18–24.

204. IFC MS 839, Omey Island, pp. 303–13.

205. Micheál O'Guiheen, *A Pity Youth Does Not Last*, trans. Tim Enright (Oxford, 2000; first published Dublin, 1953), p. 38.

206. Bridie Molloy 'The Strand', *Muintir Acla*, no. 11, Winter 1998, pp. 213–26.

207. Becker, *Seaweed Memories*, p. 98.

208. Maria Simonds-Gooding, *Fields of Vision* (Dublin, 2004), pp. 2–5; Cathal Ó Searcaigh, 'Anseo ag Stáisiún Caiseal na gCorr' ('Here at the Caiseal na gCorr Station'), trans. Gabriel Fitzmaurice, in John McDonagh (ed.), *A Fine Statement: An Irish Poet's Anthology* (Dublin, 2008), pp. 272–6.

209. Fergus Bourke, 'The Aran Islands', *Ireland of the Welcomes*, vol. 13, no. 2, July–August 1964, pp. 18–20.

210. Ní Shúillobháin, 'Valentia Fireside'; Mould, *Valentia*, p. 90.
211. Kelly, *Letters of Liam O'Flaherty*, p. 84, O'Flaherty to Edward Garnett, 27 April 1924.
212. Ibid., p. 249, O'Flaherty to A. D. Peters, July 1931, and p. 263, to Francis Stuart, 6 October 1932.
213. NFC MS 839, Inishturk, pp. 52–67.
214. Fox, *The Tory Islanders*, pp. 156–7 and p. 16.
215. Francis MacManus 'Viking Faced Cape Clear Island', *The Bell*, vol. 16, no. 2, November 1950, pp. 24–30.
216. Viney, 'The Yank in the Corner'.
217. Carney, *From the Great Blasket to America*, pp. 31–6.
218. Ó Conluain (ed.), *Islands and Authors*, pp. 95–8.
219. NFC MS 1365, Rathlin Island, pp. 94–101.
220. Tall, *Island of the White Cow*, pp. 9–14.
221. NFC MS 1365, Rathlin Island, p. 203.
222. O'Donnell, *Proud Island*, p. 65 and p. 95.
223. Ó Conluain (ed.), *Islands and Authors*, p. 102.
224. Ibid., p. 14.
225. MacManus, 'Viking Faced Cape Clear Island'.
226. Aalen and Brody, *Gola*, p. 84.
227. Becker, *Seaweed Memories*, pp. 12–19.
228. Clarke, *A Penny in the Clouds*, pp. 143–5.
229. Brian Friel, *The Gentle Island* (London, 1974), and Seamus Kelly's review, *Irish Times*, 1 December 1971.
230. *Irish Times*, 17 December 1988.
231. CCA 46/6, Case Studies of Cape Clear Island undertaken by Bolton Street Students, 1975–1995 ('Case Study of Aspects of Island Life', 'A Week in Cape Clear', 'Cape Clear Co-Op 1970: A Study of Its Formation, Aims and Early Development').
232. Ibid., Note of Eamon Lankford, 2013.

Postscript

1. *Irish Press*, 22 May 1974.
2. *Irish Independent*, 9 January 1985.
3. *Sunday Independent*, 30 May 1971.
4. Colm Tóibín (ed.), *Synge: A Celebration* (Dublin, 2005), pp. 33–44.
5. Power, *Apple on the Treetop*, p. 110.

6. *Southern Star*, 9 December 1989.

7. Anthony Toole, 'The Islandman's Dream', *Ireland of the Welcomes*, vol. 50, no. 3 May–June 2001, pp. 33–42; *Irish Times*, 6 June 2016.

8. *Irish Times*, 13 April 2013.

9. Jo Kerrigan, 'The Blaskets', *Ireland of the Welcomes*, vol. 50, no. 4, July–August 2001, pp. 24–32.

10. Christopher Moriarty, 'The Island of Achill', *Ireland of the Welcomes*, vol. 50, no. 5, September–October 2001, pp. 52–6 and *Muintir Acla*, no. 11, Winter 1998, p. 21.

11. *Donegal News*, 18 June 2010 and 30 May 2008.

12. *Sunday Business Post*, Magazine, 8 May 2016.

13. *Irish Times*, 3 May 2005.

14. Royle and Scott, 'Accessibility and the Irish Islands'.

15. *Cork Examiner*, 18 December 1992.

16. *Southern Star*, 30 January 2010, and Penelope Durell, *Discover Dursey* (Cork, 1996), pp. 156–60.

17. *Irish Times*, 8 September 2015.

18. *Irish Press*, 13 May 1994; *Cork Examiner*, 27 August 1999; *Donegal News*, 10 August 2001.

19. DED, vol. 462, no. 7, 7 March 1996.

20. Tall, *Island of the White Cow*, pp. 133–5.

21. *Boutique* (Aer Lingus inflight magazine), June–July 2017, pp. 38–9.

22. *Irish Times Magazine*, 10 December 2016.

23. www.inishmeain.com, accessed 11 October 2017.

24. *Irish Times Magazine*, 17 December 2016.

25. A reference to Rathlin Island, *Irish Times*, 22 May 2008.

26. *Irish Times Magazine*, 17 December 2016.

27. www.inismeain.com, accessed 8 August 2017.

28. *Mayo News*, 30 August 2016.

29. *Sunday Business Post*, 12 April 2015.

30. *Muintir Acla*, no. 6, Spring 1997.

31. *Western People*, 3 May 2005.

32. *Sunday Times*, 12 April 2015.

33. *Irish Farmer's Journal*, 22 August 1998.

34. Lankford, *Cape Clear Island*, pp. 115–21.

35. *Nenagh Guardian*, 11 November 2000.

36. *Irish Times*, 2 June 2014.

37. *Irish Times*, 3 June 2016.

38. *Sunday Times*, 5 July 2015.

39. *Sunday Times*, 19 April 2015, referring to Inish Beg Island off west Cork.

40. *Sunday Times*, 22 January 2017.
41. *Irish Times*, 2 October 2017.
42. *Irish Times Magazine*, 17 December 2016 and www.irishcentral.com accessed 9 January 2017.
43. Dan Casey, 'Tory Island: A Review and Apologia', *Donegal Annual*, no. 63, 2011, pp. 59–63; Peter Somerville Large, *Ireland's Islands: Landscape, Life and Legends* (Dublin, 2000), p. 9.
44. Hubert Butler, 'Influenza in Aran', in Hubert Butler, *The Sub-Prefect Should Have Held His Tongue and Other Essays* (Dublin, 1990), pp. 146–59.
45. Kanigel, *On an Irish Island*, p. 36.
46. Rachel Donnelly, 'This Island Life: Inishbofin and Inishturk', www.totallydublin.ie/arts-culture, 20 January 2015, accessed 8 August 2017.
47. Central Statistics Office, www.cso.ie CNA35, 'Population of Offshore Islands Since 1841'.

BIBLIOGRAPHY

Archives

Cape Clear Museum and Archive, Cape Clear Island, County Cork
Files 5A–21F on all aspects of the history of Cape Clear Island

Capuchin Archives, Dublin
Records of Temperance Missions given by the Capuchin Fathers of Dublin,
    1904–1947

Irish Military Archives, Dublin
Bureau of Military History Witness Statements

National Archives of Ireland, Dublin
Chief Secretary's Office Registered Papers
Dáil Éireann
Department of Health
Department of Local Government
Department of Local Government and Public Health
Department of the Taoiseach

National Folklore Collection, University College Dublin
Local Reports Congested District Board, Vols. 1–3
Schools Folklore Collection, 1937–8

MS 838, Inishark Island, Inishbofin Island
MS 839, Inishturk Island, Clare Island, Omey Island
MS 917, Tory Island
MS 1365, Rathlin Island
MS 1669, Completed Questionnaires on rural life
MS 1721, Gola Island
MS 1738, Aran Islands
MS 1768, Tom Lacey, Inishark

National Library of Ireland, Dublin
Missionary Progress of the Island and Coast Society, Annual Reports
Proceedings of the Dublin Mansion House Relief Committee

National University of Ireland Galway Archive, James Hardiman Library
Bairéad Collection
Becker Collection
Druid Theatre Company Collection
Terence Ingold Collection
Tim Robinson Collection
Etienne Rynne Collection
Shields Family Collection

Public Record Office of Northern Ireland, Belfast
Cabinet Secretariat
Coroner's Inquests, Antrim
Department of Agriculture
Department of Commerce
Department of Economic Development
Department of Education
Department of Finance
Department of Health and Local Government
Department of Home Affairs
General Post Office
Home Office
Nora Workman Diary

Raphoe Diocesan Archive, Letterkenny, Donegal
Tory Island Collection, 1889–1979

Trinity College Dublin Manuscripts
Papers of John Millington Synge

Tuam Diocesan Archive, Tuam, Galway
Administration of Islands, Boxes 10–41, 1910–1967
Memoranda by Catholic priests of the diocese who served on the Islands, 1960–1987

University College Dublin Archives
Papers of Eamon de Valera
Papers of Patrick McGilligan
Papers of Eoin MacNeill
Papers of Michael Tierney

Official Reports and Publications

Coimisiún na Galetachta: Report and Evidence (Dublin, 1926)
Dáil Éireann Debates (Irish Parliamentary Debates)
European Communities Economic and Social Committee, *Disadvantaged Island Regions* (Brussels, July 1988)
Hansard: House of Commons Debates
Ireland: National Development Plan, 2007–2013 (Dublin, 2007)
Royal Commission on Congestion in Ireland: Final Report (London, 1908)
Saorstát Éireann: Irish Free State Official Handbook, ed. Bulmer Hobson (Dublin, 1932)

Newspapers

Belfast Telegraph	*Irish Echo*	*Mayo News*
Connacht Sentinel	*Irish Examiner*	*Nenagh Guardian*
Connacht Telegraph	*Irish Farmer's Journal*	*Pall Mall Gazette*
Connacht Tribune	*Irish Independent*	*Skibbereen Eagle*
Cork Examiner	*Irish Press*	*Sligo Champion*
Daily Express	*Irish Times*	*Southern Star*
Donegal News	*The Kerryman*	*Strabane Chronicle*
Freeman's Journal	*Limerick Leader*	*Sunday Independent*
The Guardian	*Manchester Guardian*	*Sunday Times*

The Tablet
Times Pictorial

Tuam Herald
Western People

Journals and Periodicals

Archaeology Ireland
The Bell
Cathair na Mart
Crane Bag
Donegal Annual
Dublin Review
Father Matthew Record
History Ireland
Ireland Today
Ireland of the Welcomes
Irish Ecclesiastical Record
Irish Economic and Social History
Irish Geography
Irish Historical Studies

Irish Journal of Anthropology
Irish Monthly
Irish Review
Journal of the Cork Historical and
    Archaeological Society
Journal of the Galway Archaeology and
    Historical Society
Journal of the Kerry Archaeological and
    Historical Society
Mizen Journal
Muintir Acla
New Hibernia Review
New Ireland Review
Proceedings of the Royal Irish Academy

Theses

Brian Harvey, 'The Emergence of the Western Problem in the Latter Part of the Nineteenth Century', unpublished MA thesis, University College Dublin, 1986.

Jude McCarthy, 'State-Aided Island Migration, 1930–60', unpublished MA thesis, UCD, 1997.

Reference Works

James McGuire and James Quinn (eds.), A Dictionary of Irish Biography: From the Earliest Times to the Year 2009, nine vols. (Cambridge, 2009).

Websites

www.census.nationalarchives.ie
www.cso.ie
www.drb.ie
dib.Cambridge.org
www.inismeain.com
www.irishislands.info

www.landedestates.ie
www.oileain.org
www.scotlandcensus.gov.uk
www.skelligexperience.com/
    thelighthouses

Books and Articles

DIB in the following list indicates, James McGuire and James Quinn (eds.), *Dictionary of Irish Biography: From the Earliest Times to the Year 2002*, 9 vols. (Cambridge, 2009)

Aalen, F. H. and H. Brody, *Gola: The Life and Last Days of an Island Community* (Cork, 1969)

Aalen, F. H. A., Kevin Whelan and Matthew Stout (eds.), *Atlas of the Irish Rural Landscape* (Cork, 1997)

Arnold, Bruce, *Haughey: His Life and Unlucky Deeds* (London, 1993)

Arnold, Bruce, *Derek Hill* (London, 2010)

Baldacchino, Godfrey and Stephen A. Royle, 'Postcolonialism and Islands: Introduction', *Space and Culture*, vol. 13, no. 2, pp. 140–43, 2010

Ball, Stephen (ed.), *A Policeman's Ireland: Recollections of Samuel Waters, RIC* (Cork, 1999)

Barry, Kevin, *Beatlebone* (Edinburgh, 2015)

Barry, Kevin, 'Roethke in the Bughouse', *Irish Times*, 29 December 2015

Barry, Sebastian, *Prayers of Sherkin, Boss Grady's Boys: Two Plays* (London, 1991)

Barsam, Richard, *The Vision of Robert Flaherty: The Artist as Myth and Film Maker* (Indianapolis, 1988)

Beaumont, Jonathan, *Achillbeg: The Life of an Island* (Usk, 2005)

Becker, Heinrich, *Seaweed Memories: In the Jaws of the Sea* (Dublin, 2000)

Behan, Brendan, 'In the Kingdom of Kerry', *Ireland of the Welcomes*, vol. 1, no. 2, July–August 1952, p. 15

Behan, Brendan, *Brendan Behan's Island* (London, 1962)

Bolger, Patrick, *The Irish Co-Operative Movement: Its History and Development* (Dublin, 1977)

Böll, Heinrich, *Irish Journal*, trans. Leila Vennewitz (New York and London, 1967; first published 1957)

Bourke, Fergus, 'The Aran Islands', *Ireland of the Welcomes*, vol. 13, no. 2, July–August 1964, pp. 18–20

Bourke, Marie, 'Yeats, Henry and the Western Idyll', *History Ireland*, vol. 11, no. 2, Summer 2003, pp. 28–34

Bowe, Nicola Gordon, *The Life and Work of Harry Clarke* (Dublin, 1989)

Boylan, Shaun, 'James McDyer', *DIB*, vol. 5, pp. 986–7

Branach, Niall, R., 'Edward Nangle and the Achill Island Mission', *History Ireland*, vol. 8, no. 3, Autumn 2000, pp. 35–9

Breathnach, Ciara, *Poverty and Development in the West of Ireland* (Dublin, 2005)

Breathnach, Proinnsias et al., 'Aspects of Rural Development in the Scottish Highlands and Islands: Report of a Study Visit' Geography Department, Maynooth University, February 1984

Browne, Charles, R., 'Ethnography of the Mullet, Inishkea Islands and Portacloy', *Proceedings of the Royal Irish Academy*, 3rd series, vol. 3, 1893–6, pp. 587–648

Browne, Charles R., 'The Ethnography of Inishbofin and Inishark Co Galway', *Proceedings of the Royal Irish Academy*, 3rd series, vol. 17, 1894, pp. 317–70

Browne, Charles R., 'The Ethnography of Clare Island and Inishturk, Co. Mayo', *Proceedings of the Royal Irish Academy*, vol. 5, June 1897

Butler, Hubert, 'Influenza in Aran', in Hubert Butler, *The Sub-Prefect Should Have Held His Tongue and Other Essays* (Dublin, 1990)

Briody, Mícheál, *The Irish Folklore Commission, 1935–1979* (Helsinki, 2008)

Brooks Walker, Barbara, 'Achill Holiday', *Ireland of the Welcomes*, vol. 11, no. 1, May–June 1962

Callow, Simon, *Orson Welles: The Road to Xanadu* (London, 1995)

Candy, Catherine, *Priestly Fictions: Popular Irish Novelists of the Early Twentieth Century* (Dublin, 1995)

Canning, Bernard, J., *Bishops of Ireland, 1870–1987* (Donegal, 1987)

Carney, Michael J., with Gerald Hayes, *From the Great Blasket to America: The Last Memoir by an Islander* (Cork, 2013)

Casey, Dan, 'Tory Island: A Review and Apologia', *Donegal Annual*, no. 63, 2011, pp. 59–63

Clarke, Austin, *A Penny in the Clouds: More Memories of Ireland and England* (London, 1968)

Clarke, Frances and Patrick Maume, 'Emily Lawless', *DIB*, vol. 5, pp. 351–3

Clarke, Kieran, 'The Clew Bay Boating Disaster', *Cathair Na Mart*, vol. 6, no. 1, 1986, pp. 5–24

Clissmann, Anne, *Flann O'Brien: A Critical Introduction to His Writings* (Dublin, 1975)

Collins, Michael, *The Path to Freedom* (Dublin, 1922)

Collins, Timothy, 'Praeger in the West: Naturalists and Antiquarians in Connemara and the Islands, 1894–1914', *Journal of the Galway Archaeology and Historical Society*, vol. 45, 1993, pp. 124–55

Commissioners of Irish lights, *For the Safety of All: Image and Inspections of Irish Lighthouses* (Dublin, 2003)

Concannon, Kieran (ed.), *Inishbofin Through Time and Tide* (Galway, 1993)

Coombe, James, 'The *Margaret Hughes* and the Maritime Tradition of Sherkin Island', *Mizen Journal*, no. 12, 2004, pp. 60–62

Costello, Peter, *Liam O'Flaherty's Ireland* (Dublin, 1996)

Coulter, Henry, *The West of Ireland: Its Existing Condition, and Prospects.* (Dublin and London, 1862)

Cronin, Anthony, *No Laughing Matter: The Life and Times of Flann O'Brien* (London, 1989)

Cronin, Maurice, 'Joseph Guinan', *DIB*, vol. 4, pp. 310–11

Curtis, L. P., 'Ireland in 1914', in W. E. Vaughan (ed.), *A New History of Ireland*, vol. 6: *Ireland Under the Union II, 1870–1921* (Oxford, 1996), pp. 145–88

Daly, Eugene, 'Heir Island', *Mizen Journal*, no. 8, 2000, pp. 34–56

Daly, Eugene, *Heir Island: Its History and People* (Cork, 2004)

Davies, R. T., *Samuel Johnson: Selected Writings* (London, 1965)

Davitt, Michael, 'The Distress in Achill', reprinted in *Muintir Acla*, no. 6, Spring 1997, pp. 20–23

de Mórdha, Mícheál, 'Bryan Macmahon, Peig Sayers and the Publication of *Peig* in English', in Gabriel Fitzmaurice (ed.), *The Worlds of Bryan Macmahon* (Cork, 2005), pp. 107–28

de Mórdha, Mícheál, *An Island Community: The Ebb and Flow of the Great Blasket Island*, trans. Gabriel Fitzmaurice (Dublin, 2015)

Dillon, Eilís, *The Lost Island* (London, 1976; first published 1952)

Dornan, Brian, *The Inishkeas: Mayo's Lost Islands* (Dublin, 2000)

Dowling, Michelle, '"The Ireland that I would have": De Valera and the Creation of an Irish National Image', *History Ireland*, vol. 5, no. 2, Summer 1997, pp. 37–42

Dudley Edwards, Ruth, *The Seven: The Lives and Legacies of the Founding Fathers of the Irish Republic* (London, 2016)

Durell, Penelope, *Discover Dursey* (Cork, 1996)

Ellmann, Richard, *James Joyce* (Oxford, 1982; first published 1959)

Evans, Emyr Estan, *The Personality of Ireland: Habitat, Heritage and History* (Dublin, 1992; first published 1973)

Evans, Emyr Estan, *Ireland and the Atlantic Heritage: Selected Writings* (Dublin, 1996)

Feehan, John (ed.), *The Book of Aran* (Galway, 1994)

Feeney, Marie, *The Cleggan Bay Disaster* (Donegal, 2001)

Ferriter, Diarmaid, *Mothers, Maidens and Myths: A History of the Irish Countrywomen's Association* (Dublin, 1995)

Ferriter, Diarmaid, and Lawrence White, 'Francis Patrick Fahy', *DIB*, vol. 3, pp. 691–2

Ferriter, Diarmaid, 'Patrick Gallagher', *DIB*, vol. 4, pp. 11–12

Ferriter, Diarmaid, *Ambiguous Republic: Ireland in the 1970s* (London, 2012)

Figgis, Darrell, *Children of Earth* (London, 1918)

Forsythe, W., 'The Archaeology of the Kelp Industry in the Northern Islands of Ireland', *International Journal of Nautical Archaeology*, vol. 35, no. 2, October 2006, pp. 218–29

Foster, John Wilson, *Colonial Consequences: Essays in Irish Literature and Culture* (Dublin, 1991)

Foster, R. F., *W. B. Yeats: A Life*, vol. 1: *Apprentice Mage, 1865–1914* (London, 1997)

Fox, Robin, *The Tory Islanders: A People of the Celtic Fringe* (Cambridge, 1978)

Friel, Brian, *The Gentle Island* (London, 1974)

Gaughan, Anthony, *Memoirs of Constable Jeremiah Mee, RIC* (Dublin, 1975)

Gibbings, Robert, 'The Connemara Islands', *The Bell*, vol. 8, no. 5, August 1944, pp. 427–40

Gibney, John, 'Review of *An tÉireannach Fáin*', *History Ireland*, vol. 19, no. 2, March–April 2011, pp. 50–51

Gladwin, Derek and Christine Cusick (eds.), *Unfolding Irish Landscapes: Tim Robinson, Culture and Environment* (Manchester, 2016)

Gosling, Paul, 'The Archaeology of Clare Island, Co. Mayo', *Archaeology Ireland*, vol. 4, no. 1, Spring 1990, pp. 7–12

Green, A. S., H. Barbour, Douglas Hyde and Alec Wilson, 'The Connemara Islands', *Irish Review*, 4, March–November 1914, May 1914, pp. 113–27

Gregory, Lady, *Visions and Beliefs in the West of Ireland* (London, 1920)

Grene, Nicholas (ed.), *J. M. Synge and Irish Theatre* (Dublin, 2000)

Guinan, Joseph, *Island Parish* (Dublin, 1908)

Gwynn, Stephen, *A Holiday in Connemara* (London, 1909)

Haddon, A. C. and C. R. Browne, 'On the Ethnography of the Aran Islands, Co. Galway', *Proceedings of the Royal Irish Academy*, 3rd series, vol. 2, 1891–3, pp. 768–830

Harbison, Peter, 'John Windele's Visit to Skellig Michael in 1851', *Journal of the Kerry Archaeological and Historical Society*, vol. 9, 1976, pp. 125–6.

Harrison Therman, Dorothy, *Stories from Tory Island* (Dublin, 1999, first published 1989)

Hawke, Siobhán, *A Social and Economic History of Bere Island, 1900–1920* (Cork, 2004)

Healy, John, 'A Pilgrimage to Inishmurray', *Irish Monthly*, vol. 5, July 1877, pp. 433–9

Heaney, Seamus, *Death of a Naturalist* (London, 1991; first published 1966)

Healy, John, 'The Largest Island' (1965), in John Horgan (ed.), *Great Irish Reportage* (Dublin, 2013), pp. 104–12

Hedderman, B. N., *Glimpses of My Life in Aran* (London, 1917)

Henry, Paul, *An Irish Portrait: The Autobiography of Paul Henry* (London, 1951)

Hindley, Reg, *The Death of the Irish Language: A Qualified Obituary* (London, 1990)

Hindley, Reg, 'Clear Island in 1958: A Study in Geolinguistic Transition', *Irish Geography*, 27, 2, 1994, pp. 97–106

Hourican, Bridget, 'Robert Flaherty', *DIB*, vol. 3, pp. 994–6

Hughes, Brian (ed.), *Eoin MacNeill: Memoir of a Revolutionary Scholar* (Dublin, 2016)

Hunter, Jim, *The Waves of Tory: The Story of an Atlantic Community* (Coleraine, 2006)

Island and Coast Society, *Missionary Progress of the Island and Coast Society*, Annual Reports (Dublin, 1863–81)

Joyce, P. J., *John Healy, Archbishop of Tuam* (Dublin, 1931)

Kanigel, Robert, *On an Irish Island* (New York, 2012)

Kelly, A. A. (ed.), *The Letters of Liam O'Flaherty* (Dublin, 1996)

Kerrigan, Jo, 'The Blaskets', *Ireland of the Welcomes*, vol. 50, no. 4, July–August 2001, pp. 24–32

Kiberd, Declan, 'Inventing Irelands', *Crane Bag*, vol. 8, 1984, pp. 11–26

Kiberd, Declan, *Synge and the Irish Language* (London, 1993)

Keane, Maureen, 'The Inishkeas: A Look at Life There Before the Islands Were Abandoned in 1937', *Cathair Na Mart*, vol. 11, 1991, pp. 66–74

Kelley, Tom and Linde Lunney, 'Edward Walter Nangle', *DIB*, vol. 6., pp. 854–6

Kennedy, Sheila, 'Our Western Seaboard', *Ireland Today*, vol. 11, no. 12, December 1937, pp. 13–20

Kleinman-Batt, Sylvie and Elaine Garvey, 'An Absent Minded Person of the Student Type: Extracts from the Artaud File', *Dublin Review*, no. 1, Winter 2000–1, pp. 58–81

Kotsonouris, Mary, *Retreat from Revolution: The Dáil Courts, 1920–1924* (Dublin, 1994)

Lankford, Eamon, *Cape Clear Island: Its People and Landscape* (Cork, 1999)

Lawless, Emily, *Grania: The Story of an Island* (London, 1892)

Legg, Marie Louise, *Newspapers and Nationalism: The Irish Provincial Press, 1850–1892* (Dublin, 1999)

Lockley, R. M., *I Know an Island* (London, 1938)

Long, Bill, *Bright Light, White Water: The Story of Irish Lighthouses and Their People* (Dublin, 1993)

Long, Patrick, 'George Halpin', *DIB*, vol. 4, pp. 372–3

Luke, Eric, *Looking Back: The Changing Face of Ireland* (Dublin, 2016)

Mac Cárthaigh, Criostóir and Kevin Whelan (eds.), *New Survey of Clare Island*, vol. 1: *History and Cultural Landscape* (Dublin, 1999)

McCurdy, Augustine, *Rathlin's Rugged Story* (Ballycastle, 2000)

Mac Curtain, Margaret, 'Fullness Of Life: Defining Female Spirituality in Twentieth Century Ireland', in Margaret Mac Curtain, *Ariadne's Thread* (Galway, 2008), pp. 175–211

McDonagh, Martin, *The Cripple of Inishmaan* (London, 1997)

McDyer, James, *Fr McDyer of Glencolumbkille: An Autobiography* (Kerry, 1982)

McGahern, John, 'What is My Language?', in Stanley van der Ziel (ed.), *Love of the World: Essays by John McGahern* (London, 2009), pp. 26–274

McGowan, Joe, *Inishmurray; Gale, Stone and Fire* (Sligo, 1998)

McGowan, Joe, *Island Voices: Inishmurray* (Dublin, 2004)

MacIntyre, James, *Three Men on an Island* (Belfast, 1996)

MacIntyre, Tom, 'Men of the West', *Ireland of the Welcomes*, vol. 22, no. 4, November–December 1973, p. 31

McLaverty, Michael, *Call My Brother Back* (Belfast, 2003; first published London, 1939)

MacLochlainn, Alf, 'Blasket Island Life and Work', *Journal of the Kerry Archaeological and Historical Society*, 2nd series, vol. 10, 2010, pp. 115–42

McMahon, Timothy G., *Grand Opportunity: The Gaelic Revival and Irish Society 1893–1910* (New York, 2008)

McNally, Kenneth, *The Islands of Ireland* (London, 1978)

MacManus, Francis, 'Viking Faced Cape Clear Island', *The Bell*, vol. 16, no. 2, Nov. 1950, pp. 24–30

MacManus, Francis, 'Life at Europe's Edge', *Ireland of the Welcomes*, vol. 2, no. 5, January–February 1954, pp. 5–8

McNeillie, Andrew, *An Aran Keening* (Dublin, 2001)

Macken, Ultan, *Walter Macken: Dreams on Paper* (Cork, 2009)

Macken, Walter, *Rain on the Winds* (London, 1950)

Macken, Walter, 'Achill Island', *Ireland of the Welcomes*, vol. 3, no. 5, January–February 1955

Malcolm, Elizabeth, 'Temperance and Irish Nationalism', in F. S. L. Lyons and
　　R. A. J. Hawkins (eds.), *Ireland Under the Union: Varieties of Tension*
　　(Oxford, 1980), pp. 69–115

Mansion House Relief Committee, *The Irish Crisis of 1879–80: Proceedings of the
　　Dublin Mansion House Relief Committee, 1880* (Dublin, 1881)

Marquardt, Janet T. (ed.), *Françoise Henry in County Mayo: The Inishkea Journals*
　　(Dublin, 2012)

Martin, Kevin, 'How The West Was Wonderful: Some Historical Perspectives
　　on Representations of the West of Ireland in Popular Culture', *Institute of
　　Technology Blanchardstown Journal*, vol. 2, no. 2, 2001, pp. 89–94

Maume, Patrick, 'John Healy', *DIB*, vol. 4, pp. 561–4

Maume, Patrick, 'Charles James (C. J.) Haughey', *DIB*, online entry, revised
　　February 2016.

Maume, Patrick, 'A Pastoral Vision: The Novels of Canon Joseph Guinan', *New
　　Hibernia Review*, vol. 9, no. 4, Winter 2005, pp. 79–98

Meehan, Denis, 'The Island of Molaise', *Ireland of the Welcomes*, vol. 4, no. 1, May–
　　June 1955, pp. 21–3

Messenger, John C., *Inis Beag: Isle of Ireland* (Holt,1969)

Messenger, John C., 'The Irish Comic Tradition of Inis Beag', *Journal of the
　　Folklore Institute*, vol. 15, no. 3, September–December 1978, pp. 235–51

Mills, Ralph, J. (ed.), *Selected Letters of Theodore Roethke* (Seattle, 1968)

Mitchell, Angus, 'An Irish Putumayo: Roger Casement's Humanitarian Relief
　　Campaign Among the Connemara Islanders 1913–14', *Irish Economic and
　　Social History*, vol. 31, 2004, pp. 41–61

Mitchell, Frank, *Man and Environment in Valencia Island* (Dublin, 1989)

Molloy, Bridie, 'The Strand', *Muintir Acla*, no. 11, Winter 1998, pp. 213–26

Moreton, Cole, *Hungry for Home: Leaving the Blaskets: A Journey from the Edge of
　　Ireland* (London, 2000)

Moriarty, Christopher, 'The Island of Achill', *Ireland of the Welcomes*, vol. 50, no. 5,
　　September–October 2001, pp. 52–6

Morrissey, James and Brian Farrell, *Inishbofin* (Dublin, 1987)

Murphy, David, 'James Hack Tuke', *DIB*, vol. 9, pp. 512–13

Murphy, Maureen, 'Jeremiah Curtin', *DIB*, vol. 2, pp. 1114–16

Murphy, Richard, *The Kick: A Memoir* (London, 2002)

Murphy, William, *Political Imprisonment and the Irish, 1912–1921* (Oxford, 2014)

Murray, Joan, 'One Woman's Life', *Muintir Acla*, no. 6, Spring 1997, pp. 29–31

Neary, Revd John, 'History of Inishbofin and Inishark', *Irish Ecclesiastical Record*,
　　5th series, vol. 15, January–June 1920, pp. 216–28

Ní Shúillobháin, Nóra, 'Valentia Fireside – Yesterday', *Capuchin Annual*, vol. 43,
　　1976, pp. 184–98

Nic Craith, M., 'Primary Education on the Great Blasket Island, 1864–1940', *Journal of the Kerry Archaeological and Historical Society*, no, 28, 1995, pp. 77–138

Noble, Gordon (ed.), *Scottish Odysseys: The Archaeology of Islands* (London, 2008)

'Nomad', 'The Aran Islands', *Ireland of the Welcomes*, vol. 11, no. 2, July–August 1962

O'Brien, Flann, *The Poor Mouth*, trans. Patrick C. Power (London, 1993; first published Dublin, 1941)

O'Brien, Justin, *The Modern Prince* (Dublin, 2002)

Ó Catháin, Gearóid Cheaist, *The Loneliest Boy in the World: The Last Child of the Great Blasket Island* (Cork, 2014)

Ó Coigligh, Ciarán, 'Cathair Synge agus Cathaoir Synge: J. M. Synge, Baile Átha Cliath agus Oileáin Arainn', *Journal of the Galway Archaeological and Historical Society*, vol. 64, 2012, pp. 153–69

Ó Conluain, Proinsias, 'Cín lae Craoltóra', trans. Deirdre Ní Chonghaile, in Louis McRedmond (ed.), *Written on the Wind: Personal Memories of Irish Radio 1926–76* (Dublin, 1976), pp. 87–106.

Ó Conluain, Proinsias, *Islands and Authors: Pen-Pictures of Life Past and Present on the Islands of Ireland* (Cork, 1983)

O'Connor, Barbara and Michael Cronin (eds.), *Tourism in Ireland: A Critical Analysis* (Cork, 1993)

O'Connor Eimear, *Seán Keating in Context: Responses to Culture and Politics in Post Civil-War Ireland* (Dublin, 2009)

Ó Crohan, Seán, *A Day in Our Life*, trans. Tim Enright (Oxford, 1992)

Ó Crohan, Tomás, *Island Cross-Talk: Pages from a Blasket Island Diary*, trans. Tim Enright (Oxford, 2000; first published Dublin, 1928)

Ó Crohan, Tomás, *The Islandman*, trans. Robin Flower (Oxford, 2000; first published Dublin 1929)

Ó Croidheáin, Caoimhghin, *Language from Below: The Irish Language, Ideology and Power in Twentieth Century Ireland* (Oxford, 2006)

Ó Dálaigh, Micheál, 'Memories of Fishing in Cape Clear Between the Two World Wars', *Mizen Journal*, no. 9, 2001, pp. 111–28

Ó Danachair, Caoimhín, 'The Magic Islands', *Ireland of the Welcomes*, vol. 5, no. 1, May–June 1956

O'Donnell, Peadar, *Proud Island* (Dublin, 1975)

O'Donnell, Peadar, *Islanders* (Cork, 2005; first published London, 1927)

O'Donnell, Peadar, 'Kirkintilloch', *Ireland Today*, vol. 2, no. 10, October 1937, pp. 45–52

Ó Drisceoil, Donal, *Peadar O'Donnell* (Cork, 2001)

Ó Dubhshláine, Mícheál, *A Dark Day on the Blaskets* (Kerry, 2003)

O'Faoláin, Seán, *An Irish Journey* (London, 1940)

O'Faoláin, Seán, 'The Gaelic Cult', *The Bell*, vol. 9, no. 3, December 1944, pp. 185–96

O'Faoláin, Seán, 'Don Quixote O'Flaherty', *The Bell*, vol. 2, no. 3, June 1941, pp. 28–37

Ó Fathartaigh, Mícheál, 'Cumann na nGaedheal, Sea Fishing and West Galway, 1923–32', *Irish Historical Studies*, vol. 36, no. 141, May 2008, pp. 72–90

O'Flaherty, Liam, *A Tourist's Guide to Ireland* (1930)

O'Flaherty, Liam, *Skerrett* (Dublin, 1977; first published London, 1932)

O'Flaherty, Tom, *Cliffmen of the West* (London, 1935)

O'Flanagan, Donal, 'Curraghs of Aran', *Ireland of the Welcomes*, vol. 5, no. 5, January–February 1957, pp. 27–36

Ó Giolláin, Diarmuid, *Locating Irish Folklore: Tradition, Modernity, Identity* (Cork, 2000)

O'Guiheen, Micheál, *A Pity Youth Does Not Last*, trans. Tim Enright (Oxford, 2000; first published Dublin, 1953)

Ó hEithir, Breandán and Ruairi Ó hEithir, *An Aran Reader* (Dublin, 1991)

O'Laoire, Lillis, 'Field Work in Common Places: An Ethnographer's Experiences in Tory Island', *British Journal of Ethnomusicology*, vol. 12, no. 1, 2003, pp. 113–36

O'Laoire, Lillis, *On a Rock in the Middle of the Ocean: Songs and Singers in Tory Island* (Galway, 2007)

Ó Péicín, Diarmuid, with Liam Nolan, *Islanders: The True Story of One Man's Fight to Save a Way of Life* (London, 1997)

O'Regan, Liam, 'The Castle Island Evictions 1889–90', *Mizen Journal*, no. 6, 1998, pp. 116–29

O'Riagáin, Pádraig, *Language Policy and Social Reproduction: Ireland, 1893–1993* (Oxford, 1997)

O'Riordan, Turlough, 'Thomas Holmes Mason', *DIB*, vol. 6, pp. 410–11

Ó Searcaigh, Cathal, 'Anseo ag Stáisiún Caiseal na gCorr' ('Here at the Caiseal na gCorr Station'), trans. Gabriel Fitzmaurice, in John McDonagh (ed.), *A Fine Statement: An Irish Poet's Anthology* (Dublin, 2008), pp. 272–6

Ó Siocháin, Conchúr, *The Man from Cape Clear*, trans. Riobárd P Breatnach (Dublin, 1975)

O'Sullivan, Aidan, 'The Western Islands': Ireland's Atlantic Islands and the Forging of Gaelic Irish National Identities', in Gordon Noble (ed.), *Scottish Odysseys: The Archaeology of Islands* (London, 2008), pp. 172–90

O'Sullivan, Jerry and Tomás Ó Carragáin, *Inishmurray: Monks and Pilgrims in an Atlantic Landscape*, vol. 1: *Archaeological Survey and Excavations 1997–2000* (Cork, 2008)

O'Sullivan, Maurice, *Twenty Years a Growing*, trans. George Thomson (Oxford, 1953)

O'Toole, Fintan (ed.), *Modern Ireland in 100 Art Works* (Dublin, 2016)

O'Toole, Pádraig, *Aran to Africa: An Irishman's Unique Odyssey* (Galway, 2013)

Ó Tuathaigh, Gearóid, 'The State and the Irish Language: A Historical Perspective', in Caoilfhionn Nic Pháidín and Seán Ó Cearnaigh (eds.), *A New View of the Irish Language* (Dublin, 2008), pp. 26–43

Rainbird, Paul, 'Islands Out of Time: Towards a Critique of Island Archaeology', *Journal of Mediterranean Archaeology*, vol. 12, no. 2, 1999, pp. 216–34

Pataux, Agnès, *Ireland on the Edge of Europe* (Milan, 2003)

Pochin Mould, Daphne D. C., *The Rock of Truth* (London, 1953)

Pochin Mould, Daphne D. C., *Valentia: Portrait of an Island* (Dublin, 1978)

Power, Richard, *The Land of Youth: A Novel* (New York, 1964)

Power, Richard, *Apple on the Treetop*, trans. Victor Power (Dublin, 1980; first published 1958)

Praeger, Robert Lloyd, *The Botanist in Ireland* (Dublin, 1934)

Quinn, Bob and Liam Mac Con Iomaire, *Conamara: Tír Aineoil: The Unknown Country* (Galway, 1997)

Quinn, James, 'James Arthur Balfour', *DIB*, vol. 1, pp. 239–42

Raftery, Barry, *Pagan and Celtic Ireland: The Enigma of the Irish Iron Age* (London, 1994)

Reader, John, 'Shark Men', *Ireland of the Welcomes*, vol. 13, no. 5, January–February 1965, p. 10

Rivers, Elizabeth, *Stranger in Aran* (Dublin, 1946)

Robinson, Henry A., *Memories: Wise and Otherwise* (London, 1923)

Robinson, Henry A., *Further Memories of Irish Life* (London, 1924)

Robinson, Tim, 'The Impossible Isles', *Ireland of the Welcomes*, vol. 30, no. 4, July–August 1981, pp. 18–19

Robinson, Tim, 'Place/Person/Book', in J. M. Synge, *The Aran Islands* (Penguin, 1992; first published 1907)

Robinson, Tim, *Stones of Aran: Pilgrimage* (Dublin, 1986)

Robinson, Tim, *Stones of Aran: Labyrinth* (New York, 2009; first published 1995)

Robinson, Tim, *Connemara: A Little Gaelic Kingdom* (London, 2011)

Royle, Stephen A., 'Irish Famine Relief in the Early Nineteenth Century: The 1822 Famine on the Aran Islands', *Irish Economic and Social History*, vol. 11, 1984, pp. 44–59

Royle, Stephen A., 'A Dispersed Pressure Group: Comhdháil na nOileán: The Federation of the Islands of Ireland', *Irish Geography*, vol. 19, 1986, pp. 92–5

Royle, Stephen A., 'Leaving the "Dreadful Rocks": Irish Island Emigration and Its Legacy', *History Ireland*, no. 4, Spring 1998, pp. 34–8

Royle, Stephen A., 'From Marginality to Resurgence: The Case of the Irish Islands', *Skima: The International Journal for Research into Island Cultures*, vol. 2, no. 2, 2008, pp. 42–54

Royle, Stephen A. and Derek Scott, 'Accessibility and the Irish Islands', *Geography: Journal of the Geographical Association*, vol. 81, no. 2, 1996, pp. 111–19

Ryan, Michael (ed.), *Irish Archaeology* (Dublin, 1994)

Saddlemyer, Ann, 'J. M. Synge', *Ireland of the Welcomes*, vol. 19, no. 6, March–April 1971, pp. 6–13

Saddlemyer, Ann (ed.), *The Playboy of the Western World and Other Plays* (Oxford, 2008)

Sayers, Peig, *Peig: The Autobiography of Peig Sayers of the Great Blasket Island*, trans. Bryan MacMahon (Dublin, 1974; first published 1936)

Sayers, Peig, *Labharfad Le Cách* (*I Will Speak to You All*), trans. Bo Almqvist and Pádraig Ó Héalaí (Dublin, 2009)

Scally, Brendan, 'A Journey to Achill, 1947', *Cathair Na Mart*, vol. 8, no. 1, 1988, pp. 118–22

Schafer, Joseph (ed.), *Memoirs of Jeremiah Curtin* (Madison, WI, 1940)

Scheper-Hughes, Nancy, *Saints, Scholars and Schizophrenics: Mental Illness in Rural Ireland* (Berkeley, 1979)

Seager, Allan, *The Glass House: The Life of Theodore Roethke* (Ann Arbor, MI, 2002; first published New York, 1968)

Sheeran, Patrick F., *The Novels of Liam O'Flaherty: A Study in Romantic Realism* (Dublin, 1976)

Simonds-Gooding, Maria, *Fields of Vision* (Dublin, 2004)

Siocháin, Séamas, *Roger Casement: Imperialist, Rebel, Revolutionary* (Dublin, 2008)

Sisson, Elaine, 'The Aran Islands and the Travel Essays', in P. J. Matthews (ed.), *The Cambridge Companion to J. M. Synge* (Cambridge, 2009), pp. 52–64

Smith, Denis, *Aran Islands: A Personal Journey* (New York, 1980)

Somerville Large, Peter, *Ireland's Islands: Landscape, Life and Legends* (Dublin, 2000)

Sweeney, Bernadette and Marie Kelly (eds.), *The Theatre of Tom MacIntyre: Strays from the Ether* (Dublin, 2010)

Symons, Arthur, *Cities and Sea Coasts and Islands* (Evanston, IL, 1998; first published New York, 1918)

Synge, J. M., 'A Story from Inishmaan', *New Ireland Review*, vol. 10, September 1898 – February 1899, pp. 153–7

Synge, J. M., *The Aran Islands*, ed. and intro. Tim Robinson (Harmondsworth, 1992; first published London, 1907)

Synge, J. M., *Riders to the Sea*, in Ann Saddlemyer (ed.), *The Playboy of the Western World and Other Plays* (Oxford, 2008), pp. 1–13

Tall, Deborah, *The Island of the White Cow: Memories of an Irish Island* (London, 1986)

Taylor, Richard, M., *The Lighthouses of Ireland* (Cork, 2004)

Tóibín, Colm, 'The Mystery of Inis Meáin', *The Guardian*, 12 May 2007

Tóibín, Colm (ed.), *Synge: A Celebration* (Dublin, 2005)

Toner, Jerome, *Rural Ireland: Some of Its Problems* (1955)

Toole, Anthony, 'The Islandman's Dream', *Ireland of the Welcomes*, vol. 50, no. 3 May–June 2001, pp. 33–42

van der Ziel, Stanley, *John McGahern and the Imagination of Tradition* (Cork, 2016)

Walsh, Ciarán, 'Charles R. Browne, the Irish "Headhunter"', *Irish Journal of Anthropology*, vol. 16, no. 1, 2013, pp. 16–23

Walsh, David, *Oileáin: The Irish Islands Guide* (Dublin, 2004)

Whelan, Kevin, 'Landscape and Society on Clare Island, 1700–1900', in Criostóir Mac Cárthaigh and Kevin Whelan (eds.), *New Survey of Clare Island*, vol. 1: *History and Cultural Landscape* (Dublin, 1999), pp. 73–99

Wilde, William, R., 'On the Battle of Moytura', *Proceedings of the Royal Irish Academy*, 1836–1869, vol. 9, 1864–6, pp. 546–50

Yeats, W. B., *Synge and the Ireland of His Time* (Dublin, 1911)

Yeats, W. B., *Essays and Introductions* (London, 1961)

LIST OF ILLUSTRATIONS

13 Dublin Opinion magazine, June 1933.

14 Gearóid O Catháin. Photo: Donal MacMonagle, / macmonagle.com

15 Jacket of Liam O'Flaherty's novel Skerrett.

16 J. M. Synge's photograph of Aran men on the beach.
Papers of John Millington Synge [MS11332_44] Copyright 2009 The Board of Trinity College Dublin.

17 Painter Jack B. Yeats' frontispiece of Synge's The Aran Islands (1907). ©
Estate of Jack B Yeats / DACS

18 A still from the film The Door Ajar (2011) by Patrick Jolley, courtesy of the Patrick Jolley Estate

19 Theodore Roethke, Seattle, 1963. Photos: University of Washington Libraries, Special Collections, [MPH328]

20 The Back of Tory Island (1960) by Derek Hill. Oil on canvas. Collection Irish Museum of Modern Art

21 Tory Island aerial view. Photo: Kevin Dwyer.

22 Island Voting 1992. Photo: Frank Miller / Irish Times.

23 Tim Robinson. Photo David Whittaker / Wavestone Press

24 Peadar O'Donnell (1966). Photo: courtesy of RTÉ Archives (ref: 2595/095).

25 Charles Haughey on Inishvickillane. Photo: Colman Doyle / National Library of Ireland.

26 Gerard Dillon's (1916–1971) Island People (1950). Oil onboard. Reproduced with the agreement of the Gerard Dillon Estate / Collection of Crawford Art Gallery, Cork

While every effort has been made to contact copyright-holders of illustrations, the author and publishers would be grateful for information about any illustrations where they have been unable to trace them, and would be glad to make amendments in further editions.

INDEX